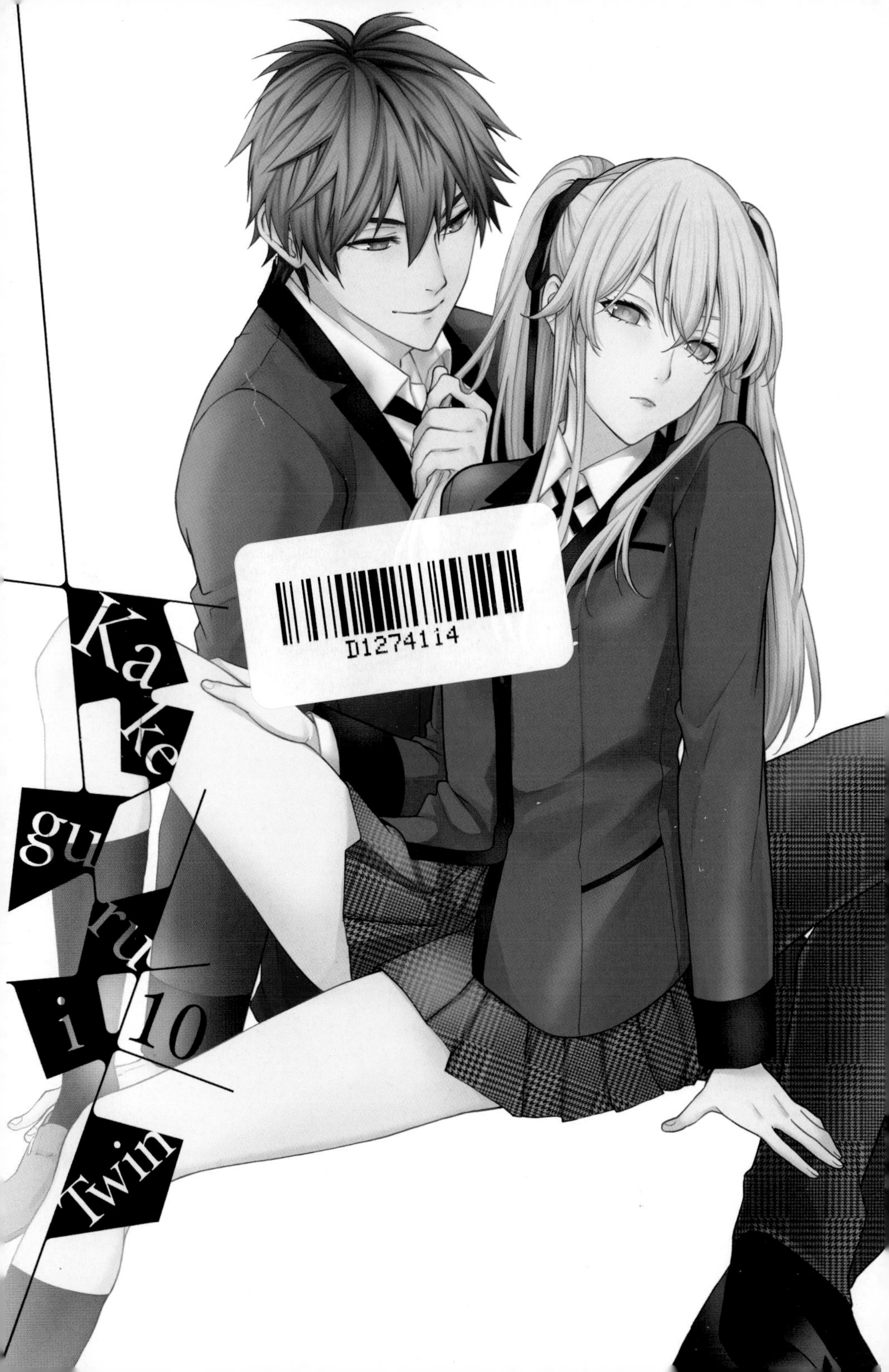
Kakegurui
10
Twin

(10)

KAKEGURUI TWIN

CHAPTER FORTY-NINE: THE SCORE-SETTLING GIRL ———————————— 3

CHAPTER FIFTY: THE OBJECTIFIED GIRL —————————————— 33

CHAPTER FIFTY-ONE: THE FIGHTING GIRLS ———————————— 67

CHAPTER FIFTY-TWO: THE CONTEMPTUOUS GIRL ——————————— 95

CHAPTER FIFTY-THREE: THE FRUSTRATED GIRL ————————————— 135

CHAPTER FIFTY-FOUR: THE INVIGORATING GIRL ——————————— 171

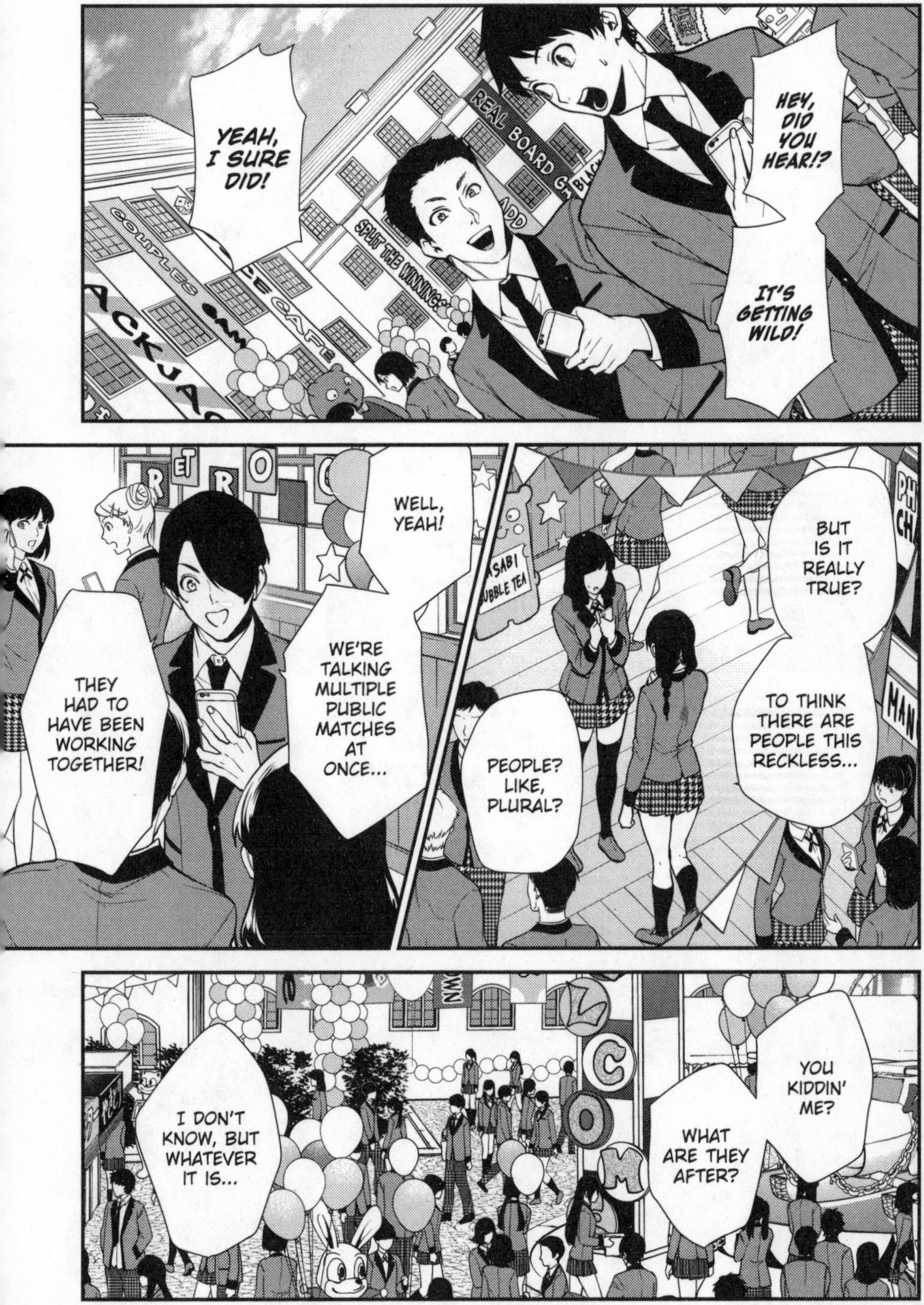
HEY, DID YOU HEAR!?
IT'S GETTING WILD!
YEAH, I SURE DID!
BUT IS IT REALLY TRUE?
TO THINK THERE ARE PEOPLE THIS RECKLESS...
PEOPLE? LIKE, PLURAL?
WELL, YEAH!
WE'RE TALKING MULTIPLE PUBLIC MATCHES AT ONCE...
THEY HAD TO HAVE BEEN WORKING TOGETHER!
YOU KIDDIN' ME?
WHAT ARE THEY AFTER?
I DON'T KNOW, BUT WHATEVER IT IS...

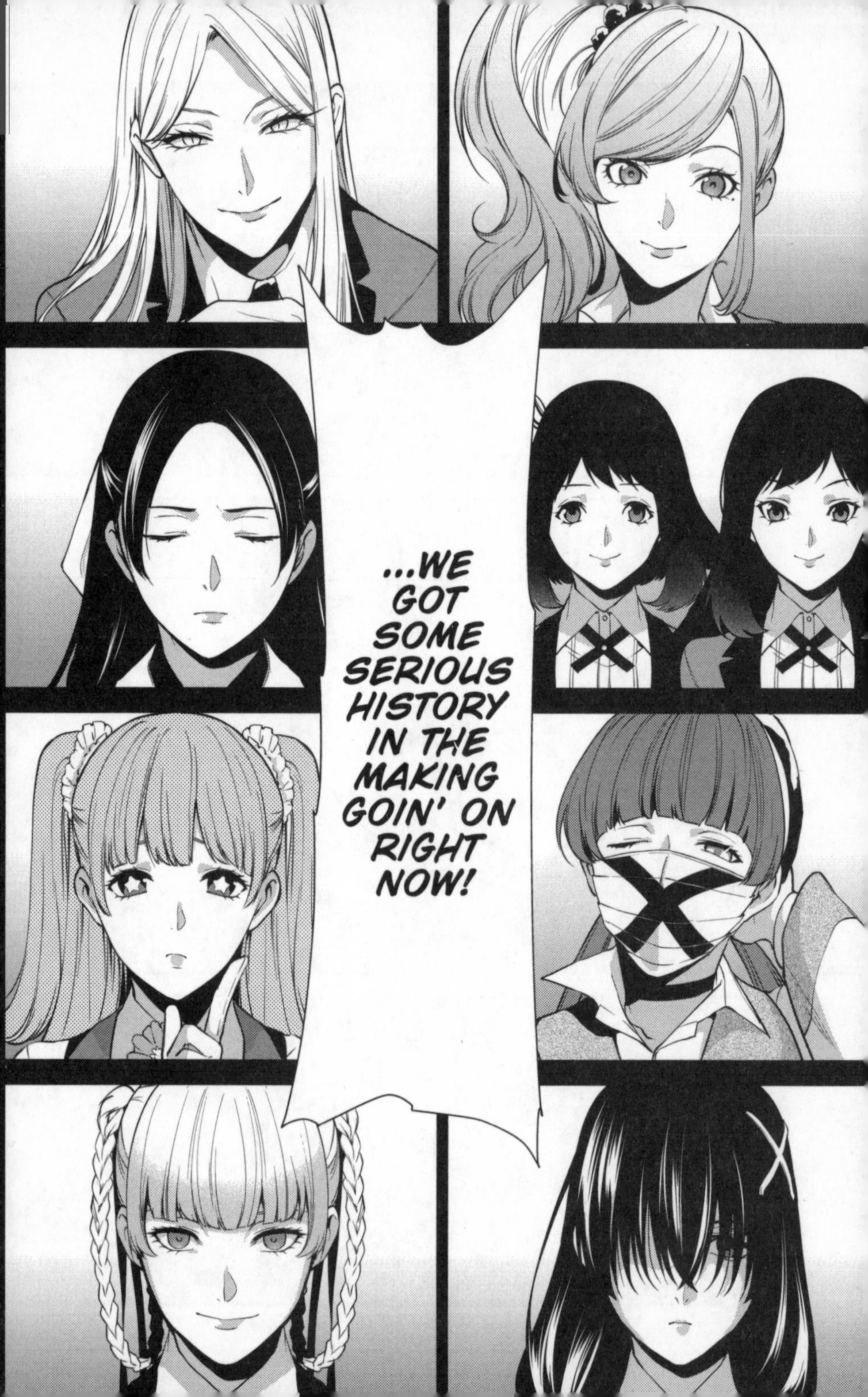
...WE GOT SOME SERIOUS HISTORY IN THE MAKING GOIN' ON RIGHT NOW!

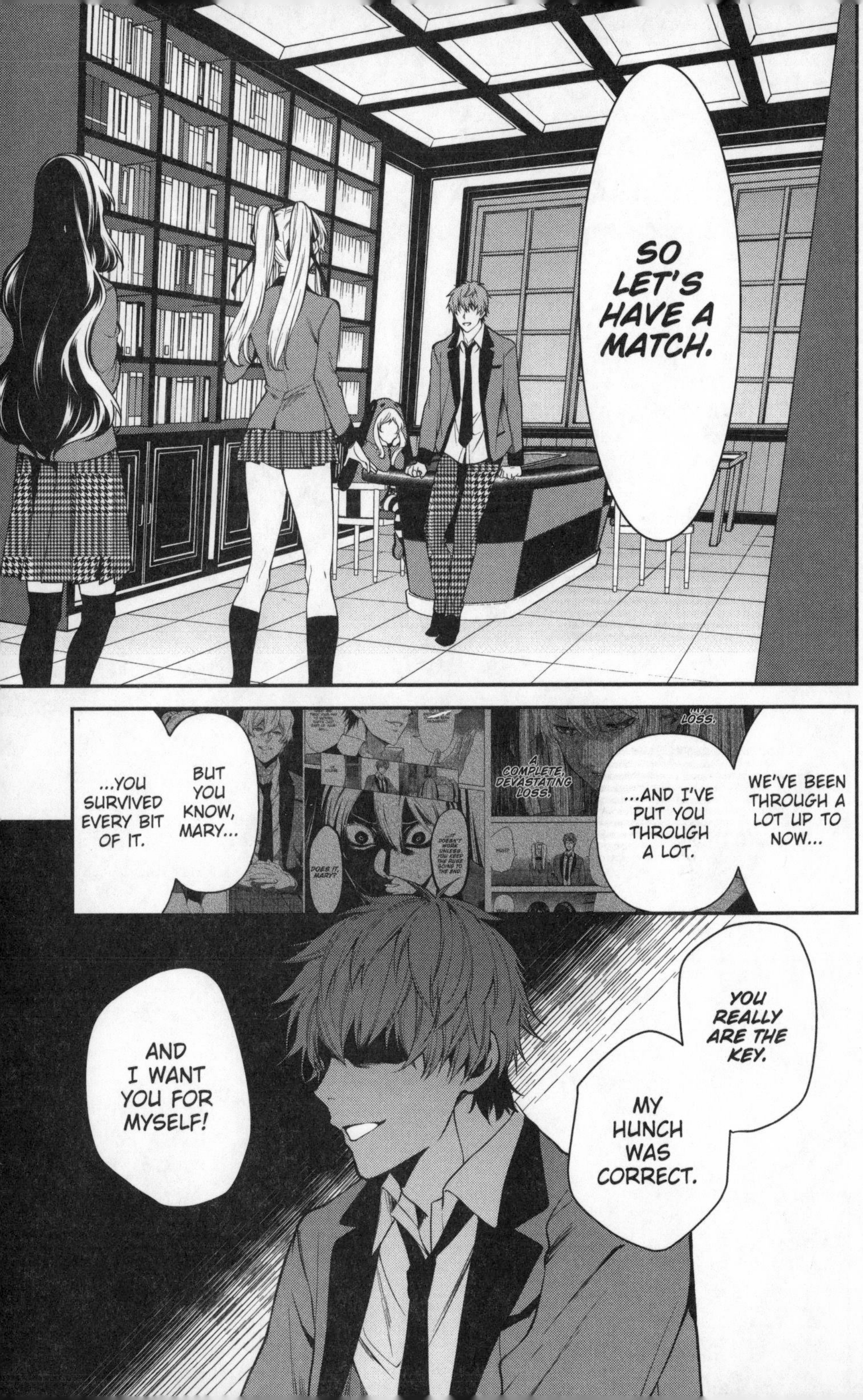
SO LET'S HAVE A MATCH.
WE'VE BEEN THROUGH A LOT UP TO NOW...
...AND I'VE PUT YOU THROUGH A LOT.
MY LOSS.
A COMPLETE, DEVASTATING LOSS.
DOES IT, MARY?
BUT YOU KNOW, MARY...
...YOU SURVIVED EVERY BIT OF IT.
YOU REALLY ARE THE KEY.
MY HUNCH WAS CORRECT.
AND I WANT YOU FOR MYSELF!

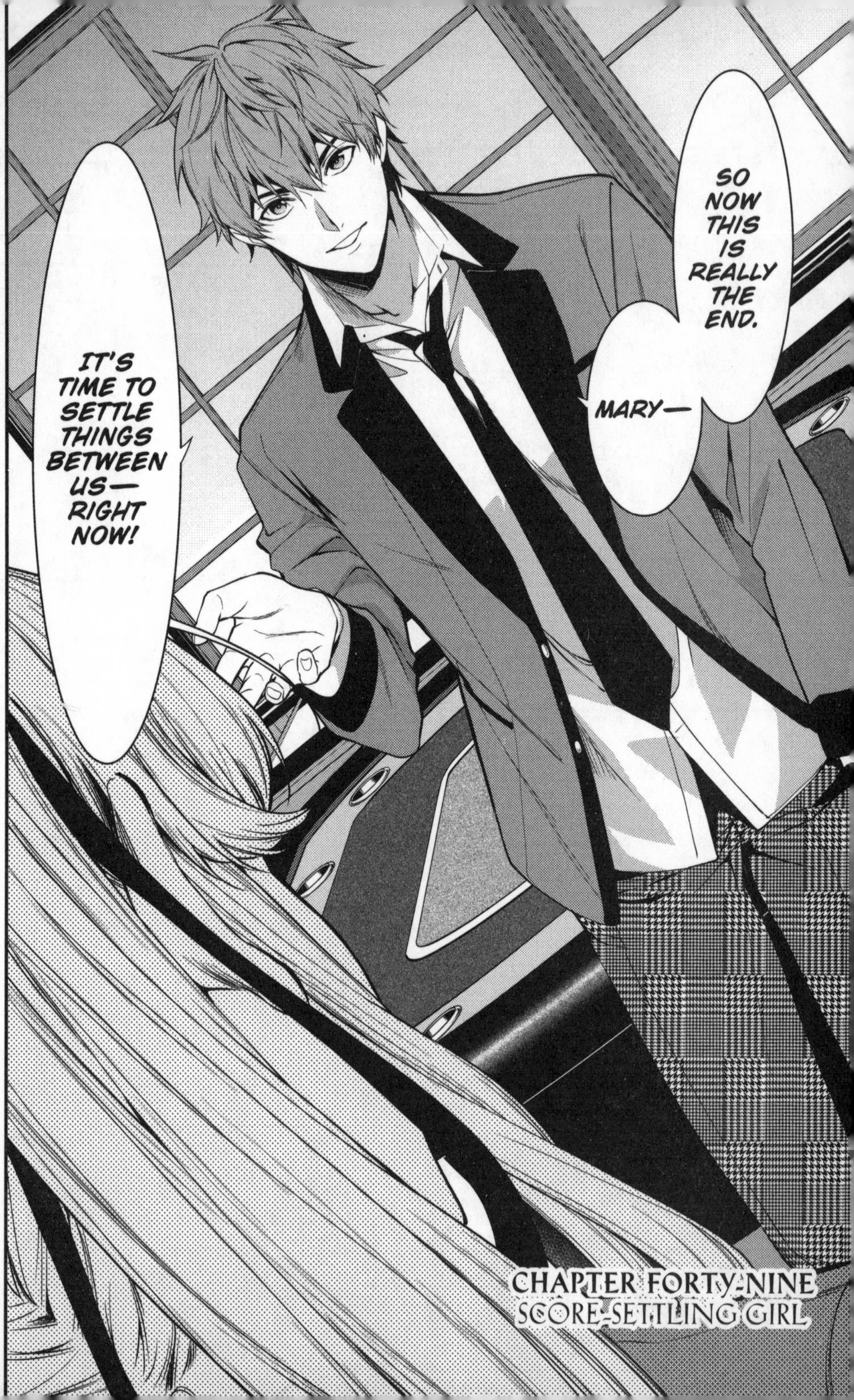
SO NOW THIS IS REALLY THE END.
MARY—
IT'S TIME TO SETTLE THINGS BETWEEN US— RIGHT NOW!

CHAPTER FORTY-NINE
SCORE-SETTLING GIRL

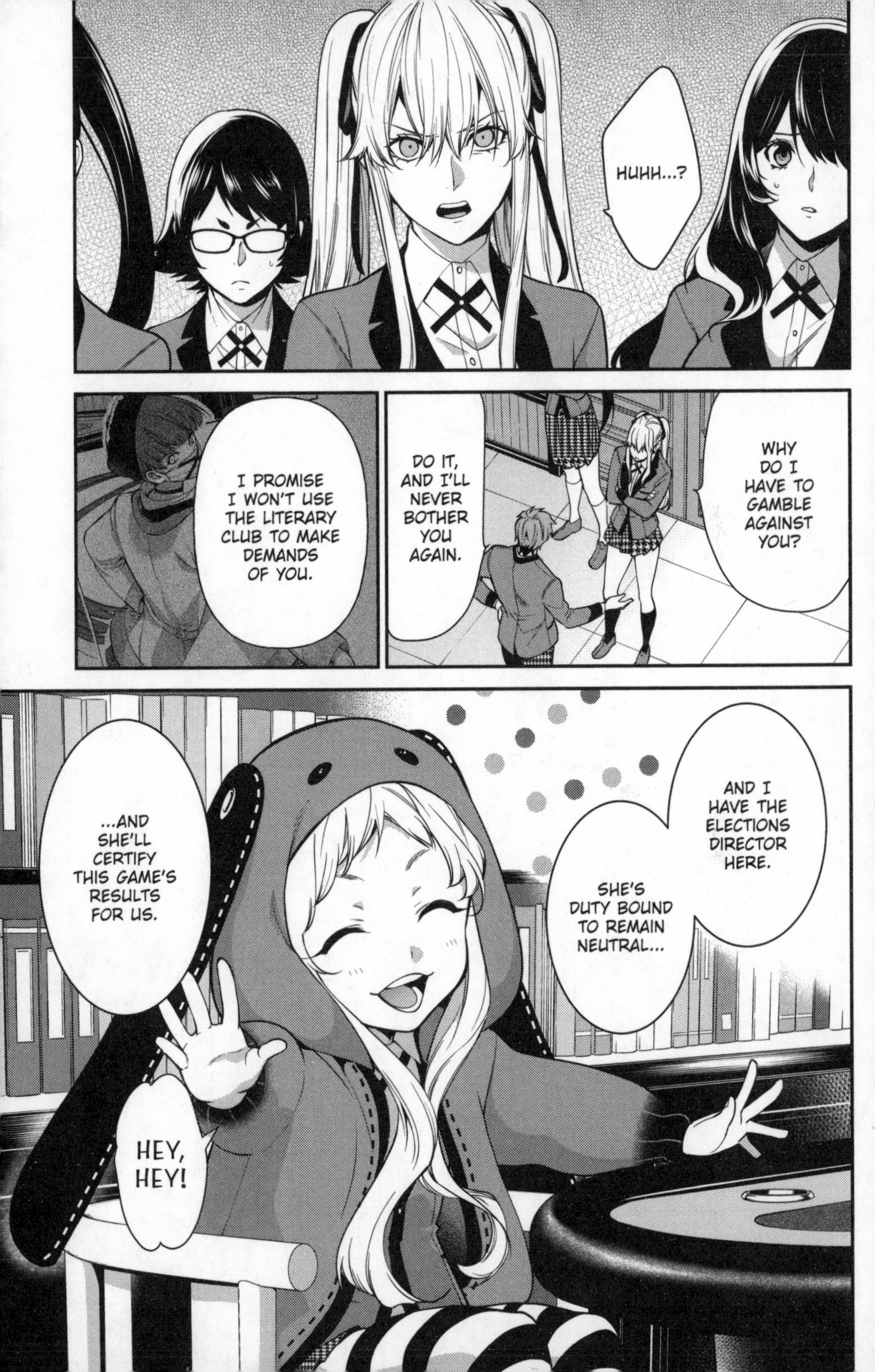
HUHH...?
WHY DO I HAVE TO GAMBLE AGAINST YOU?
DO IT, AND I'LL NEVER BOTHER YOU AGAIN.
I PROMISE I WON'T USE THE LITERARY CLUB TO MAKE DEMANDS OF YOU.
AND I HAVE THE ELECTIONS DIRECTOR HERE.
SHE'S DUTY BOUND TO REMAIN NEUTRAL...
...AND SHE'LL CERTIFY THIS GAME'S RESULTS FOR US.
HEY, HEY!

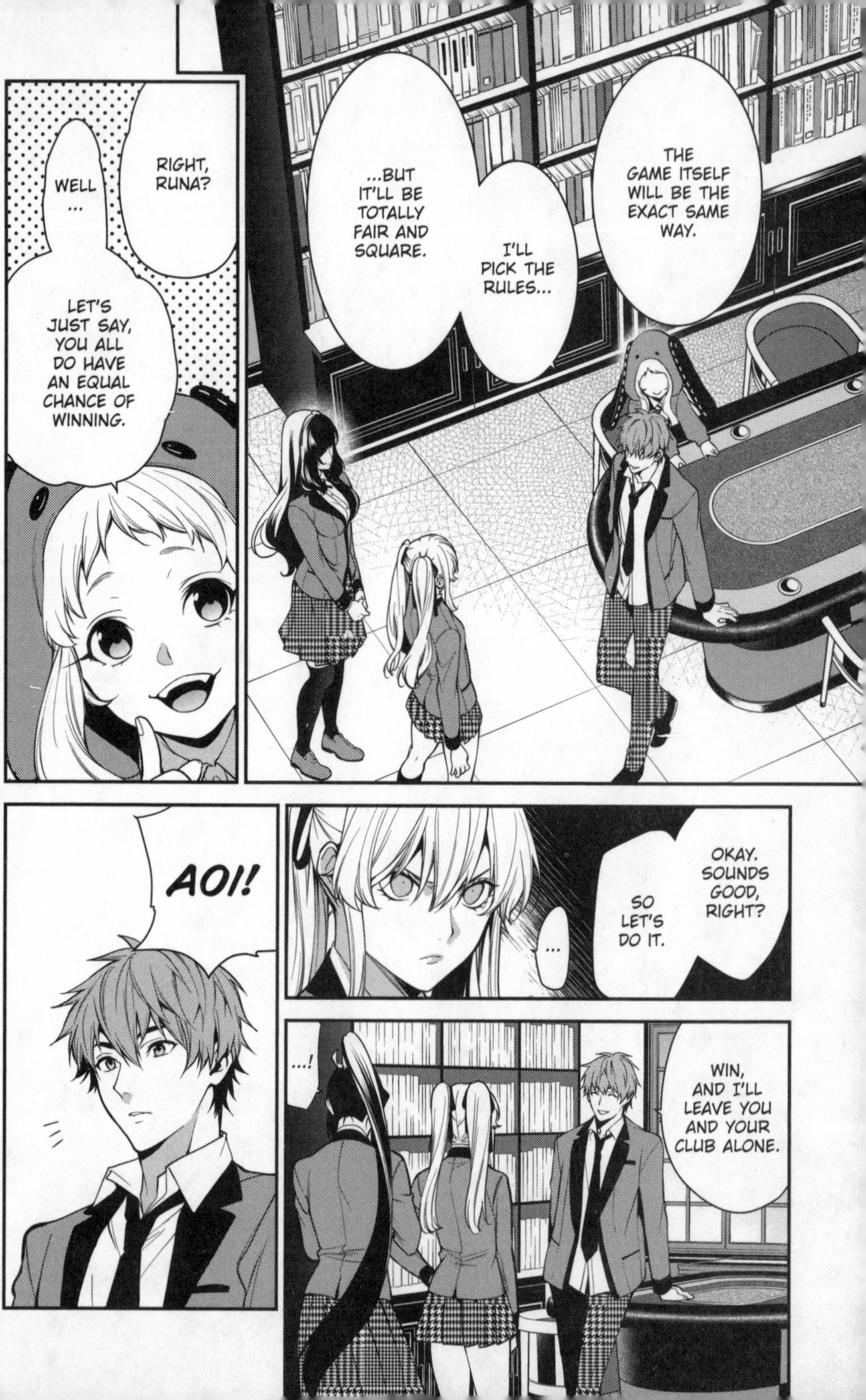
THE GAME ITSELF WILL BE THE EXACT SAME WAY.
I'LL PICK THE RULES...
...BUT IT'LL BE TOTALLY FAIR AND SQUARE.
RIGHT, RUNA?
WELL ...
LET'S JUST SAY, YOU ALL DO HAVE AN EQUAL CHANCE OF WINNING.
OKAY. SOUNDS GOOD, RIGHT?
SO LET'S DO IT.
...
WIN, AND I'LL LEAVE YOU AND YOUR CLUB ALONE.
...!
AOI!

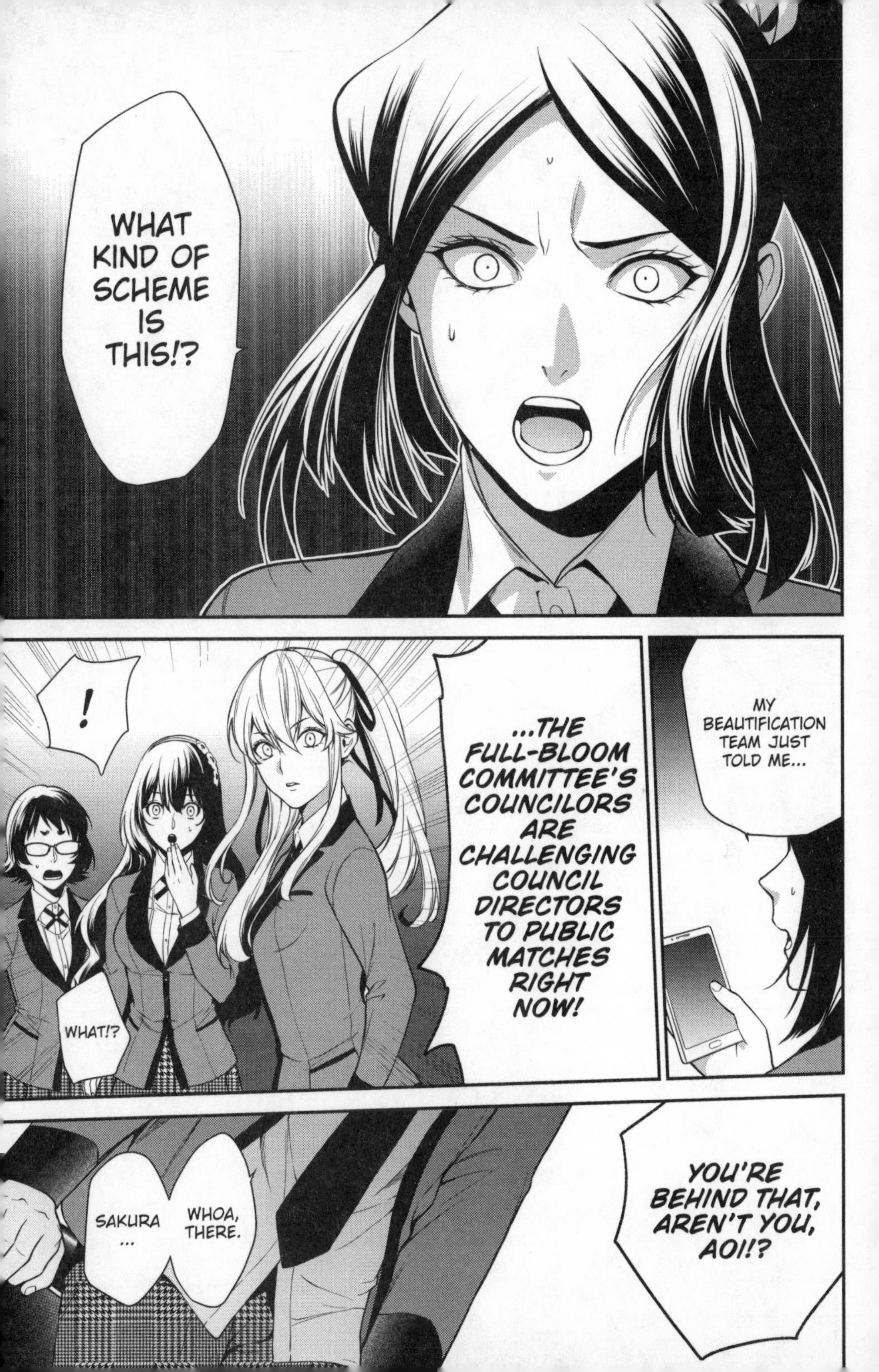
WHAT KIND OF SCHEME IS THIS!?
MY BEAUTIFICATION TEAM JUST TOLD ME...
...THE FULL-BLOOM COMMITTEE'S COUNCILORS ARE CHALLENGING COUNCIL DIRECTORS TO PUBLIC MATCHES RIGHT NOW!
!
WHAT!?
YOU'RE BEHIND THAT, AREN'T YOU, AOI!?
WHOA, THERE.
SAKURA ...

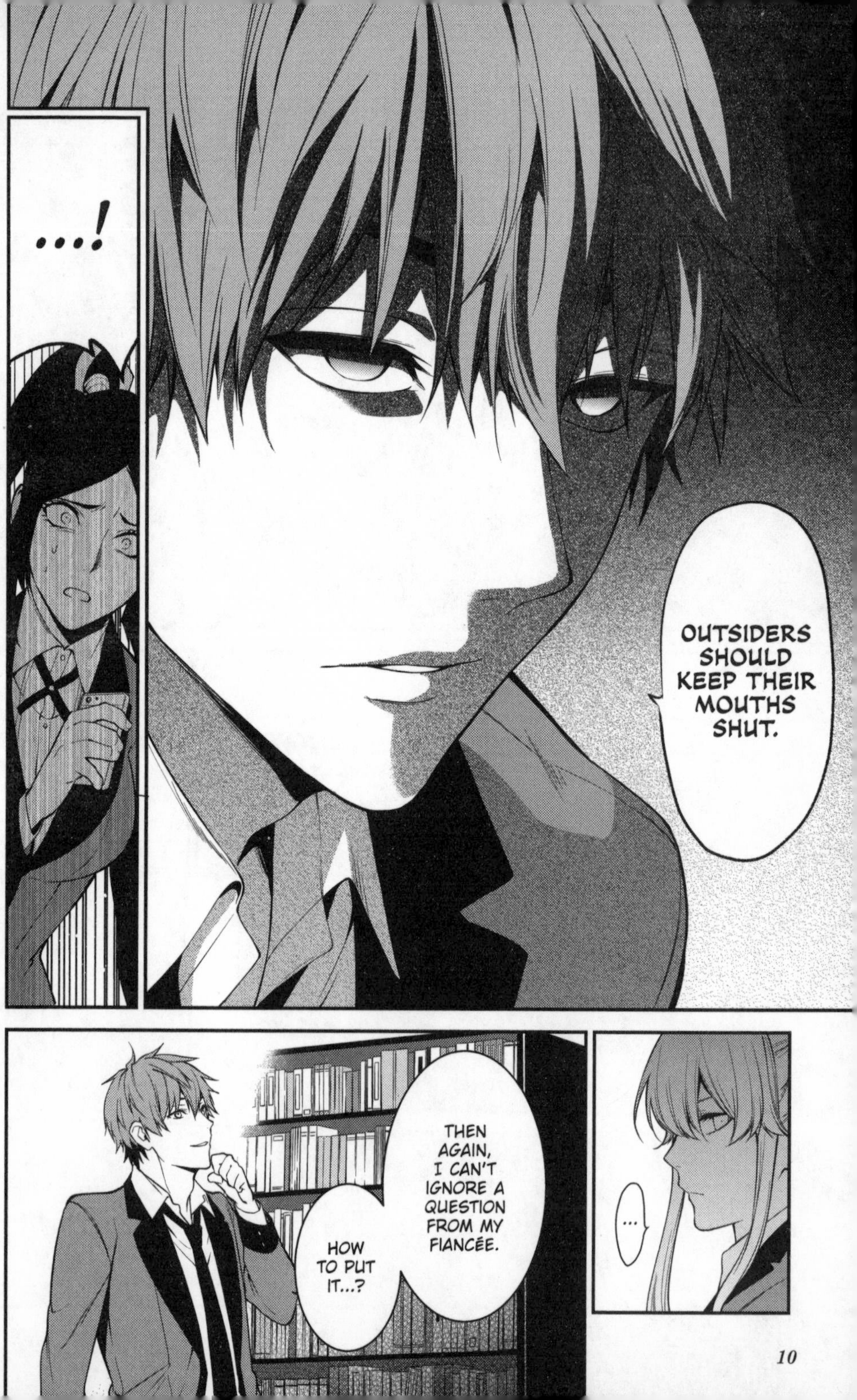
OUTSIDERS SHOULD KEEP THEIR MOUTHS SHUT.
...!
...
THEN AGAIN, I CAN'T IGNORE A QUESTION FROM MY FIANCÉE.
HOW TO PUT IT...?

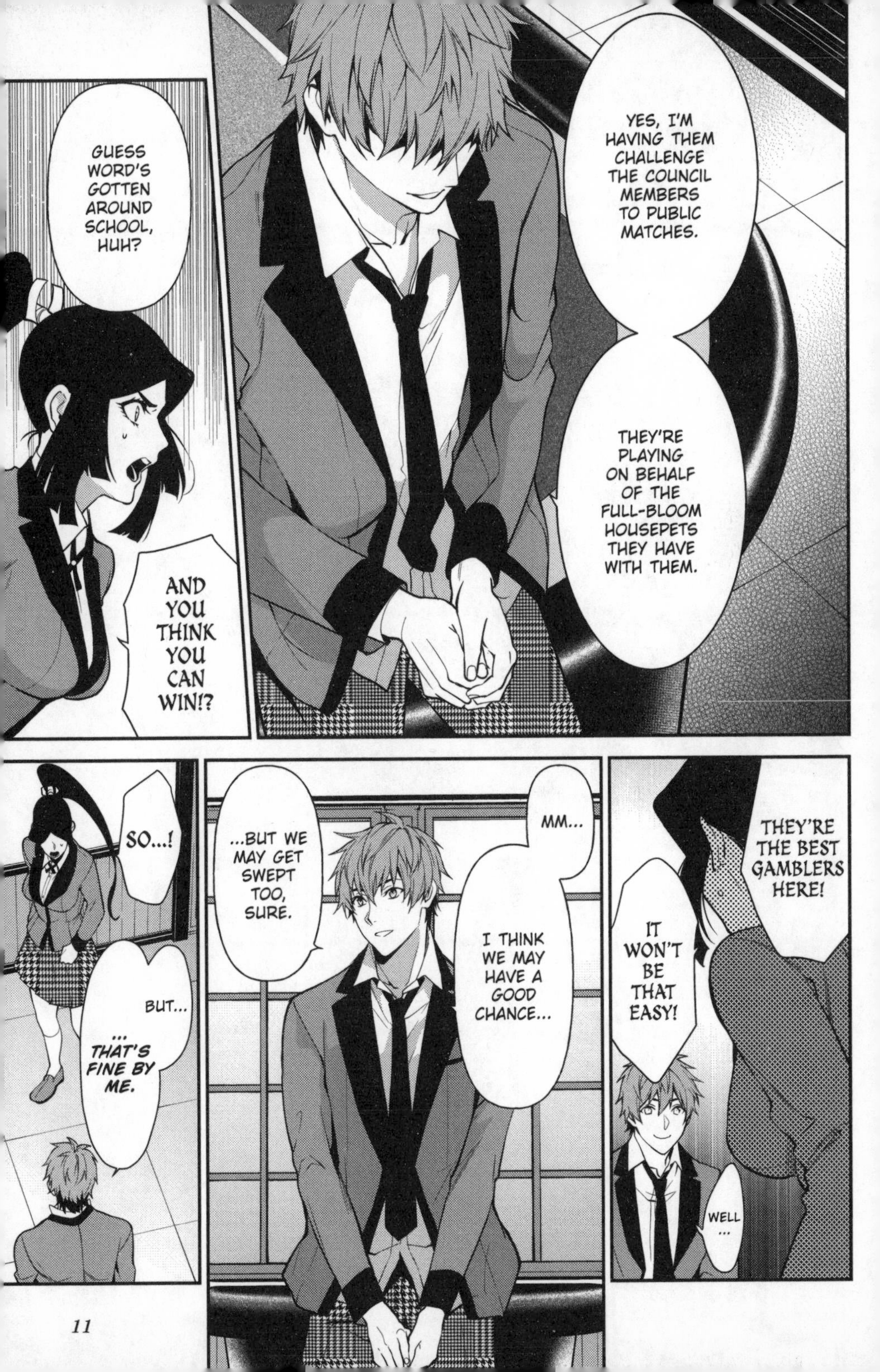
YES, I'M HAVING THEM CHALLENGE THE COUNCIL MEMBERS TO PUBLIC MATCHES.
THEY'RE PLAYING ON BEHALF OF THE FULL-BLOOM HOUSEPETS THEY HAVE WITH THEM.
GUESS WORD'S GOTTEN AROUND SCHOOL, HUH?
AND YOU THINK YOU CAN WIN!?
THEY'RE THE BEST GAMBLERS HERE!
IT WON'T BE THAT EASY!
WELL...
MM...
I THINK WE MAY HAVE A GOOD CHANCE...
...BUT WE MAY GET SWEPT TOO, SURE.
SO...!
BUT...
...THAT'S FINE BY ME.

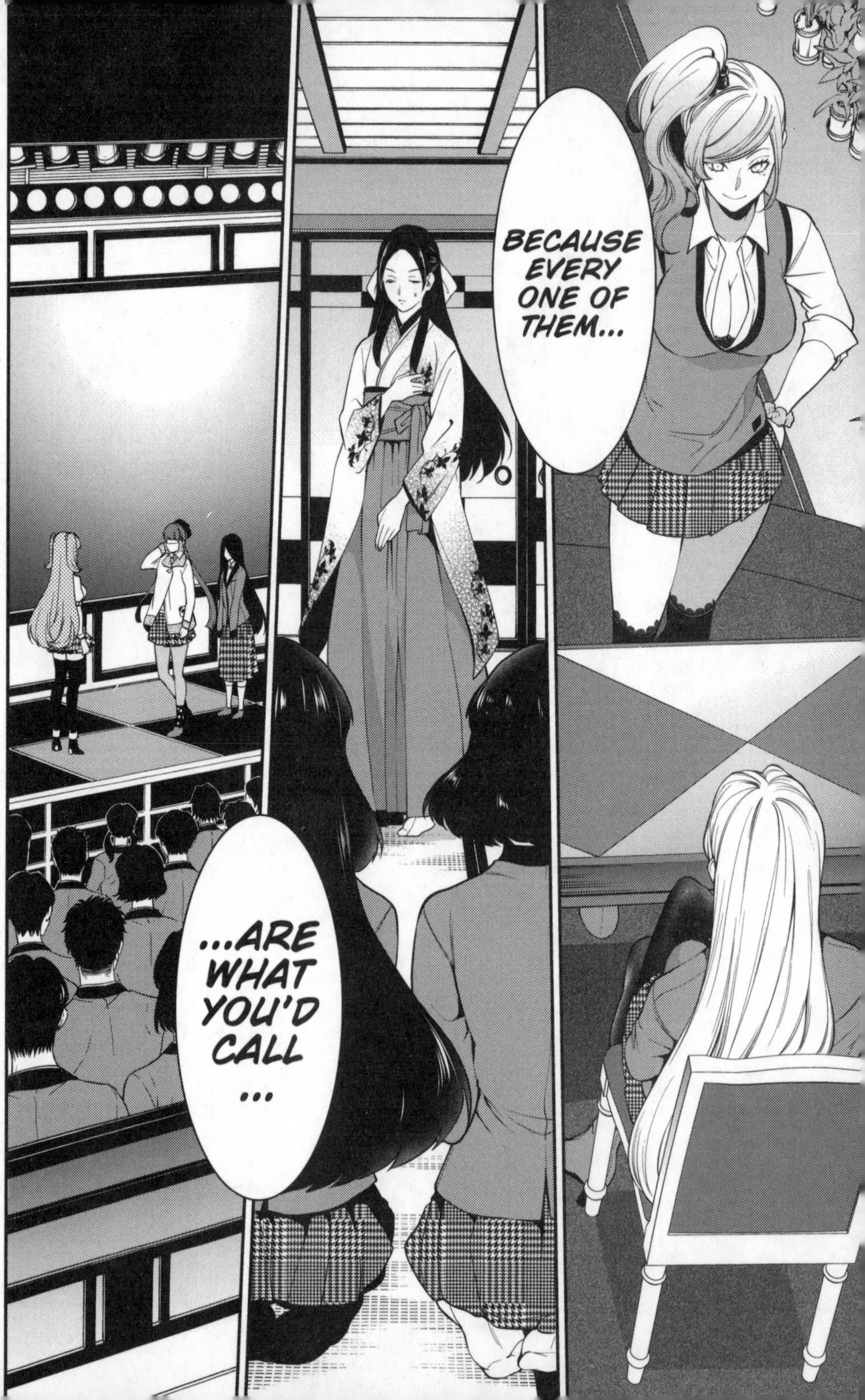
BECAUSE EVERY ONE OF THEM...
...ARE WHAT YOU'D CALL ...

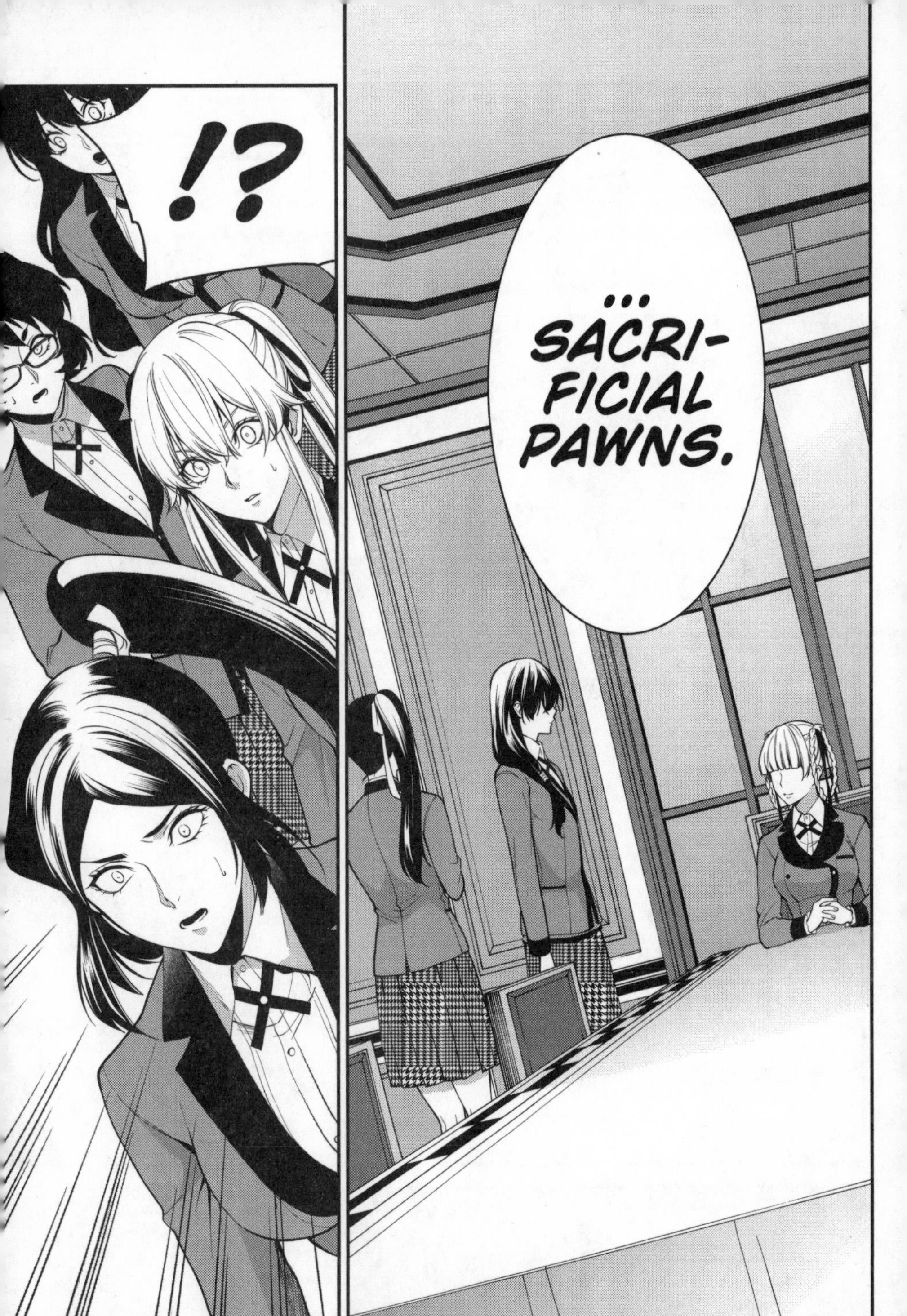

...SACRI-
FICIAL
PAWNS.
!?

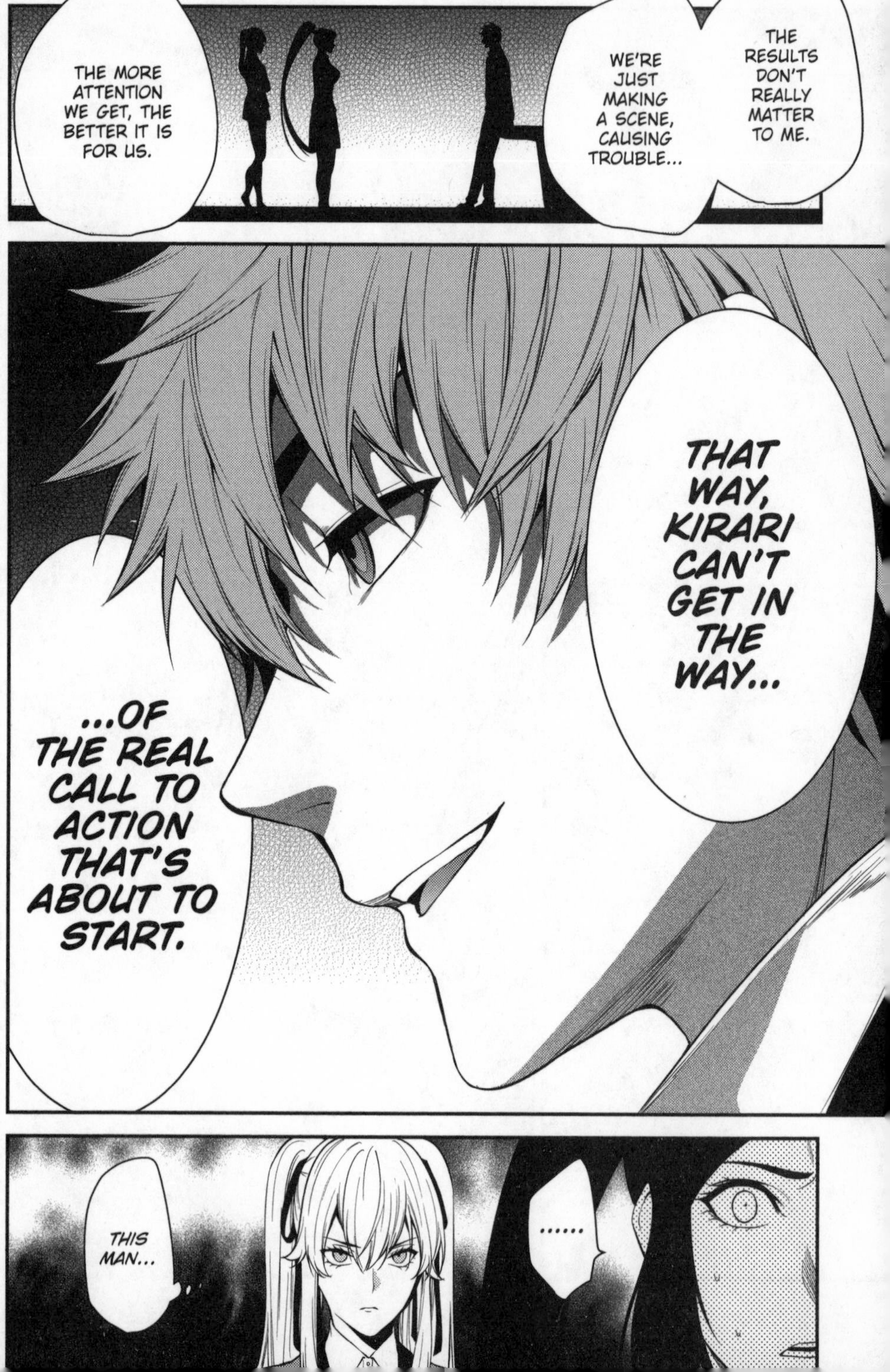
THE RESULTS DON'T REALLY MATTER TO ME.
WE'RE JUST MAKING A SCENE, CAUSING TROUBLE...
THE MORE ATTENTION WE GET, THE BETTER IT IS FOR US.
THAT WAY, KIRARI CAN'T GET IN THE WAY...
...OF THE REAL CALL TO ACTION THAT'S ABOUT TO START.
......
THIS MAN...

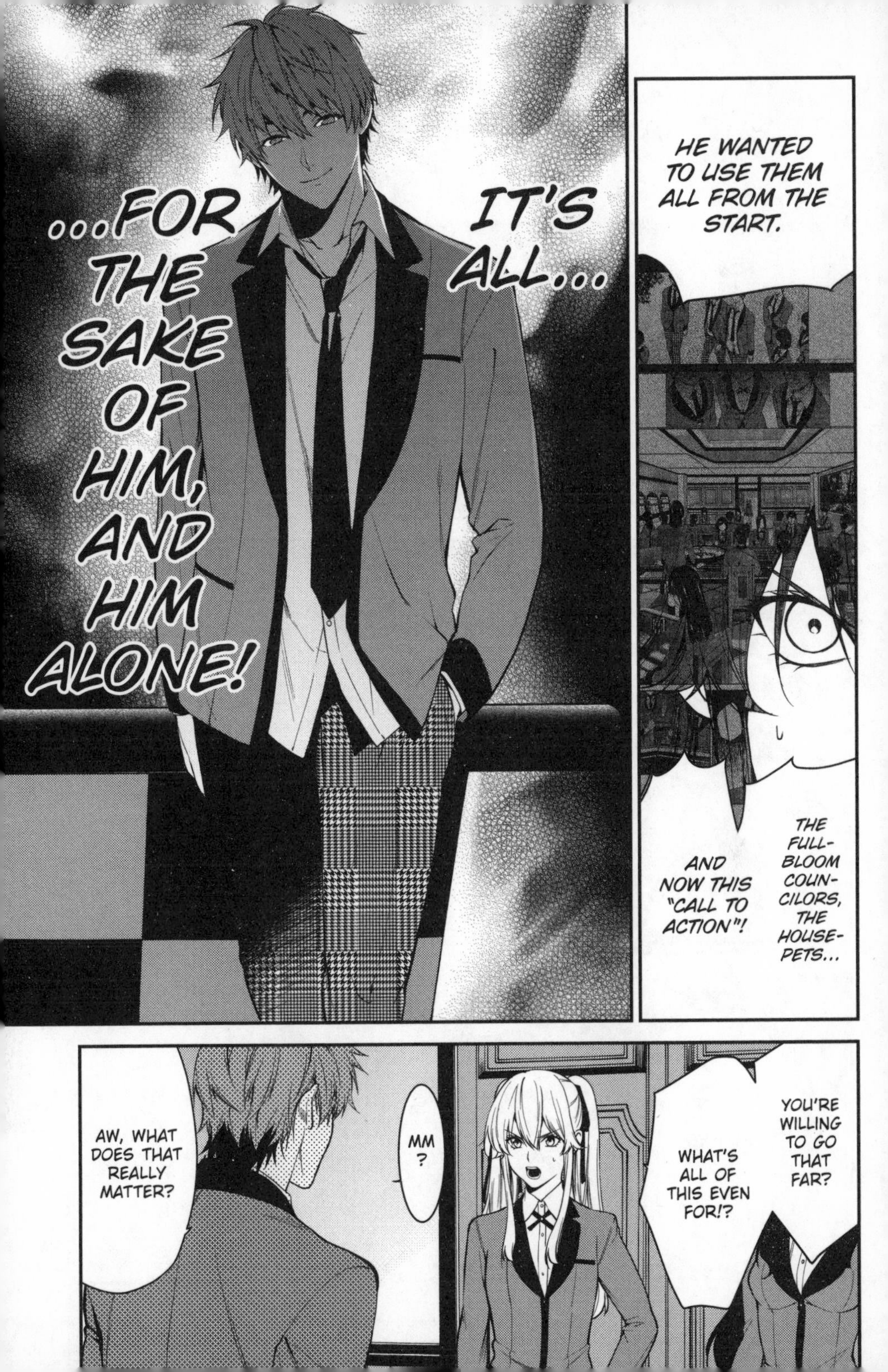
HE WANTED TO USE THEM ALL FROM THE START.
THE FULL-BLOOM COUNCILORS, THE HOUSE-PETS...
AND NOW THIS "CALL TO ACTION"!
IT'S ALL...
...FOR THE SAKE OF HIM, AND HIM ALONE!
YOU'RE WILLING TO GO THAT FAR?
WHAT'S ALL OF THIS EVEN FOR!?
MM?
AW, WHAT DOES THAT REALLY MATTER?

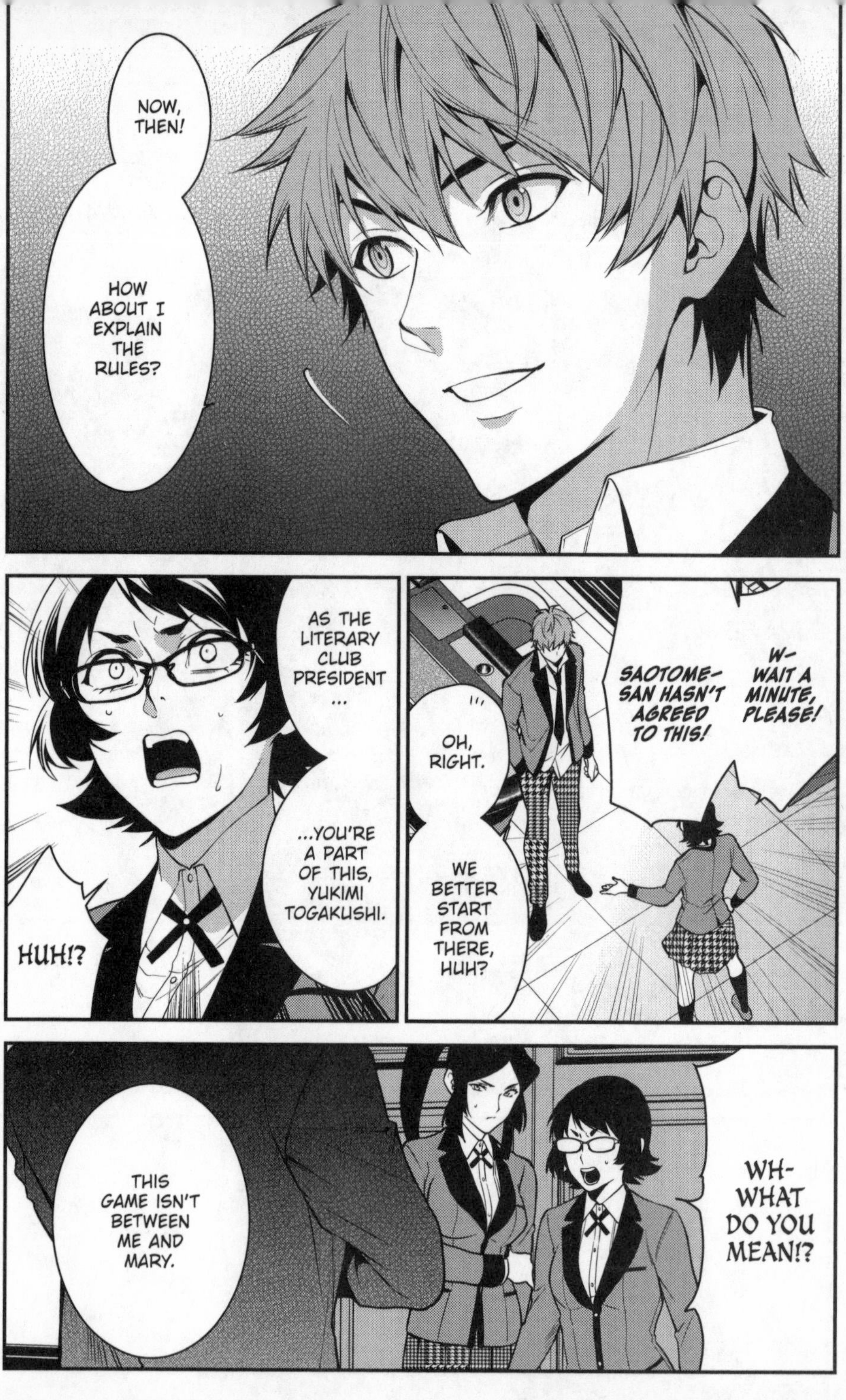
NOW, THEN!
HOW ABOUT I EXPLAIN THE RULES?
W-WAIT A MINUTE, PLEASE!
SAOTOME-SAN HASN'T AGREED TO THIS!
!!
OH, RIGHT.
WE BETTER START FROM THERE, HUH?
AS THE LITERARY CLUB PRESIDENT ...
...YOU'RE A PART OF THIS, YUKIMI TOGAKUSHI.
HUH!?
THIS GAME ISN'T BETWEEN ME AND MARY.
WH-WHAT DO YOU MEAN!?

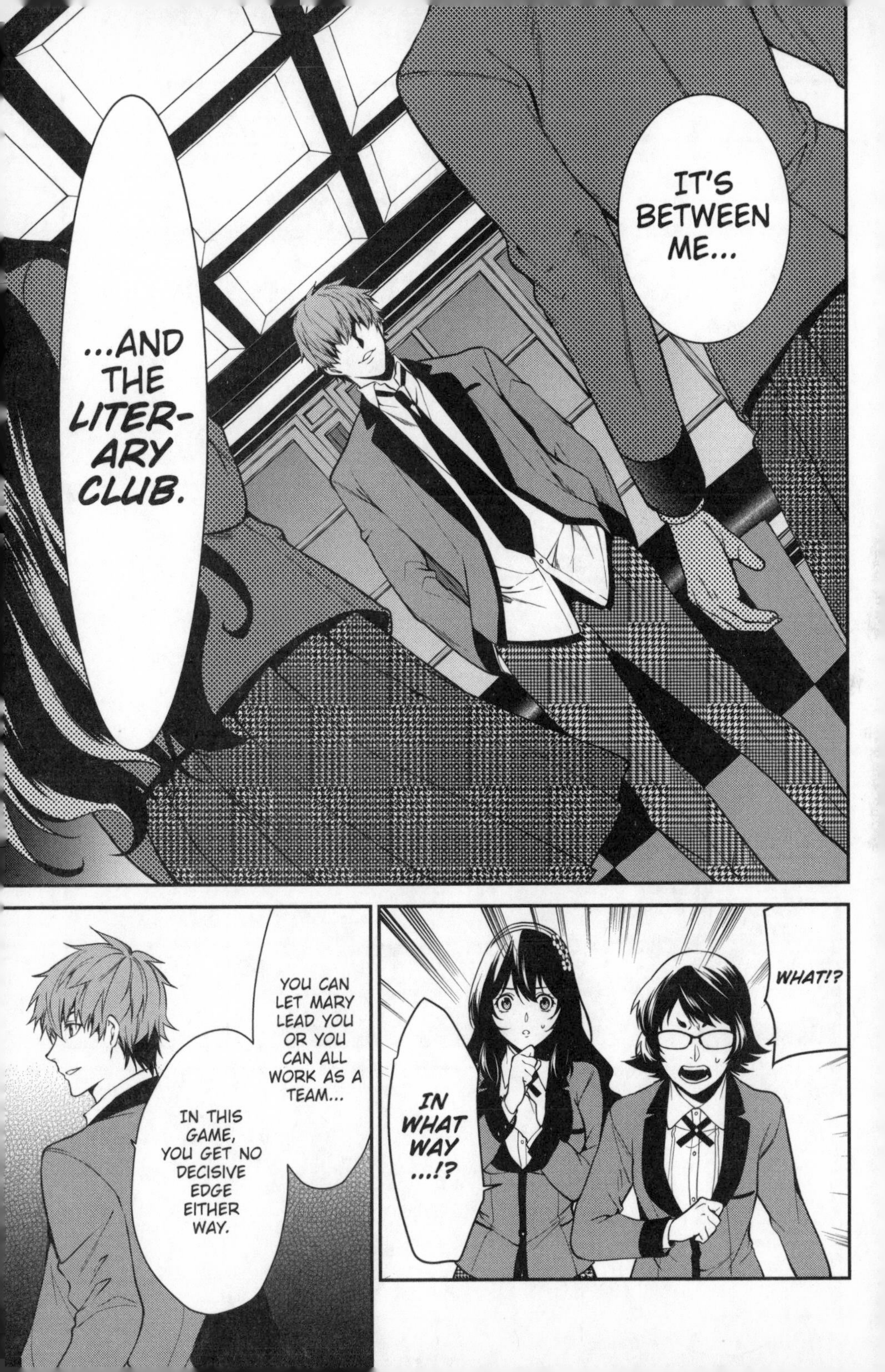
IT'S BETWEEN ME...
...AND THE LITER-ARY CLUB.
WHAT!?
IN WHAT WAY ...!?
YOU CAN LET MARY LEAD YOU OR YOU CAN ALL WORK AS A TEAM...
IN THIS GAME, YOU GET NO DECISIVE EDGE EITHER WAY.

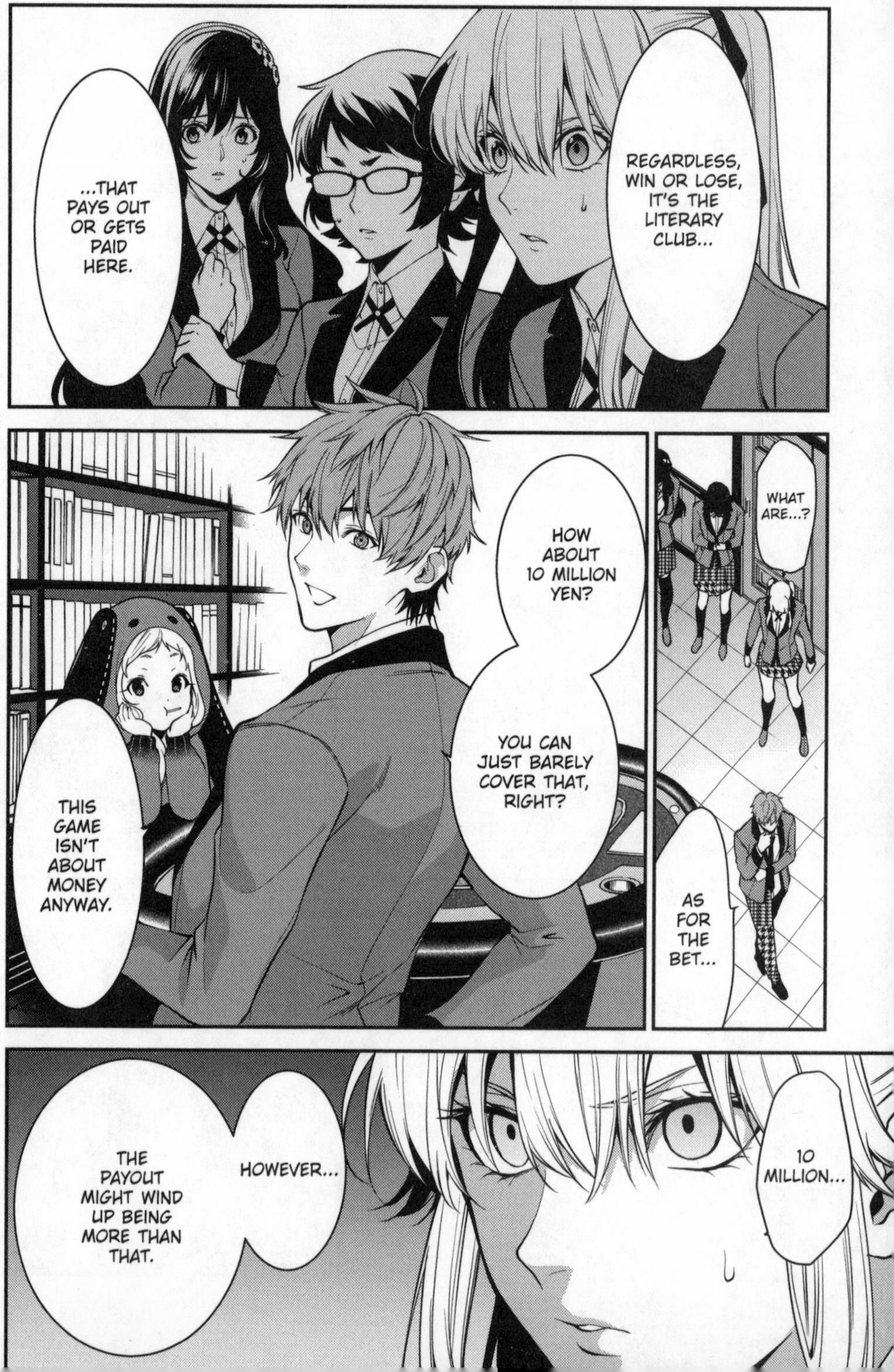
REGARDLESS, WIN OR LOSE, IT'S THE LITERARY CLUB...
...THAT PAYS OUT OR GETS PAID HERE.
WHAT ARE...?
AS FOR THE BET...
HOW ABOUT 10 MILLION YEN?
YOU CAN JUST BARELY COVER THAT, RIGHT?
THIS GAME ISN'T ABOUT MONEY ANYWAY.
10 MILLION...
HOWEVER...
THE PAYOUT MIGHT WIND UP BEING MORE THAN THAT.

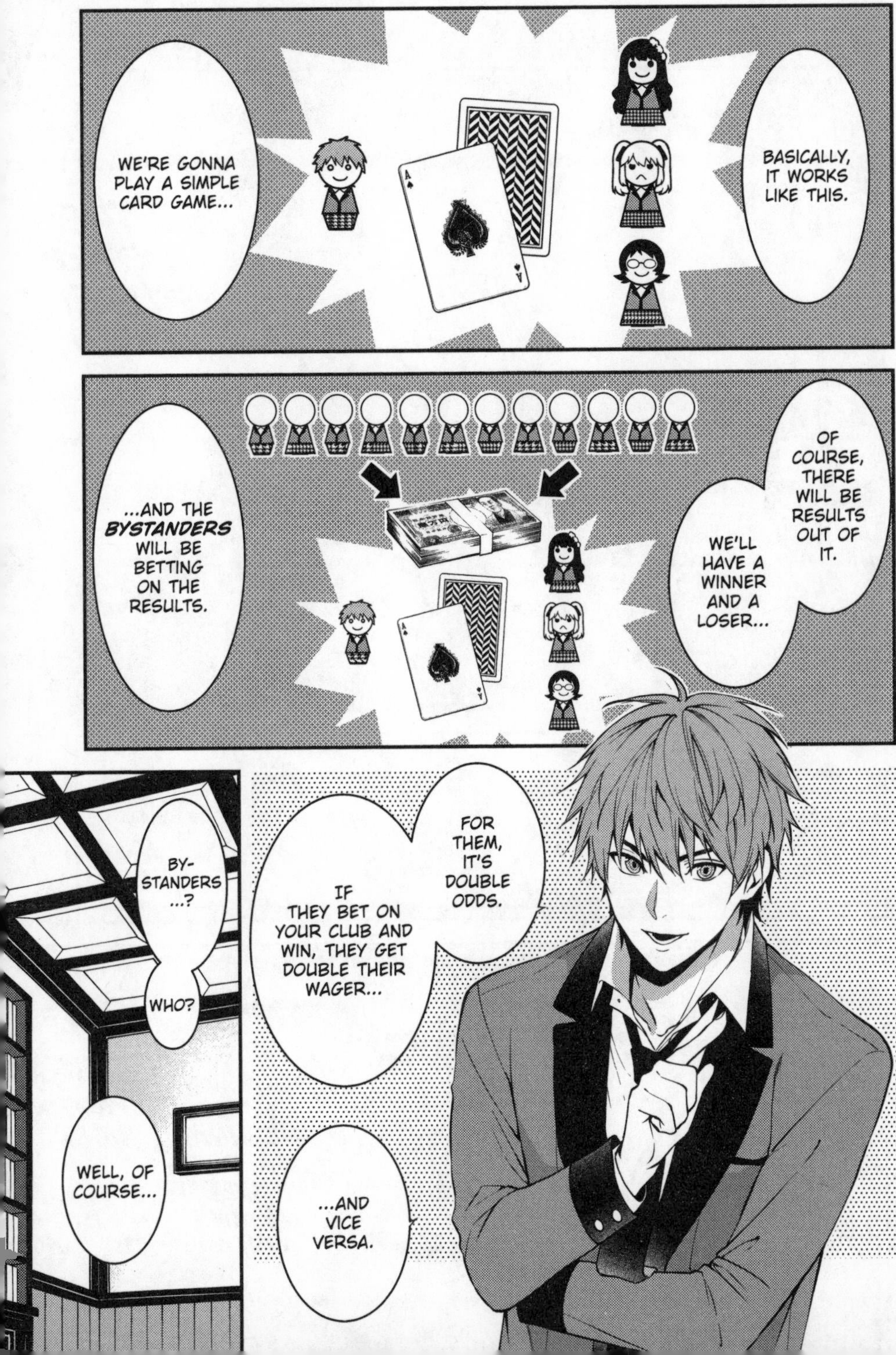
BASICALLY, IT WORKS LIKE THIS.
WE'RE GONNA PLAY A SIMPLE CARD GAME...
OF COURSE, THERE WILL BE RESULTS OUT OF IT.
WE'LL HAVE A WINNER AND A LOSER...
...AND THE BYSTANDERS WILL BE BETTING ON THE RESULTS.
FOR THEM, IT'S DOUBLE ODDS.
IF THEY BET ON YOUR CLUB AND WIN, THEY GET DOUBLE THEIR WAGER...
...AND VICE VERSA.
BY-STANDERS...?
WHO?
WELL, OF COURSE...

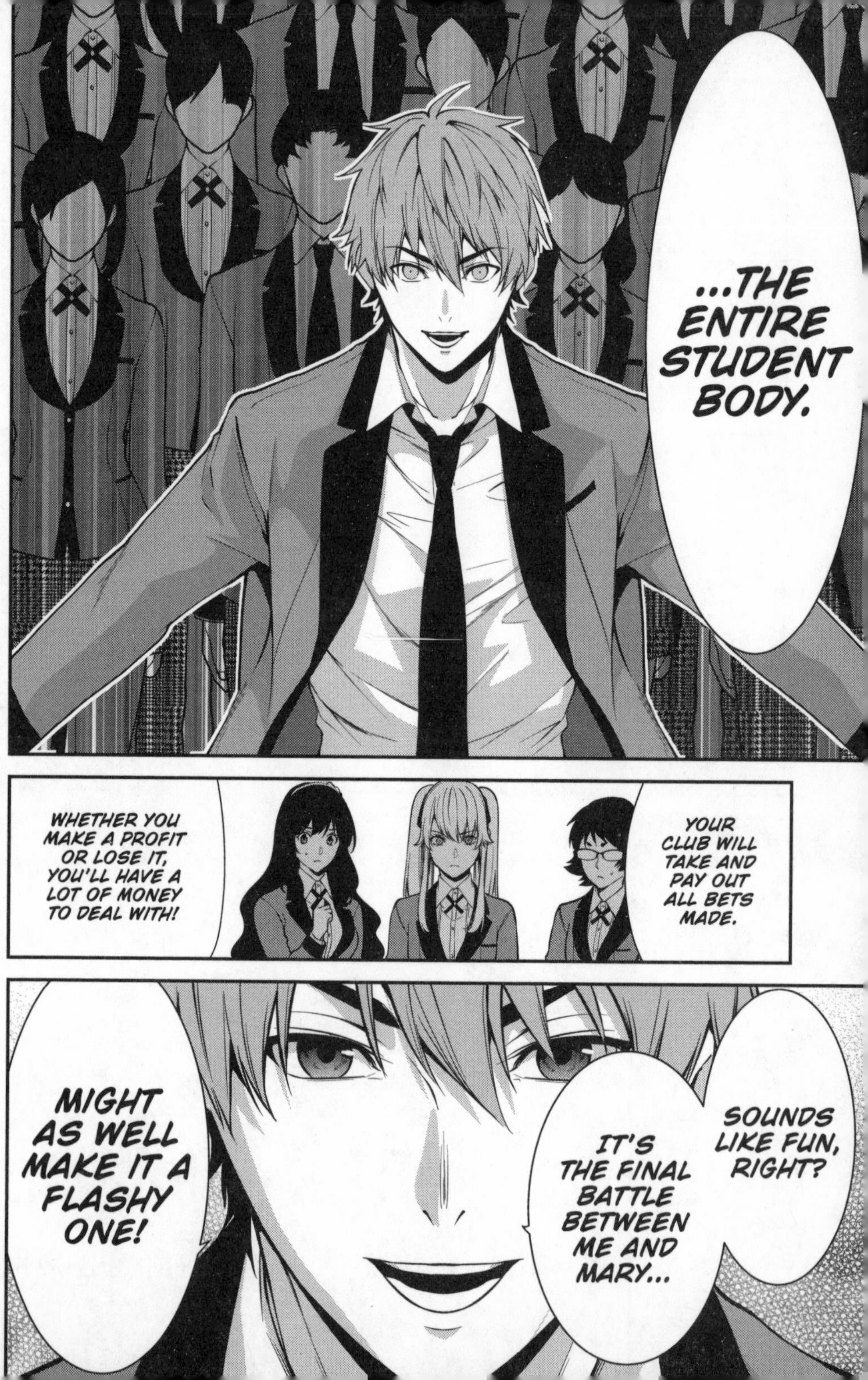
...THE ENTIRE STUDENT BODY.
YOUR CLUB WILL TAKE AND PAY OUT ALL BETS MADE.
WHETHER YOU MAKE A PROFIT OR LOSE IT, YOU'LL HAVE A LOT OF MONEY TO DEAL WITH!
SOUNDS LIKE FUN, RIGHT?
IT'S THE FINAL BATTLE BETWEEN ME AND MARY...
MIGHT AS WELL MAKE IT A FLASHY ONE!

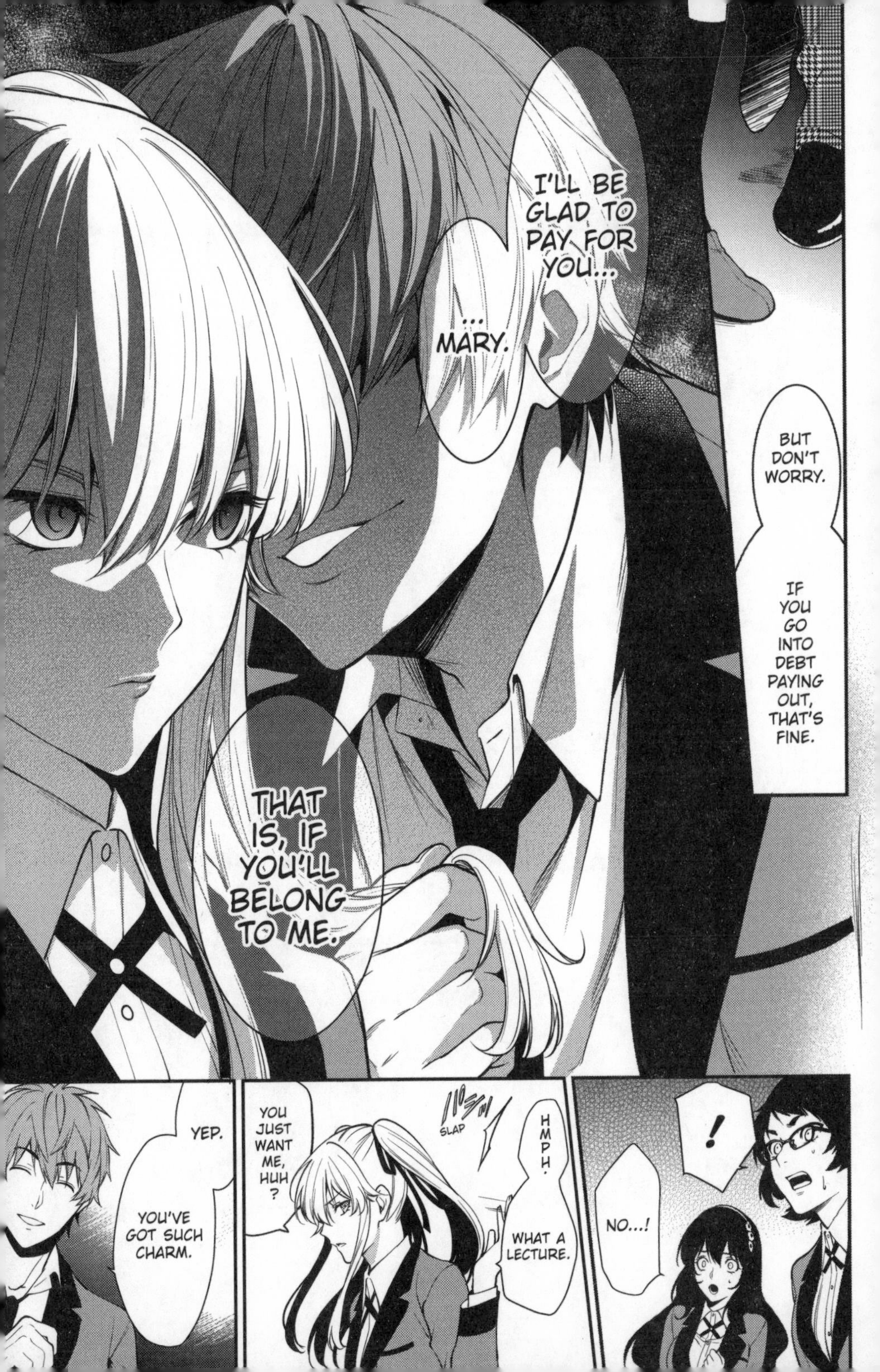
BUT DON'T WORRY.
IF YOU GO INTO DEBT PAYING OUT, THAT'S FINE.
I'LL BE GLAD TO PAY FOR YOU...
...MARY.
THAT IS, IF YOU'LL BELONG TO ME.
!
NO...!
HMPH.
WHAT A LECTURE.
パシッ
SLAP
YOU JUST WANT ME, HUH?
YEP.
YOU'VE GOT SUCH CHARM.

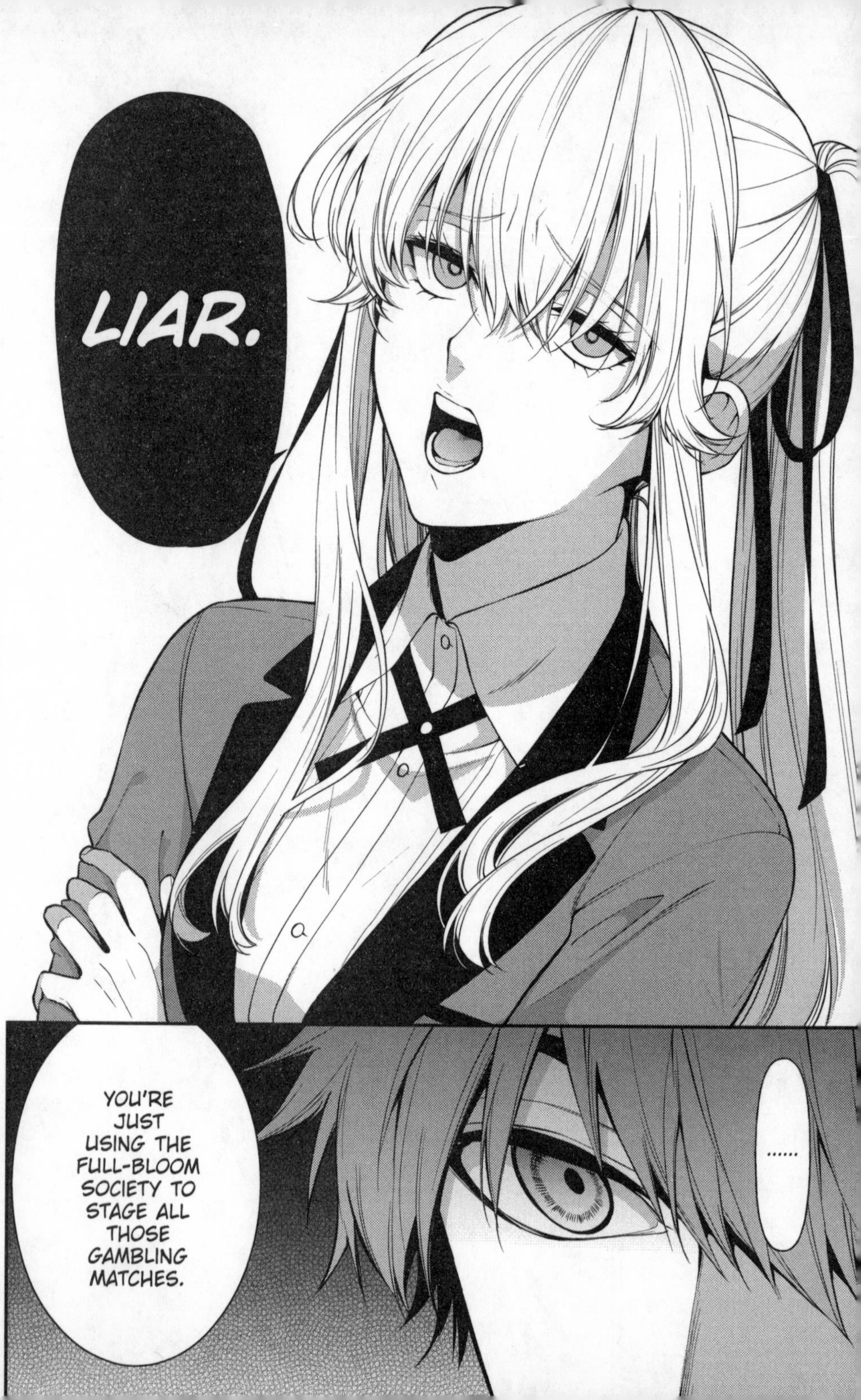
LIAR.
YOU'RE JUST USING THE FULL-BLOOM SOCIETY TO STAGE ALL THOSE GAMBLING MATCHES.
......

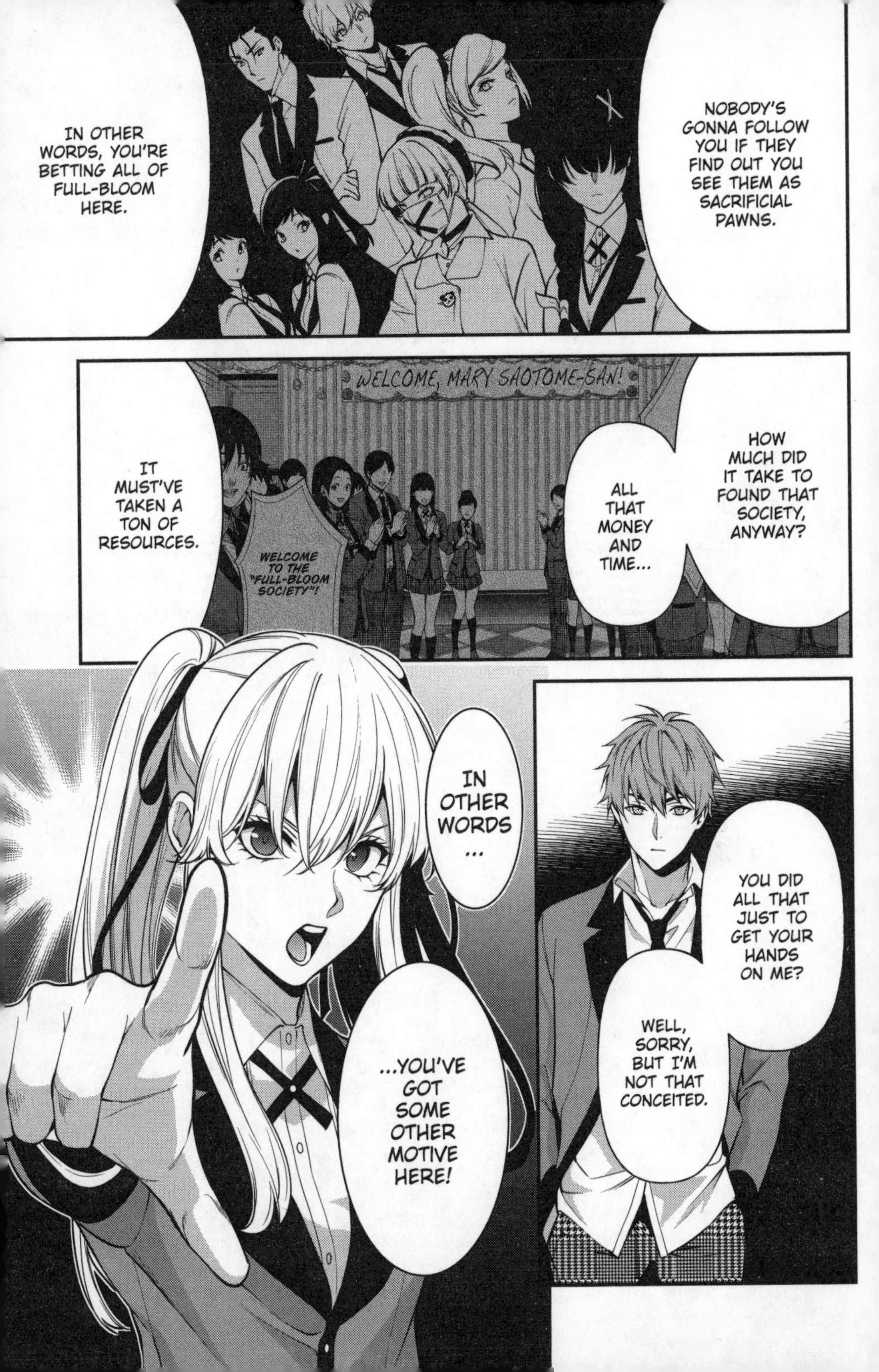
NOBODY'S GONNA FOLLOW YOU IF THEY FIND OUT YOU SEE THEM AS SACRIFICIAL PAWNS.
IN OTHER WORDS, YOU'RE BETTING ALL OF FULL-BLOOM HERE.
WELCOME, MARY SAOTOME-SAN!
HOW MUCH DID IT TAKE TO FOUND THAT SOCIETY, ANYWAY?
ALL THAT MONEY AND TIME...
IT MUST'VE TAKEN A TON OF RESOURCES.
WELCOME TO THE "FULL-BLOOM SOCIETY"!
YOU DID ALL THAT JUST TO GET YOUR HANDS ON ME?
WELL, SORRY, BUT I'M NOT THAT CONCEITED.
IN OTHER WORDS ...
...YOU'VE GOT SOME OTHER MOTIVE HERE!

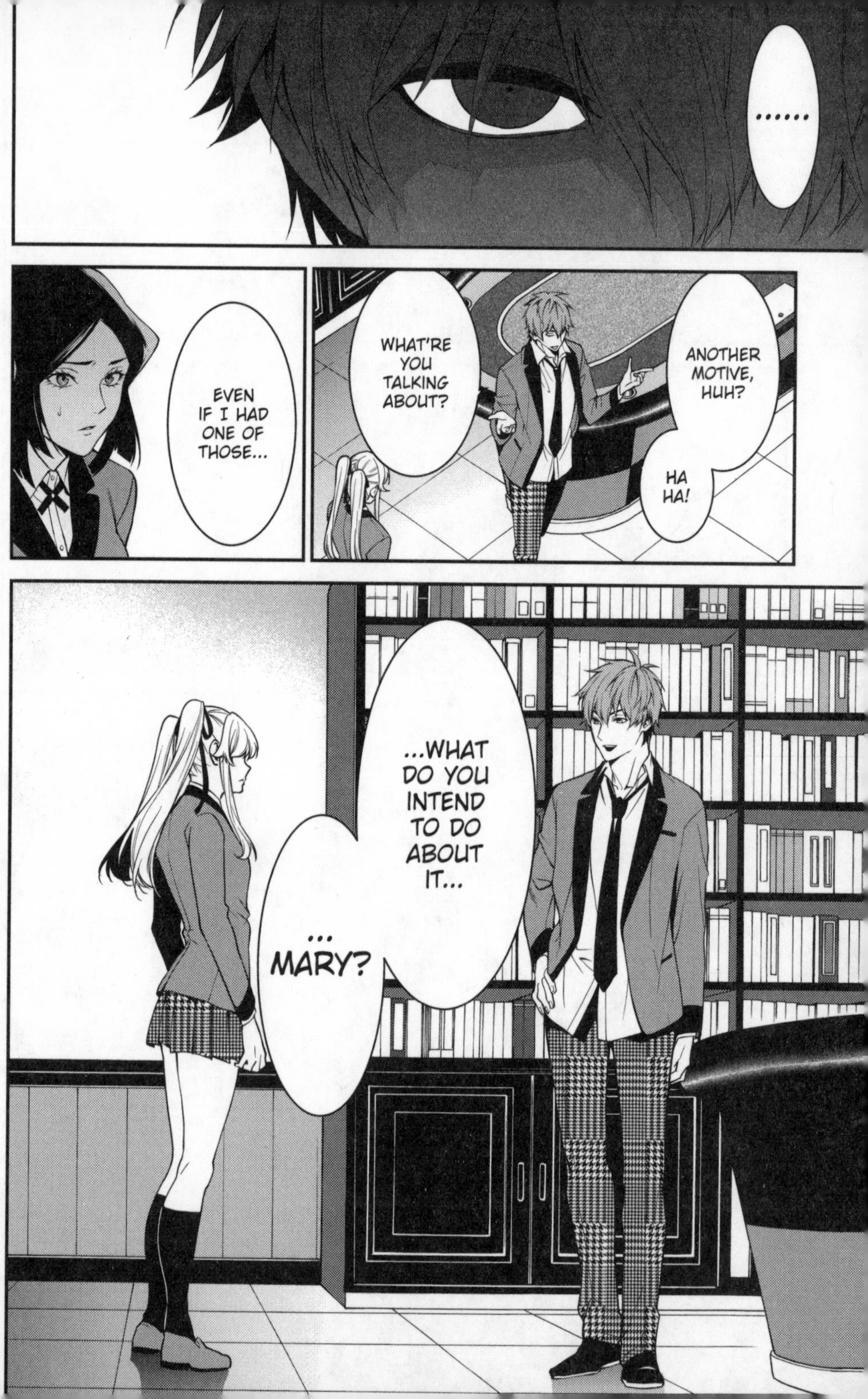
......
ANOTHER MOTIVE, HUH?
HA HA!
WHAT'RE YOU TALKING ABOUT?
EVEN IF I HAD ONE OF THOSE...
...WHAT DO YOU INTEND TO DO ABOUT IT...
... MARY?

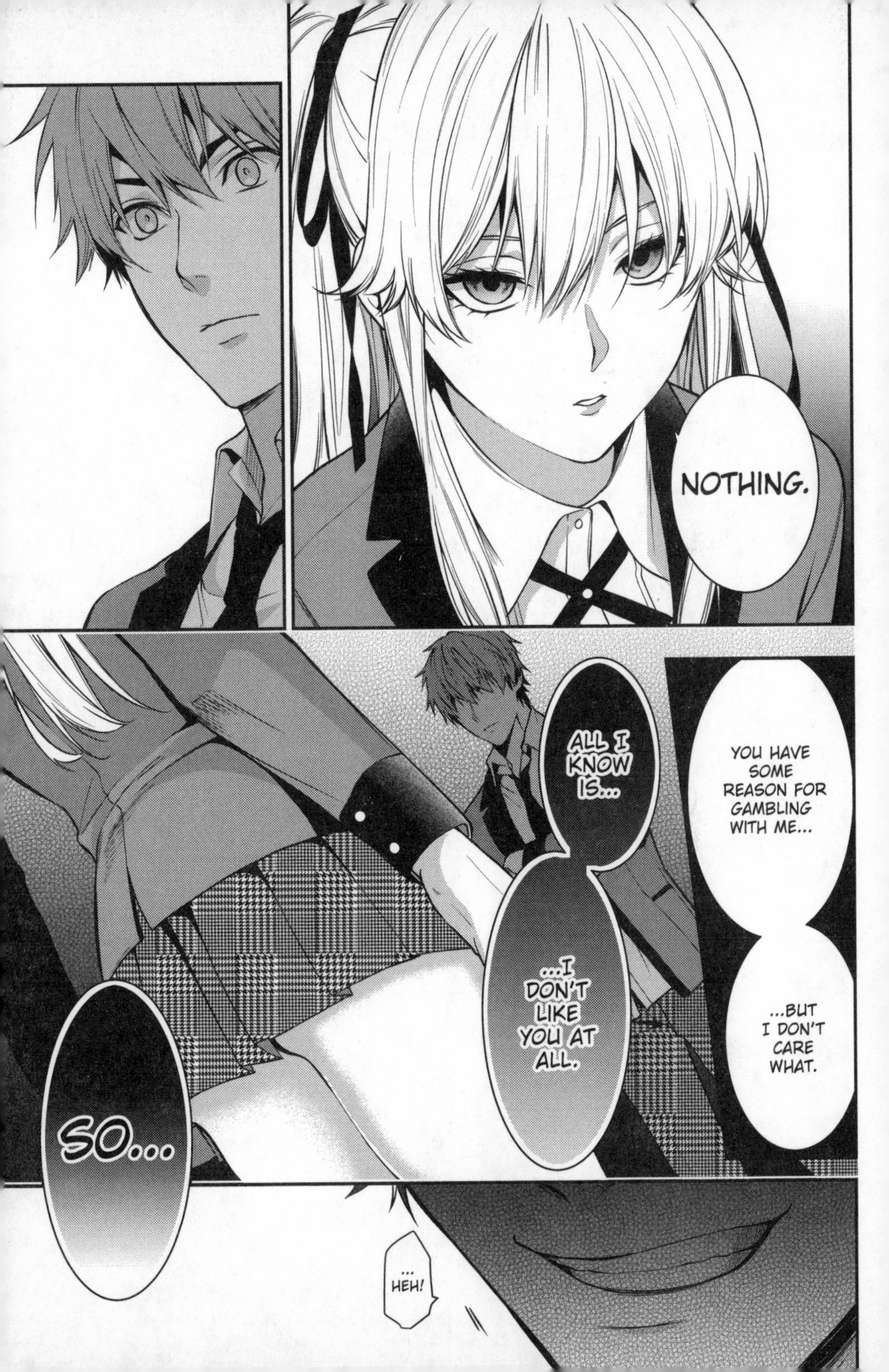
NOTHING.
YOU HAVE SOME REASON FOR GAMBLING WITH ME...
...BUT I DON'T CARE WHAT.
ALL I KNOW IS...
...I DON'T LIKE YOU AT ALL.
SO...
...HEH!

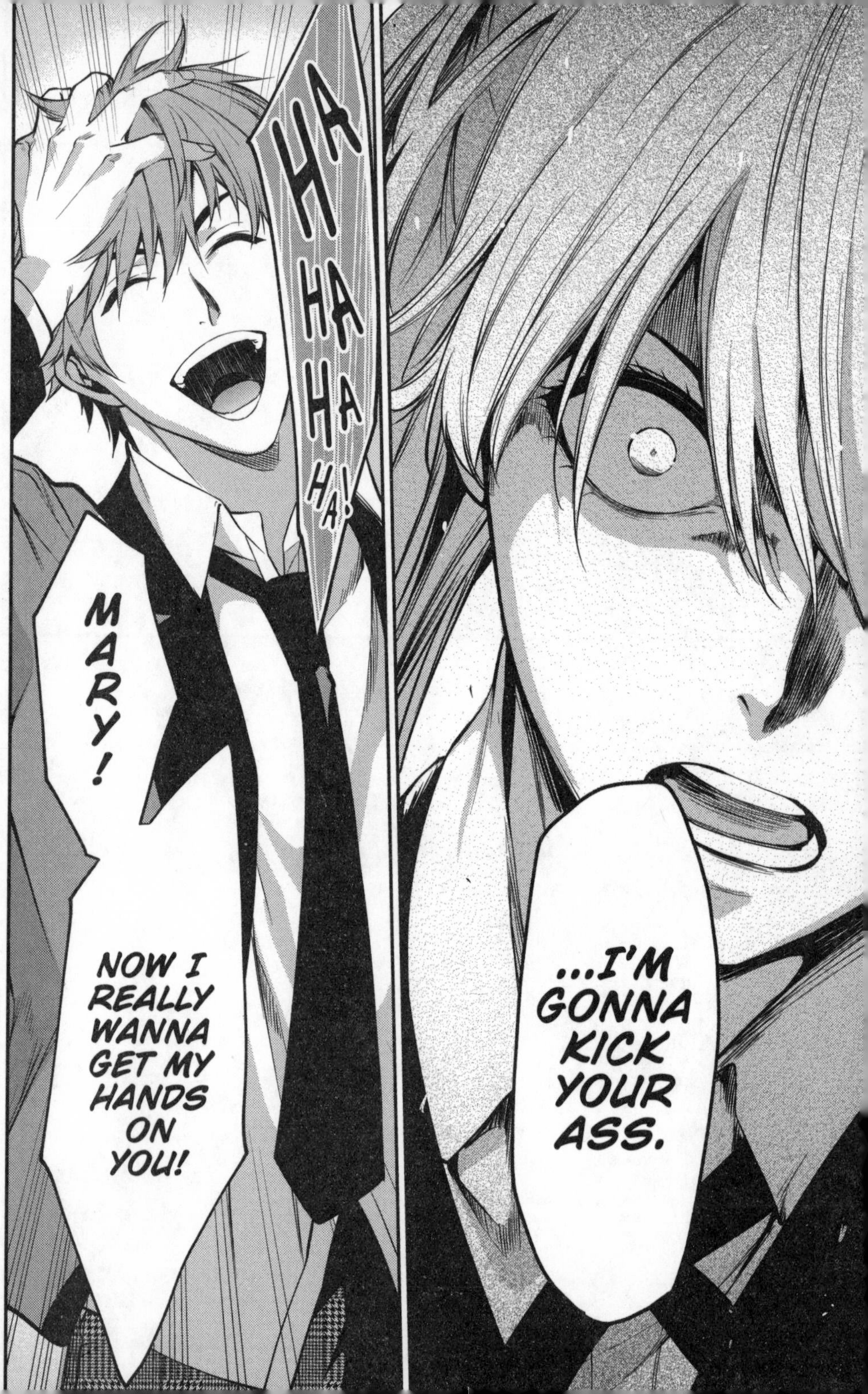
...I'M GONNA KICK YOUR ASS.
HA HA HA HA HA!
MARY!
NOW I REALLY WANNA GET MY HANDS ON YOU!

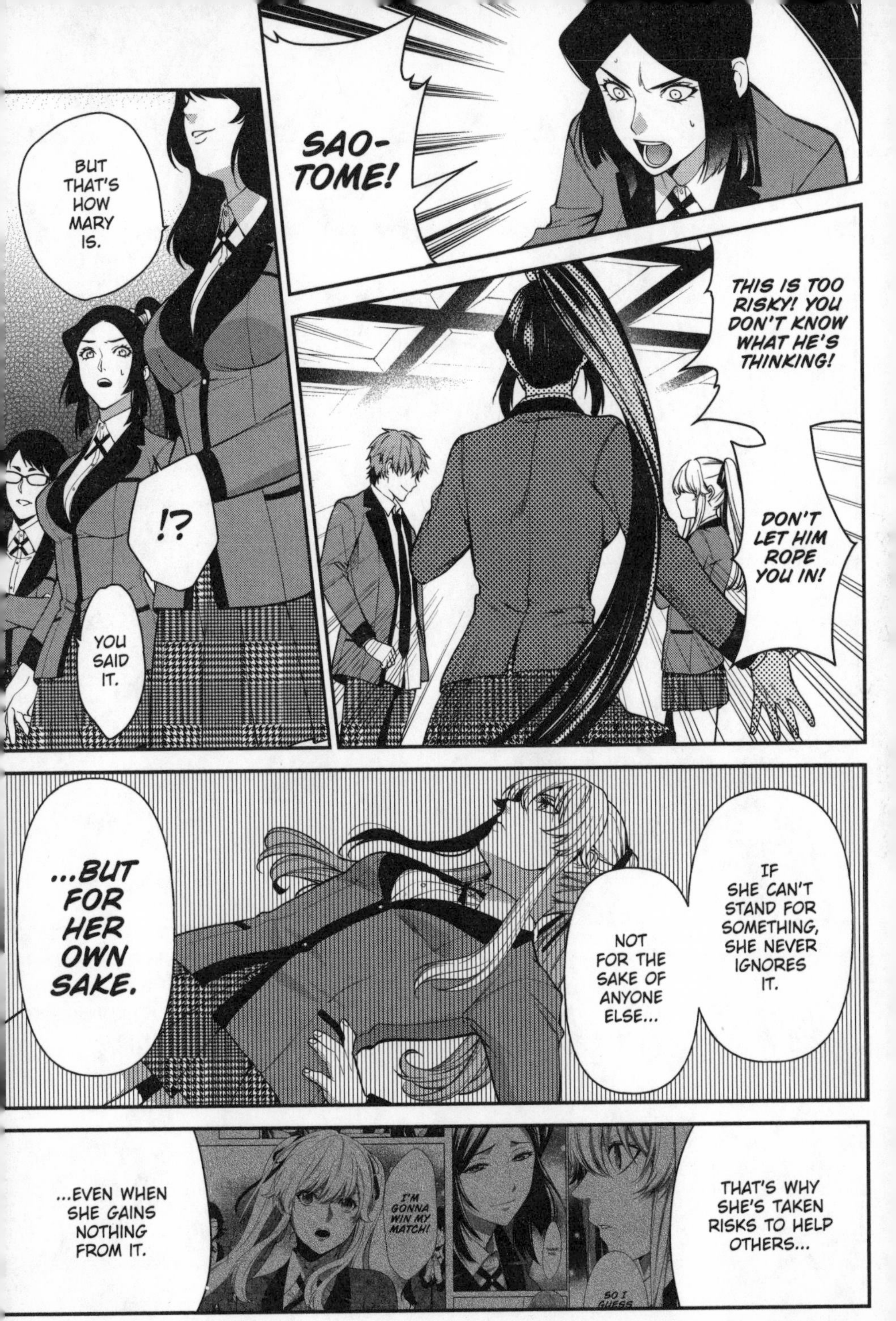
SAO-TOME!
THIS IS TOO RISKY! YOU DON'T KNOW WHAT HE'S THINKING!
DON'T LET HIM ROPE YOU IN!
BUT THAT'S HOW MARY IS.
!?
YOU SAID IT.
IF SHE CAN'T STAND FOR SOMETHING, SHE NEVER IGNORES IT.
NOT FOR THE SAKE OF ANYONE ELSE...
...BUT FOR HER OWN SAKE.
THAT'S WHY SHE'S TAKEN RISKS TO HELP OTHERS...
I'M GONNA WIN MY MATCH!
...EVEN WHEN SHE GAINS NOTHING FROM IT.

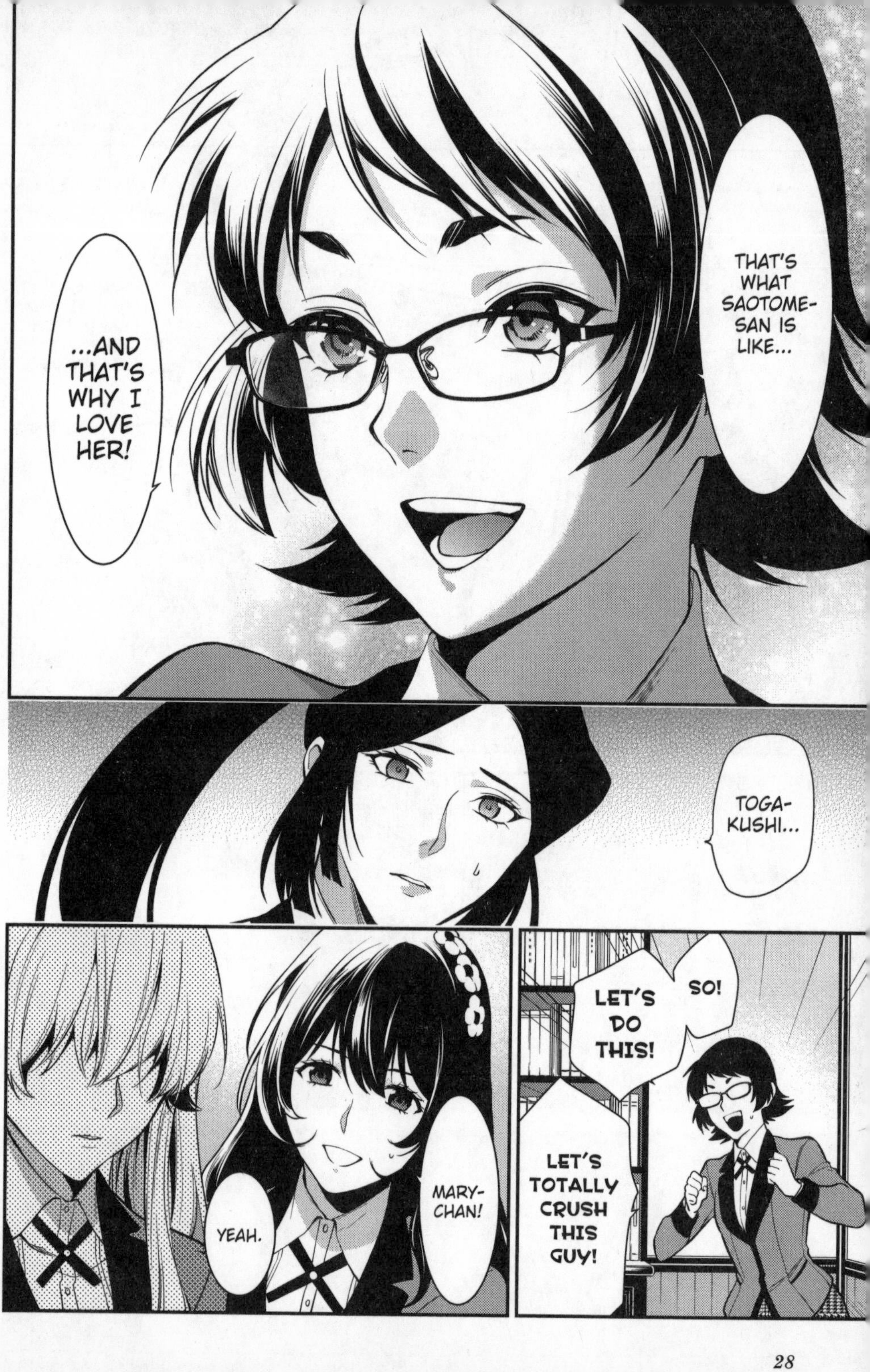
THAT'S WHAT SAOTOME-SAN IS LIKE...
...AND THAT'S WHY I LOVE HER!
TOGA-KUSHI...
SO!
LET'S DO THIS!
LET'S TOTALLY CRUSH THIS GUY!
MARY-CHAN!
YEAH.

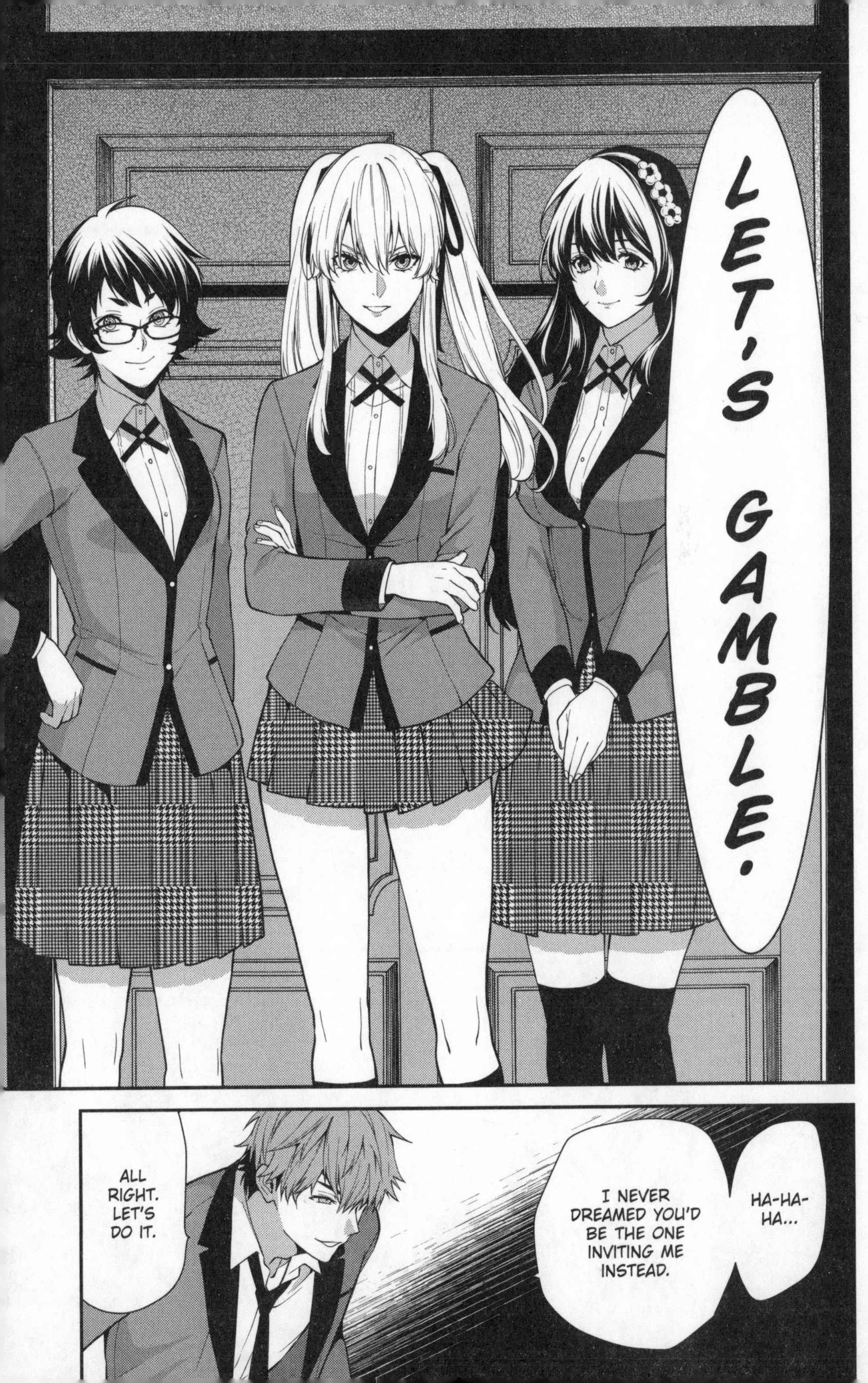
LET'S GAMBLE.
HA-HA-HA...
I NEVER DREAMED YOU'D BE THE ONE INVITING ME INSTEAD.
ALL RIGHT. LET'S DO IT.

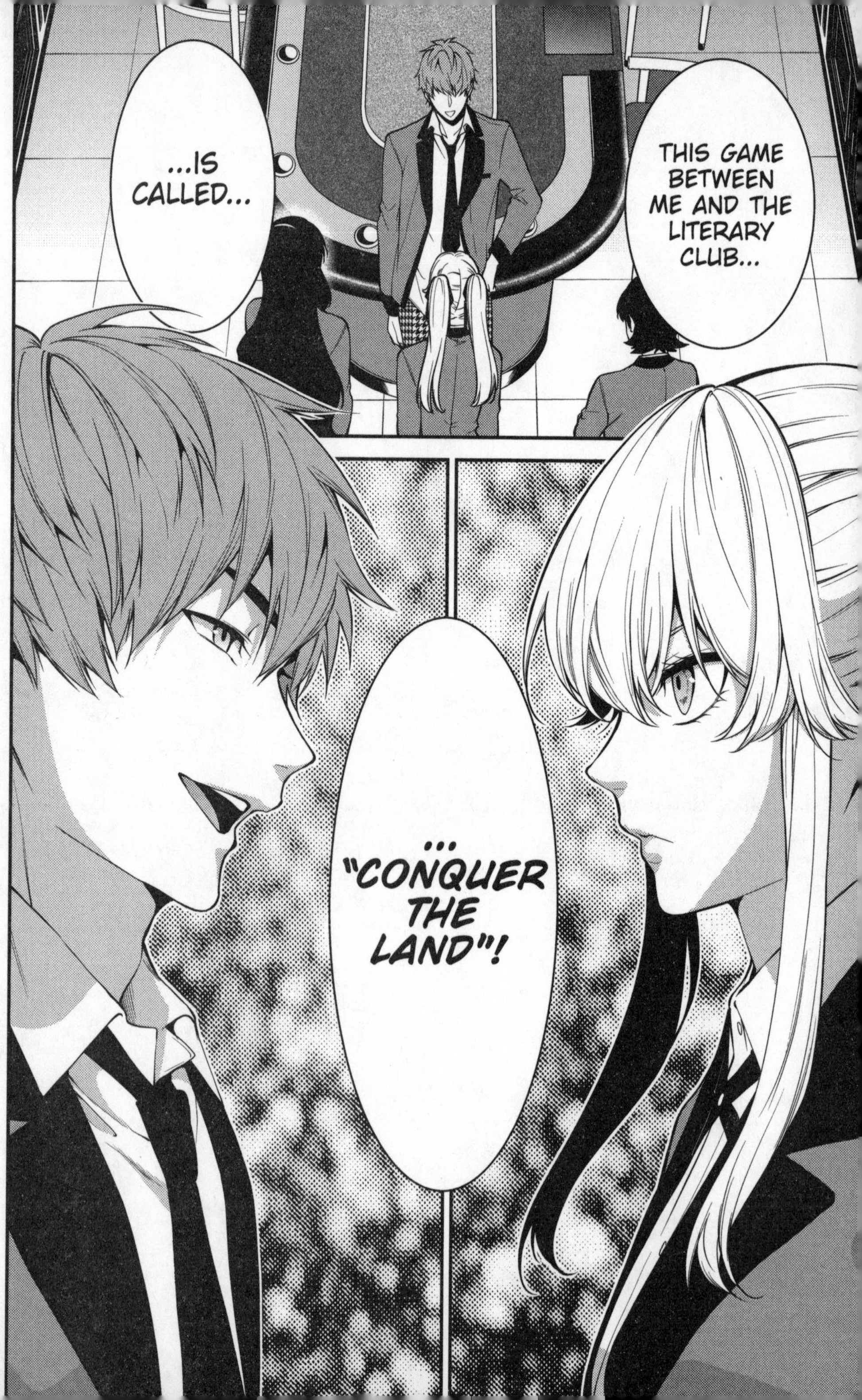
THIS GAME BETWEEN ME AND THE LITERARY CLUB...
...IS CALLED...
... "CONQUER THE LAND"!

Kakegurui Twin

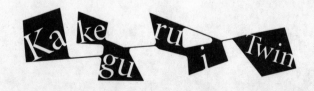

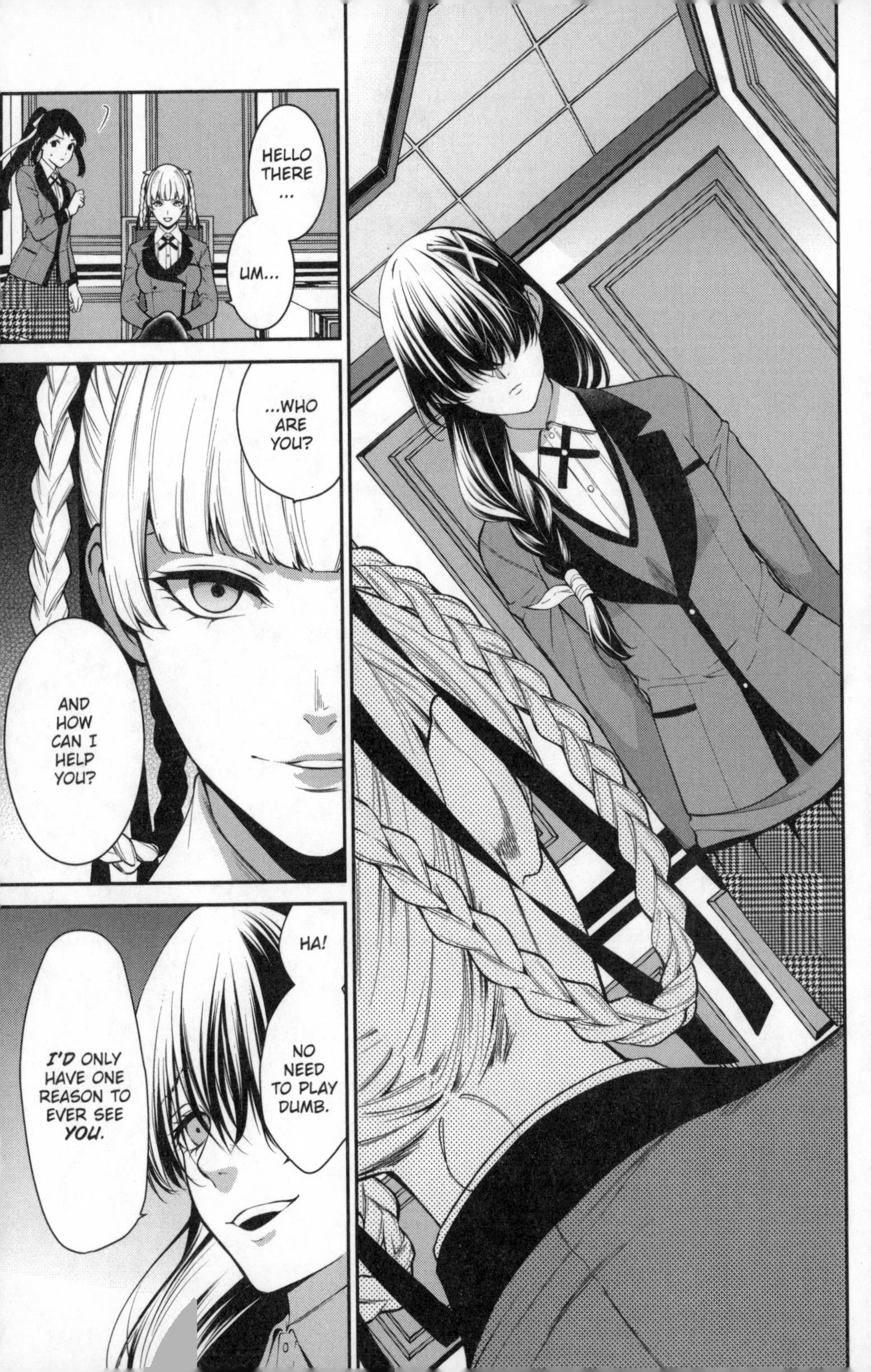
HELLO THERE ...
UM...
...WHO ARE YOU?
AND HOW CAN I HELP YOU?
HA!
NO NEED TO PLAY DUMB.
I'D ONLY HAVE ONE REASON TO EVER SEE *YOU*.

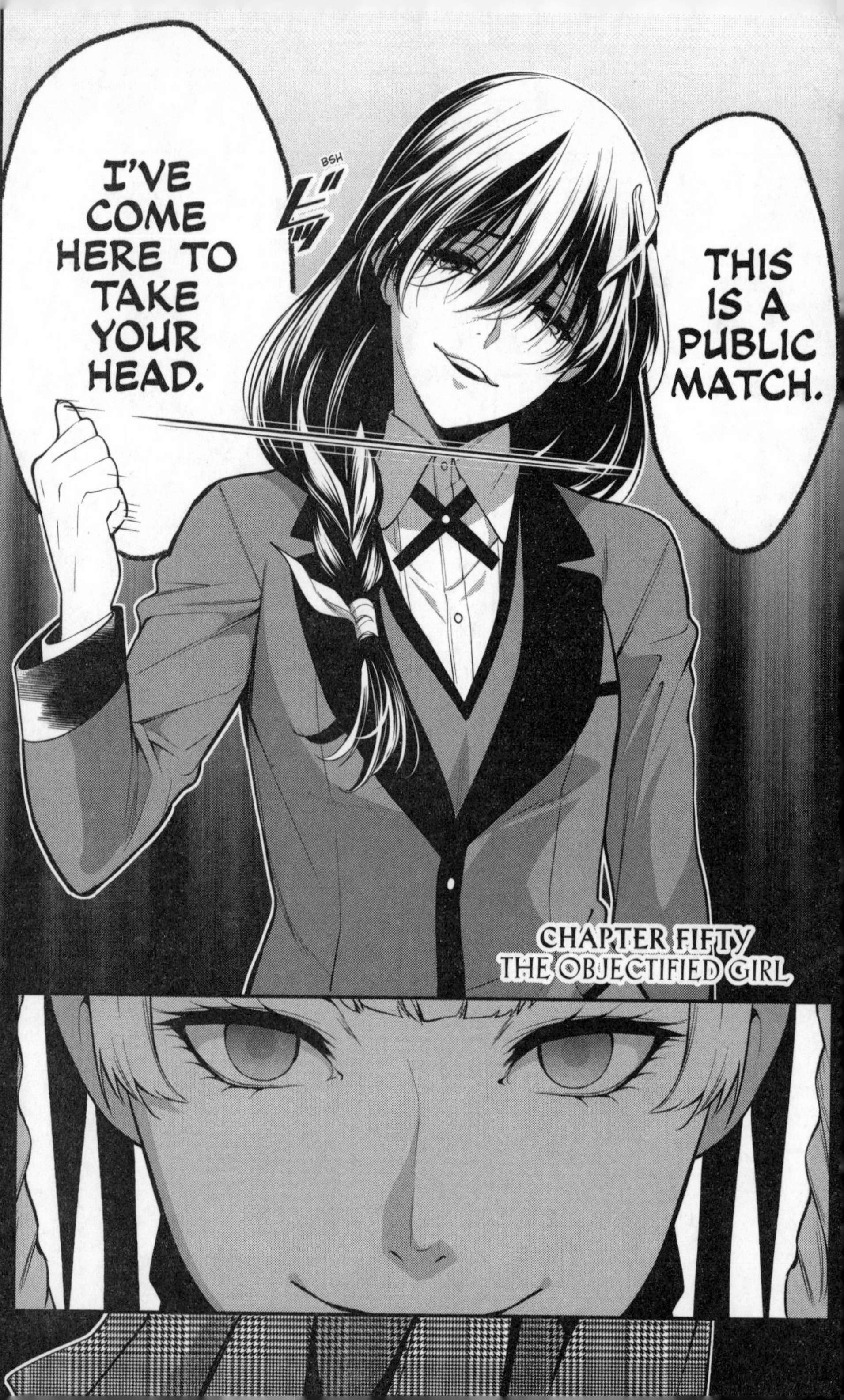
THIS IS A PUBLIC MATCH.
BSH
I'VE COME HERE TO TAKE YOUR HEAD.
CHAPTER FIFTY
THE OBJECTIFIED GIRL

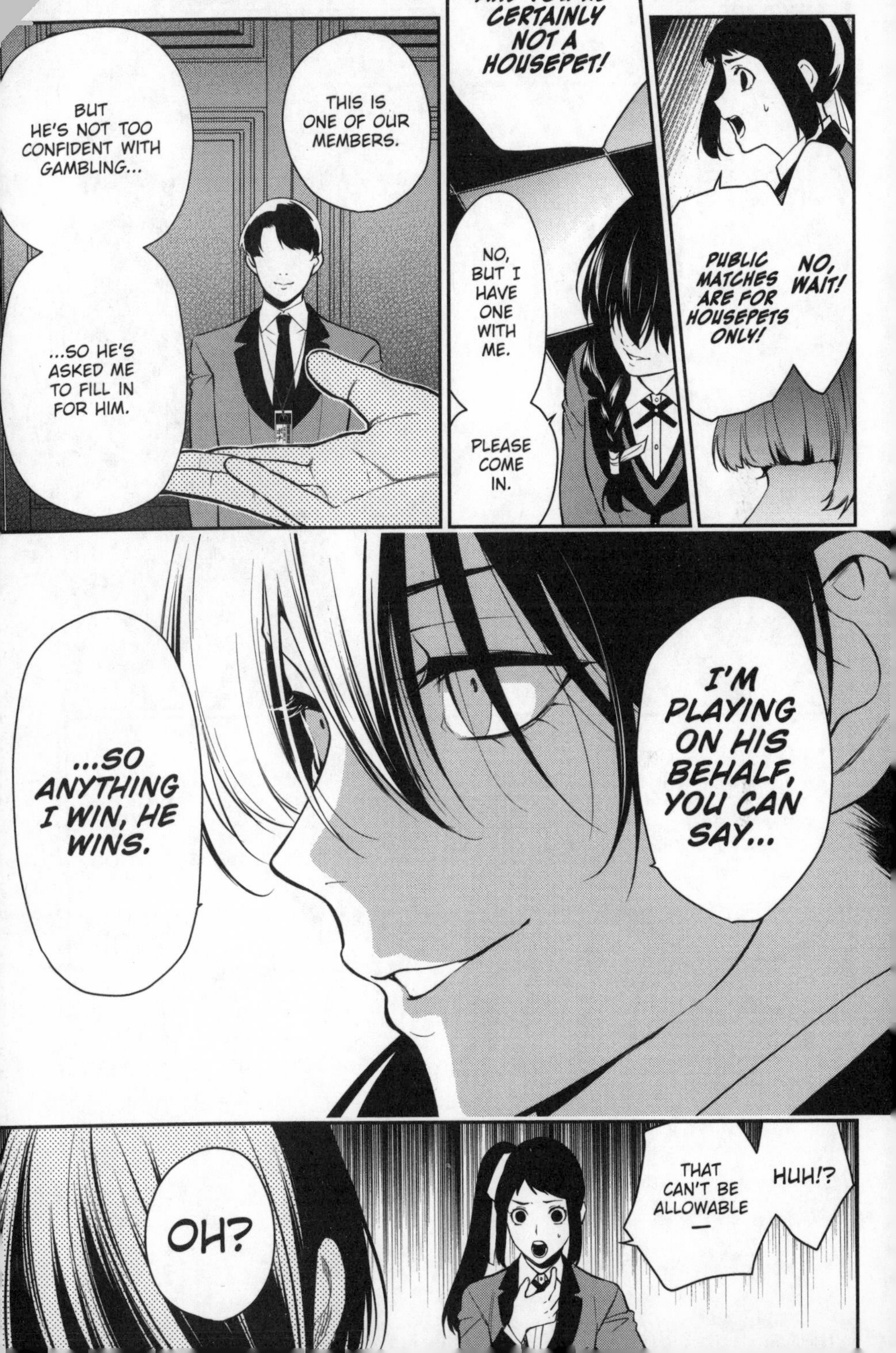
NO, WAIT!
PUBLIC MATCHES ARE FOR HOUSEPETS ONLY!
AND YOU'RE CERTAINLY NOT A HOUSEPET!
NO, BUT I HAVE ONE WITH ME.
PLEASE COME IN.
THIS IS ONE OF OUR MEMBERS.
BUT HE'S NOT TOO CONFIDENT WITH GAMBLING...
...SO HE'S ASKED ME TO FILL IN FOR HIM.
I'M PLAYING ON HIS BEHALF, YOU CAN SAY...
...SO ANYTHING I WIN, HE WINS.
HUH!?
THAT CAN'T BE ALLOWABLE —
OH?

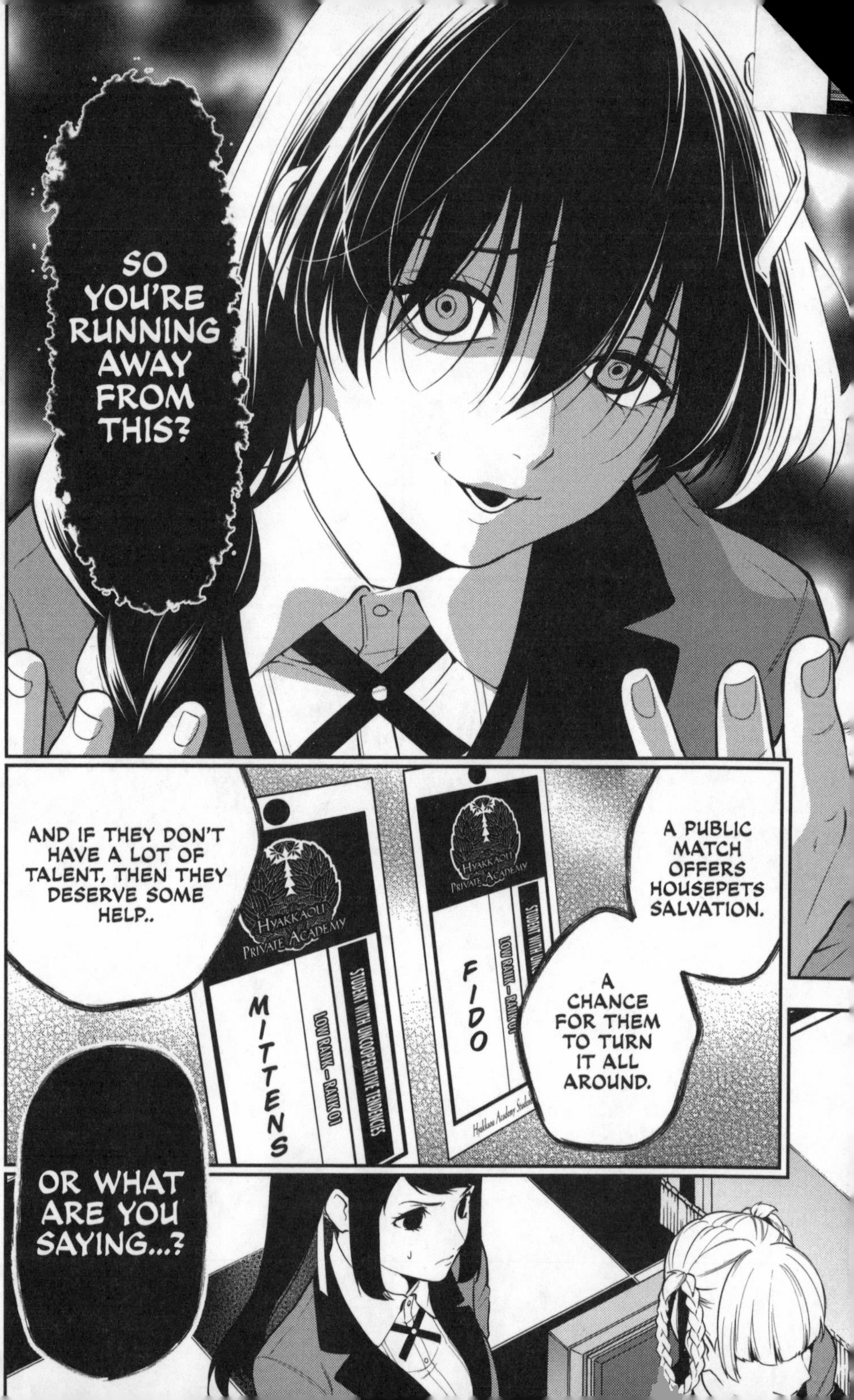
SO YOU'RE RUNNING AWAY FROM THIS?
A PUBLIC MATCH OFFERS HOUSEPETS SALVATION.
A CHANCE FOR THEM TO TURN IT ALL AROUND.
AND IF THEY DON'T HAVE A LOT OF TALENT, THEN THEY DESERVE SOME HELP..
HYAKKAOU PRIVATE ACADEMY
FIDO
HYAKKAOU PRIVATE ACADEMY
STUDENT WITH UNCOOPERATIVE TENDENCIES
LOW RANK—RANK 01
MITTENS
OR WHAT ARE YOU SAYING...?

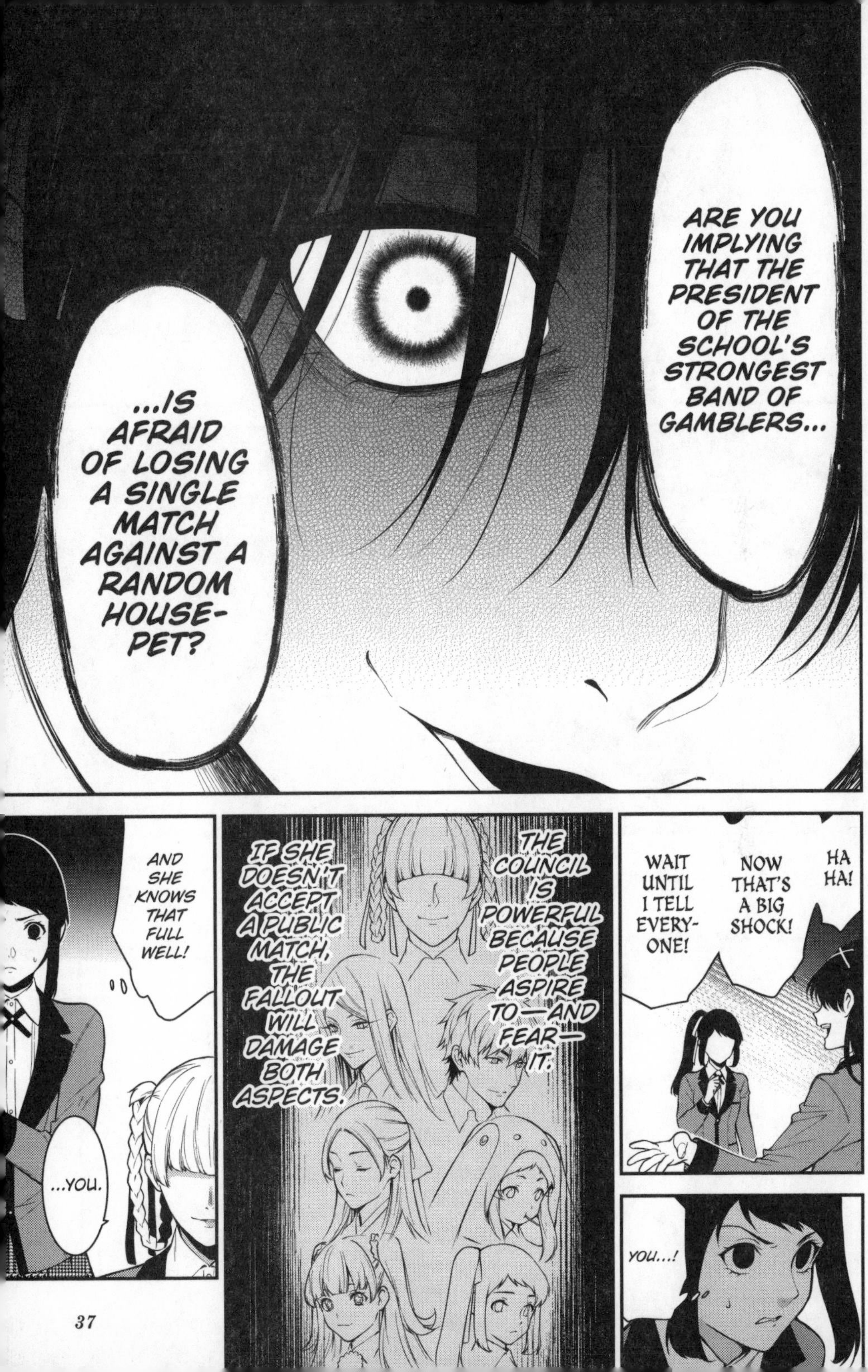

ARE YOU IMPLYING THAT THE PRESIDENT OF THE SCHOOL'S STRONGEST BAND OF GAMBLERS...
...IS AFRAID OF LOSING A SINGLE MATCH AGAINST A RANDOM HOUSE-PET?
HA HA!
NOW THAT'S A BIG SHOCK!
WAIT UNTIL I TELL EVERY-ONE!
YOU...!
THE COUNCIL IS POWERFUL BECAUSE PEOPLE ASPIRE TO—AND FEAR—IT.
IF SHE DOESN'T ACCEPT A PUBLIC MATCH, THE FALLOUT WILL DAMAGE BOTH ASPECTS.
AND SHE KNOWS THAT FULL WELL!
...YOU.

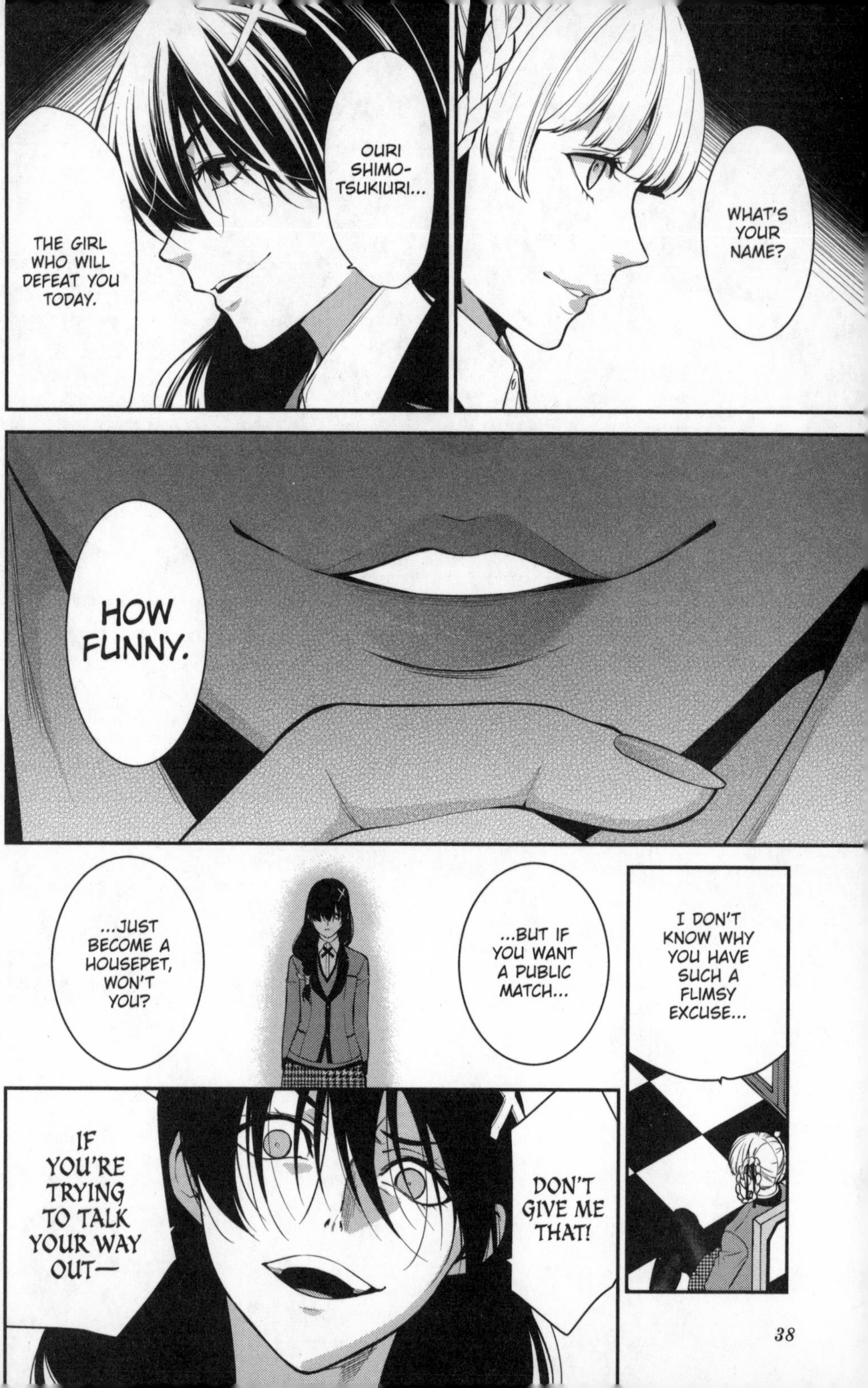
WHAT'S YOUR NAME?
OURI SHIMO-TSUKIURI...
THE GIRL WHO WILL DEFEAT YOU TODAY.
HOW FUNNY.
I DON'T KNOW WHY YOU HAVE SUCH A FLIMSY EXCUSE...
...BUT IF YOU WANT A PUBLIC MATCH...
...JUST BECOME A HOUSEPET, WON'T YOU?
DON'T GIVE ME THAT!
IF YOU'RE TRYING TO TALK YOUR WAY OUT—

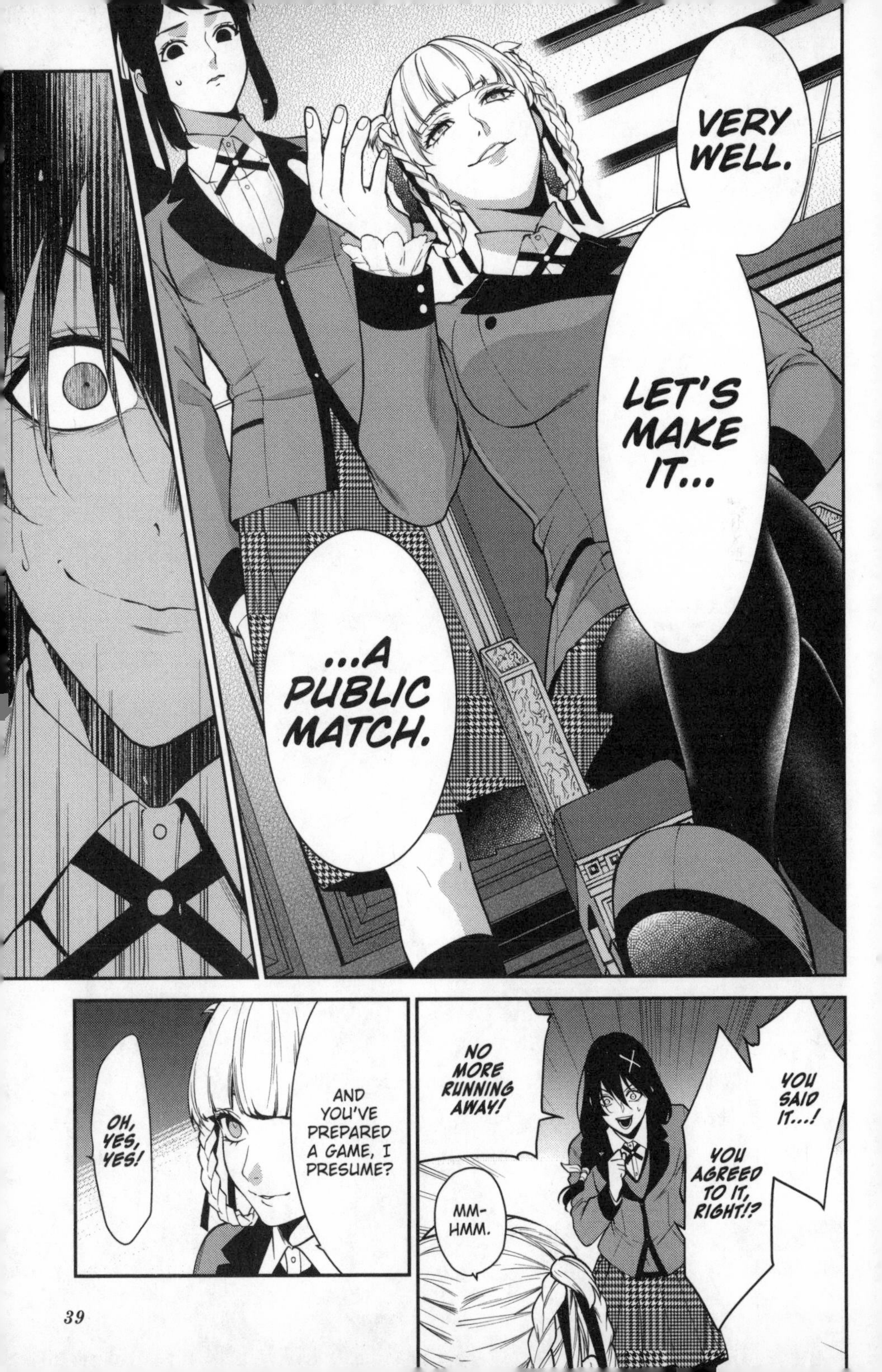
VERY WELL.
LET'S MAKE IT...
...A PUBLIC MATCH.
YOU SAID IT...!
YOU AGREED TO IT, RIGHT!?
NO MORE RUNNING AWAY!
MM-HMM.
AND YOU'VE PREPARED A GAME, I PRESUME?
OH, YES, YES!

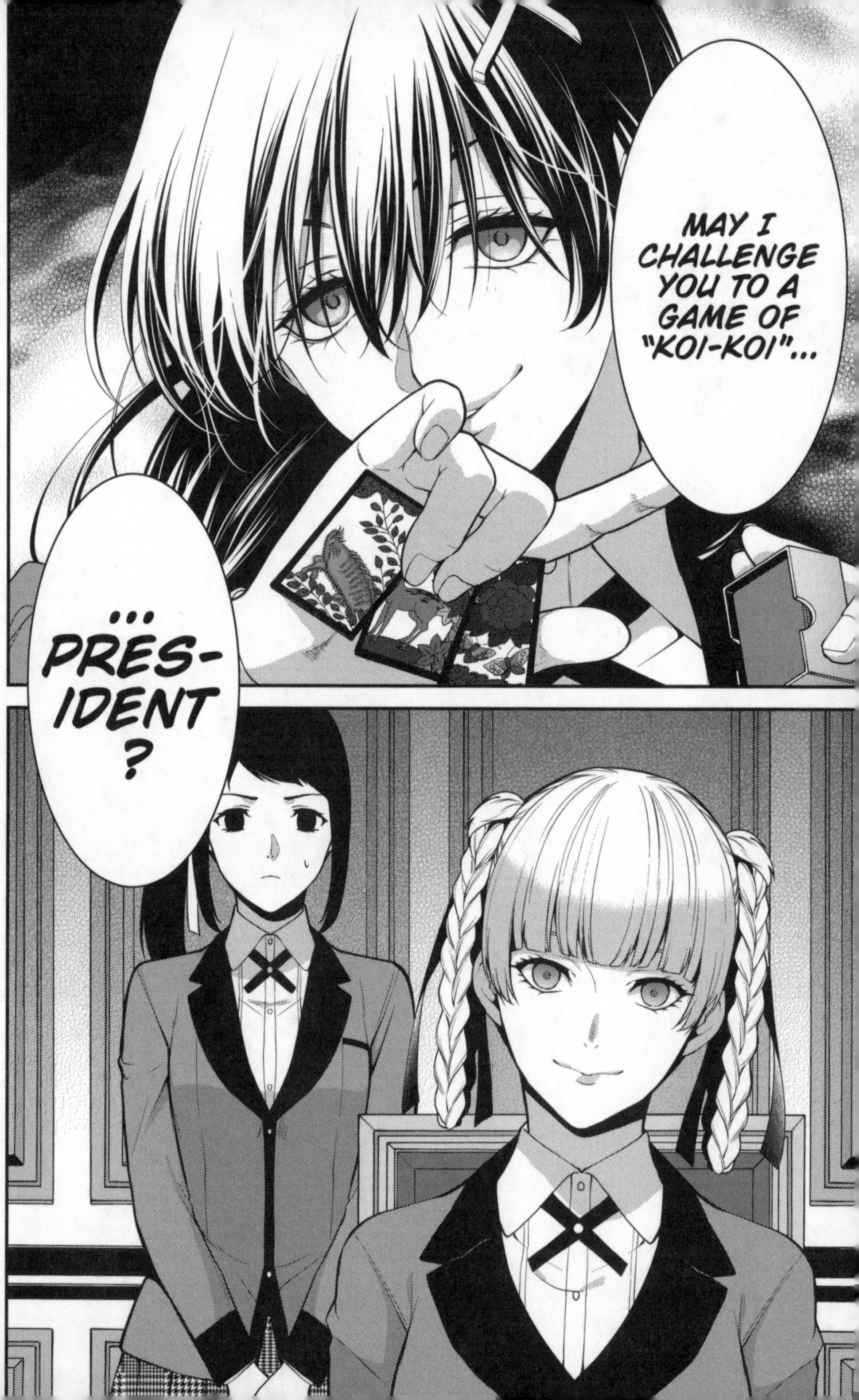
MAY I CHALLENGE YOU TO A GAME OF "KOI-KOI"...
... PRES-IDENT ?

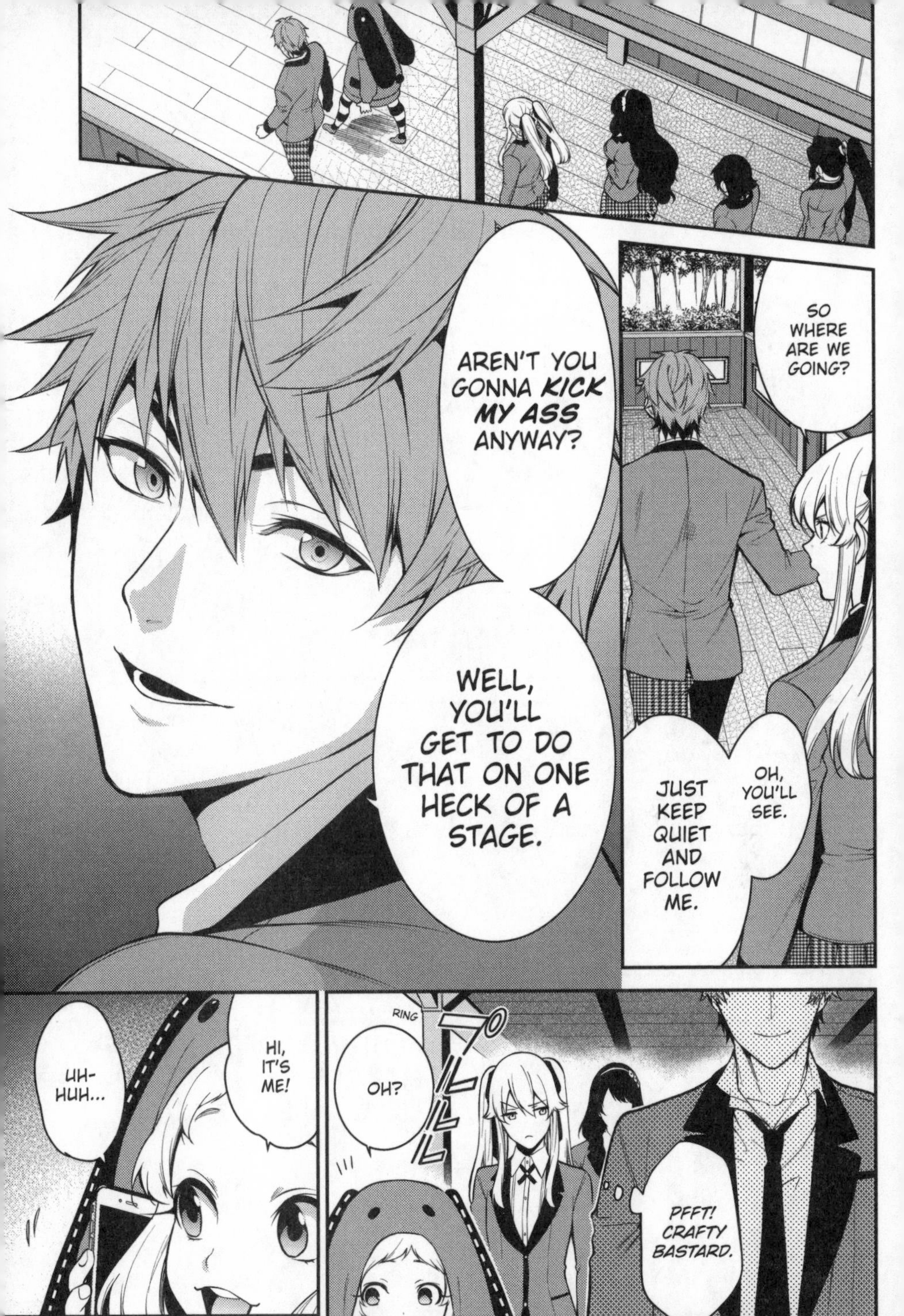
SO WHERE ARE WE GOING?
OH, YOU'LL SEE.
JUST KEEP QUIET AND FOLLOW ME.
AREN'T YOU GONNA *KICK MY ASS* ANYWAY?
WELL, YOU'LL GET TO DO THAT ON ONE HECK OF A STAGE.
RING
OH?
PFFT! CRAFTY BASTARD.
HI, IT'S ME!
UH-HUH...

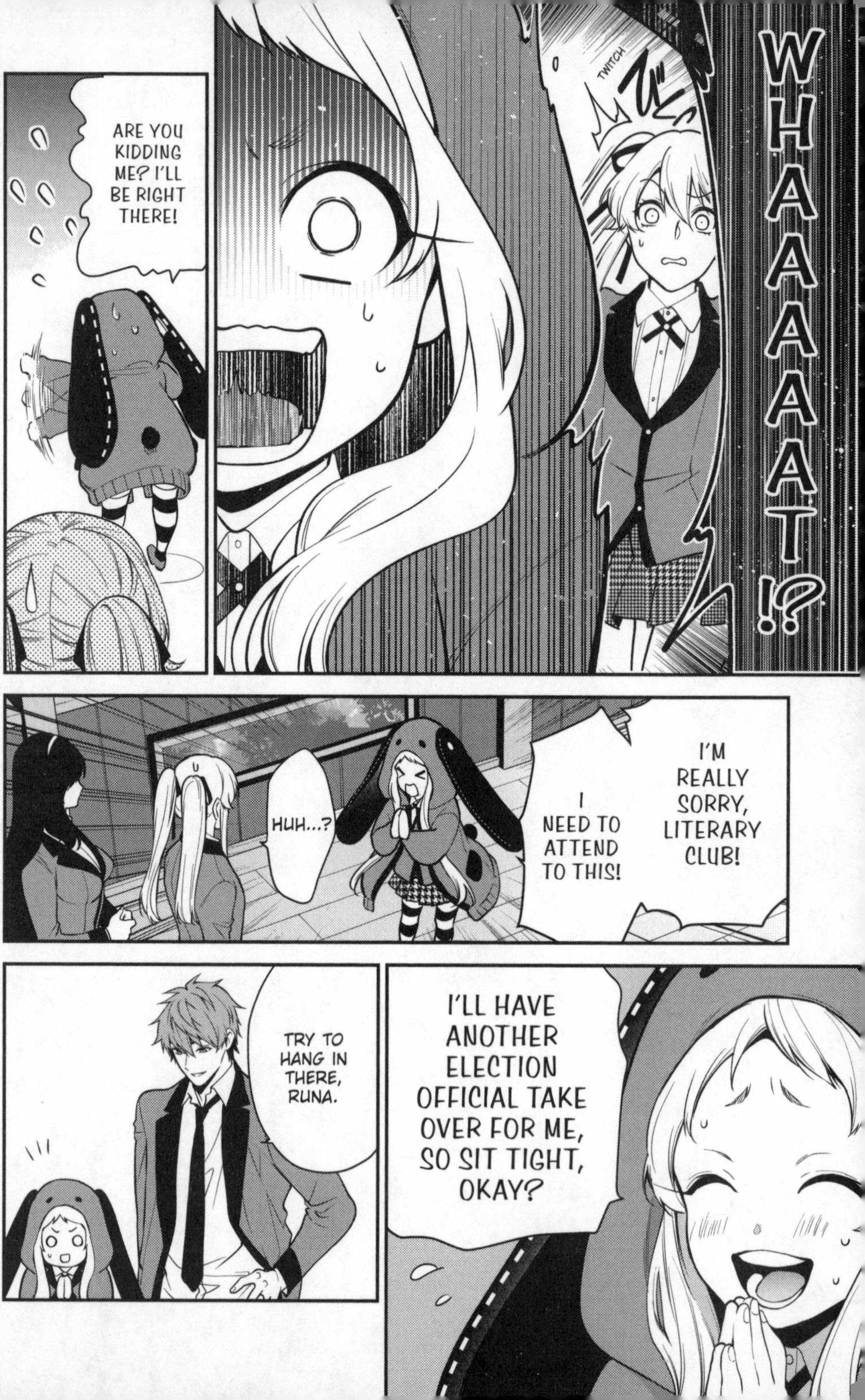
TWITCH
WHAAAAAT!?
ARE YOU KIDDING ME? I'LL BE RIGHT THERE!
I'M REALLY SORRY, LITERARY CLUB!
I NEED TO ATTEND TO THIS!
HUH...?
I'LL HAVE ANOTHER ELECTION OFFICIAL TAKE OVER FOR ME, SO SIT TIGHT, OKAY?
TRY TO HANG IN THERE, RUNA.

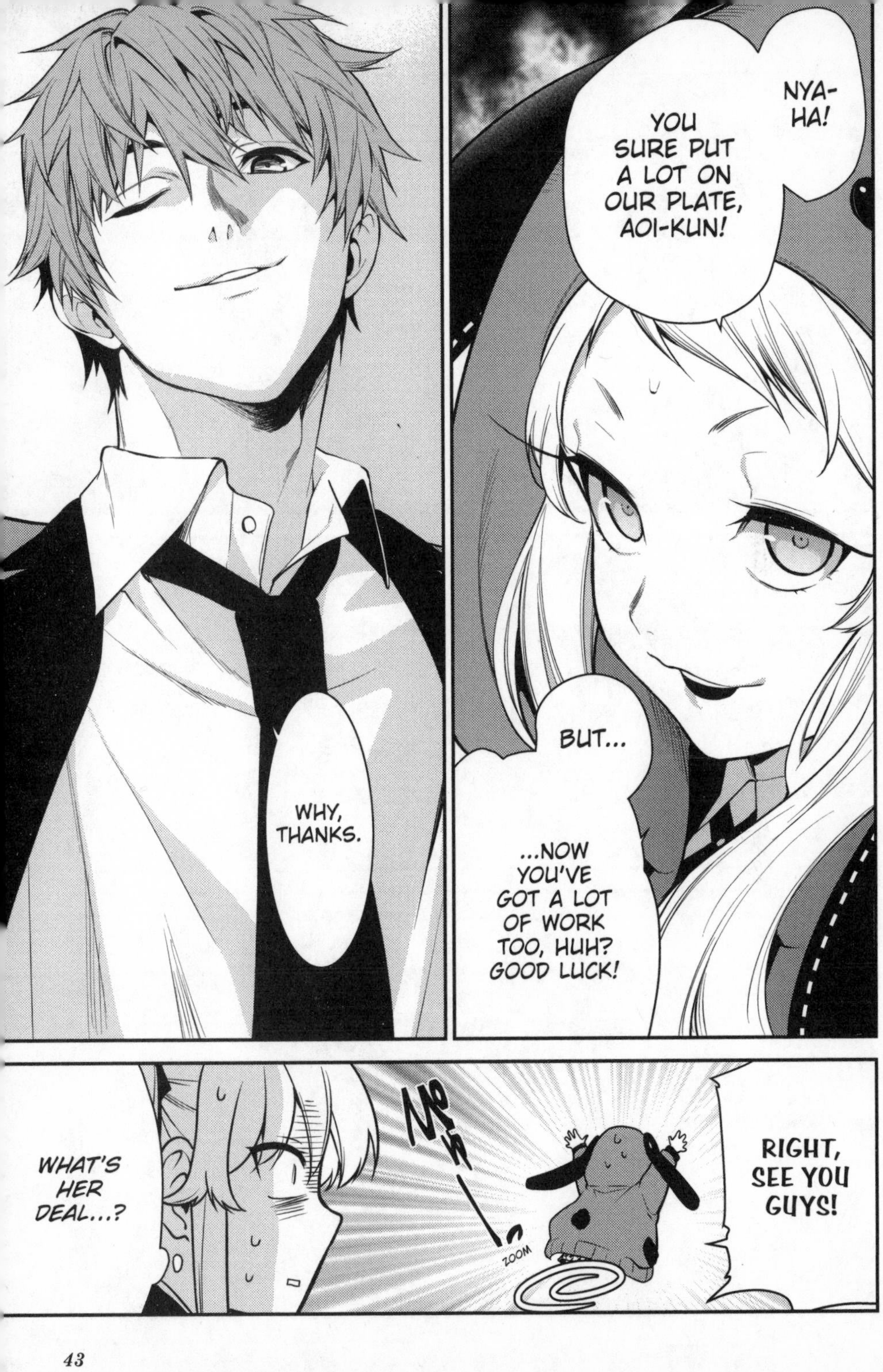
NYA-HA!
YOU SURE PUT A LOT ON OUR PLATE, AOI-KUN!
BUT...
...NOW YOU'VE GOT A LOT OF WORK TOO, HUH? GOOD LUCK!
WHY, THANKS.
RIGHT, SEE YOU GUYS!
ZOOM
WHAT'S HER DEAL...?

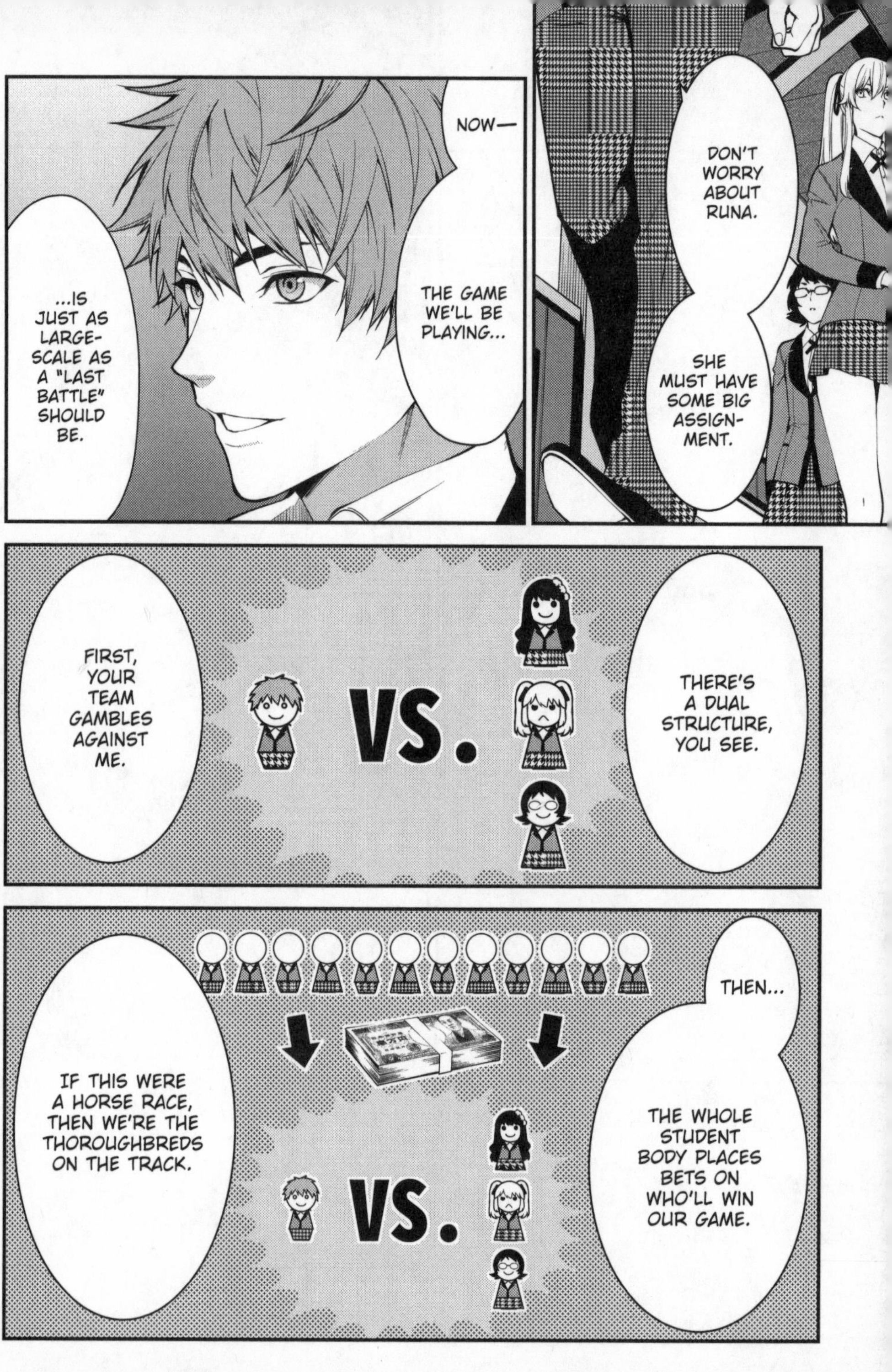
DON'T WORRY ABOUT RUNA.
SHE MUST HAVE SOME BIG ASSIGNMENT.
NOW—
THE GAME WE'LL BE PLAYING...
...IS JUST AS LARGE-SCALE AS A "LAST BATTLE" SHOULD BE.
THERE'S A DUAL STRUCTURE, YOU SEE.
VS.
FIRST, YOUR TEAM GAMBLES AGAINST ME.
THEN...
THE WHOLE STUDENT BODY PLACES BETS ON WHO'LL WIN OUR GAME.
VS.
IF THIS WERE A HORSE RACE, THEN WE'RE THE THOROUGHBREDS ON THE TRACK.

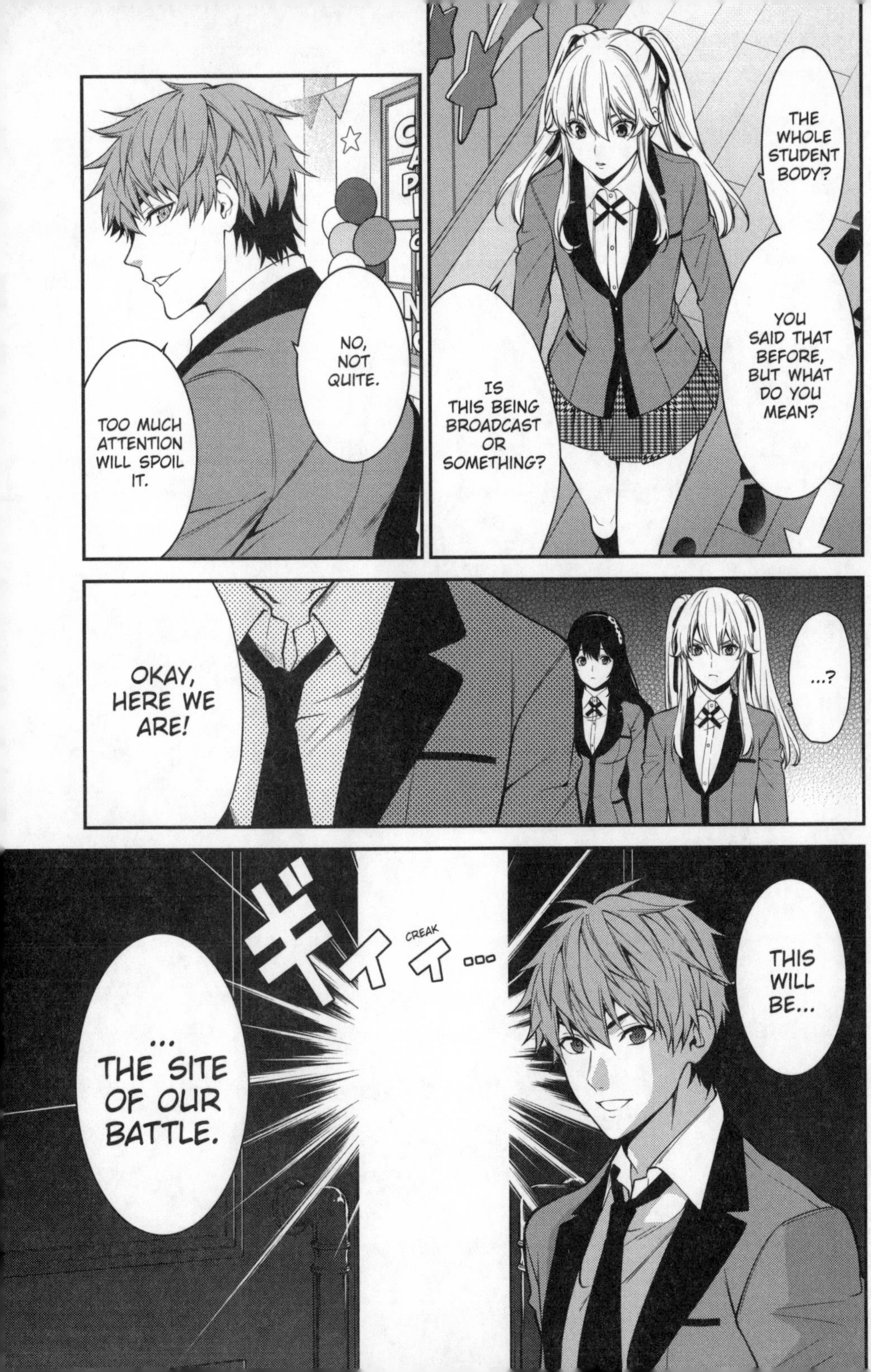
THE WHOLE STUDENT BODY?
YOU SAID THAT BEFORE, BUT WHAT DO YOU MEAN?
IS THIS BEING BROADCAST OR SOMETHING?
NO, NOT QUITE.
TOO MUCH ATTENTION WILL SPOIL IT.
...?
OKAY, HERE WE ARE!
THIS WILL BE...
ギィイ...
CREAK
... THE SITE OF OUR BATTLE.

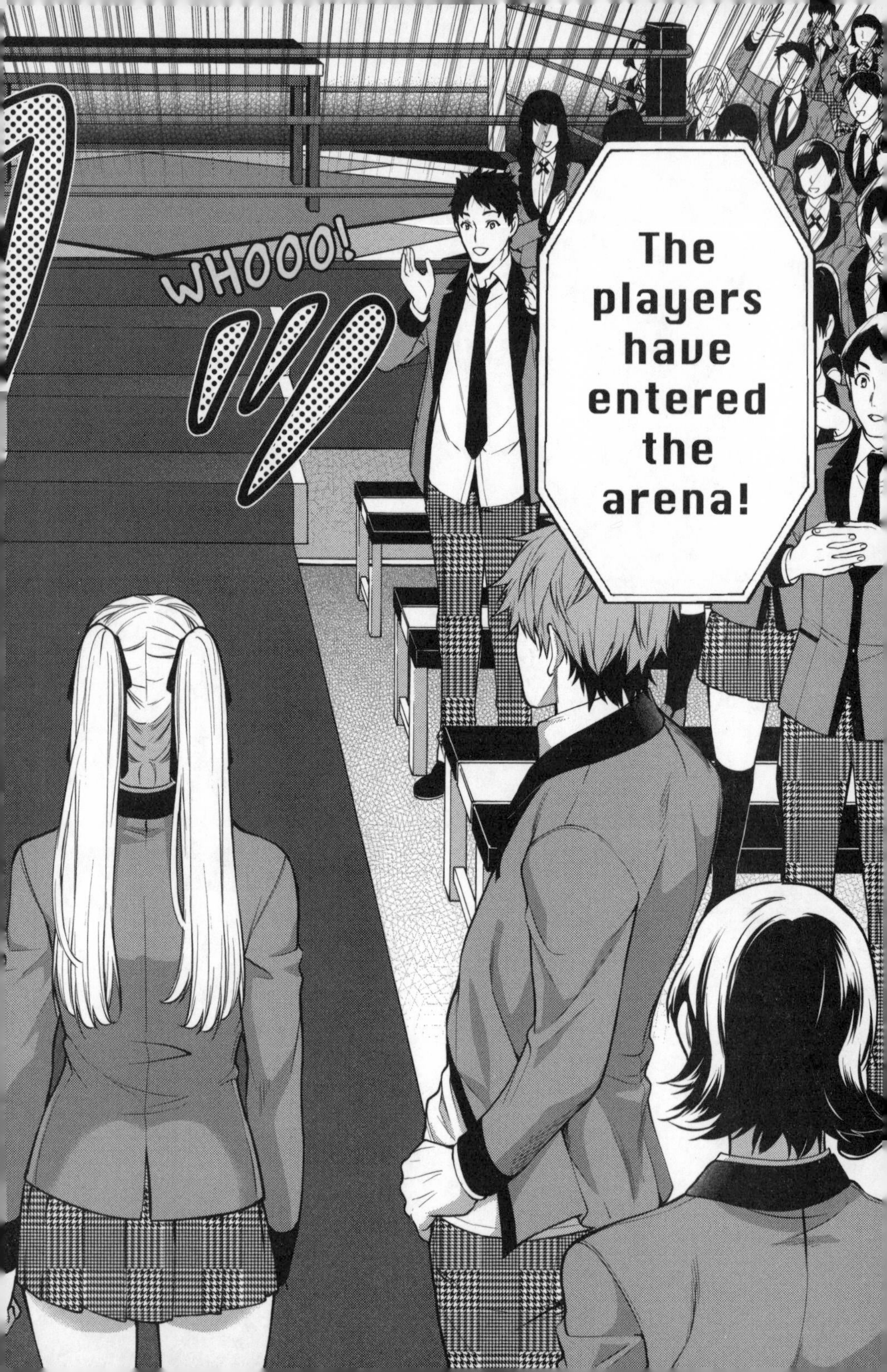
The players have entered the arena!
WHOOO!

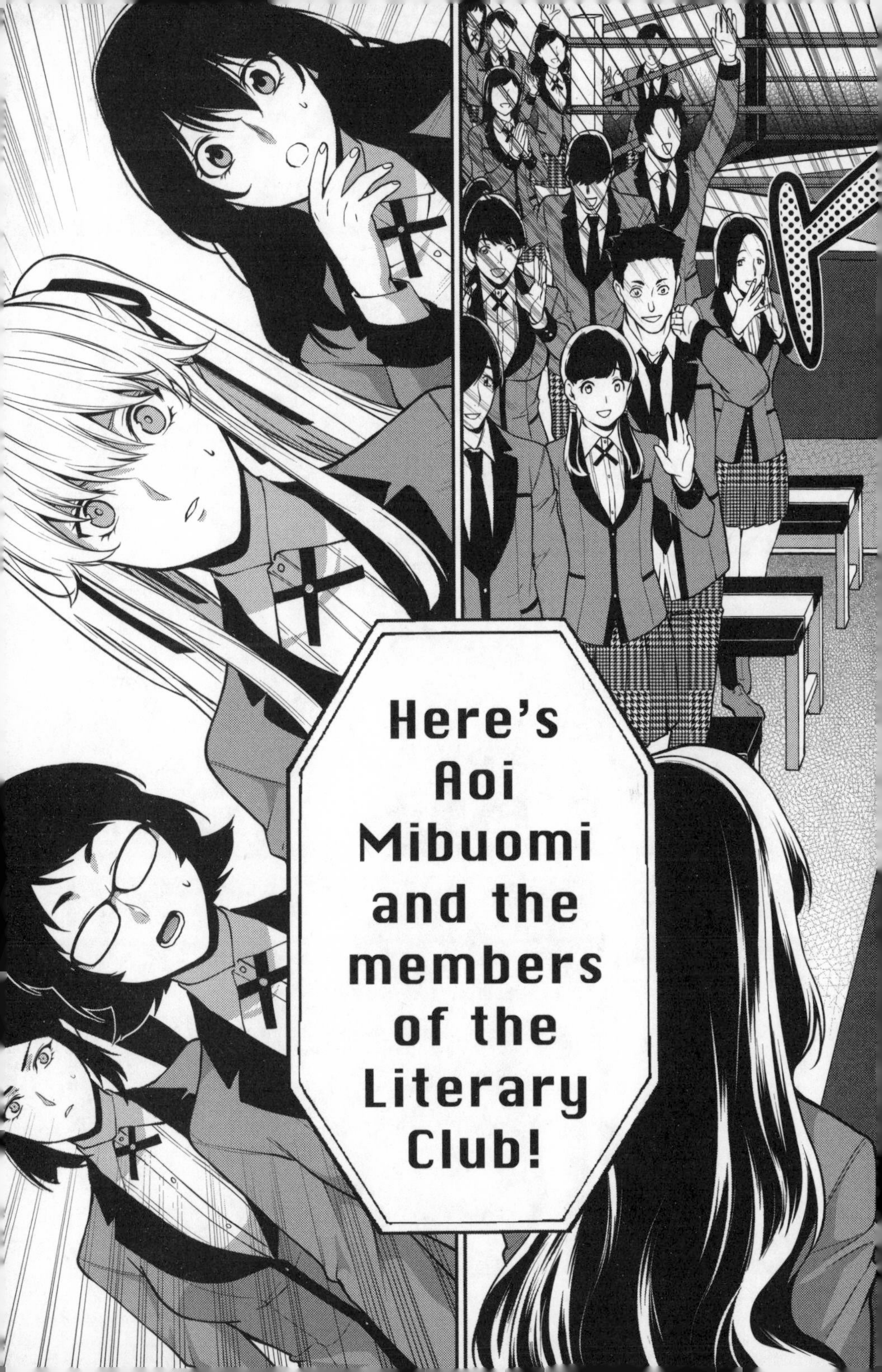
Here's Aoi Mibuomi and the members of the Literary Club!

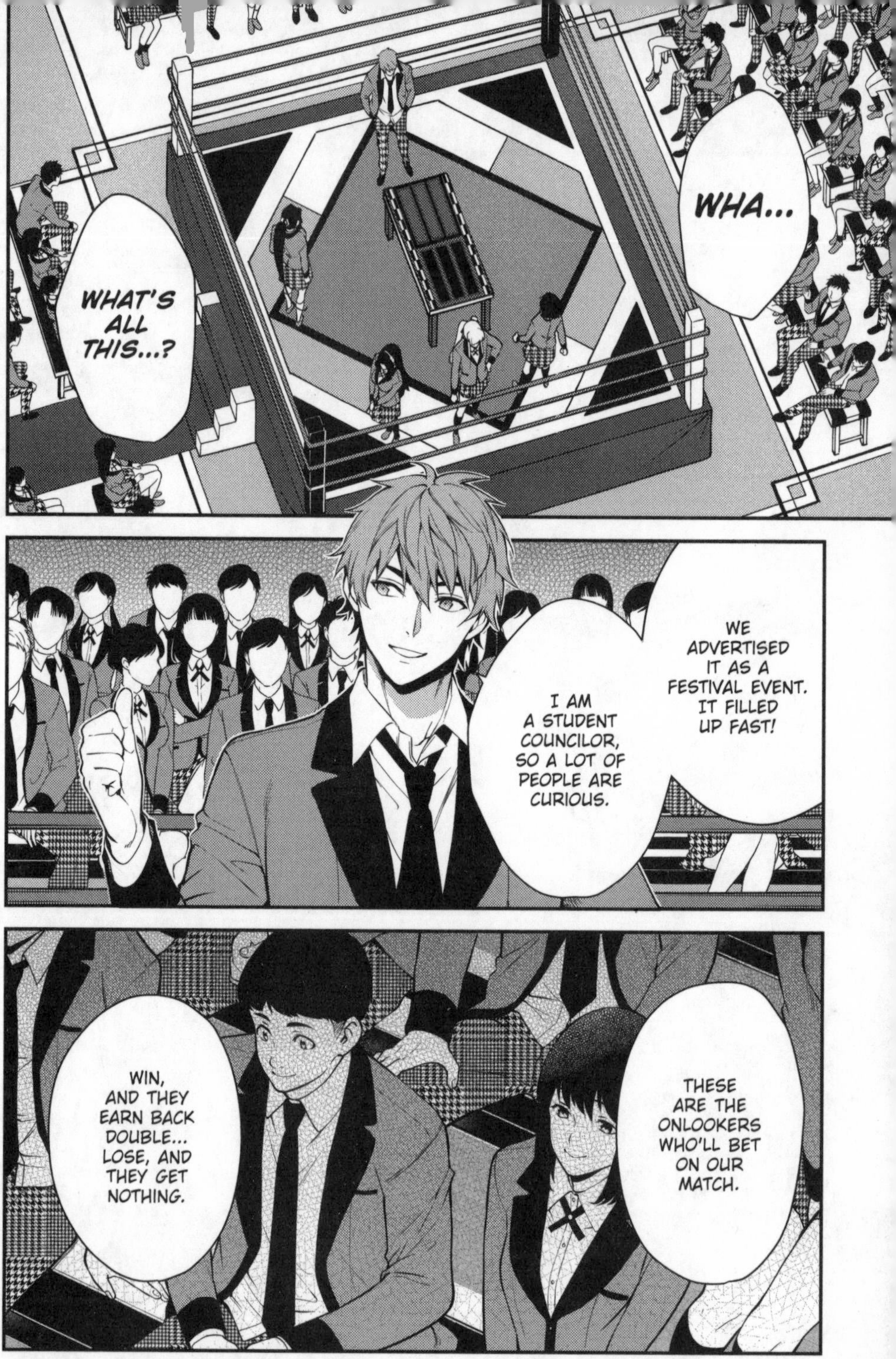
WHA...
WHAT'S ALL THIS...?
WE ADVERTISED IT AS A FESTIVAL EVENT. IT FILLED UP FAST!
I AM A STUDENT COUNCILOR, SO A LOT OF PEOPLE ARE CURIOUS.
THESE ARE THE ONLOOKERS WHO'LL BET ON OUR MATCH.
WIN, AND THEY EARN BACK DOUBLE... LOSE, AND THEY GET NOTHING.

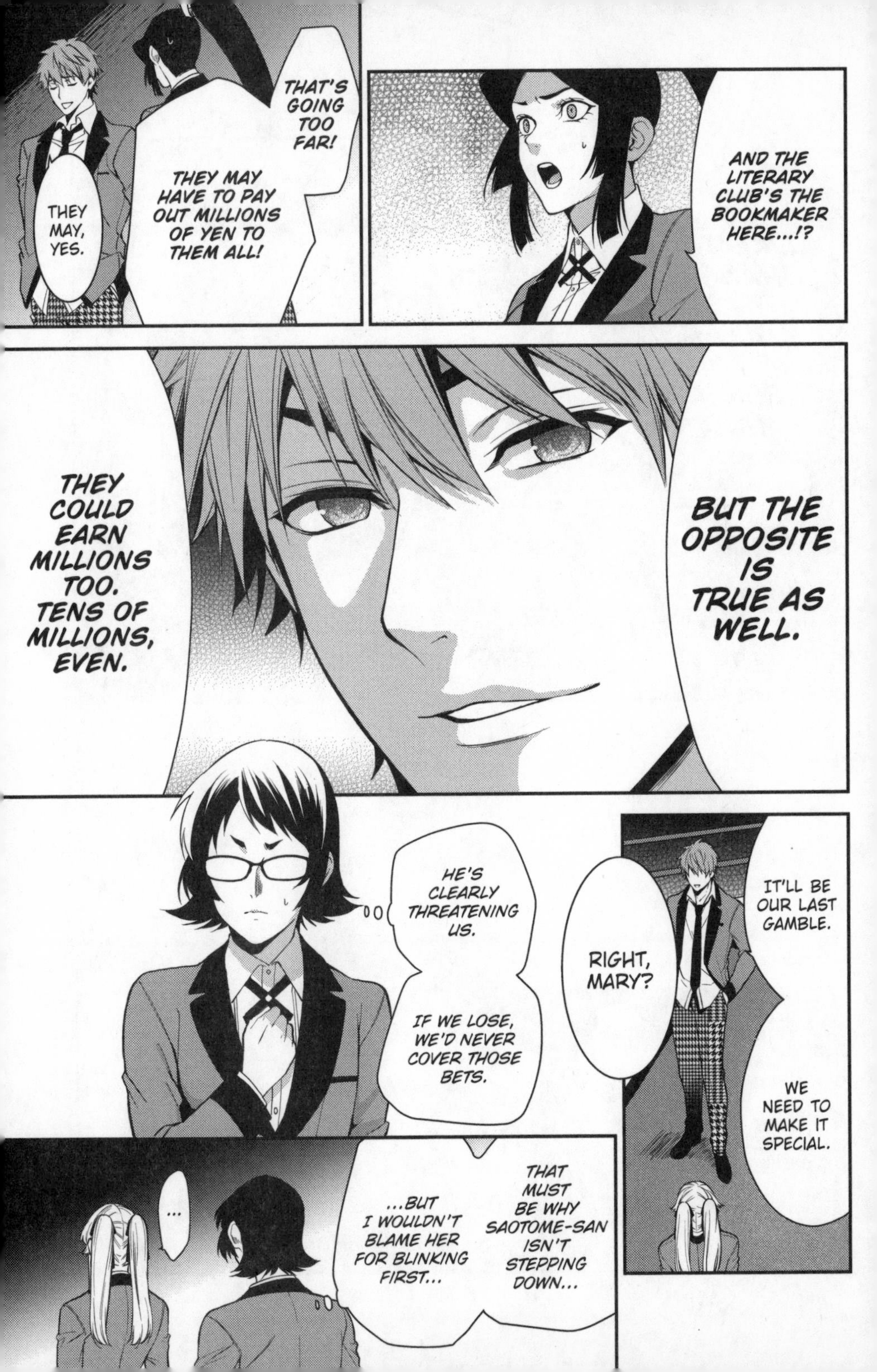
AND THE LITERARY CLUB'S THE BOOKMAKER HERE...!?
THAT'S GOING TOO FAR!
THEY MAY HAVE TO PAY OUT MILLIONS OF YEN TO THEM ALL!
THEY MAY, YES.
BUT THE OPPOSITE IS TRUE AS WELL.
THEY COULD EARN MILLIONS TOO. TENS OF MILLIONS, EVEN.
IT'LL BE OUR LAST GAMBLE.
RIGHT, MARY?
WE NEED TO MAKE IT SPECIAL.
HE'S CLEARLY THREATENING US.
IF WE LOSE, WE'D NEVER COVER THOSE BETS.
THAT MUST BE WHY SAOTOME-SAN ISN'T STEPPING DOWN...
...BUT I WOULDN'T BLAME HER FOR BLINKING FIRST...
...

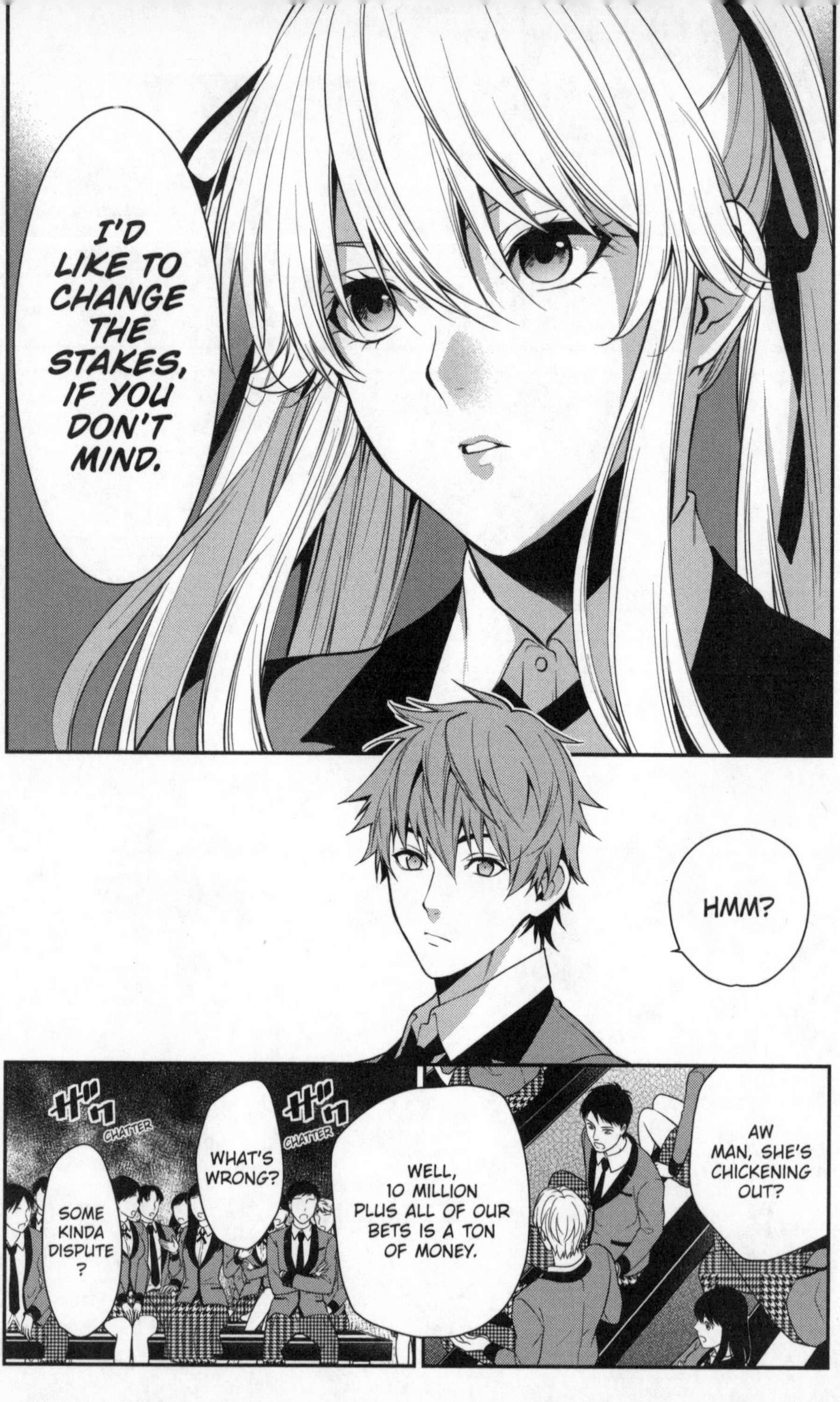
I'D LIKE TO CHANGE THE STAKES, IF YOU DON'T MIND.
HMM?
AW MAN, SHE'S CHICKENING OUT?
WELL, 10 MILLION PLUS ALL OF OUR BETS IS A TON OF MONEY.
CHATTER
WHAT'S WRONG?
CHATTER
SOME KINDA DISPUTE?

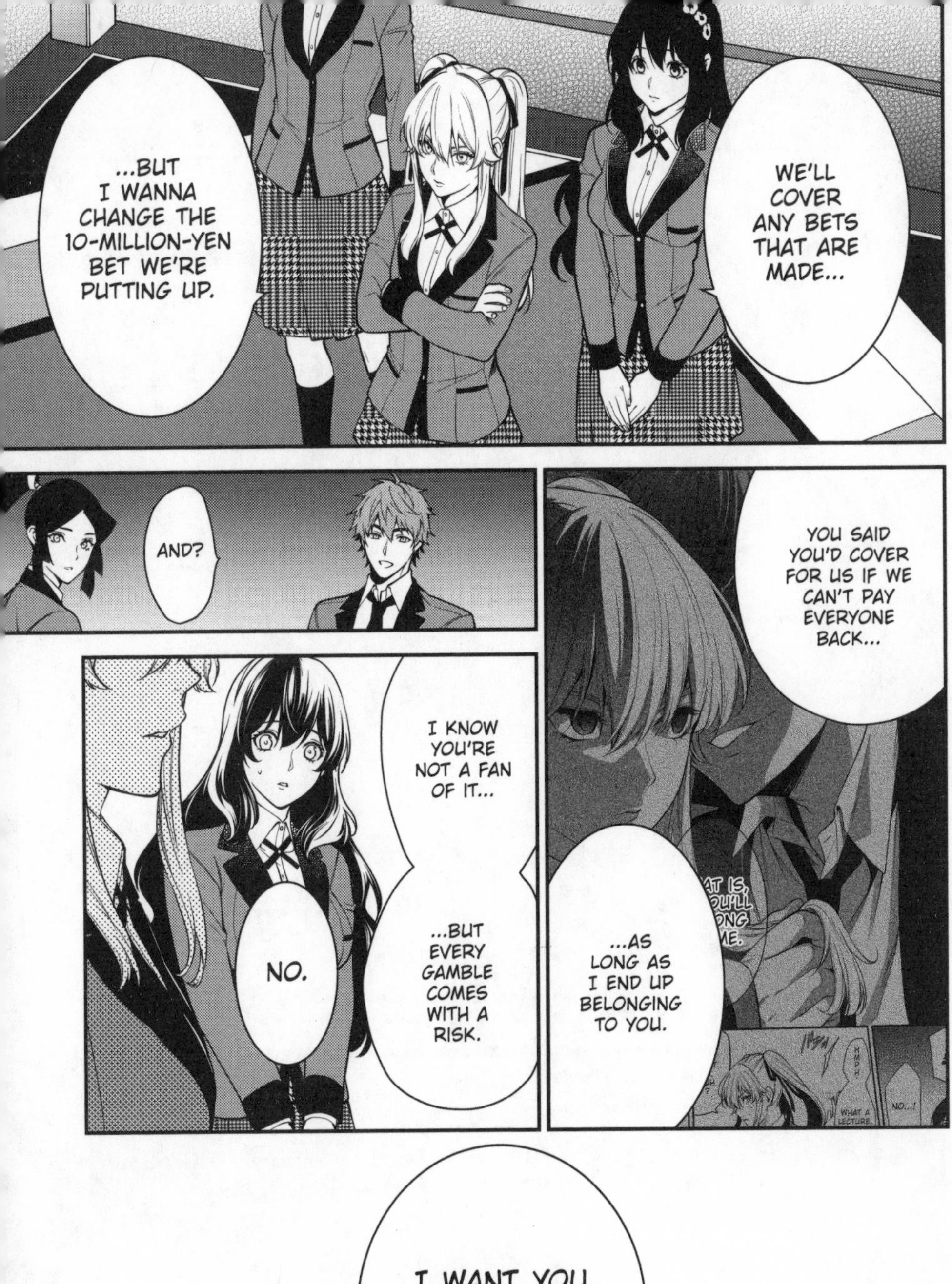
WE'LL COVER ANY BETS THAT ARE MADE...
...BUT I WANNA CHANGE THE 10-MILLION-YEN BET WE'RE PUTTING UP.
YOU SAID YOU'D COVER FOR US IF WE CAN'T PAY EVERYONE BACK...
...AS LONG AS I END UP BELONGING TO YOU.
HMPH
WHAT A LECTURE
NO...!
AND?
I KNOW YOU'RE NOT A FAN OF IT...
...BUT EVERY GAMBLE COMES WITH A RISK.
NO.
I WANT YOU TO TAKE THE SAME RISK.

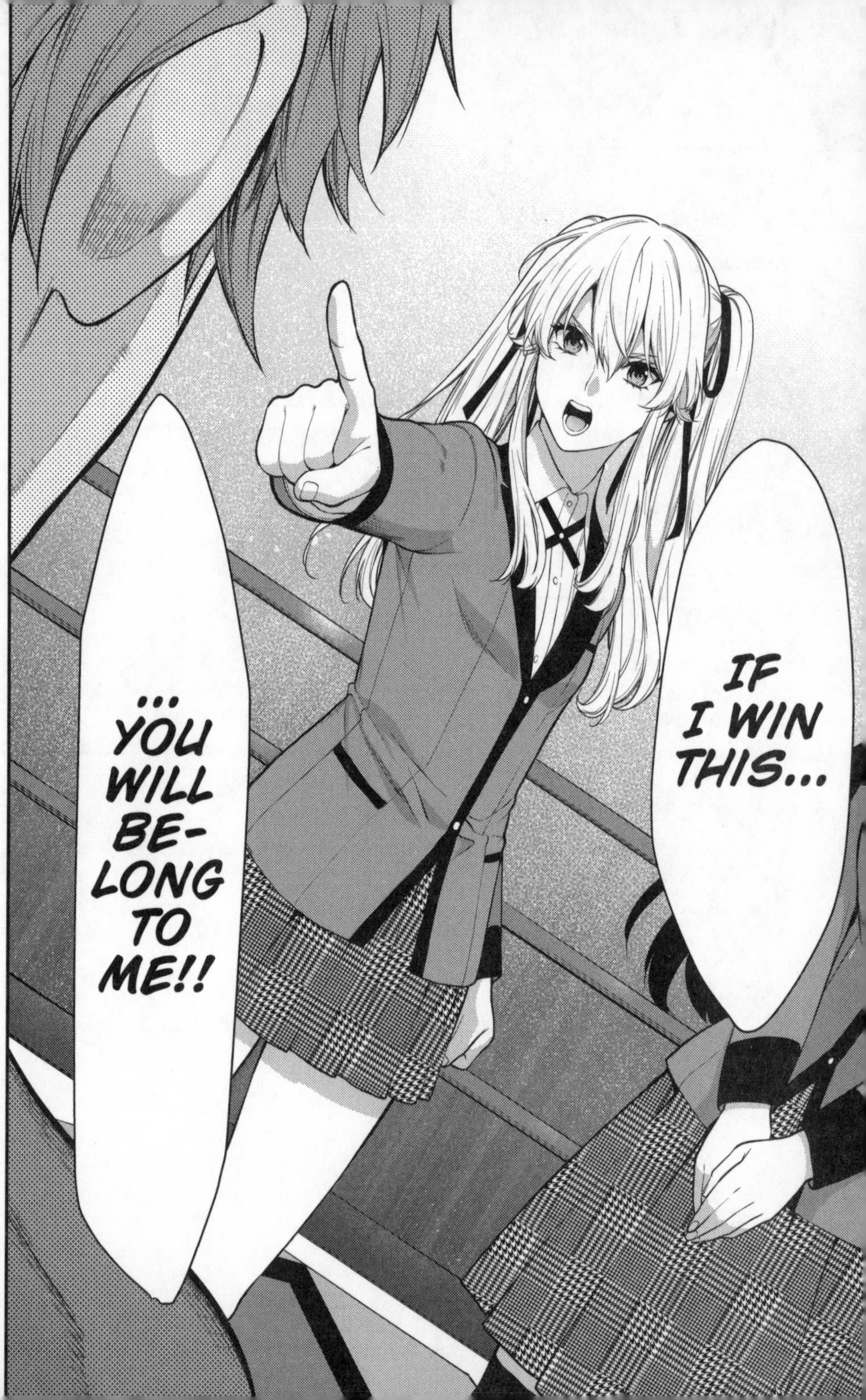
IF I WIN THIS...
...YOU WILL BE-LONG TO ME!!

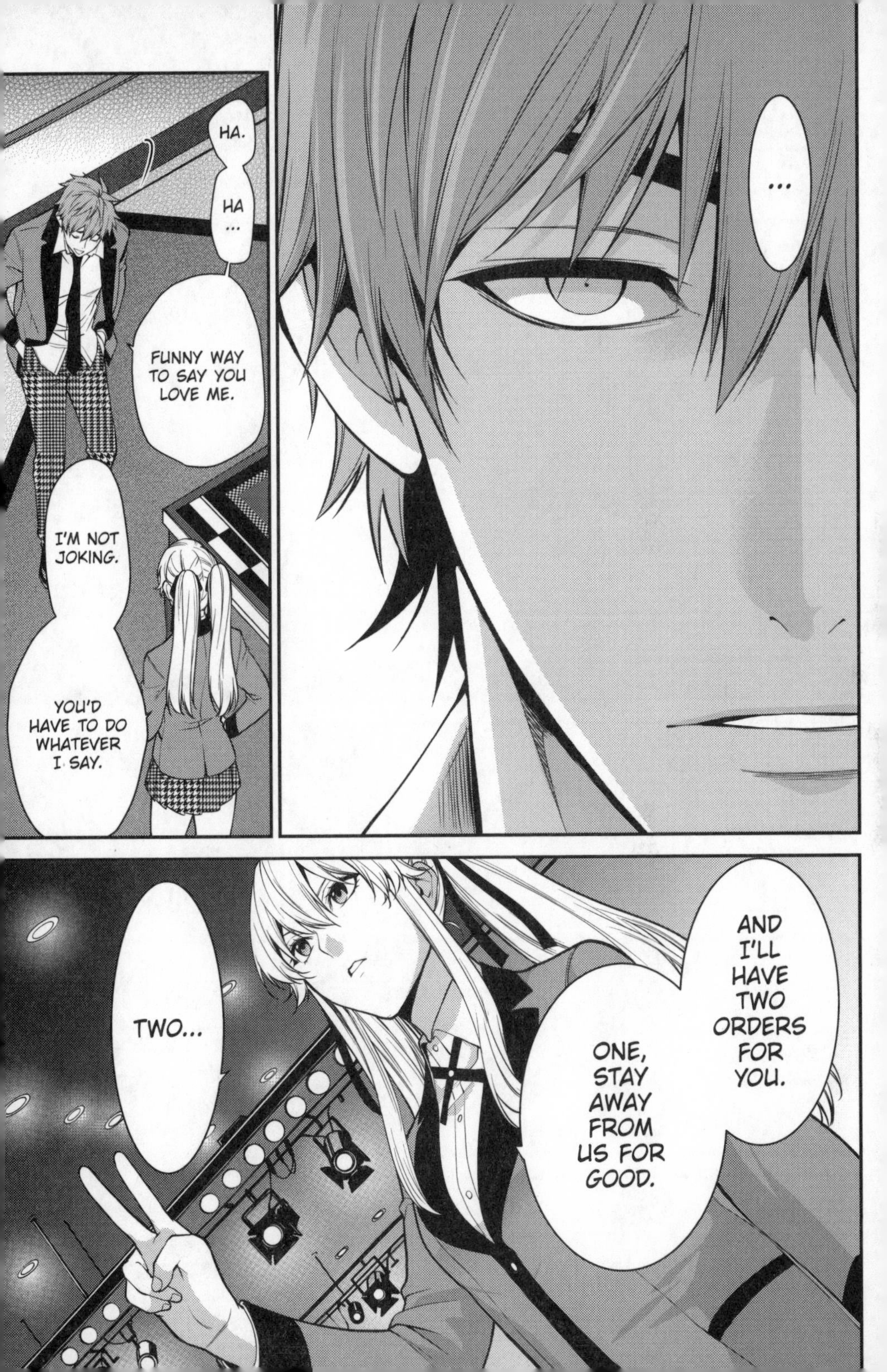
...
HA.
HA ...
FUNNY WAY TO SAY YOU LOVE ME.
I'M NOT JOKING.
YOU'D HAVE TO DO WHATEVER I SAY.
AND I'LL HAVE TWO ORDERS FOR YOU.
ONE, STAY AWAY FROM US FOR GOOD.
TWO...

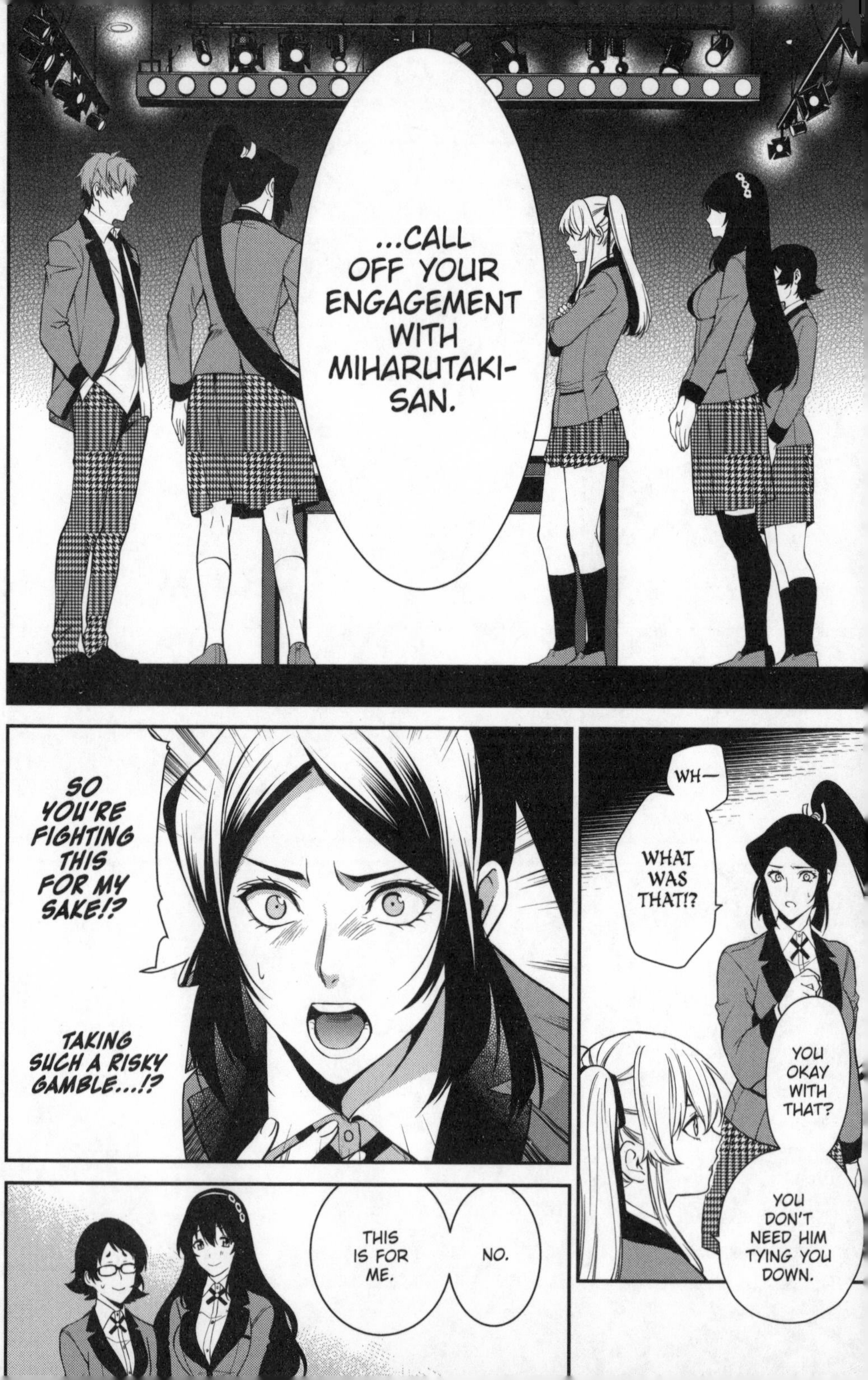
...CALL OFF YOUR ENGAGEMENT WITH MIHARUTAKI-SAN.
WH—
WHAT WAS THAT!?
YOU OKAY WITH THAT?
YOU DON'T NEED HIM TYING YOU DOWN.
SO YOU'RE FIGHTING THIS FOR MY SAKE!?
TAKING SUCH A RISKY GAMBLE...!?
NO.
THIS IS FOR ME.

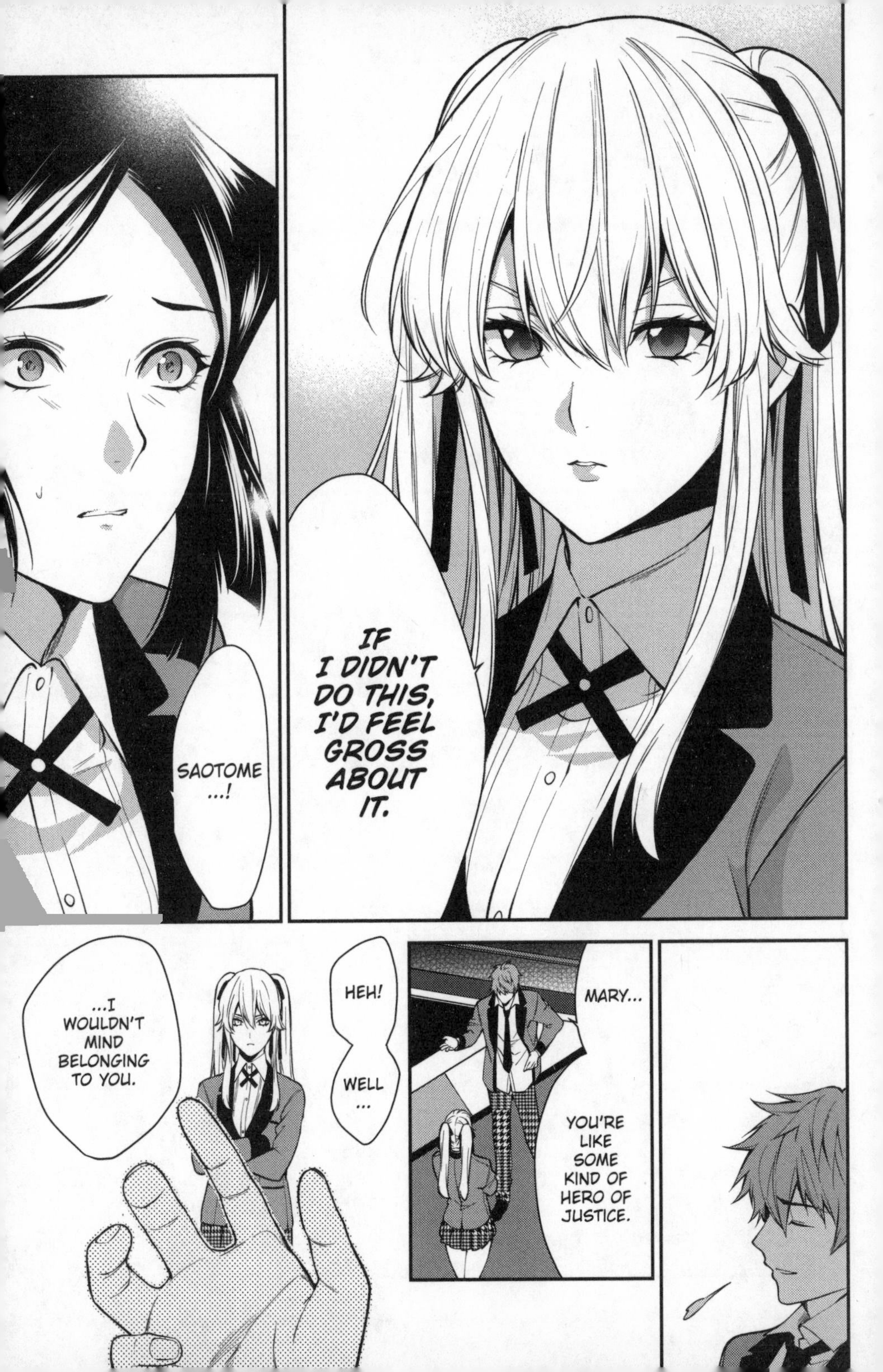
IF I DIDN'T DO THIS, I'D FEEL GROSS ABOUT IT.
SAOTOME ...!
MARY...
YOU'RE LIKE SOME KIND OF HERO OF JUSTICE.
HEH!
WELL ...
...I WOULDN'T MIND BELONGING TO YOU.

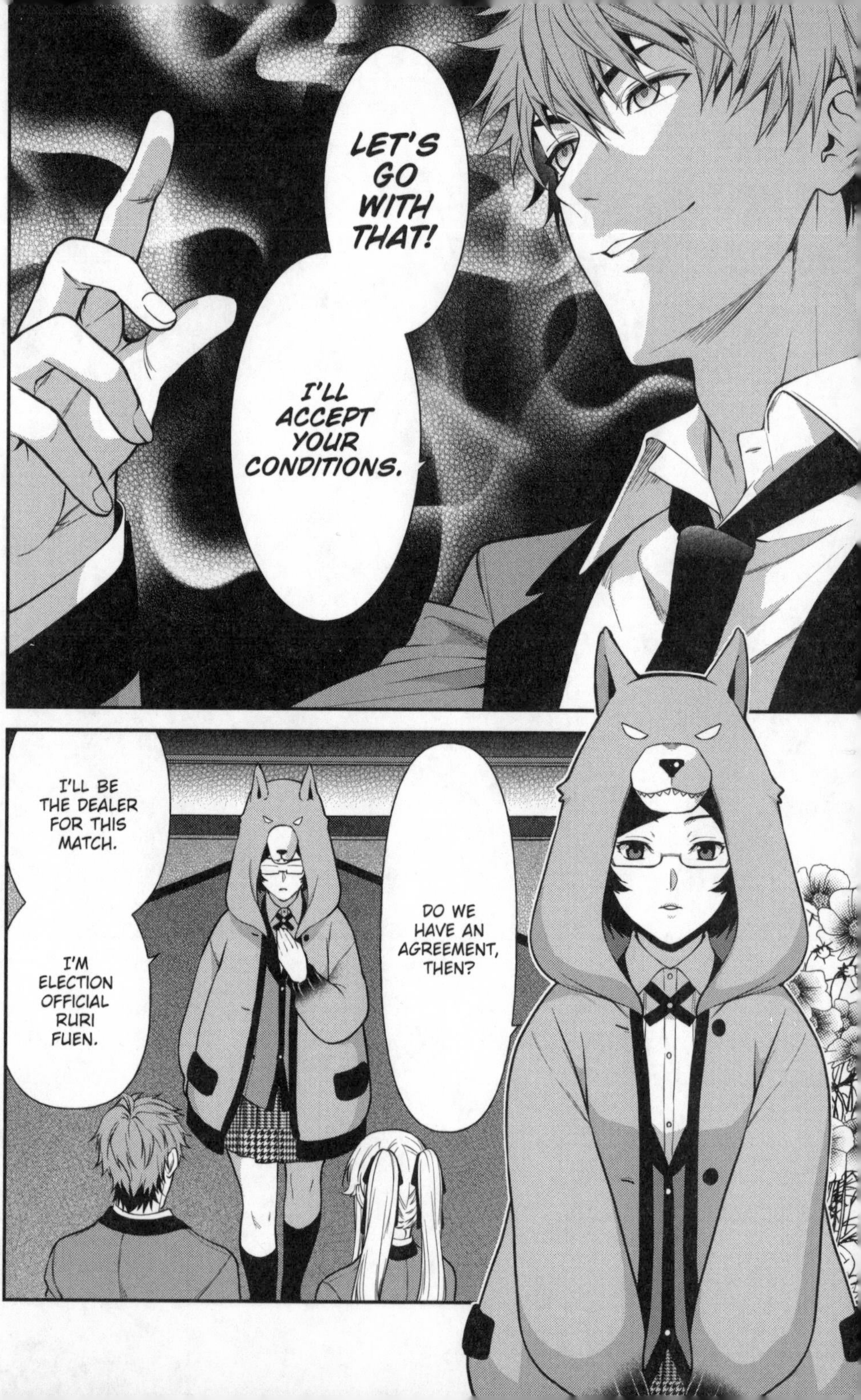
LET'S GO WITH THAT!
I'LL ACCEPT YOUR CONDITIONS.
DO WE HAVE AN AGREEMENT, THEN?
I'LL BE THE DEALER FOR THIS MATCH.
I'M ELECTION OFFICIAL RURI FUEN.

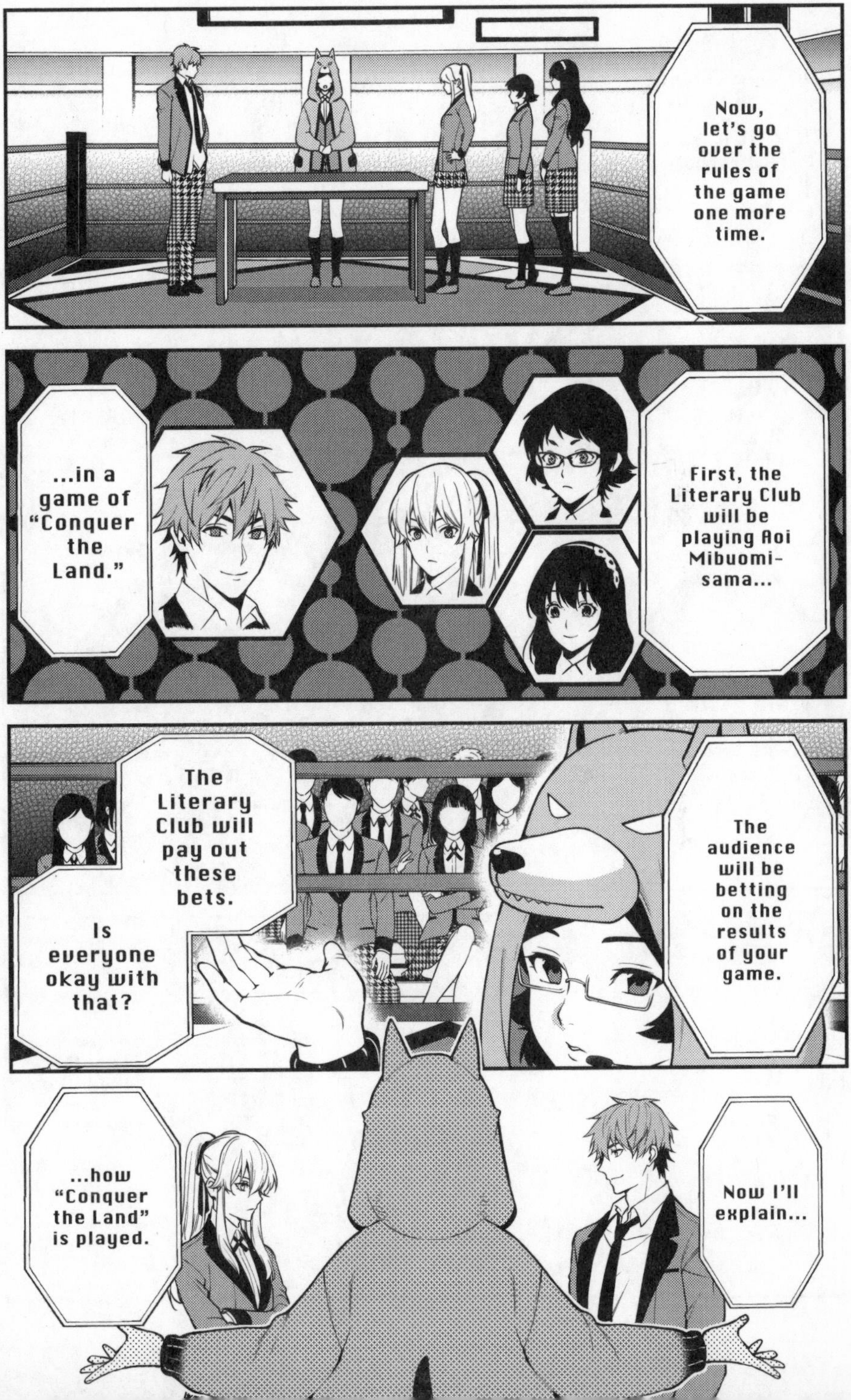
Now, let's go over the rules of the game one more time.
First, the Literary Club will be playing Aoi Mibuomi-sama...
...in a game of "Conquer the Land."
The audience will be betting on the results of your game.
The Literary Club will pay out these bets.
Is everyone okay with that?
Now I'll explain...
...how "Conquer the Land" is played.

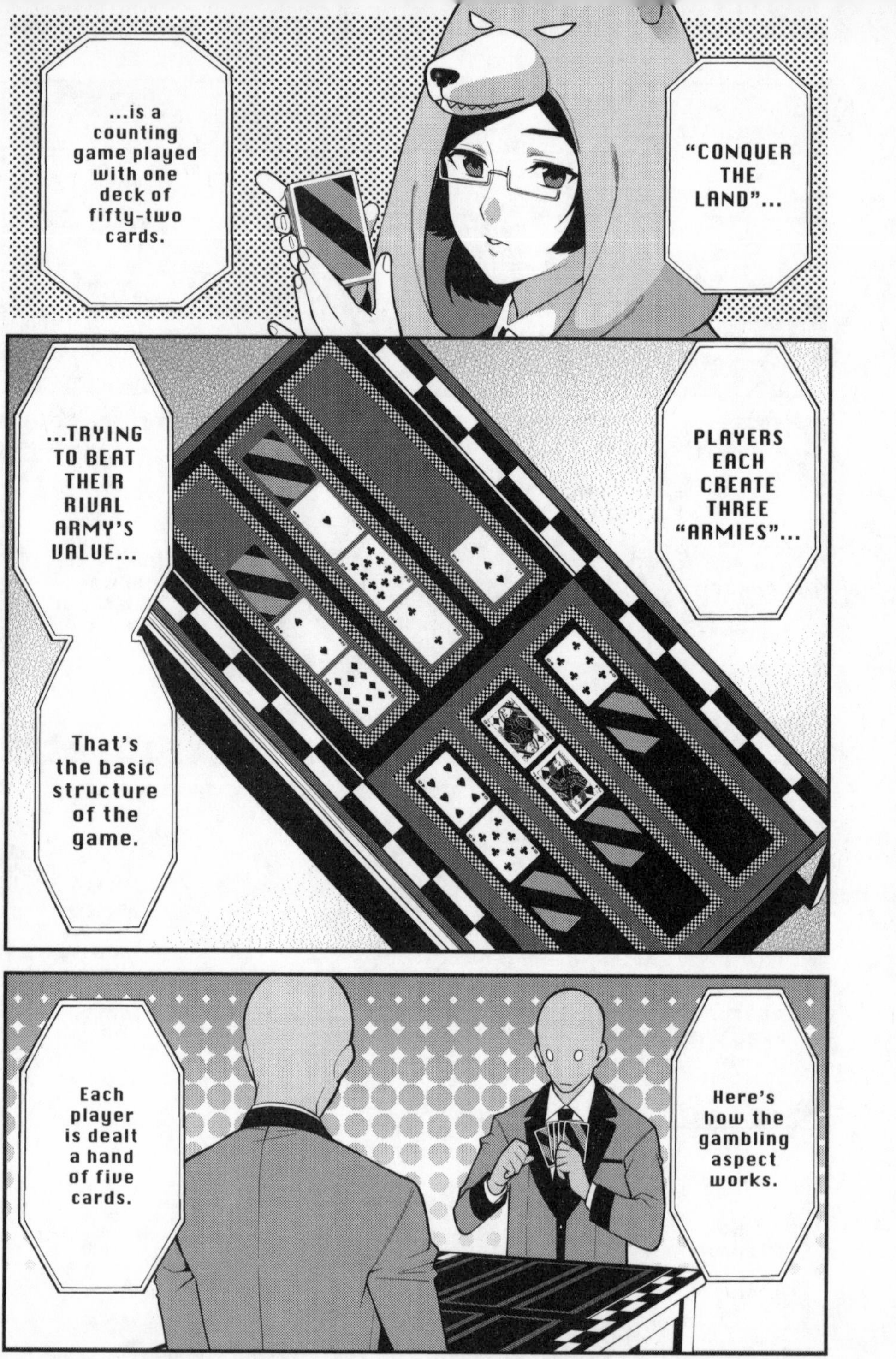
"CONQUER THE LAND"...
...is a counting game played with one deck of fifty-two cards.
PLAYERS EACH CREATE THREE "ARMIES"...
...TRYING TO BEAT THEIR RIVAL ARMY'S VALUE...
That's the basic structure of the game.
Here's how the gambling aspect works.
Each player is dealt a hand of five cards.

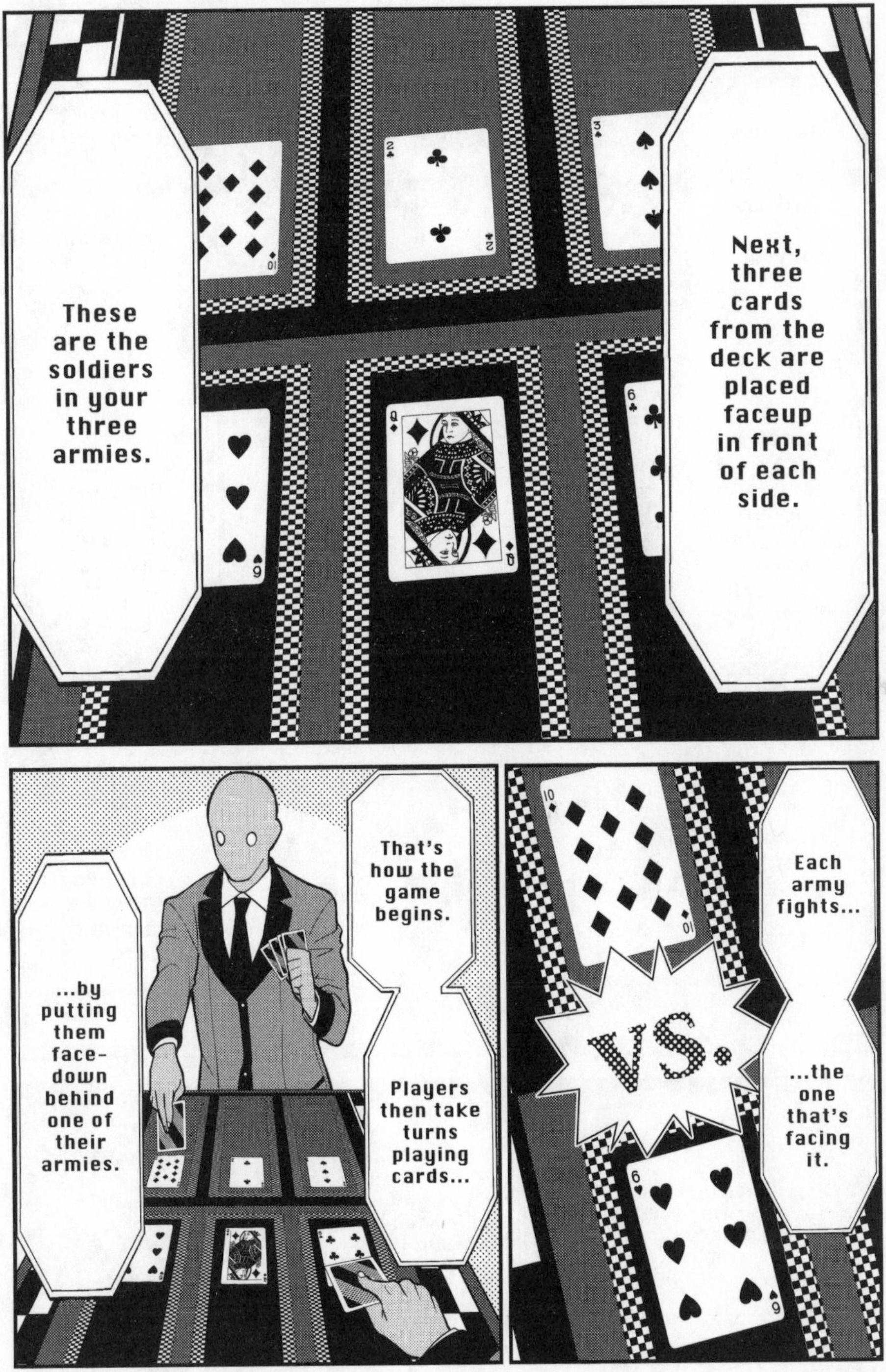
Next, three cards from the deck are placed faceup in front of each side.
These are the soldiers in your three armies.
Each army fights...
VS.
...the one that's facing it.
That's how the game begins.
Players then take turns playing cards...
...by putting them face-down behind one of their armies.

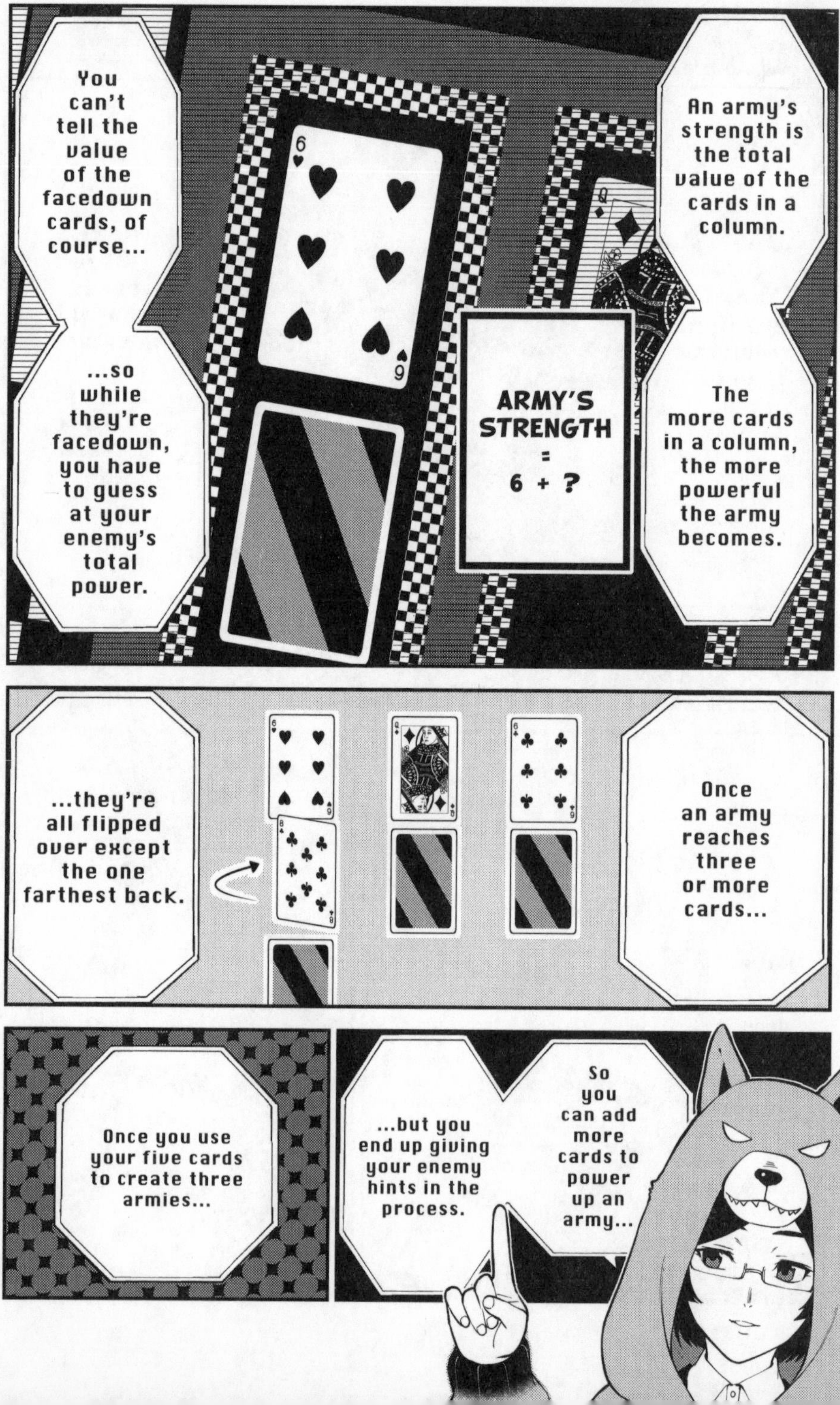
An army's strength is the total value of the cards in a column.
The more cards in a column, the more powerful the army becomes.
ARMY'S STRENGTH = 6 + ?
You can't tell the value of the facedown cards, of course...
...so while they're facedown, you have to guess at your enemy's total power.
Once an army reaches three or more cards...
...they're all flipped over except the one farthest back.
So you can add more cards to power up an army...
...but you end up giving your enemy hints in the process.
Once you use your five cards to create three armies...

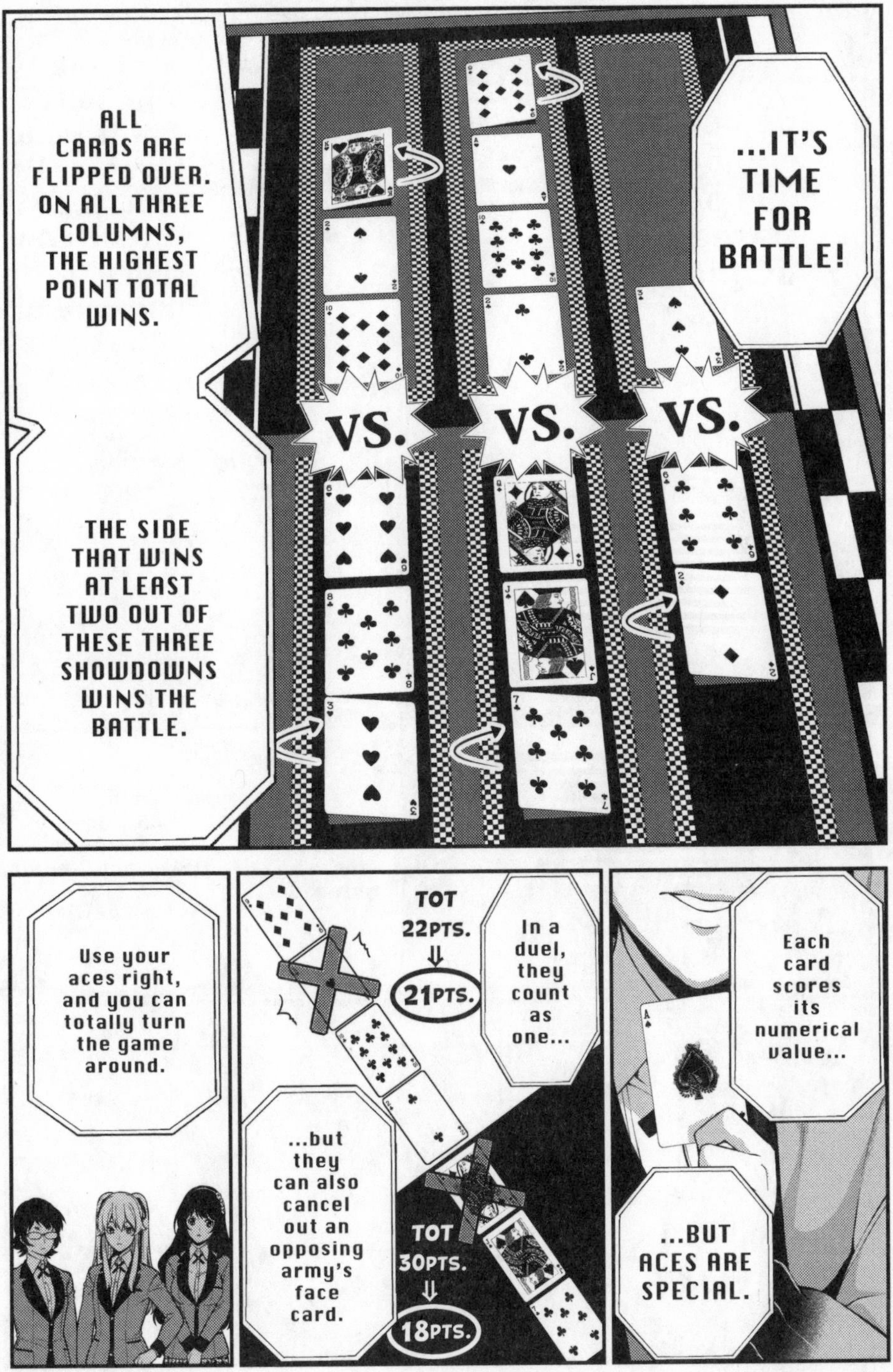
...IT'S TIME FOR BATTLE!
ALL CARDS ARE FLIPPED OVER. ON ALL THREE COLUMNS, THE HIGHEST POINT TOTAL WINS.
VS.
VS.
VS.
THE SIDE THAT WINS AT LEAST TWO OUT OF THESE THREE SHOWDOWNS WINS THE BATTLE.
Each card scores its numerical value...
...BUT ACES ARE SPECIAL.
In a duel, they count as one...
TOT 22PTS.
21PTS.
...but they can also cancel out an opposing army's face card.
TOT 30PTS.
18PTS.
Use your aces right, and you can totally turn the game around.

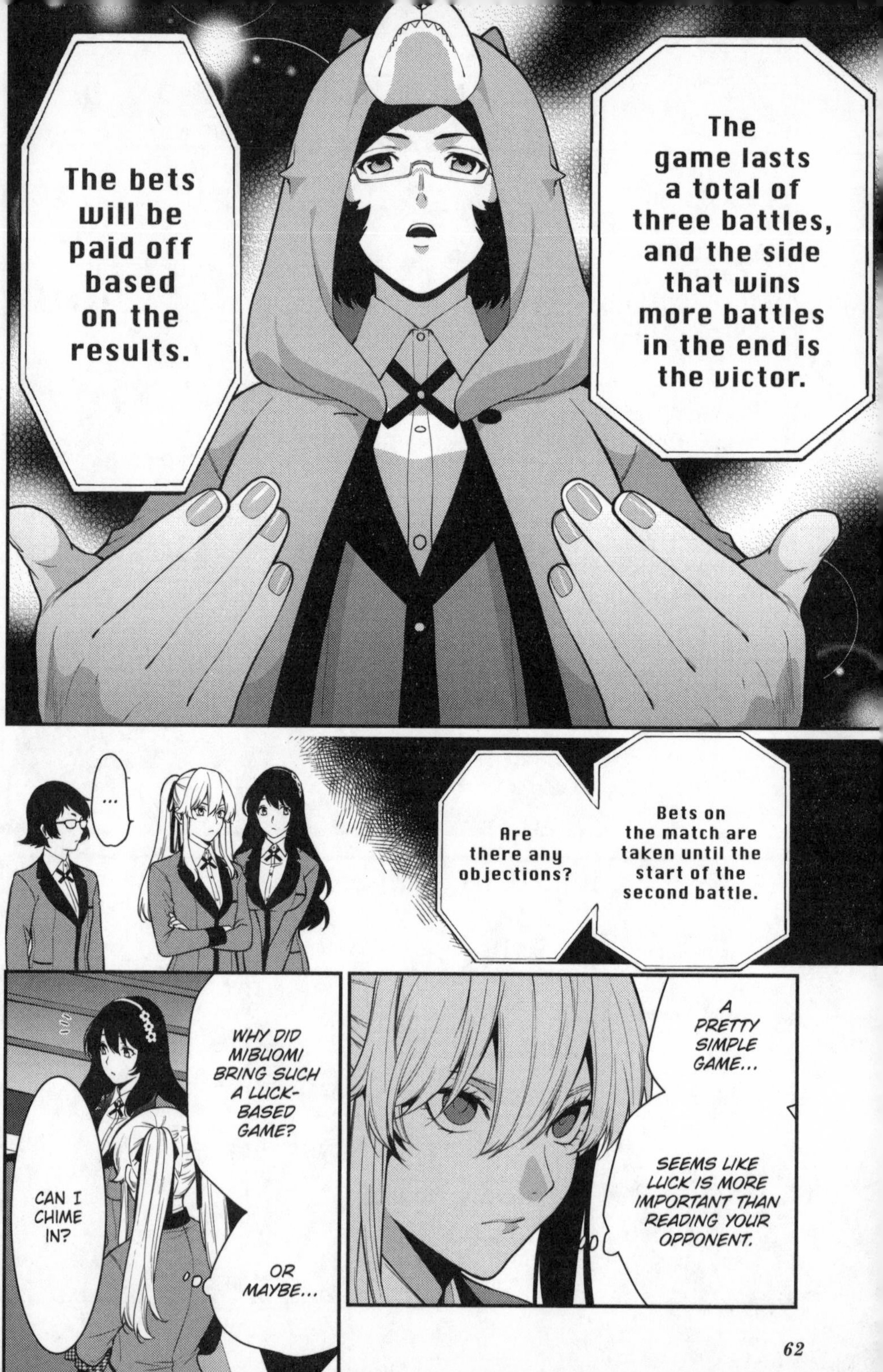
The game lasts a total of three battles, and the side that wins more battles in the end is the victor.
The bets will be paid off based on the results.
Bets on the match are taken until the start of the second battle.
Are there any objections?
...
A PRETTY SIMPLE GAME...
SEEMS LIKE LUCK IS MORE IMPORTANT THAN READING YOUR OPPONENT.
WHY DID MIBUOMI BRING SUCH A LUCK-BASED GAME?
OR MAYBE...
CAN I CHIME IN?

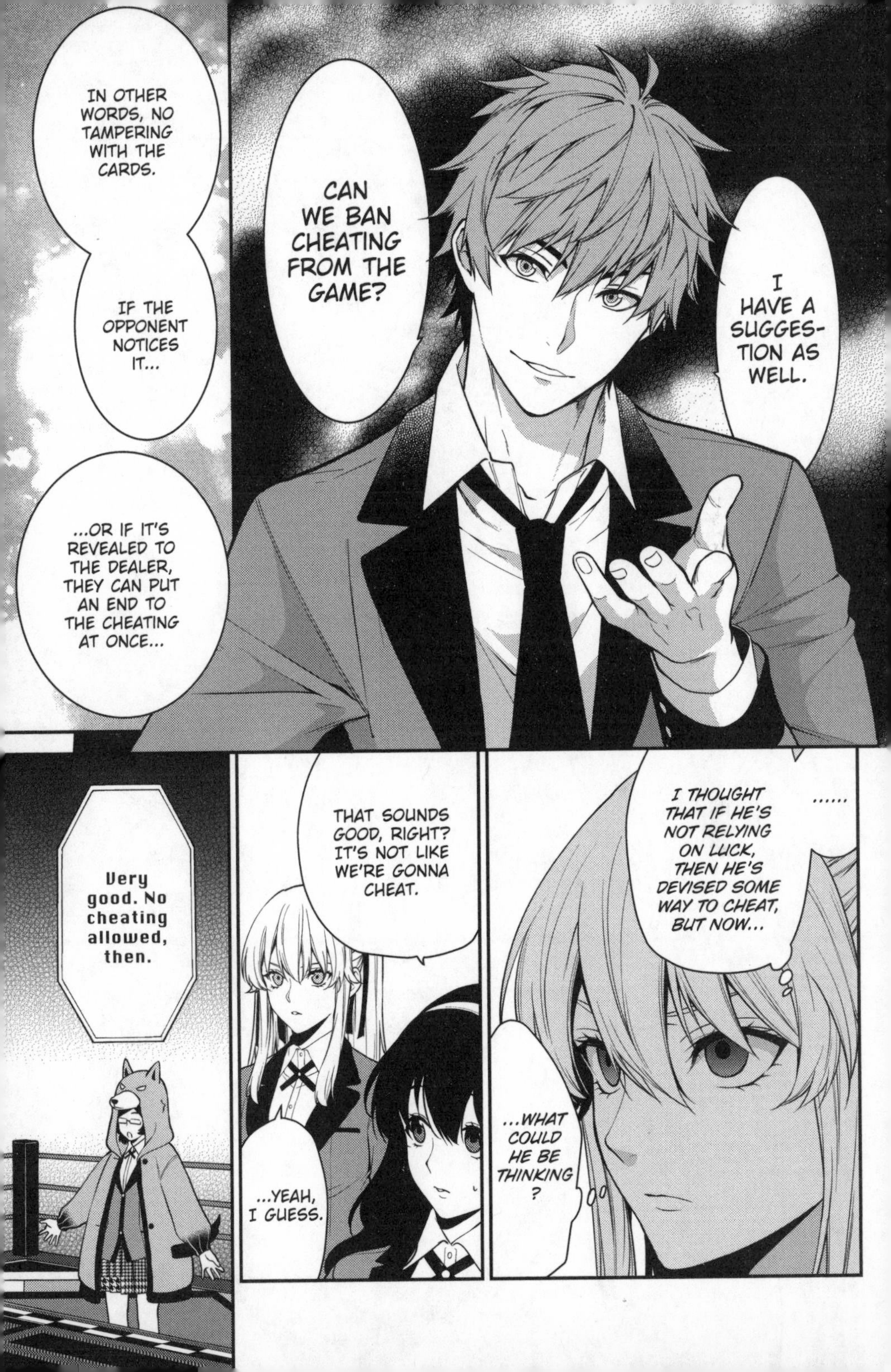
I HAVE A SUGGES-TION AS WELL.
CAN WE BAN CHEATING FROM THE GAME?
IN OTHER WORDS, NO TAMPERING WITH THE CARDS.
IF THE OPPONENT NOTICES IT...
...OR IF IT'S REVEALED TO THE DEALER, THEY CAN PUT AN END TO THE CHEATING AT ONCE...
......
I THOUGHT THAT IF HE'S NOT RELYING ON LUCK, THEN HE'S DEVISED SOME WAY TO CHEAT, BUT NOW...
...WHAT COULD HE BE THINKING?
THAT SOUNDS GOOD, RIGHT? IT'S NOT LIKE WE'RE GONNA CHEAT.
...YEAH, I GUESS.
Very good. No cheating allowed, then.

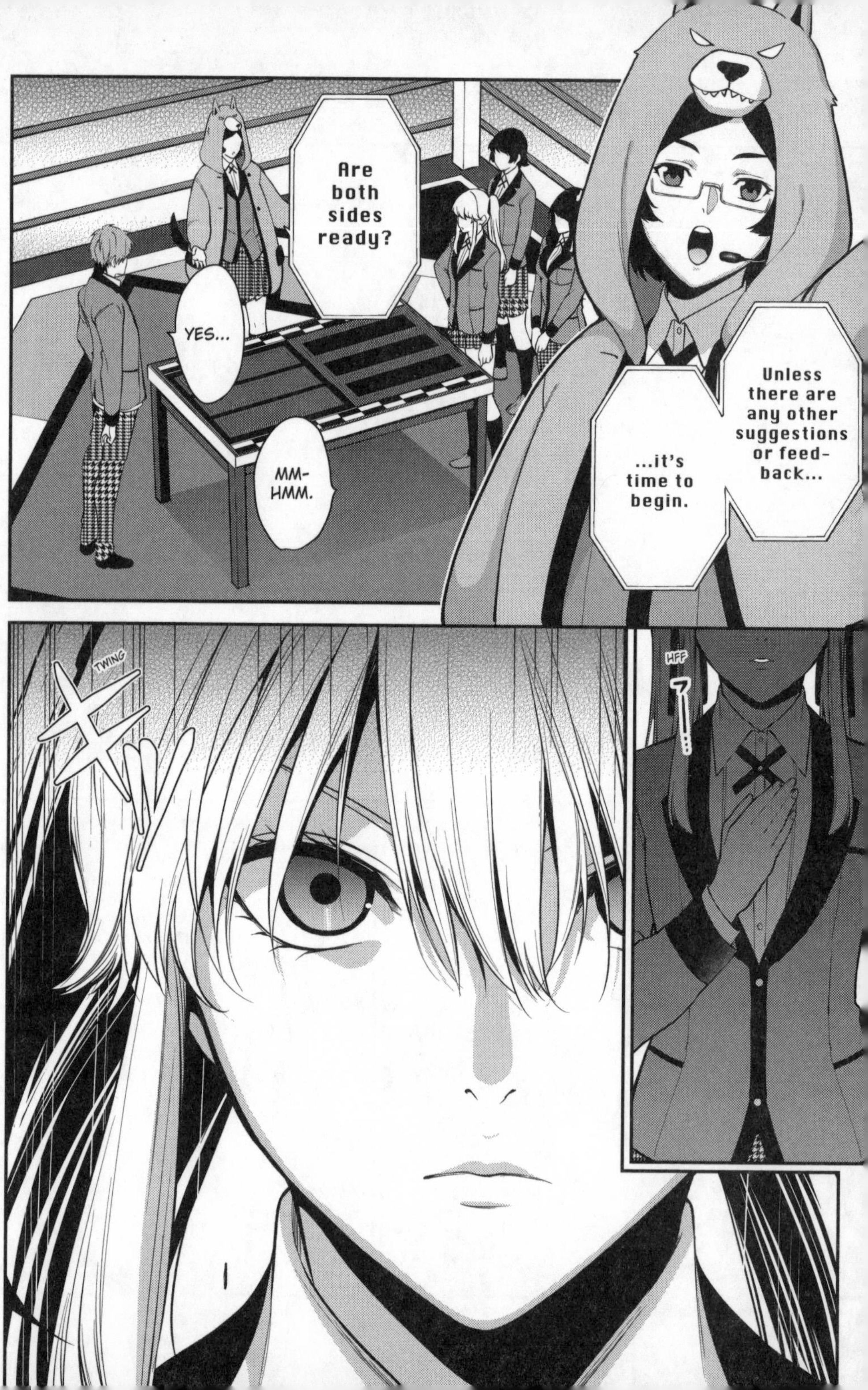
Unless there are any other suggestions or feed-back...
...it's time to begin.
Are both sides ready?
YES...
MM-HMM.
HFF
TWING

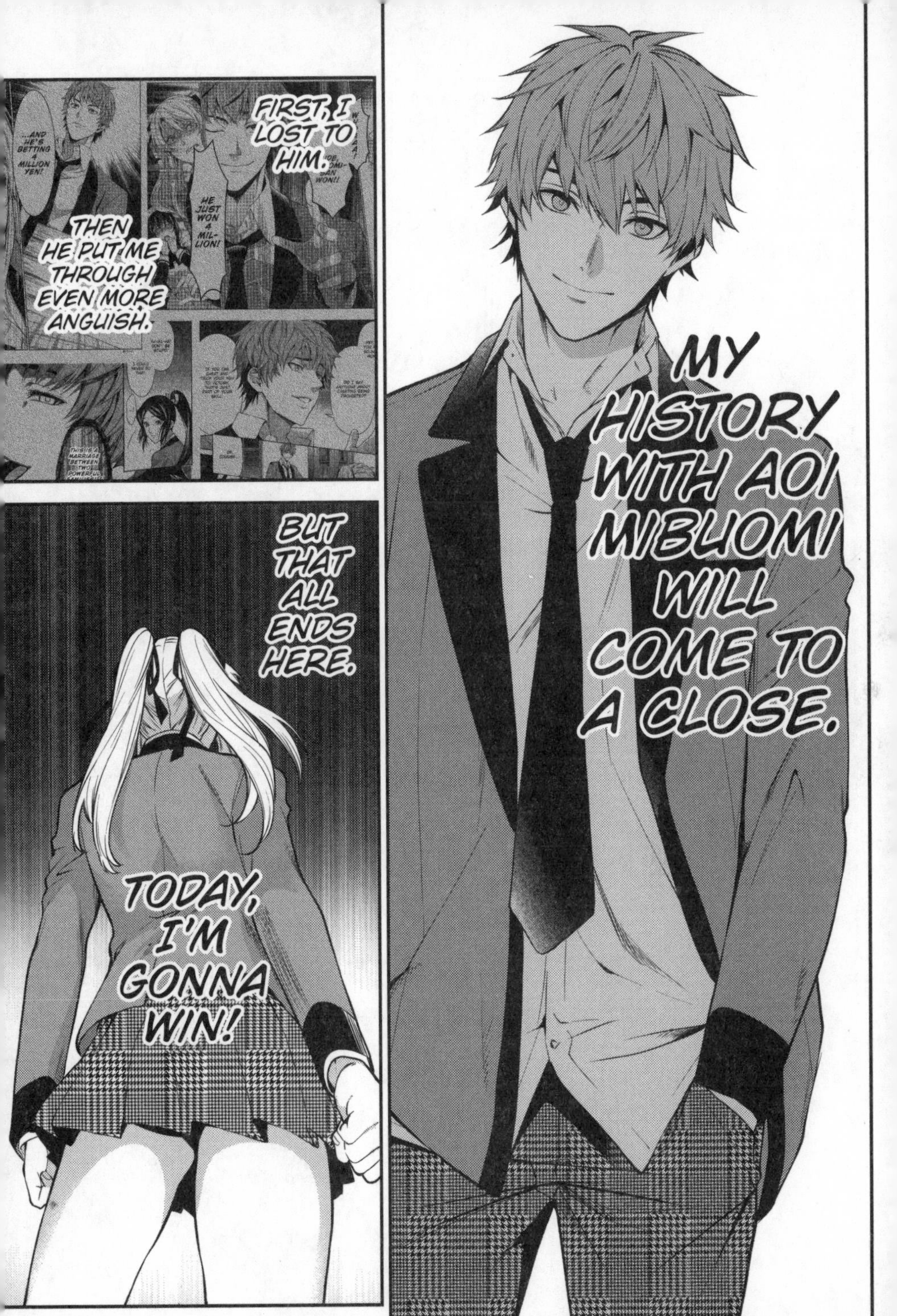
MY HISTORY WITH AOI MIBUOMI WILL COME TO A CLOSE.
FIRST, I LOST TO HIM.
HE JUST WON 4 MIL-LION!
...AND HE'S BETTING 4 MILLION YEN!
THEN HE PUT ME THROUGH EVEN MORE ANGUISH.
BUT THAT ALL ENDS HERE.
TODAY, I'M GONNA WIN!

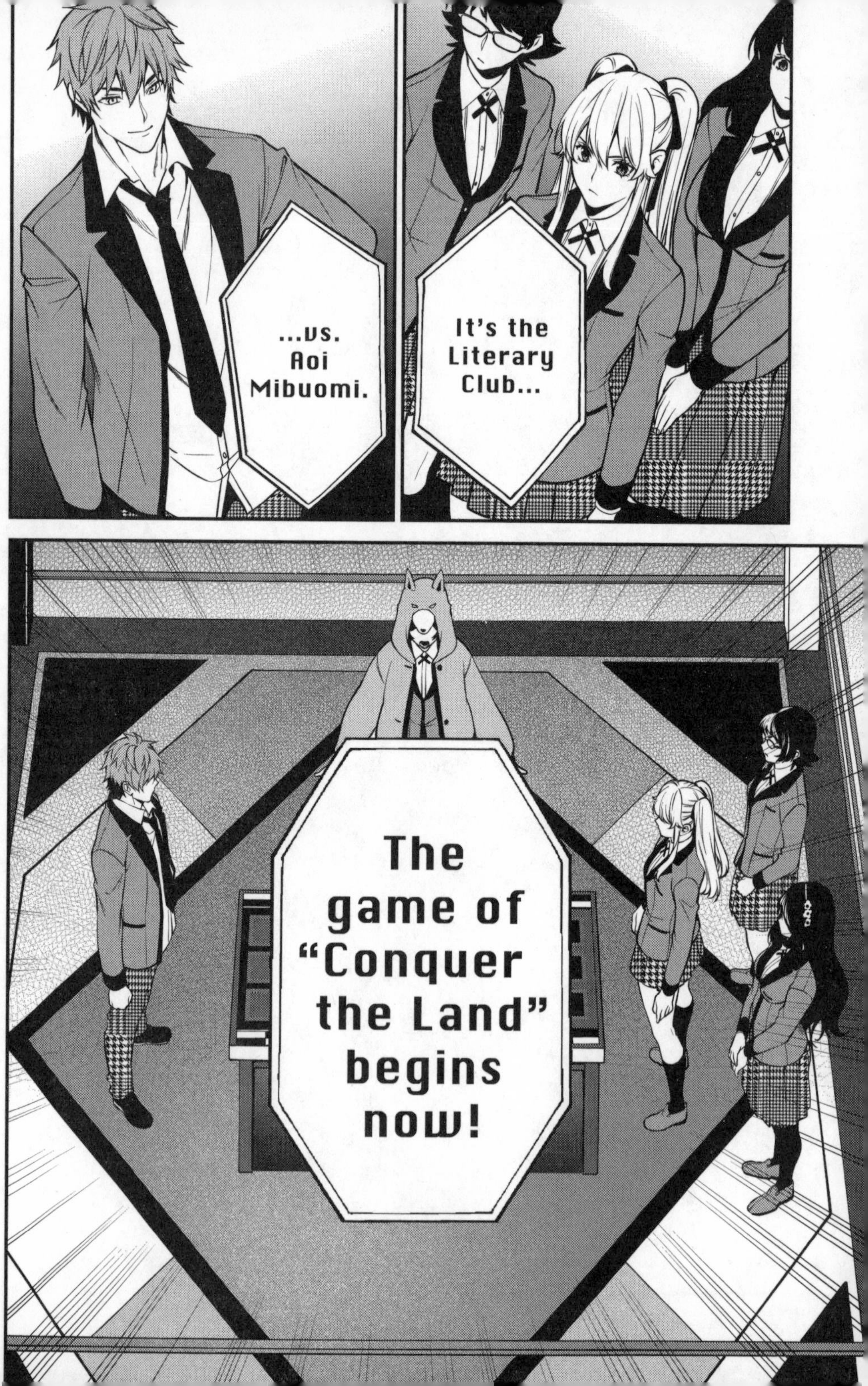
It's the Literary Club...
...vs. Aoi Mibuomi.
The game of "Conquer the Land" begins now!

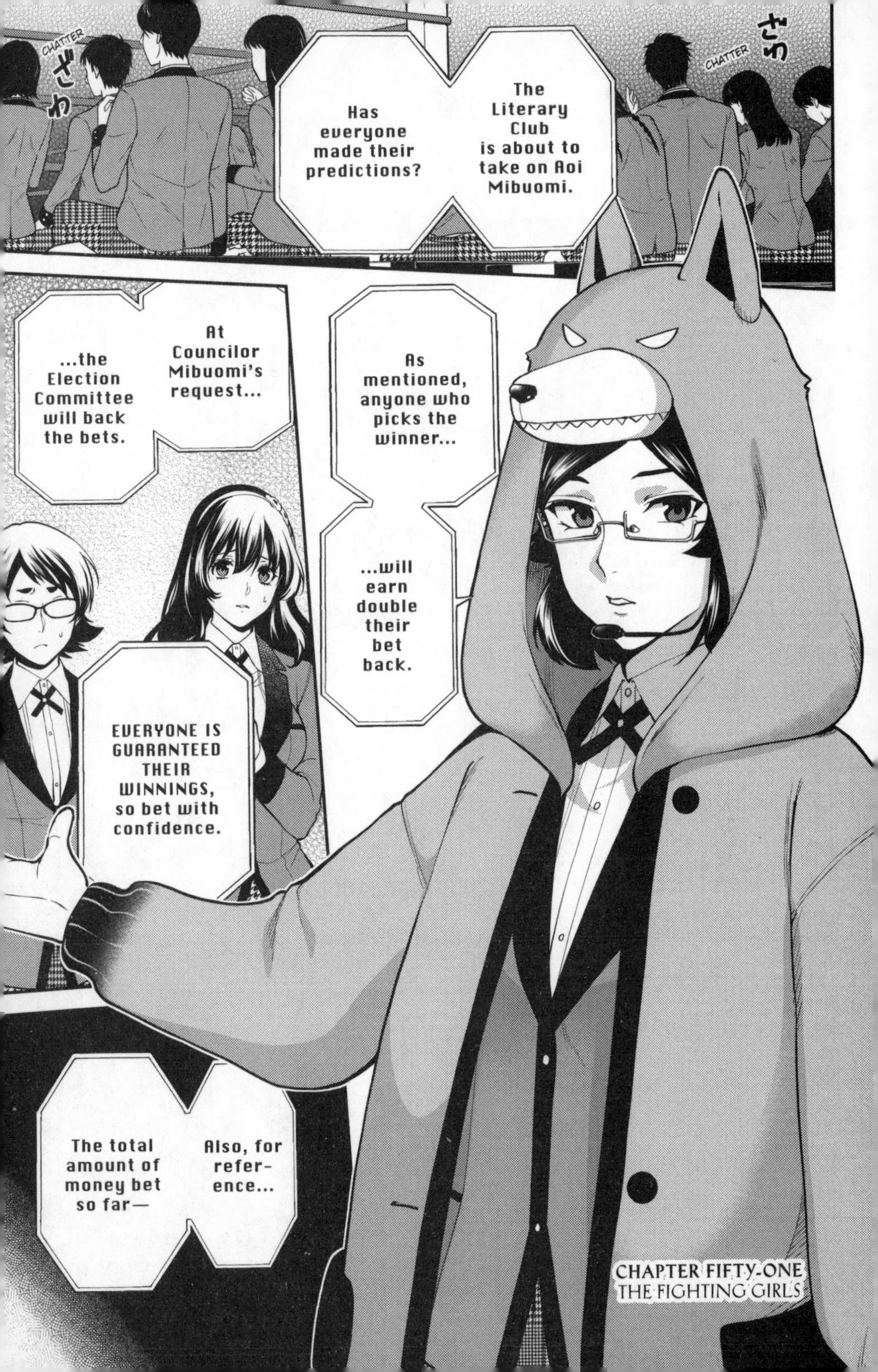
ざわ
CHATTER
CHATTER
ざわ
The Literary Club is about to take on Aoi Mibuomi.
Has everyone made their predictions?
As mentioned, anyone who picks the winner...
...will earn double their bet back.
At Councilor Mibuomi's request...
...the Election Committee will back the bets.
EVERYONE IS GUARANTEED THEIR WINNINGS, so bet with confidence.
Also, for reference...
The total amount of money bet so far—

CHAPTER FIFTY-ONE
THE FIGHTING GIRLS

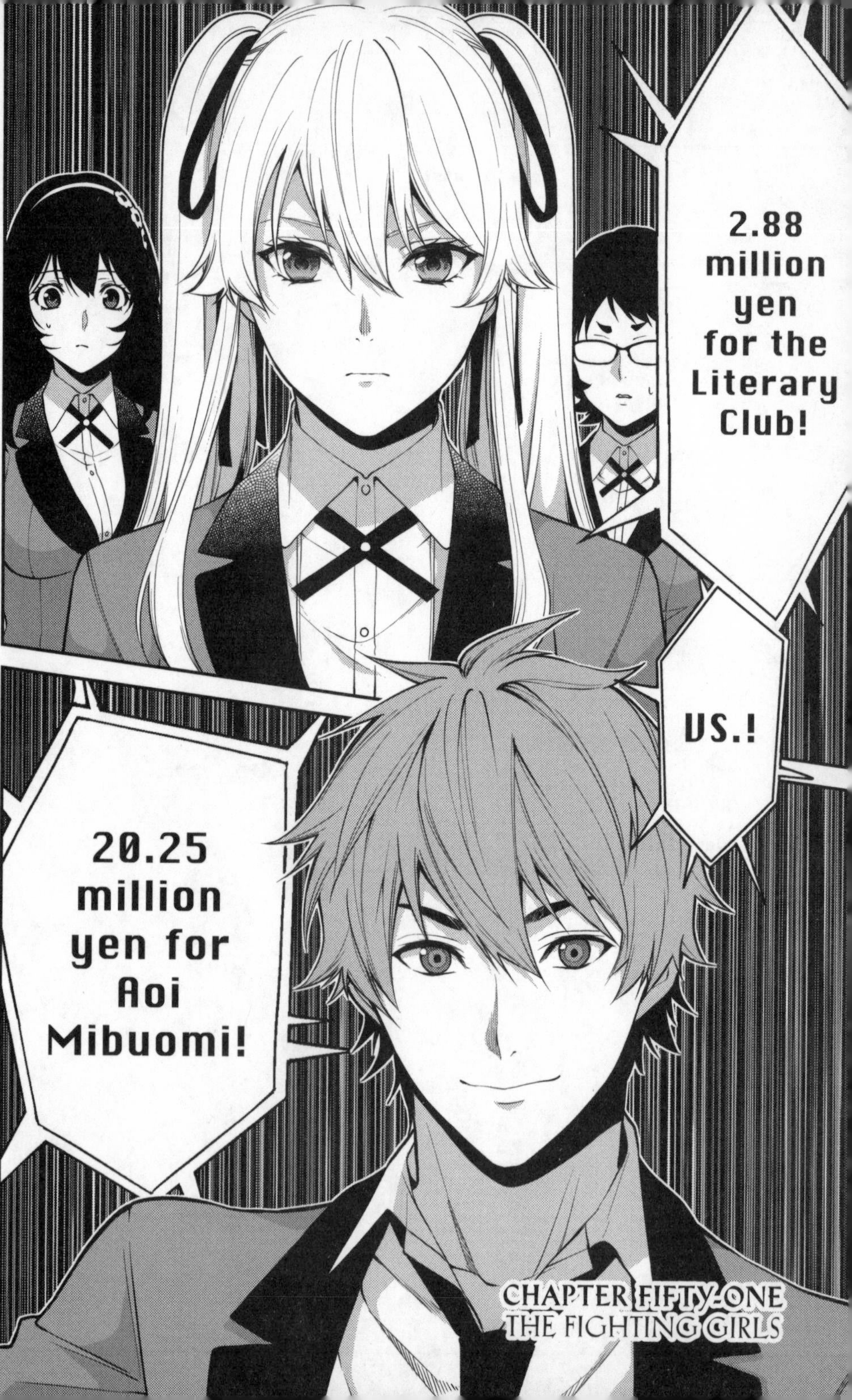
2.88 million yen for the Literary Club!
VS.!
20.25 million yen for Aoi Mibuomi!
CHAPTER FIFTY-ONE
THE FIGHTING GIRLS

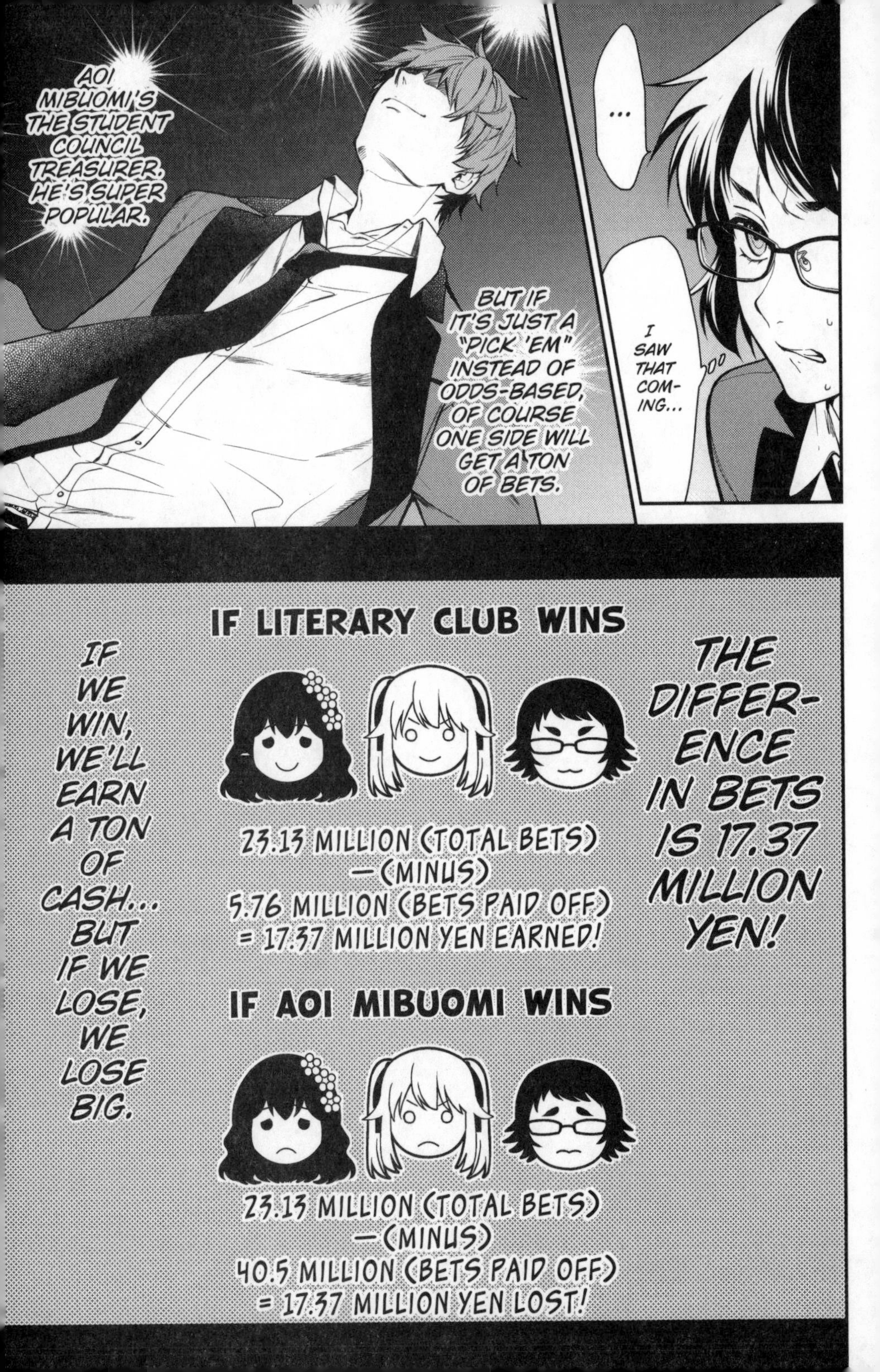
...
I SAW THAT COMING...
AOI MIBUOMI'S THE STUDENT COUNCIL TREASURER. HE'S SUPER POPULAR.
BUT IF IT'S JUST A "PICK 'EM" INSTEAD OF ODDS-BASED, OF COURSE ONE SIDE WILL GET A TON OF BETS.
THE DIFFERENCE IN BETS IS 17.37 MILLION YEN!
IF LITERARY CLUB WINS
23.13 MILLION (TOTAL BETS) —(MINUS) 5.76 MILLION (BETS PAID OFF) = 17.37 MILLION YEN EARNED!
IF AOI MIBUOMI WINS
23.13 MILLION (TOTAL BETS) —(MINUS) 40.5 MILLION (BETS PAID OFF) = 17.37 MILLION YEN LOST!
IF WE WIN, WE'LL EARN A TON OF CASH... BUT IF WE LOSE, WE LOSE BIG.

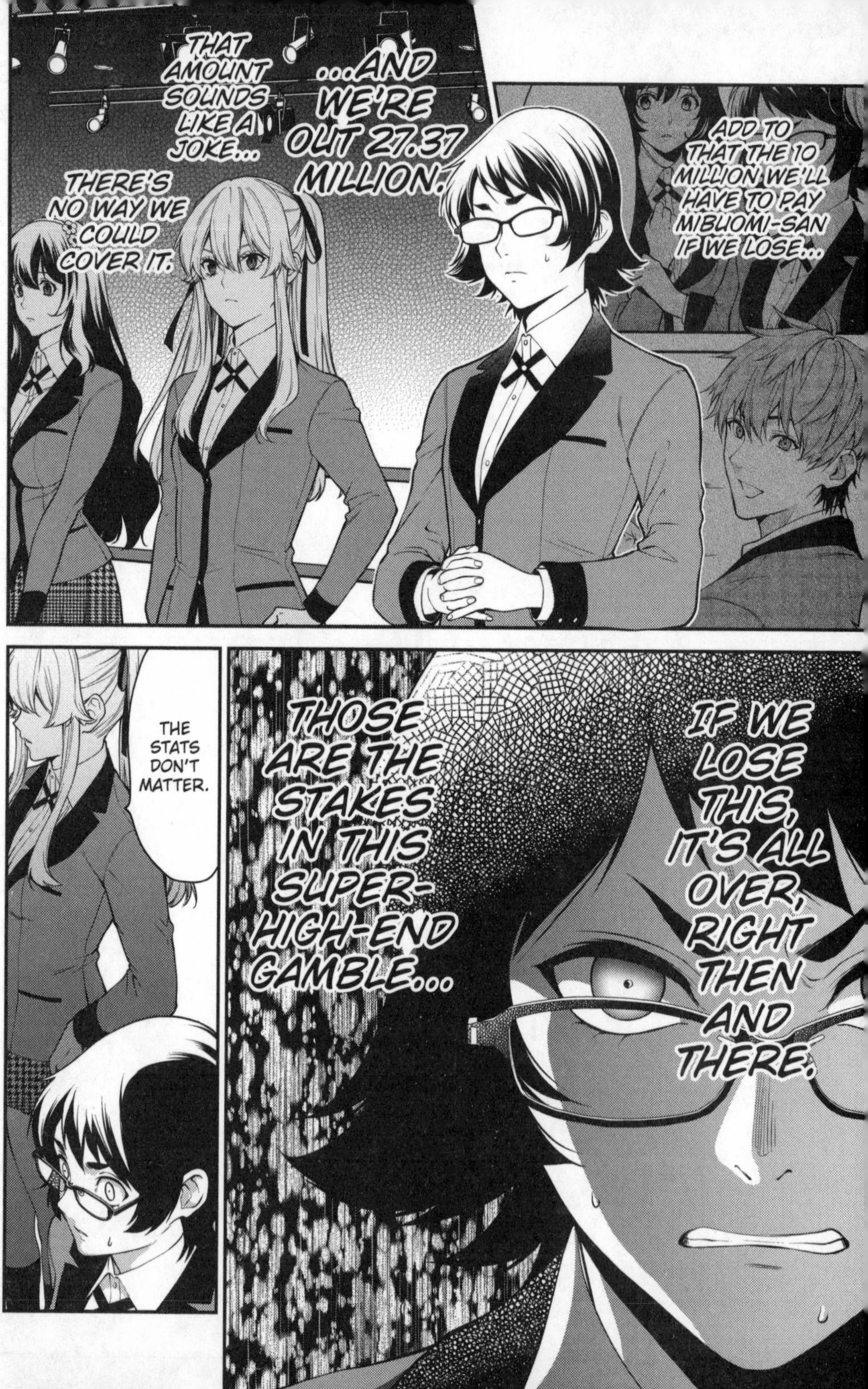
...AND WE'RE OUT 27.37 MILLION.
THAT AMOUNT SOUNDS LIKE A JOKE...
THERE'S NO WAY WE COULD COVER IT.
ADD TO THAT THE 10 MILLION WE'LL HAVE TO PAY MIBUOMI-SAN IF WE LOSE...
THOSE ARE THE STAKES IN THIS SUPER-HIGH-END GAMBLE...
IF WE LOSE THIS, IT'S ALL OVER, RIGHT THEN AND THERE.
THE STATS DON'T MATTER.

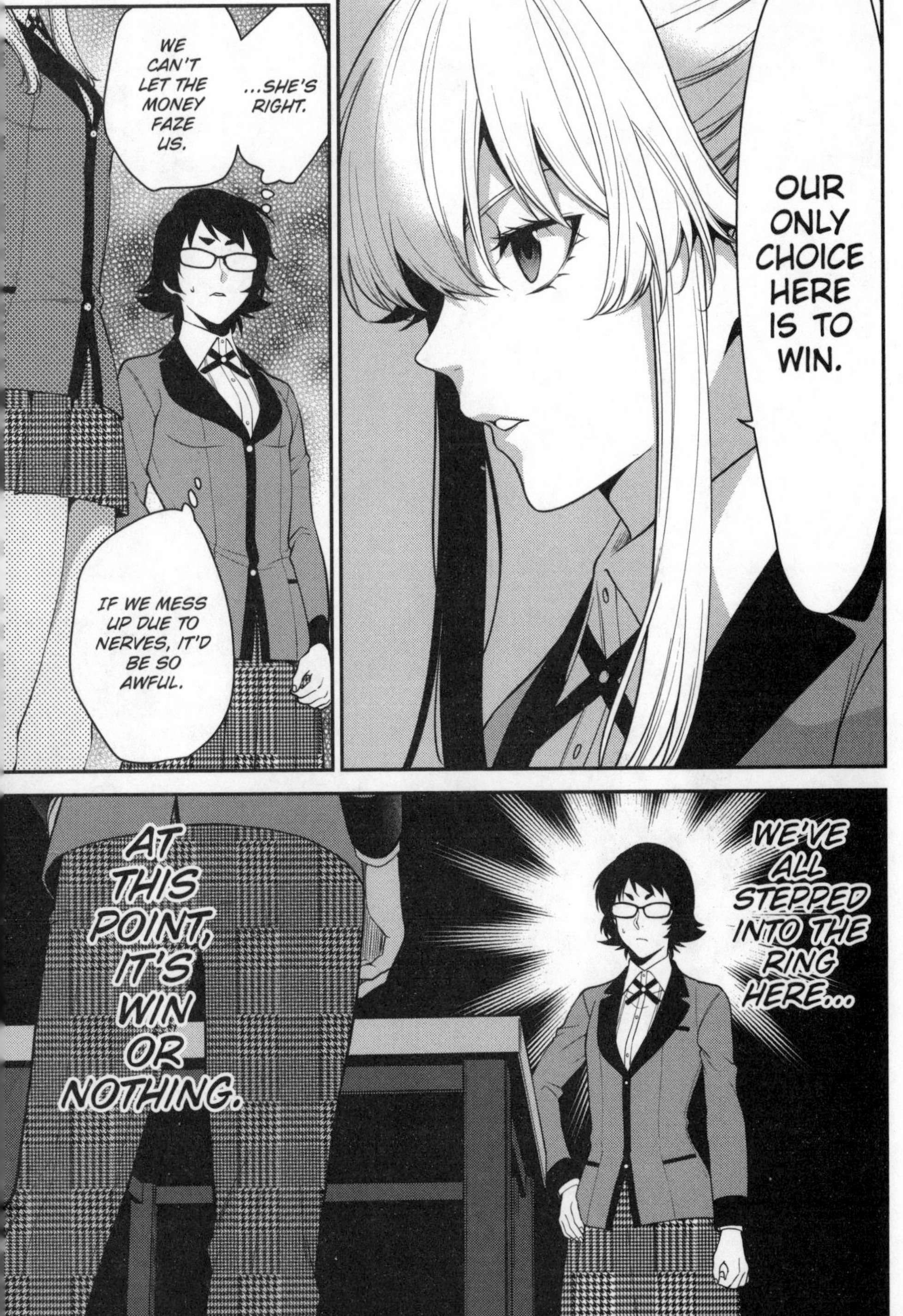
OUR ONLY CHOICE HERE IS TO WIN.
...SHE'S RIGHT.
WE CAN'T LET THE MONEY FAZE US.
IF WE MESS UP DUE TO NERVES, IT'D BE SO AWFUL.
WE'VE ALL STEPPED INTO THE RING HERE...
AT THIS POINT, IT'S WIN OR NOTHING.

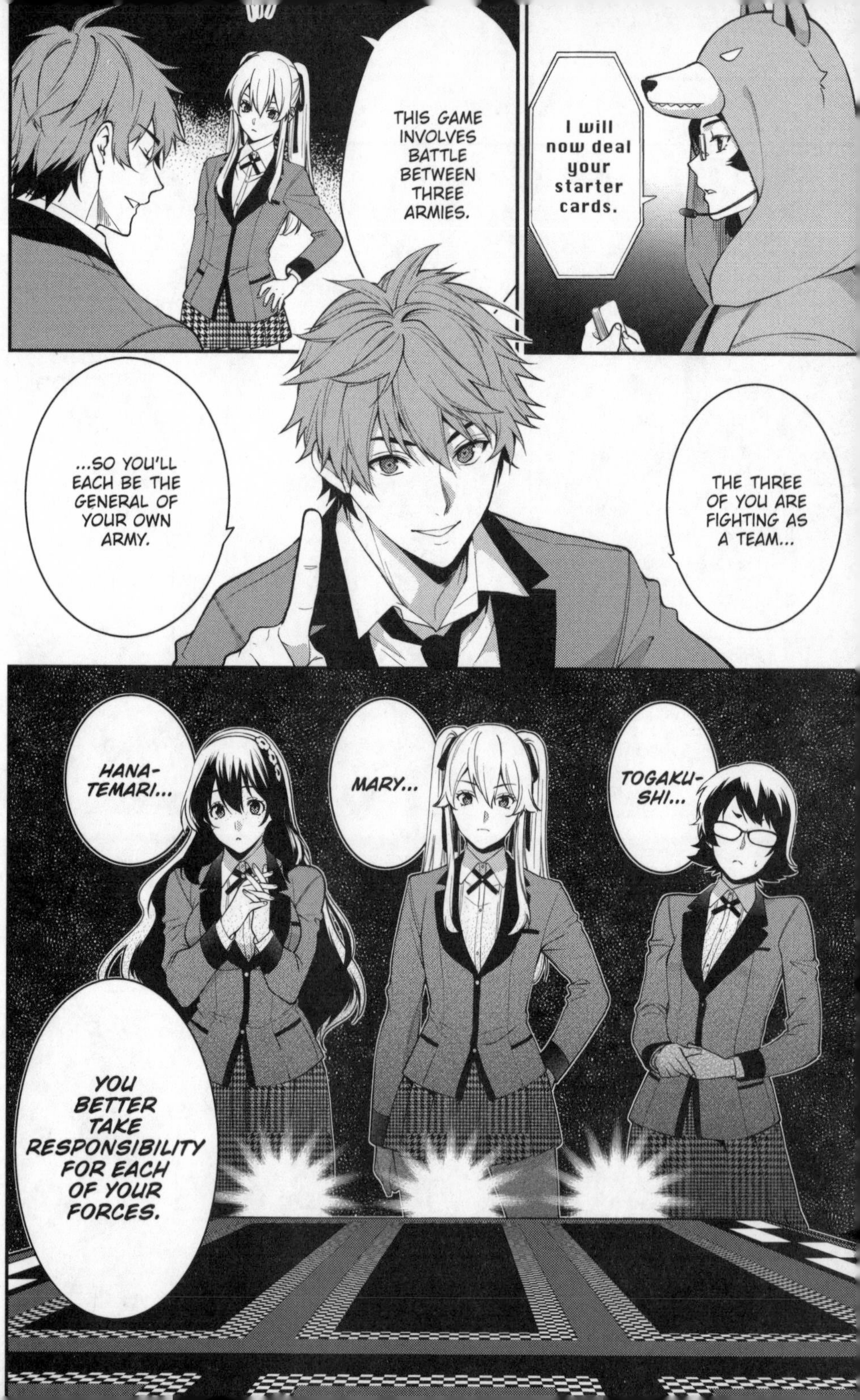
I will now deal your starter cards.
THIS GAME INVOLVES BATTLE BETWEEN THREE ARMIES.
THE THREE OF YOU ARE FIGHTING AS A TEAM...
...SO YOU'LL EACH BE THE GENERAL OF YOUR OWN ARMY.
TOGAKU-SHI...
MARY...
HANA-TEMARI...
YOU BETTER TAKE RESPONSIBILITY FOR EACH OF YOUR FORCES.

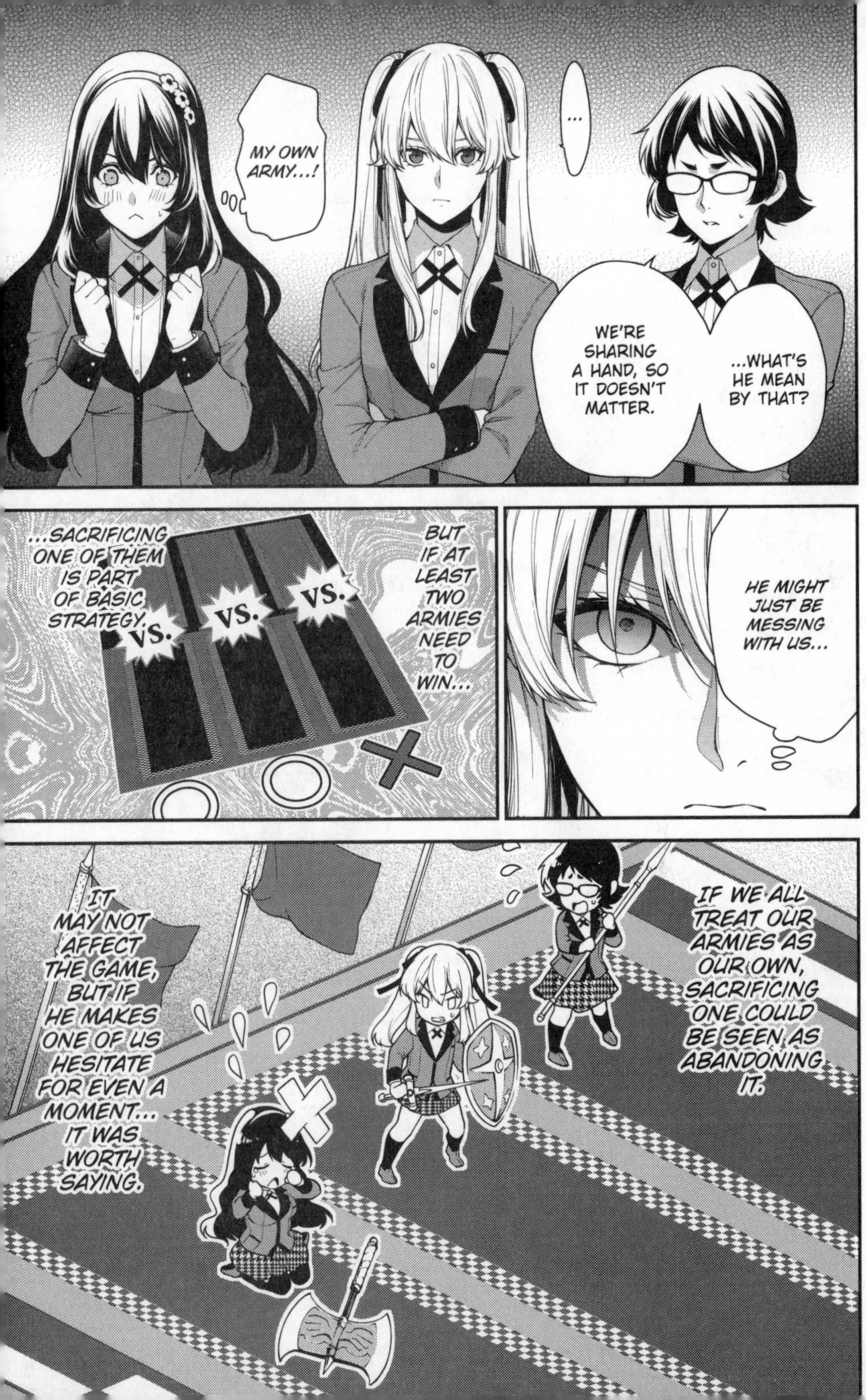
...
...WHAT'S HE MEAN BY THAT?
WE'RE SHARING A HAND, SO IT DOESN'T MATTER.
MY OWN ARMY...!
HE MIGHT JUST BE MESSING WITH US...
BUT IF AT LEAST TWO ARMIES NEED TO WIN...
VS.
VS.
VS.
...SACRIFICING ONE OF THEM IS PART OF BASIC STRATEGY.
IF WE ALL TREAT OUR ARMIES AS OUR OWN, SACRIFICING ONE COULD BE SEEN AS ABANDONING IT.
IT MAY NOT AFFECT THE GAME, BUT IF HE MAKES ONE OF US HESITATE FOR EVEN A MOMENT... IT WAS WORTH SAYING.

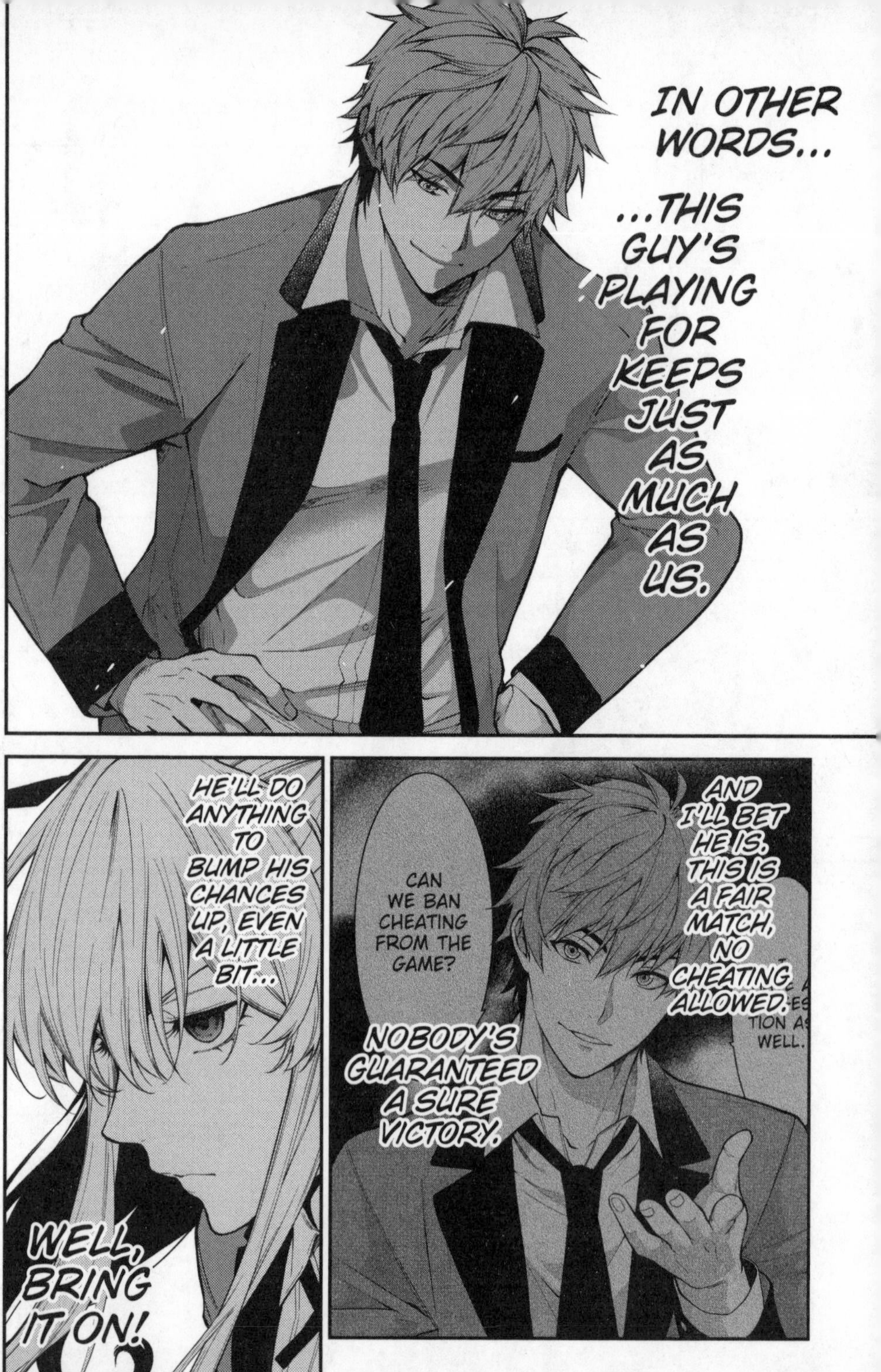
IN OTHER WORDS...
...THIS GUY'S PLAYING FOR KEEPS JUST AS MUCH AS US.
AND I'LL BET HE IS. THIS IS A FAIR MATCH, NO CHEATING ALLOWED.
CAN WE BAN CHEATING FROM THE GAME?
NOBODY'S GUARANTEED A SURE VICTORY.
HE'LL DO ANYTHING TO BUMP HIS CHANCES UP, EVEN A LITTLE BIT...
WELL, BRING IT ON!

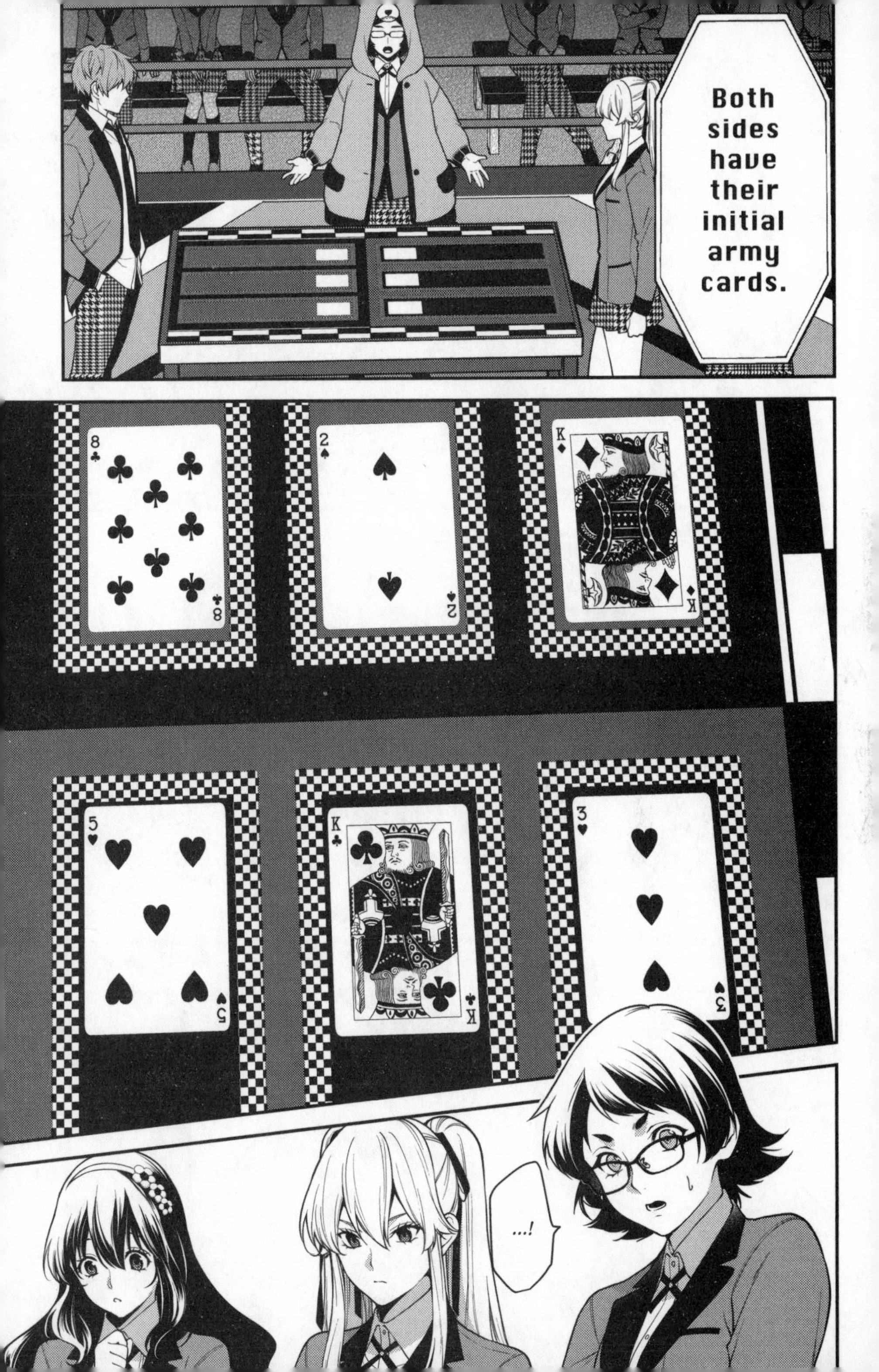
Both sides have their initial army cards.
...!

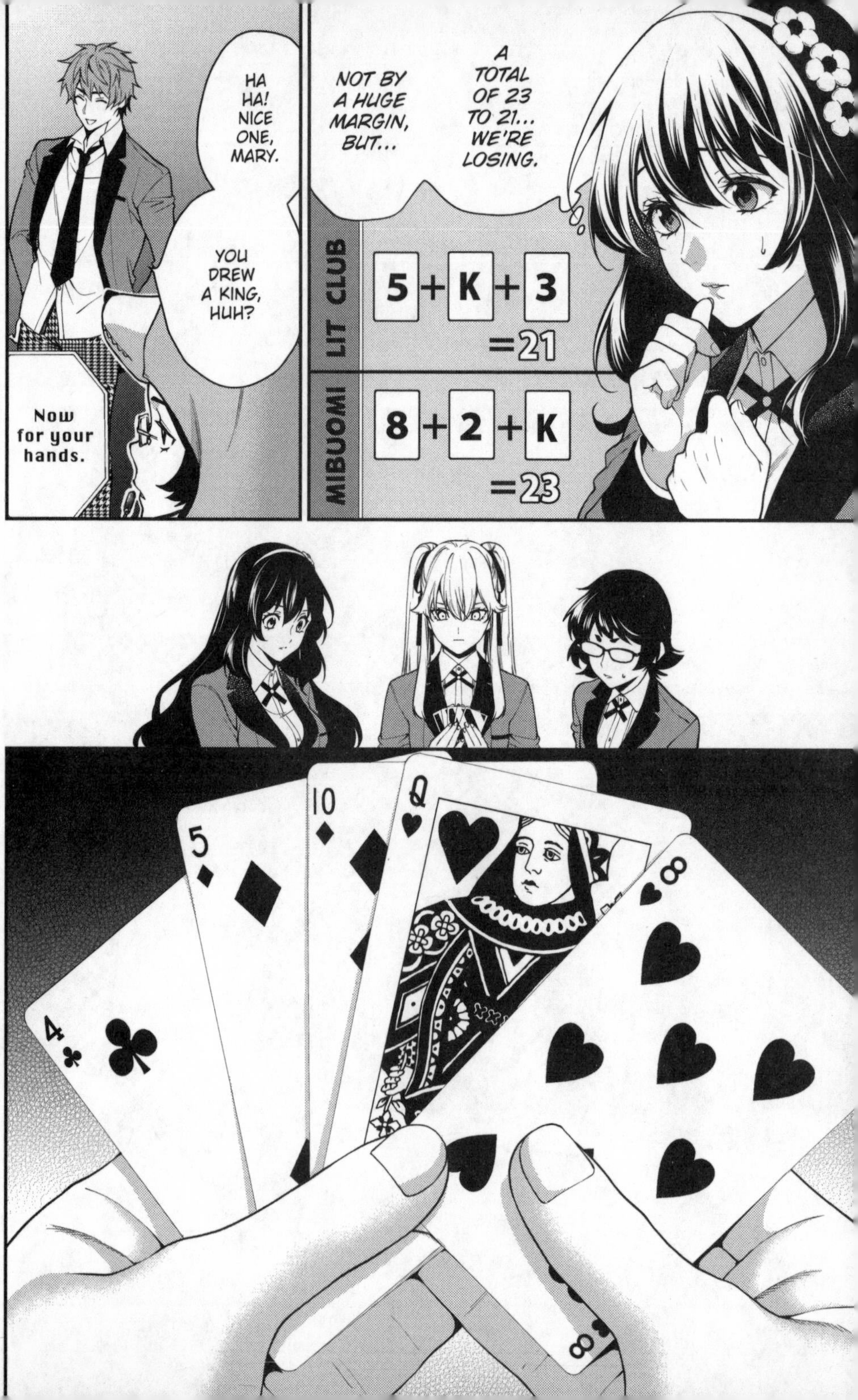
A TOTAL OF 23 TO 21... WE'RE LOSING.
NOT BY A HUGE MARGIN, BUT...
LIT CLUB
5 + K + 3
=21
MIBUOMI
8 + 2 + K
=23
HA HA! NICE ONE, MARY.
YOU DREW A KING, HUH?
Now for your hands.

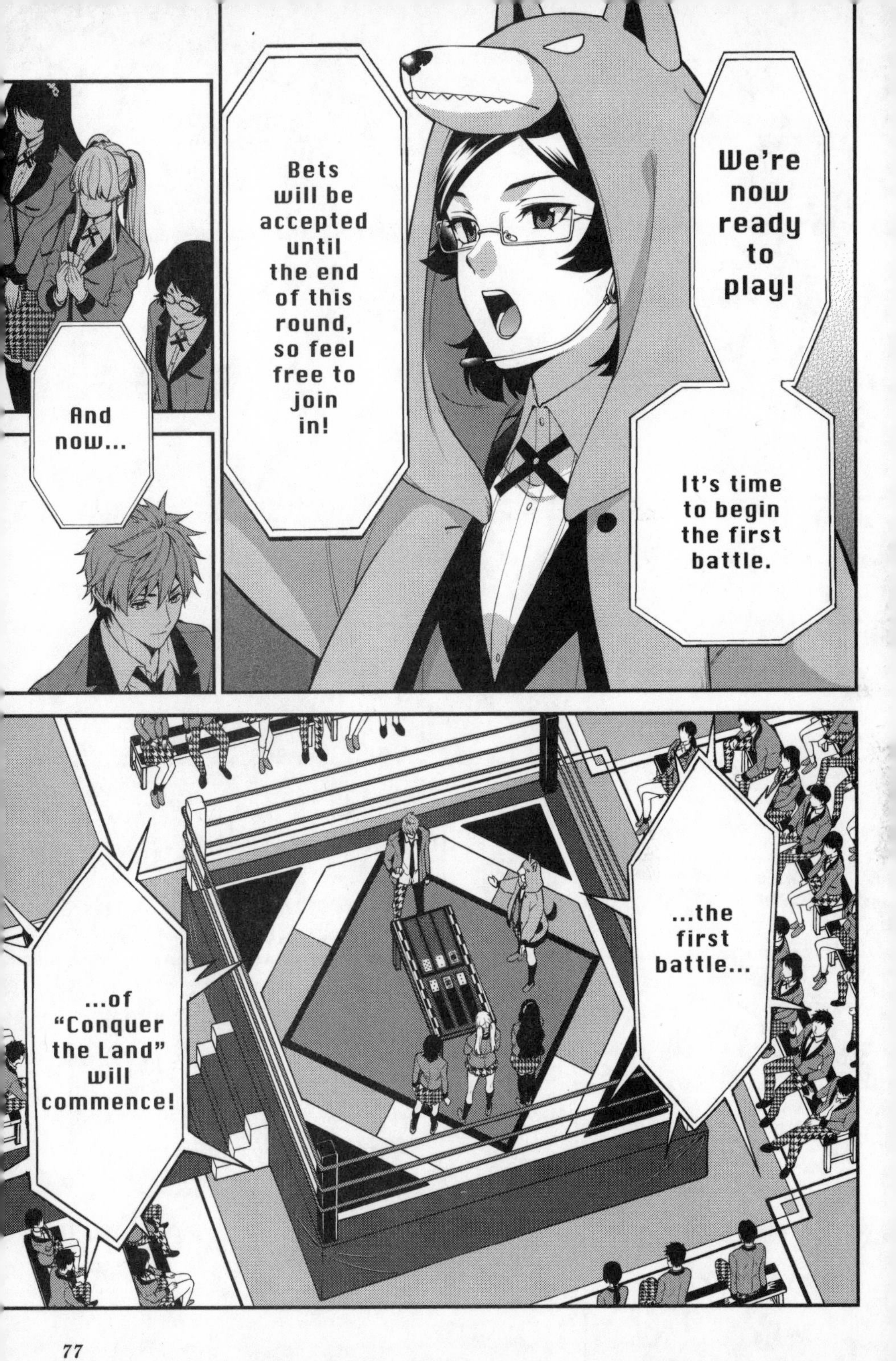
We're now ready to play!
Bets will be accepted until the end of this round, so feel free to join in!
It's time to begin the first battle.
And now...
...the first battle...
...of "Conquer the Land" will commence!

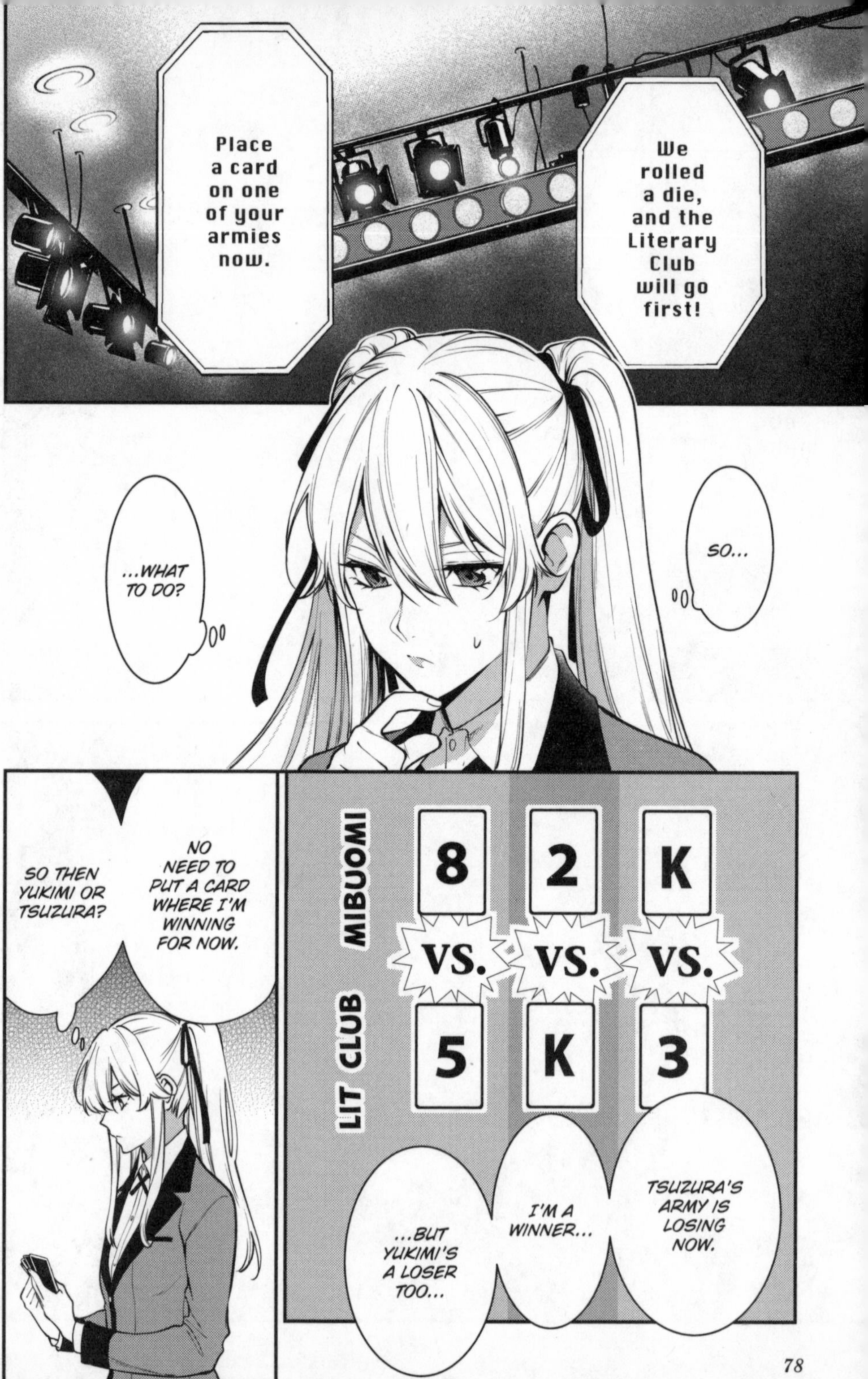
We rolled a die, and the Literary Club will go first!
Place a card on one of your armies now.
SO...
...WHAT TO DO?
MIBUOMI
8
2
K
VS.
VS.
VS.
LIT CLUB
5
K
3
TSUZURA'S ARMY IS LOSING NOW.
I'M A WINNER...
...BUT YUKIMI'S A LOSER TOO...
NO NEED TO PUT A CARD WHERE I'M WINNING FOR NOW.
SO THEN YUKIMI OR TSUZURA?

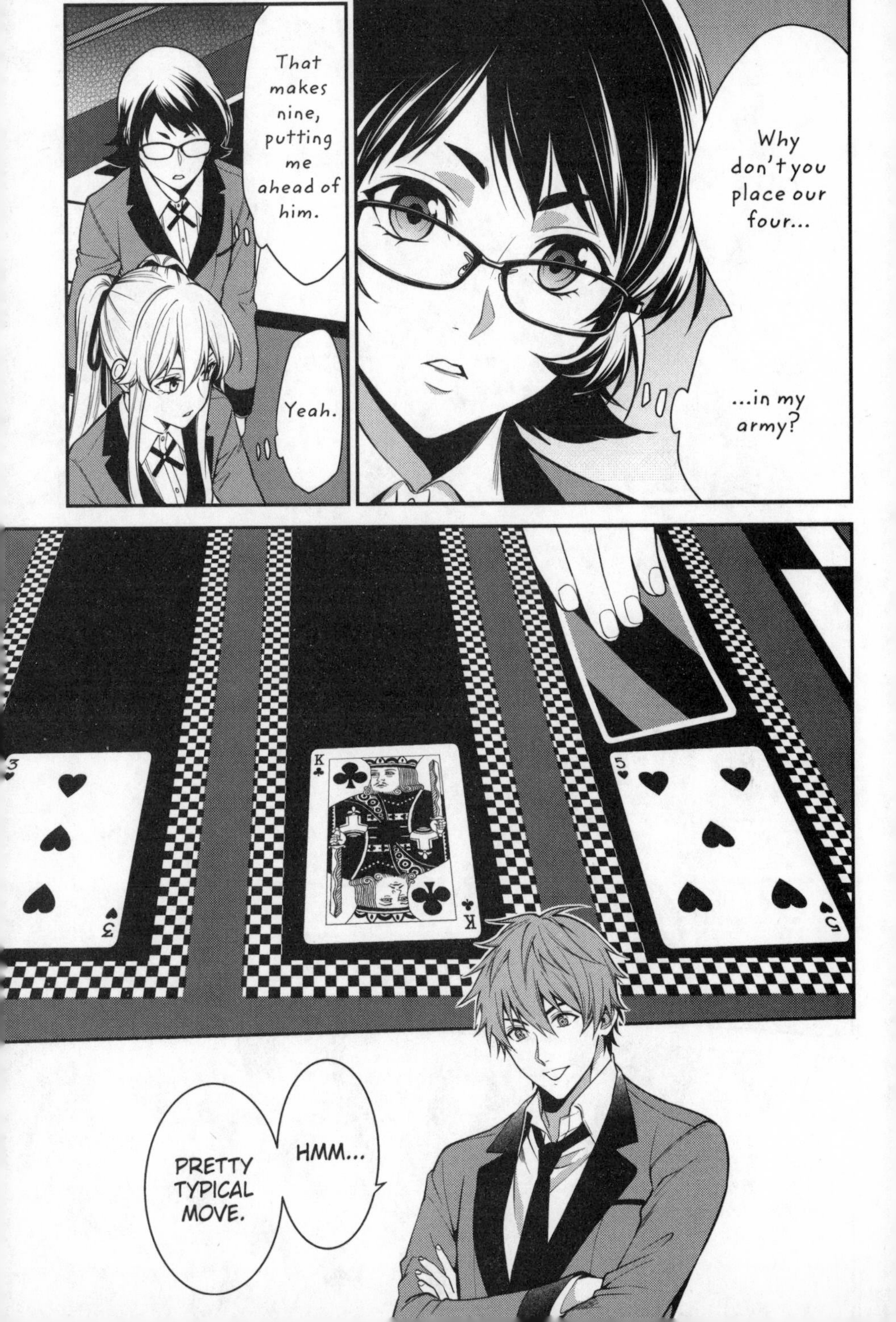
Why don't you place our four...
...in my army?
That makes nine, putting me ahead of him.
Yeah.
HMM...
PRETTY TYPICAL MOVE.

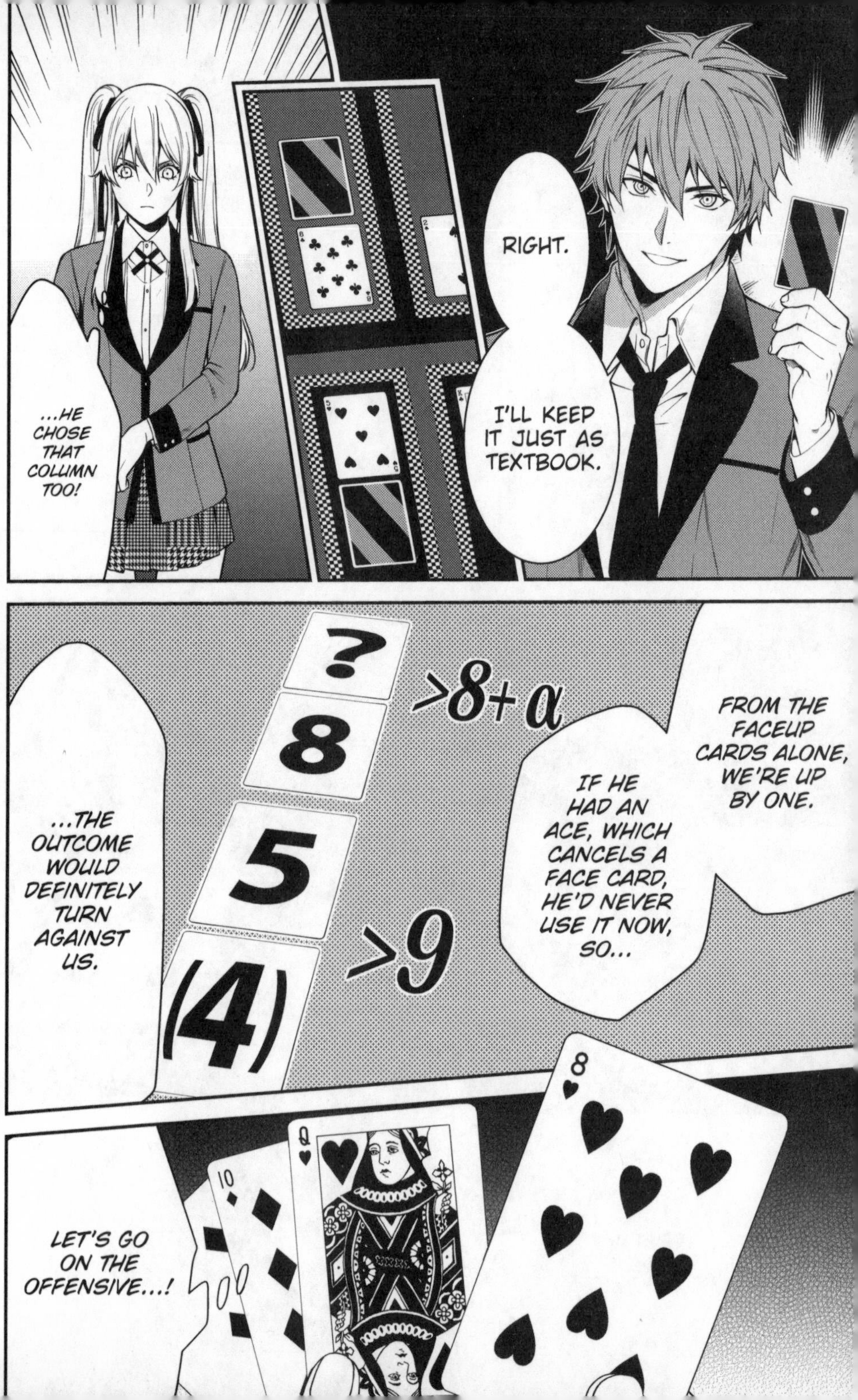
RIGHT.
I'LL KEEP IT JUST AS TEXTBOOK.
...HE CHOSE THAT COLUMN TOO!
FROM THE FACEUP CARDS ALONE, WE'RE UP BY ONE.
IF HE HAD AN ACE, WHICH CANCELS A FACE CARD, HE'D NEVER USE IT NOW, SO...
?
>8+α
8
5
>9
(4)
...THE OUTCOME WOULD DEFINITELY TURN AGAINST US.
LET'S GO ON THE OFFENSIVE...!

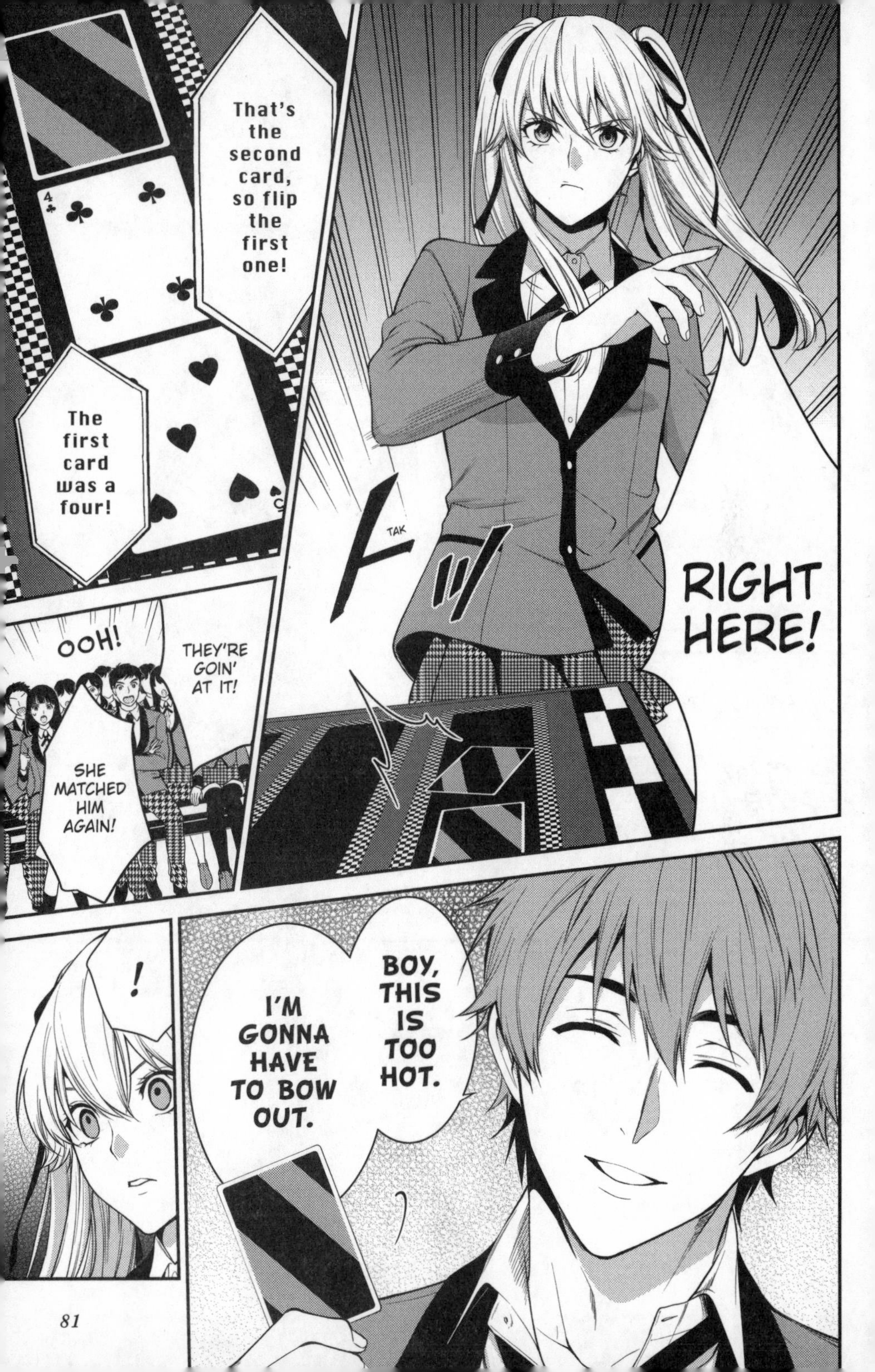
TAK
RIGHT HERE!
That's the second card, so flip the first one!
The first card was a four!
THEY'RE GOIN' AT IT!
OOH!
SHE MATCHED HIM AGAIN!
BOY, THIS IS TOO HOT.
I'M GONNA HAVE TO BOW OUT.
!

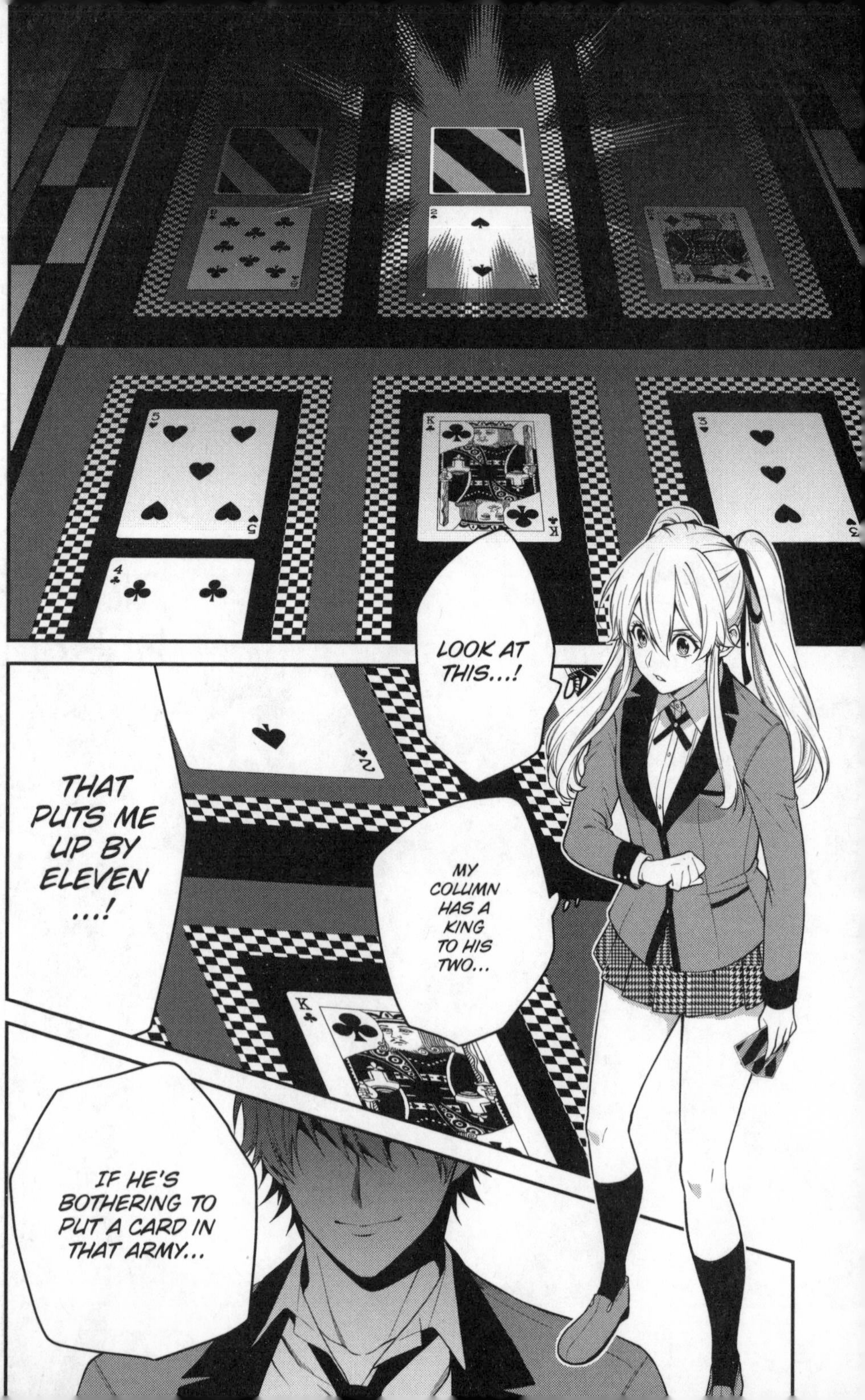
LOOK AT THIS...!
MY COLUMN HAS A KING TO HIS TWO...
THAT PUTS ME UP BY ELEVEN ...!
IF HE'S BOTHERING TO PUT A CARD IN THAT ARMY...

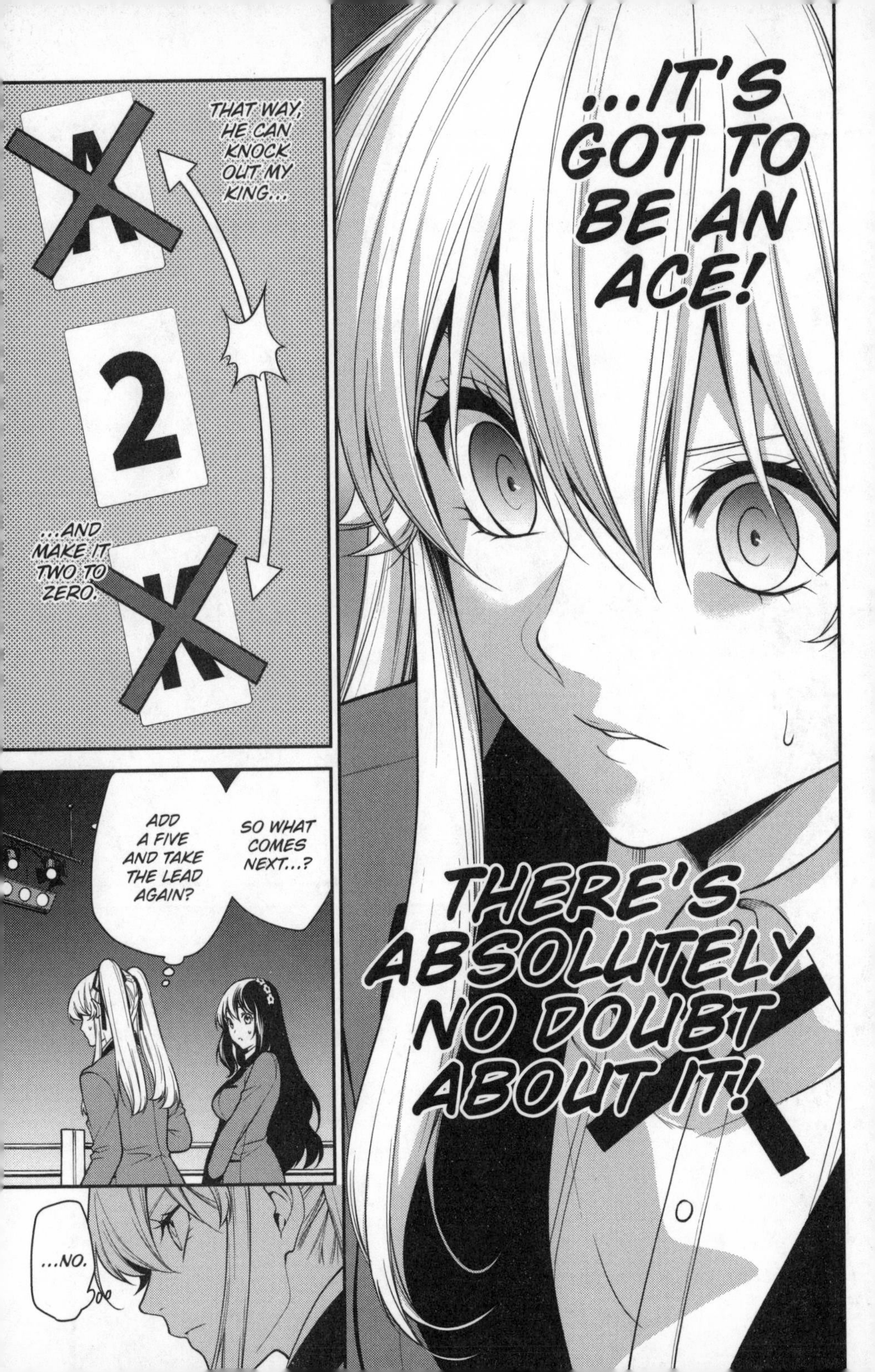
...IT'S GOT TO BE AN ACE!
THERE'S ABSOLUTELY NO DOUBT ABOUT IT!
THAT WAY, HE CAN KNOCK OUT MY KING...
2
...AND MAKE IT TWO TO ZERO.
SO WHAT COMES NEXT...?
ADD A FIVE AND TAKE THE LEAD AGAIN?
...NO.

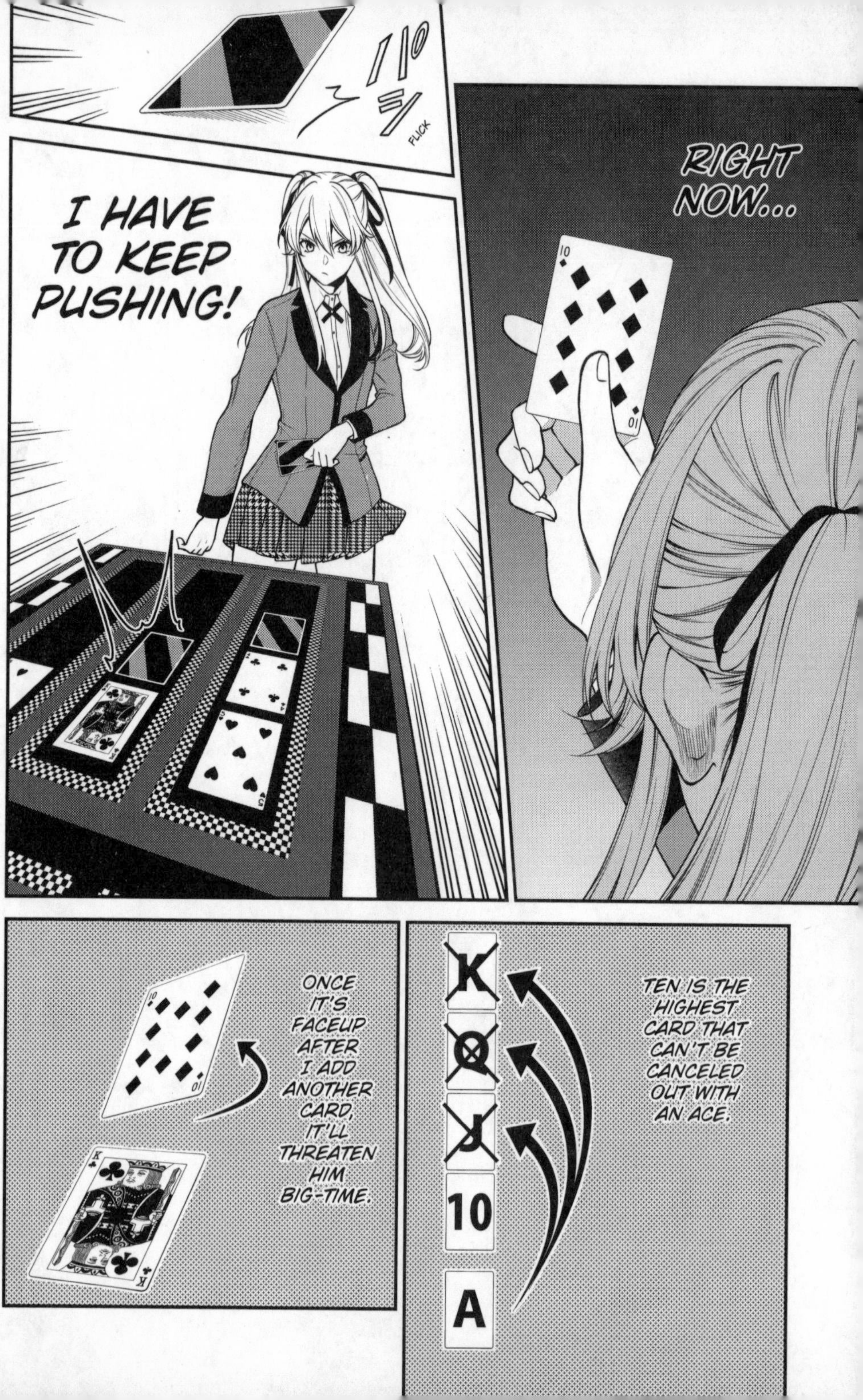

RIGHT NOW...
FLICK
I HAVE TO KEEP PUSHING!
TEN IS THE HIGHEST CARD THAT CAN'T BE CANCELED OUT WITH AN ACE.
K
Q
J
10
A
ONCE IT'S FACEUP AFTER I ADD ANOTHER CARD, IT'LL THREATEN HIM BIG-TIME.

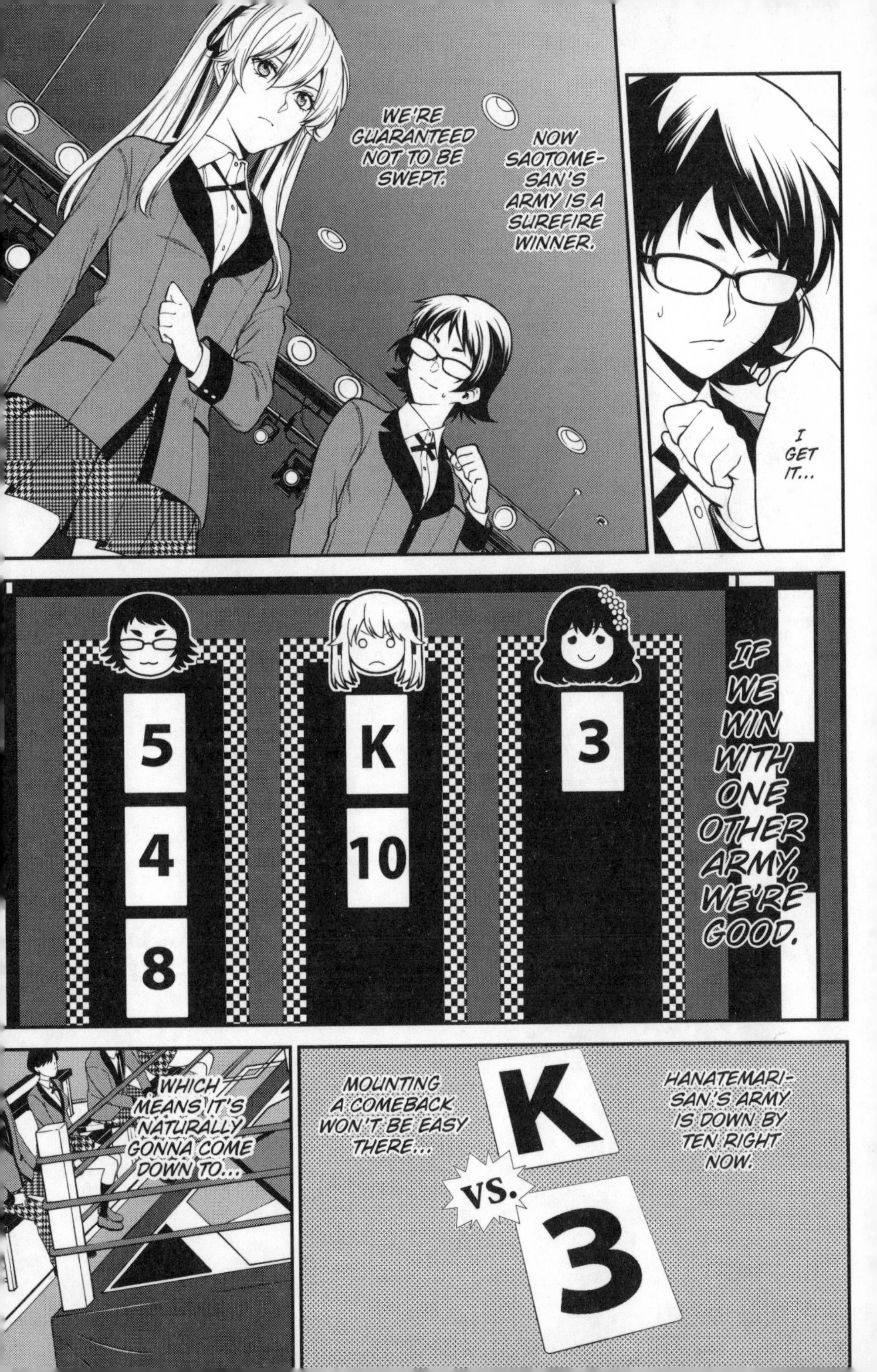
I GET IT...
NOW SAOTOME-SAN'S ARMY IS A SUREFIRE WINNER.
WE'RE GUARANTEED NOT TO BE SWEPT.
IF WE WIN WITH ONE OTHER ARMY, WE'RE GOOD.
3
K
10
5
4
8
HANATEMARI-SAN'S ARMY IS DOWN BY TEN RIGHT NOW.
K
VS.
3
MOUNTING A COMEBACK WON'T BE EASY THERE...
WHICH MEANS IT'S NATURALLY GONNA COME DOWN TO...

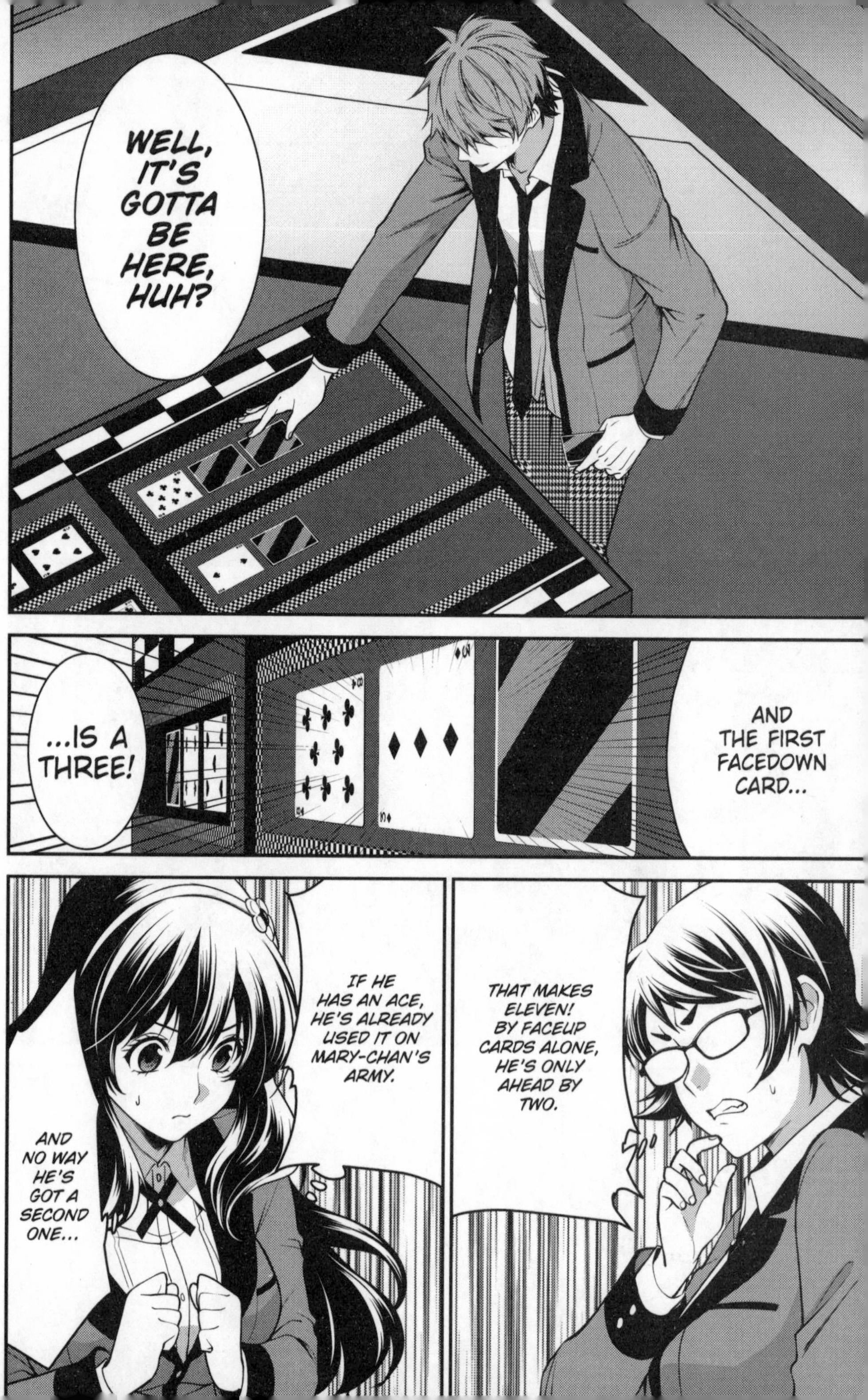
WELL, IT'S GOTTA BE HERE, HUH?
AND THE FIRST FACEDOWN CARD...
...IS A THREE!
THAT MAKES ELEVEN! BY FACEUP CARDS ALONE, HE'S ONLY AHEAD BY TWO.
IF HE HAS AN ACE, HE'S ALREADY USED IT ON MARY-CHAN'S ARMY.
AND NO WAY HE'S GOT A SECOND ONE...

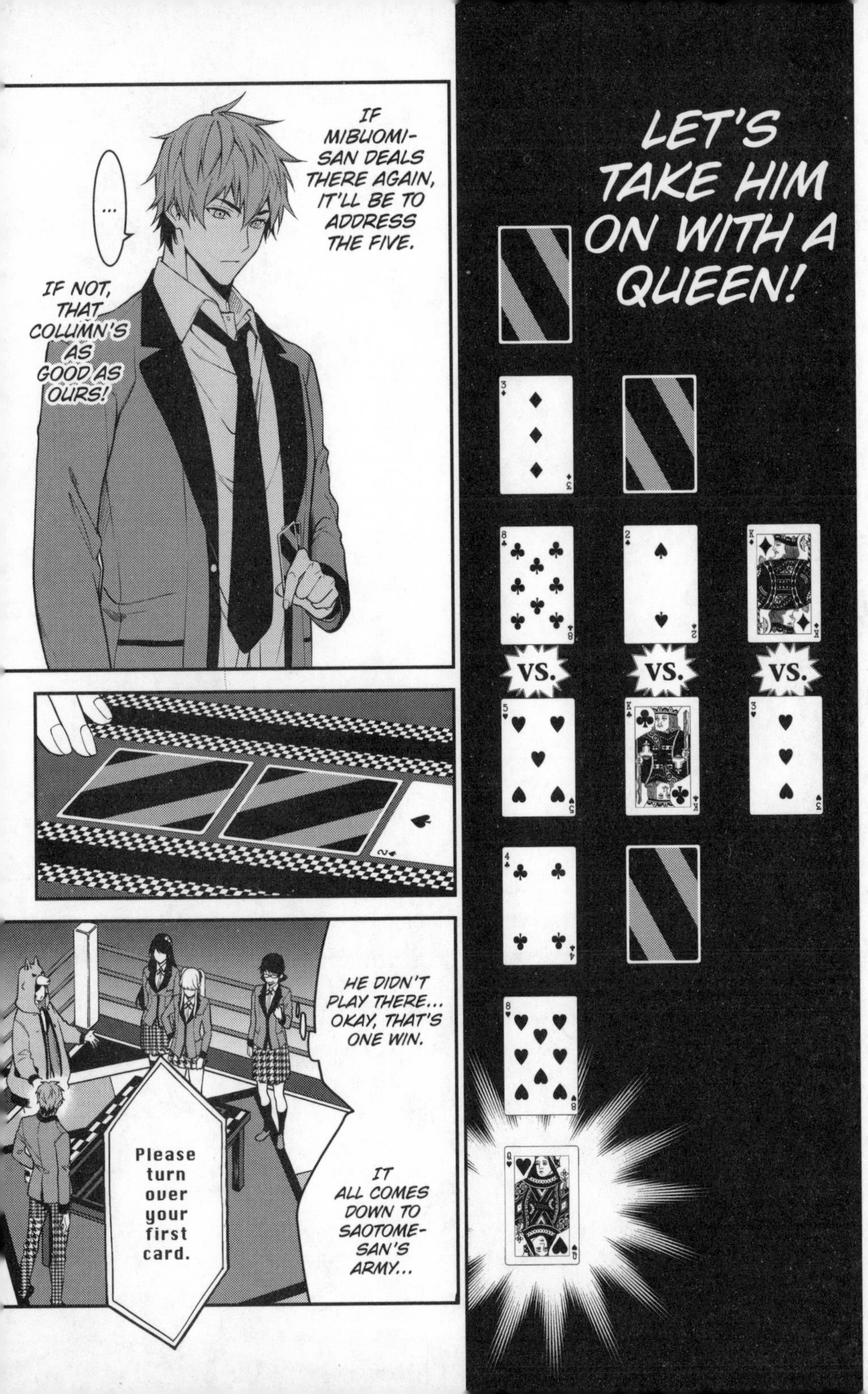
LET'S TAKE HIM ON WITH A QUEEN!
VS.
VS.
VS.
IF MIBUOMI-SAN DEALS THERE AGAIN, IT'LL BE TO ADDRESS THE FIVE.
...
IF NOT, THAT COLUMN'S AS GOOD AS OURS!
HE DIDN'T PLAY THERE... OKAY, THAT'S ONE WIN.
IT ALL COMES DOWN TO SAOTOME-SAN'S ARMY...
Please turn over your first card.

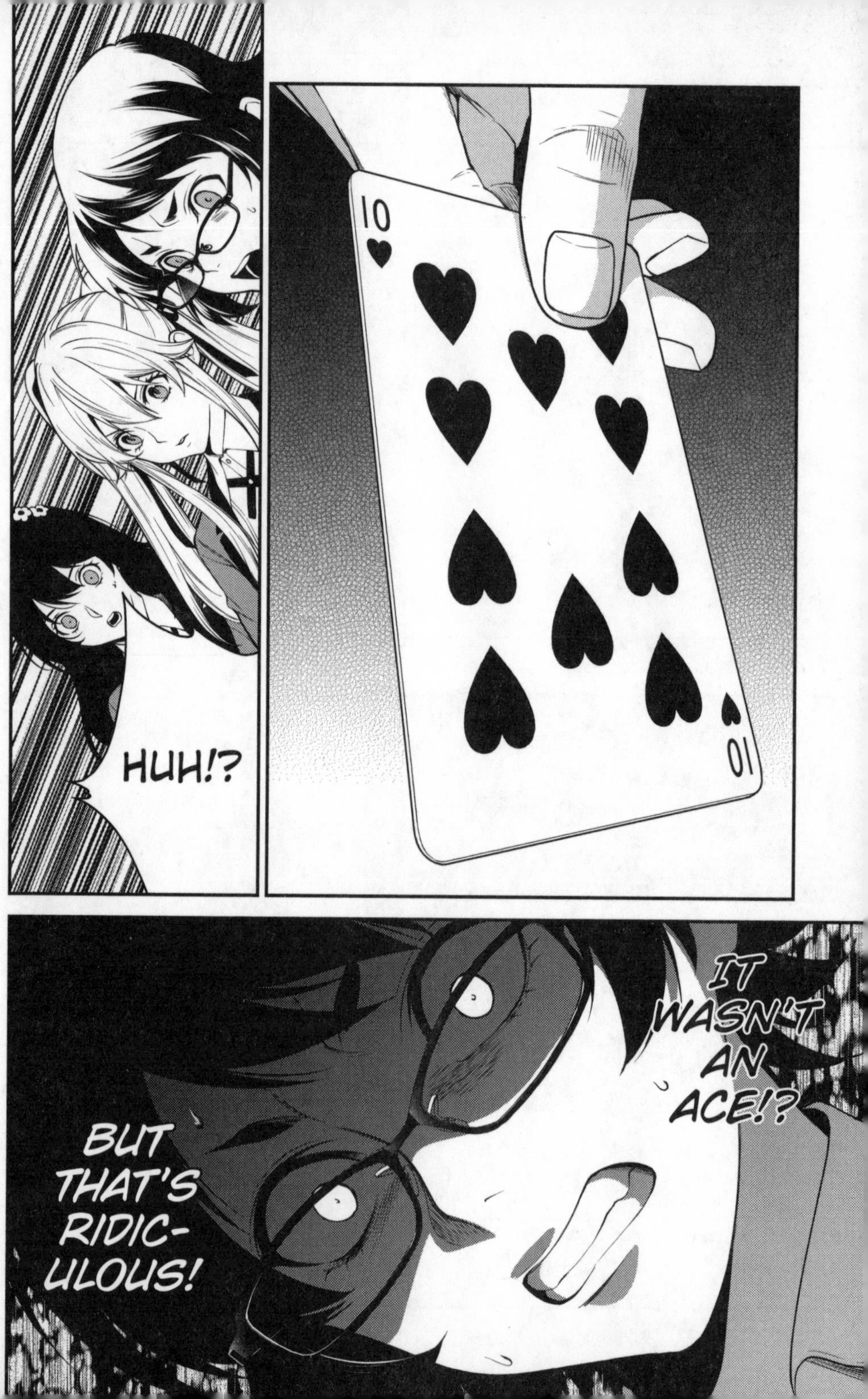
HUH!?
IT WASN'T AN ACE!?
BUT THAT'S RIDIC-ULOUS!

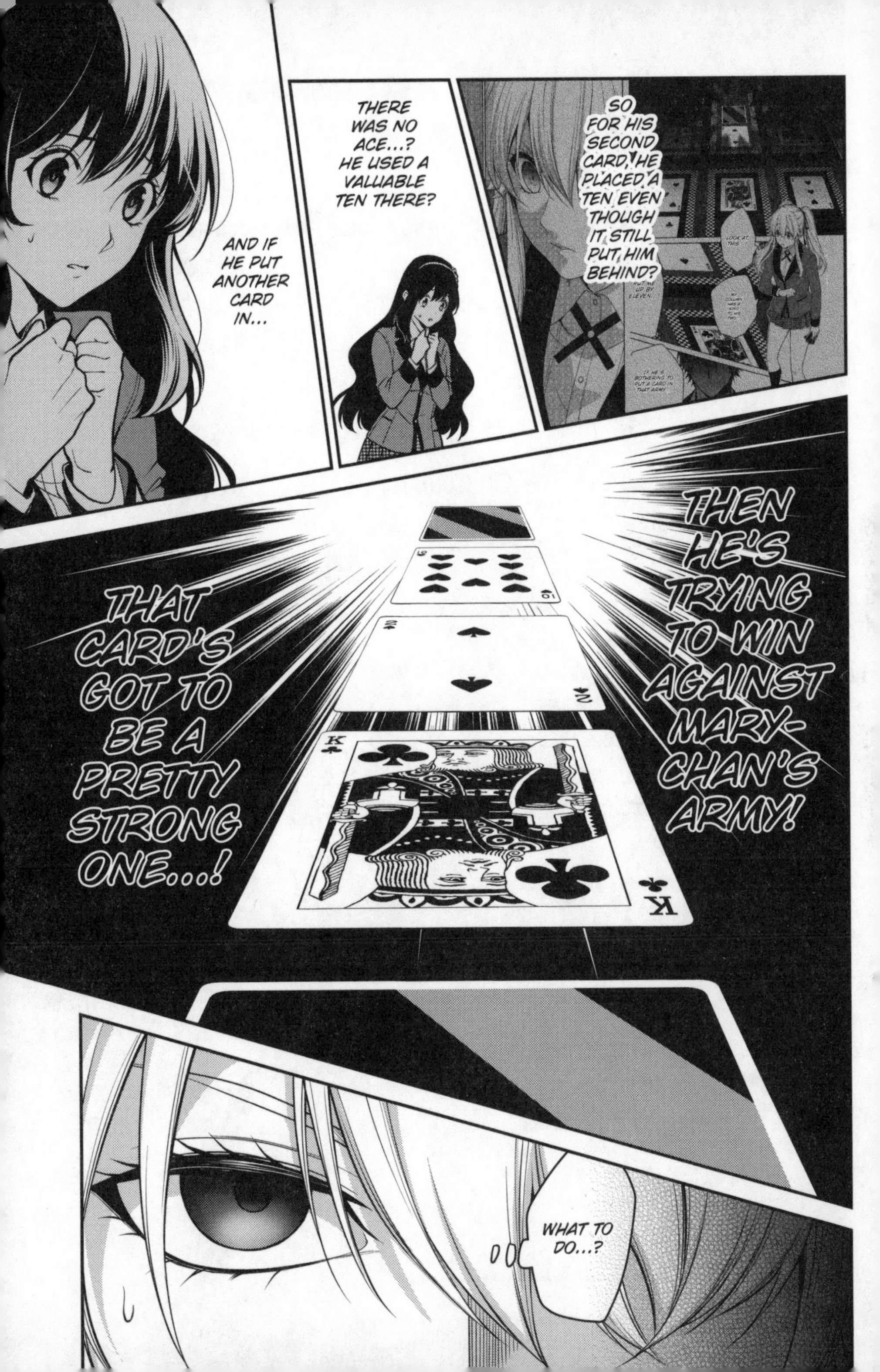
SO FOR HIS SECOND CARD, HE PLACED A TEN EVEN THOUGH IT STILL PUT HIM BEHIND?
LOOK AT THIS...!
PUT ME UP BY ELEVEN...!
MY COLUMN HAS A KING TO HIS TWO.
IF HE'S BOTHERING TO PUT A CARD IN THAT ARMY...
THERE WAS NO ACE...? HE USED A VALUABLE TEN THERE?
AND IF HE PUT ANOTHER CARD IN...
THEN HE'S TRYING TO WIN AGAINST MARY-CHAN'S ARMY!
THAT CARD'S GOT TO BE A PRETTY STRONG ONE...!
WHAT TO DO...?

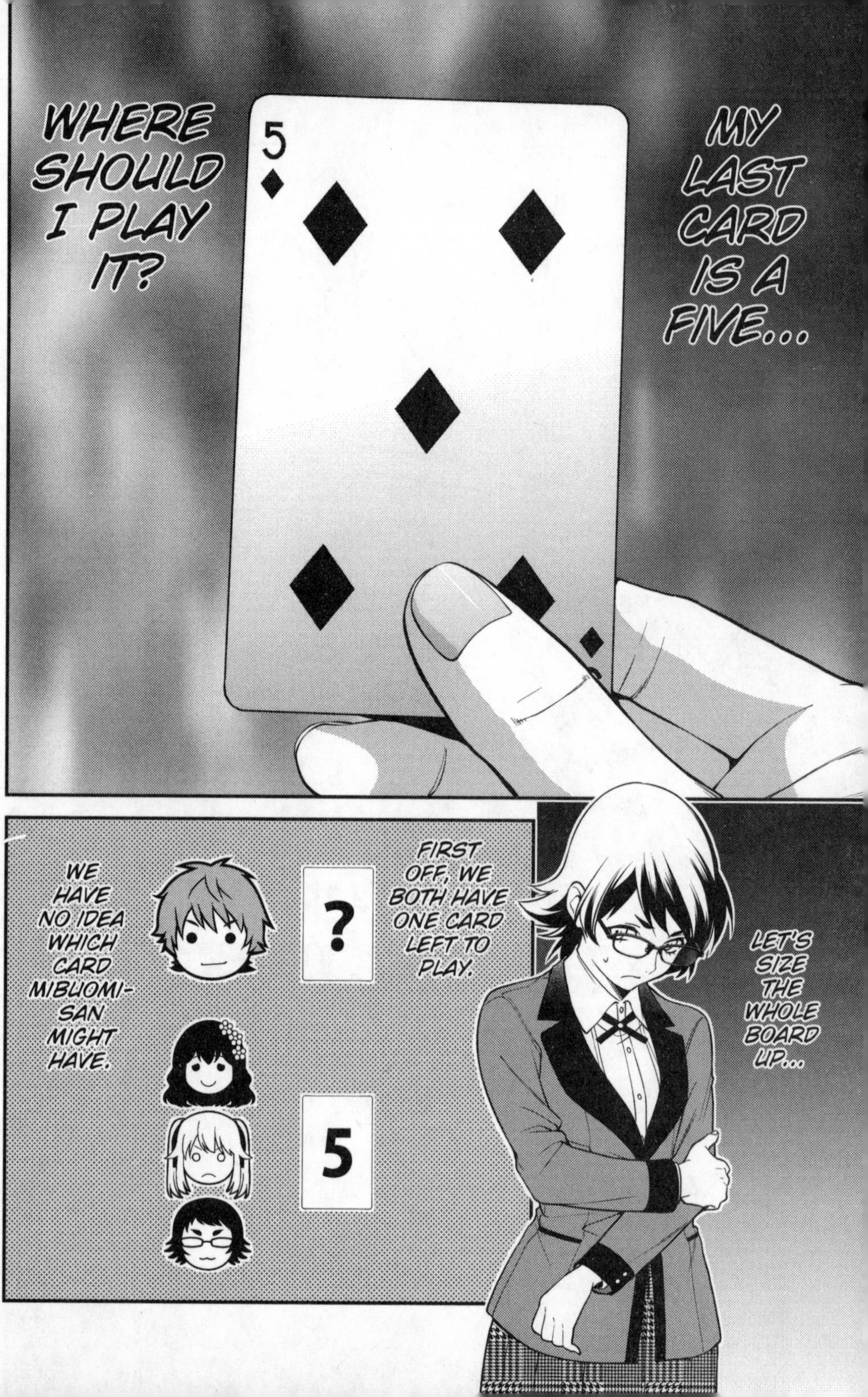

MY LAST CARD IS A FIVE...
WHERE SHOULD I PLAY IT?
LET'S SIZE THE WHOLE BOARD UP...
FIRST OFF, WE BOTH HAVE ONE CARD LEFT TO PLAY.
WE HAVE NO IDEA WHICH CARD MIBUOMI-SAN MIGHT HAVE.
?
5

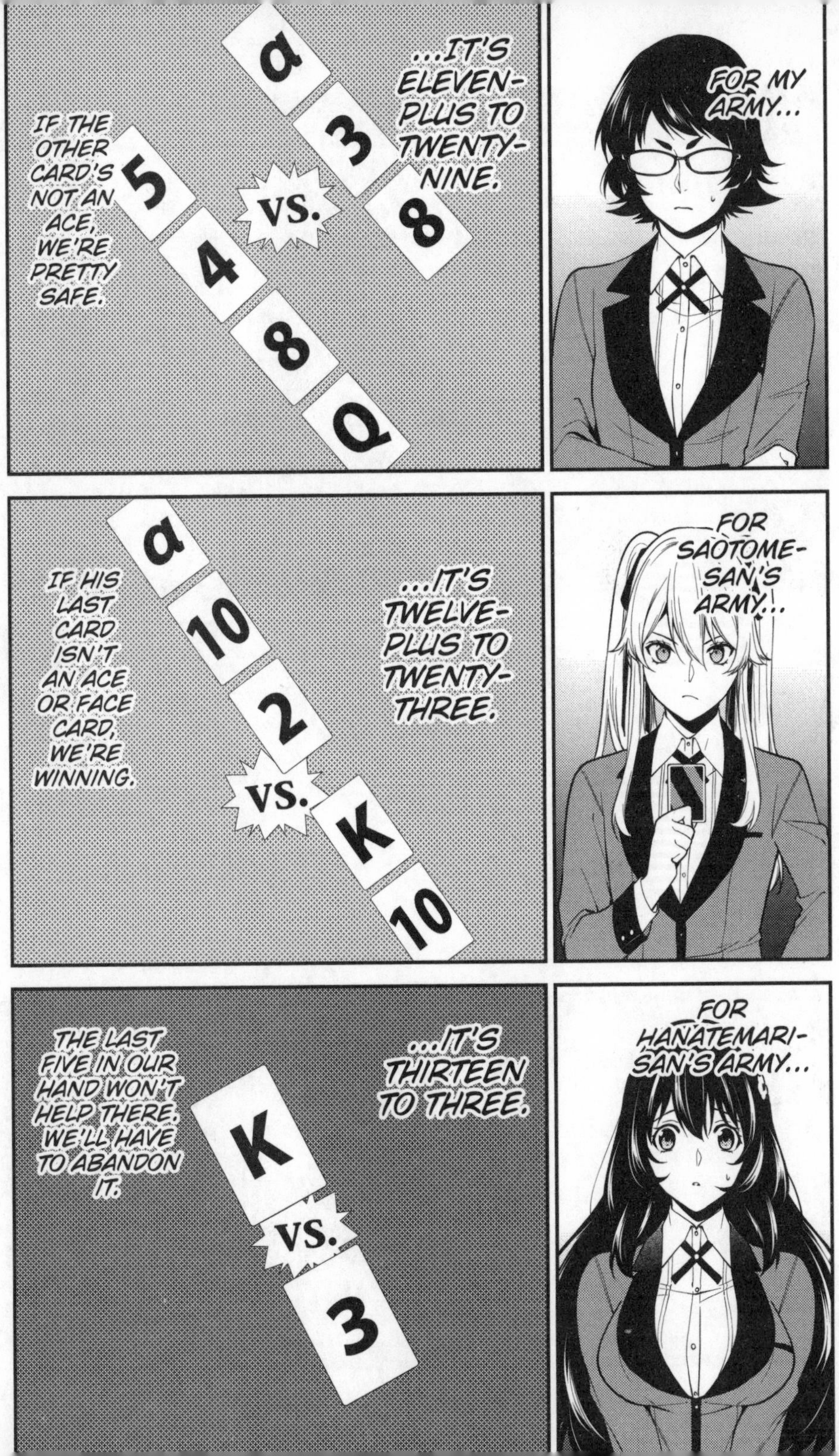
FOR MY ARMY...
...IT'S ELEVEN-PLUS TO TWENTY-NINE.
IF THE OTHER CARD'S NOT AN ACE, WE'RE PRETTY SAFE.
FOR SAOTOME-SAN'S ARMY...
...IT'S TWELVE-PLUS TO TWENTY-THREE.
IF HIS LAST CARD ISN'T AN ACE OR FACE CARD, WE'RE WINNING.
FOR HANATEMARI-SAN'S ARMY...
...IT'S THIRTEEN TO THREE.
THE LAST FIVE IN OUR HAND WON'T HELP THERE. WE'LL HAVE TO ABANDON IT.

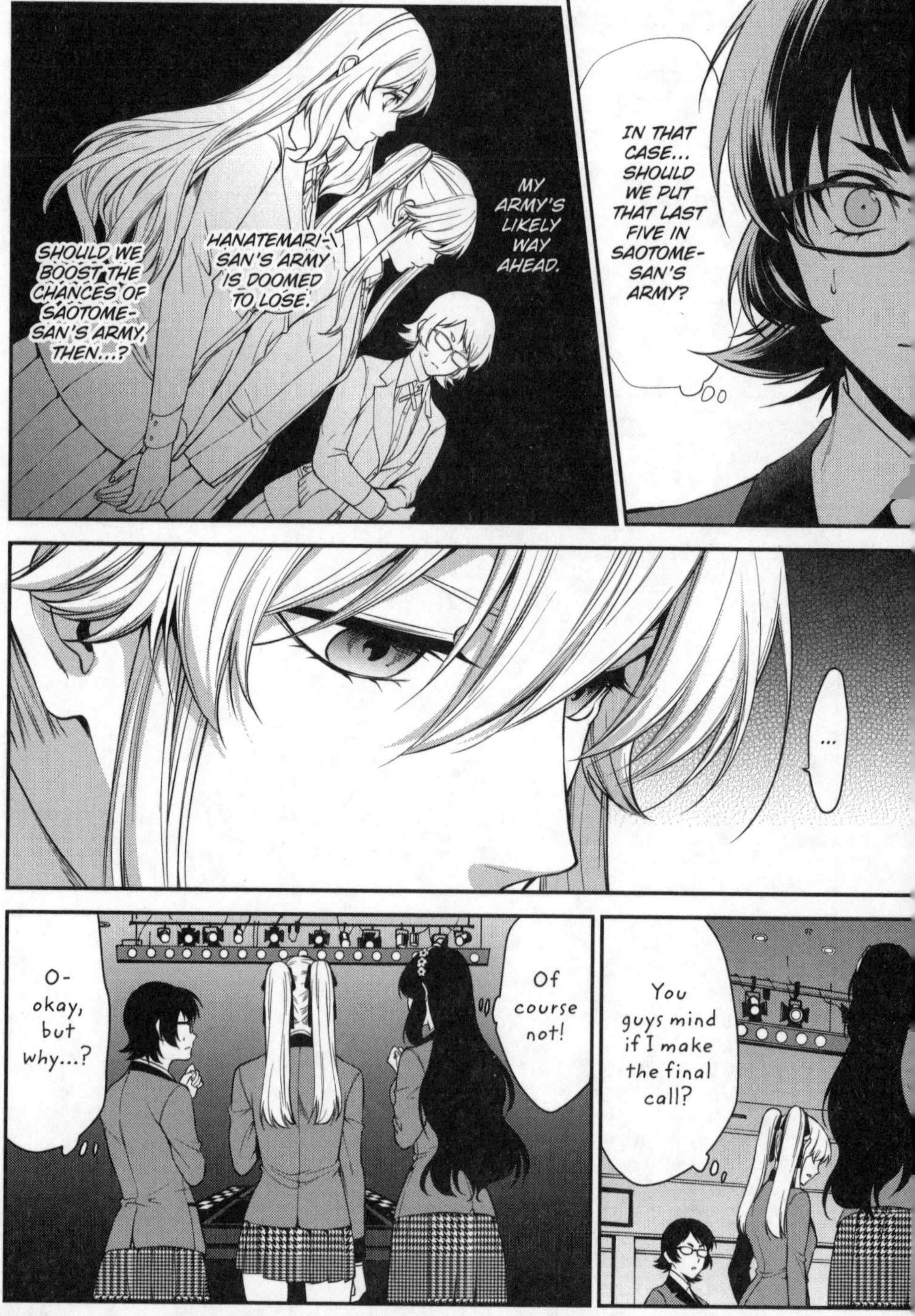
IN THAT CASE... SHOULD WE PUT THAT LAST FIVE IN SAOTOME-SAN'S ARMY?
MY ARMY'S LIKELY WAY AHEAD.
HANATEMARI-SAN'S ARMY IS DOOMED TO LOSE.
SHOULD WE BOOST THE CHANCES OF SAOTOME-SAN'S ARMY, THEN...?
...
You guys mind if I make the final call?
Of course not!
O-okay, but why...?

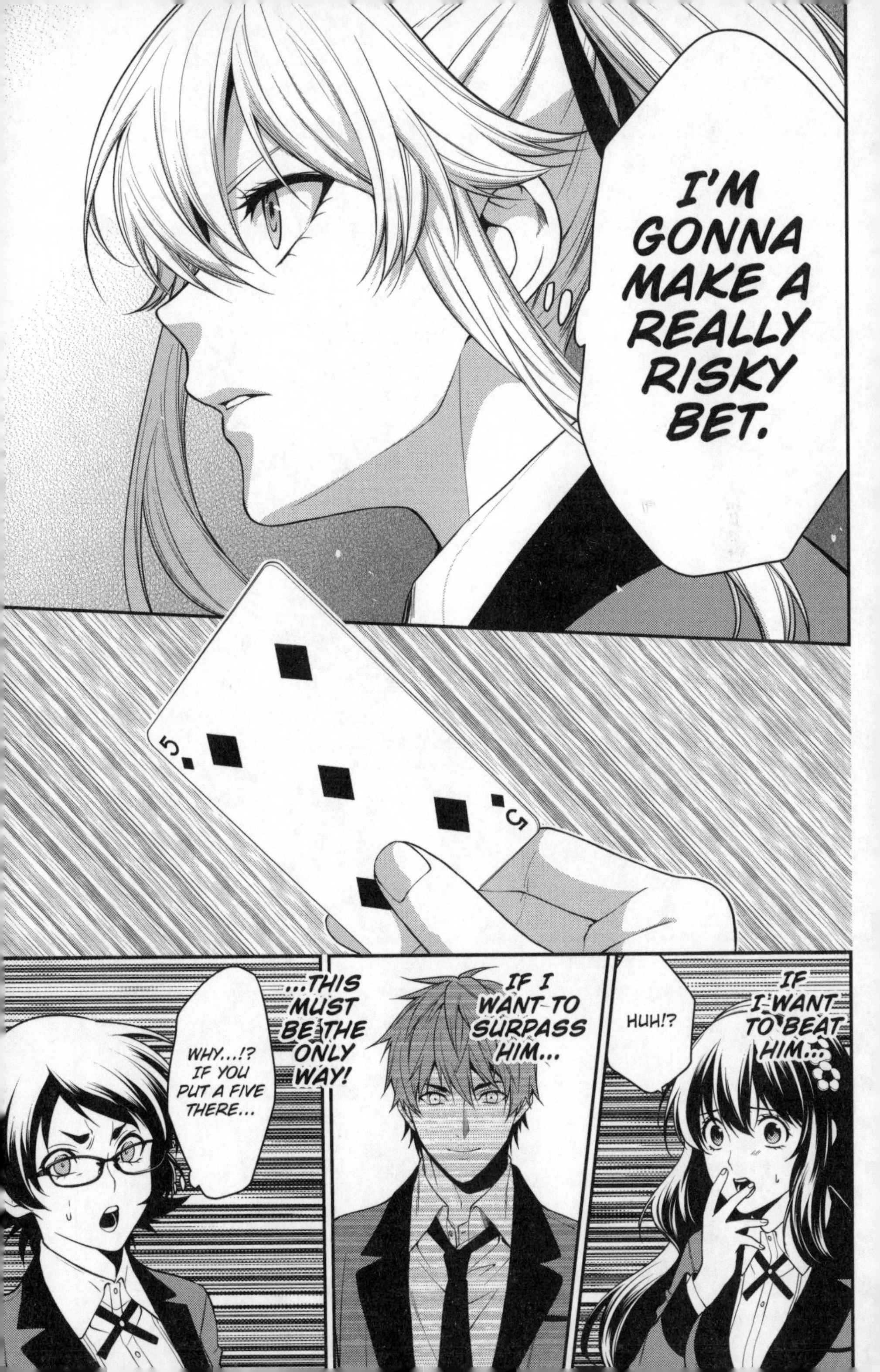
I'M GONNA MAKE A REALLY RISKY BET.
IF I WANT TO BEAT HIM...
HUH!?
IF I WANT TO SURPASS HIM...
...THIS MUST BE THE ONLY WAY!
WHY...!? IF YOU PUT A FIVE THERE...

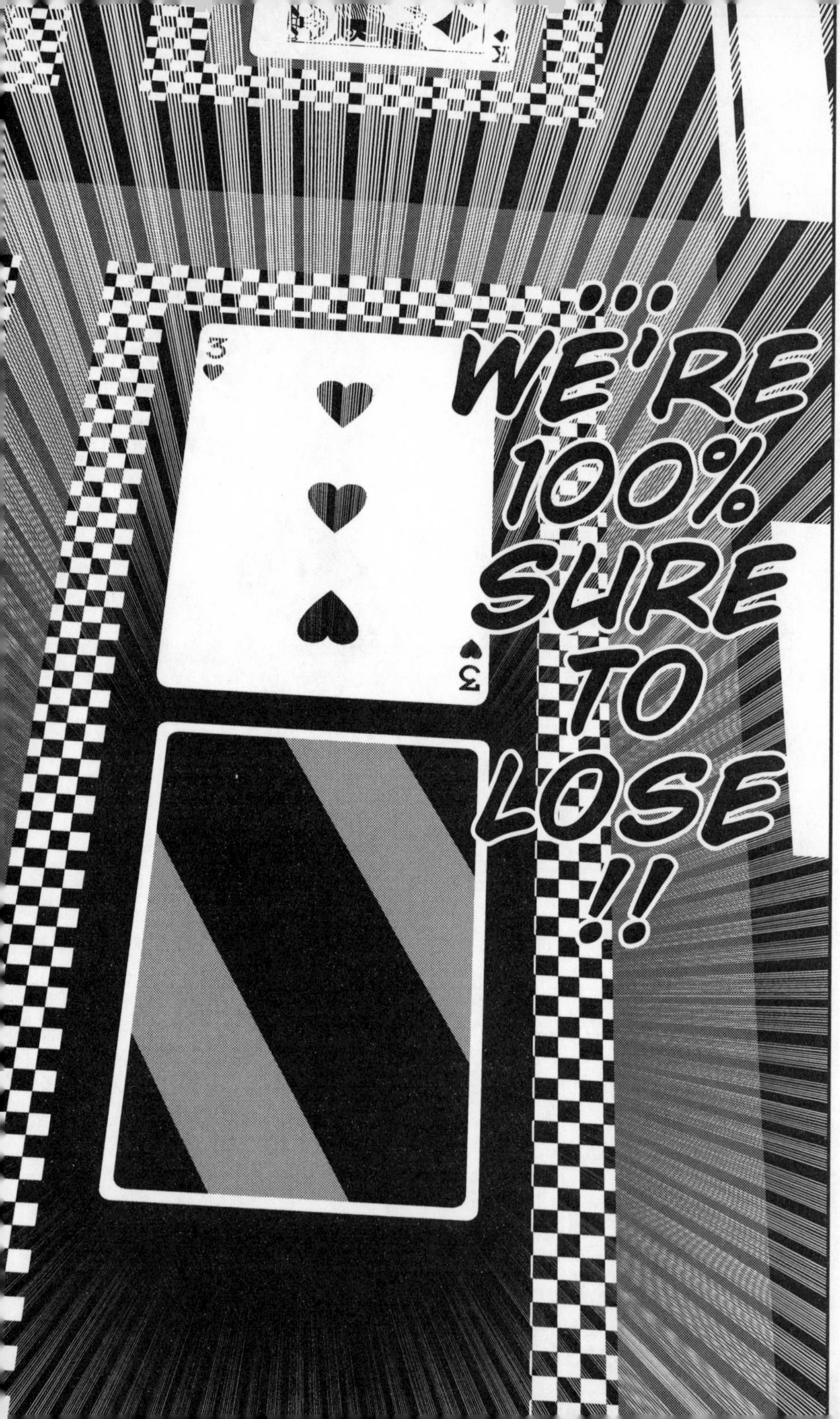
...WE'RE 100% SURE TO LOSE!!

CHAPTER FIFTY-TWO
THE CONTEMPTUOUS GIRL

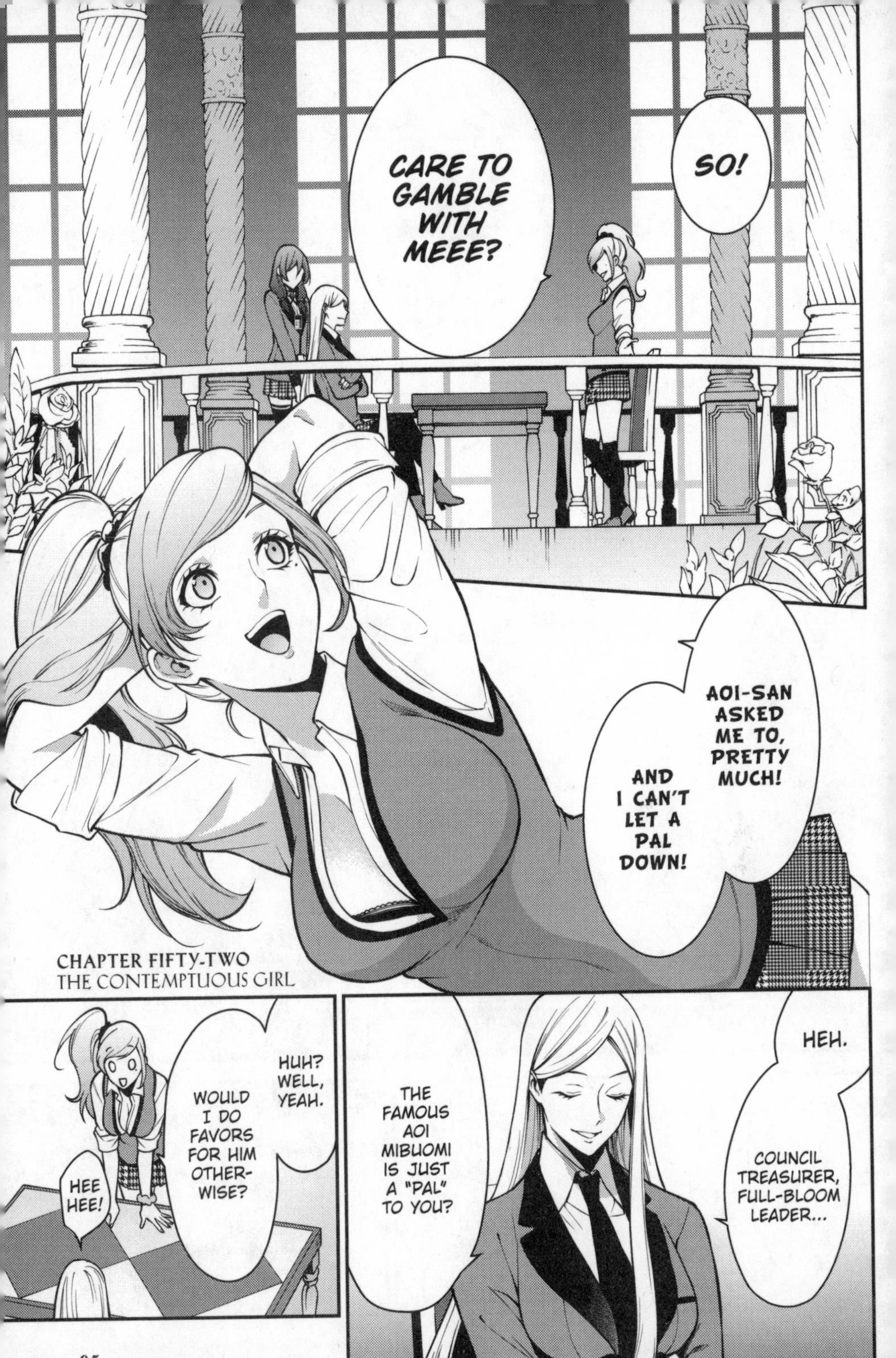
SO!
CARE TO GAMBLE WITH MEEE?
AOI-SAN ASKED ME TO, PRETTY MUCH!
AND I CAN'T LET A PAL DOWN!
HEH.
COUNCIL TREASURER, FULL-BLOOM LEADER...
THE FAMOUS AOI MIBUOMI IS JUST A "PAL" TO YOU?
HUH? WELL, YEAH.
WOULD I DO FAVORS FOR HIM OTHER-WISE?
HEE HEE!

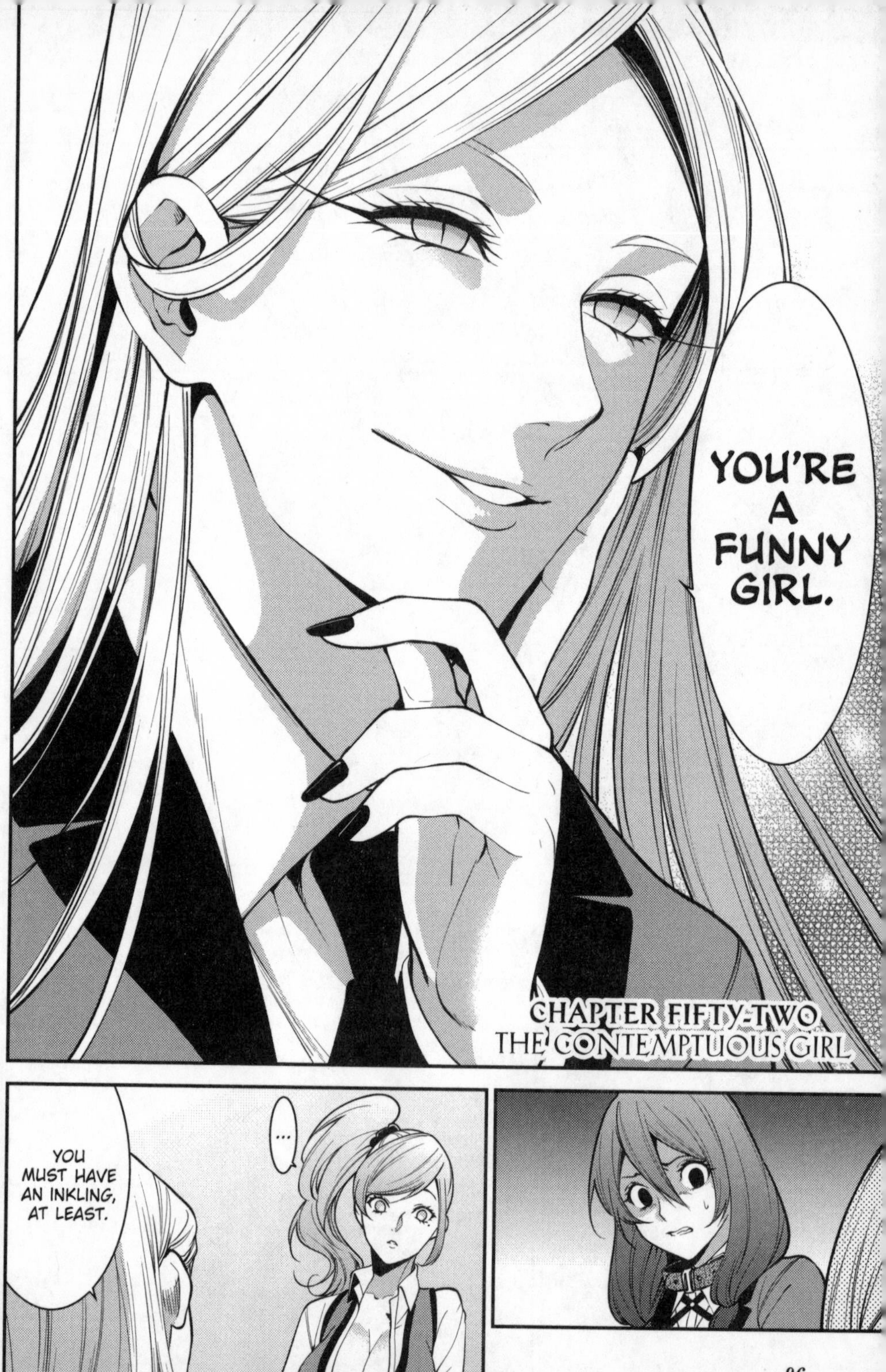
YOU'RE A FUNNY GIRL.
CHAPTER FIFTY-TWO
THE CONTEMPTUOUS GIRL
...
YOU MUST HAVE AN INKLING, AT LEAST.

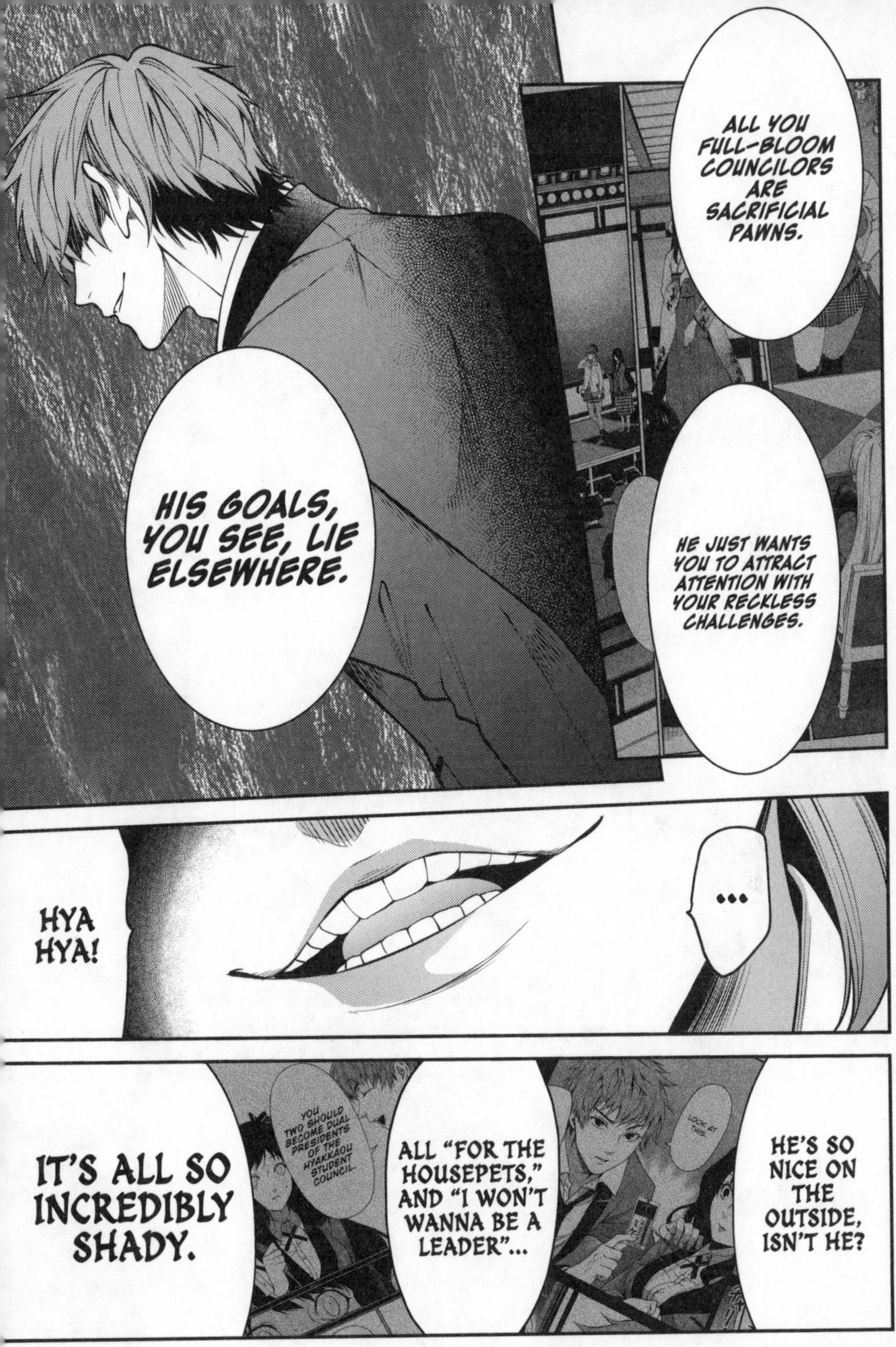
ALL YOU FULL-BLOOM COUNCILORS ARE SACRIFICIAL PAWNS.
HE JUST WANTS YOU TO ATTRACT ATTENTION WITH YOUR RECKLESS CHALLENGES.
HIS GOALS, YOU SEE, LIE ELSEWHERE.
...
HYA HYA!
HE'S SO NICE ON THE OUTSIDE, ISN'T HE?
LOOK AT THIS.
ALL "FOR THE HOUSEPETS," AND "I WON'T WANNA BE A LEADER"...
YOU TWO SHOULD BECOME DUAL PRESIDENTS OF THE HYAKKAOU STUDENT COUNCIL.
IT'S ALL SO INCREDIBLY SHADY.

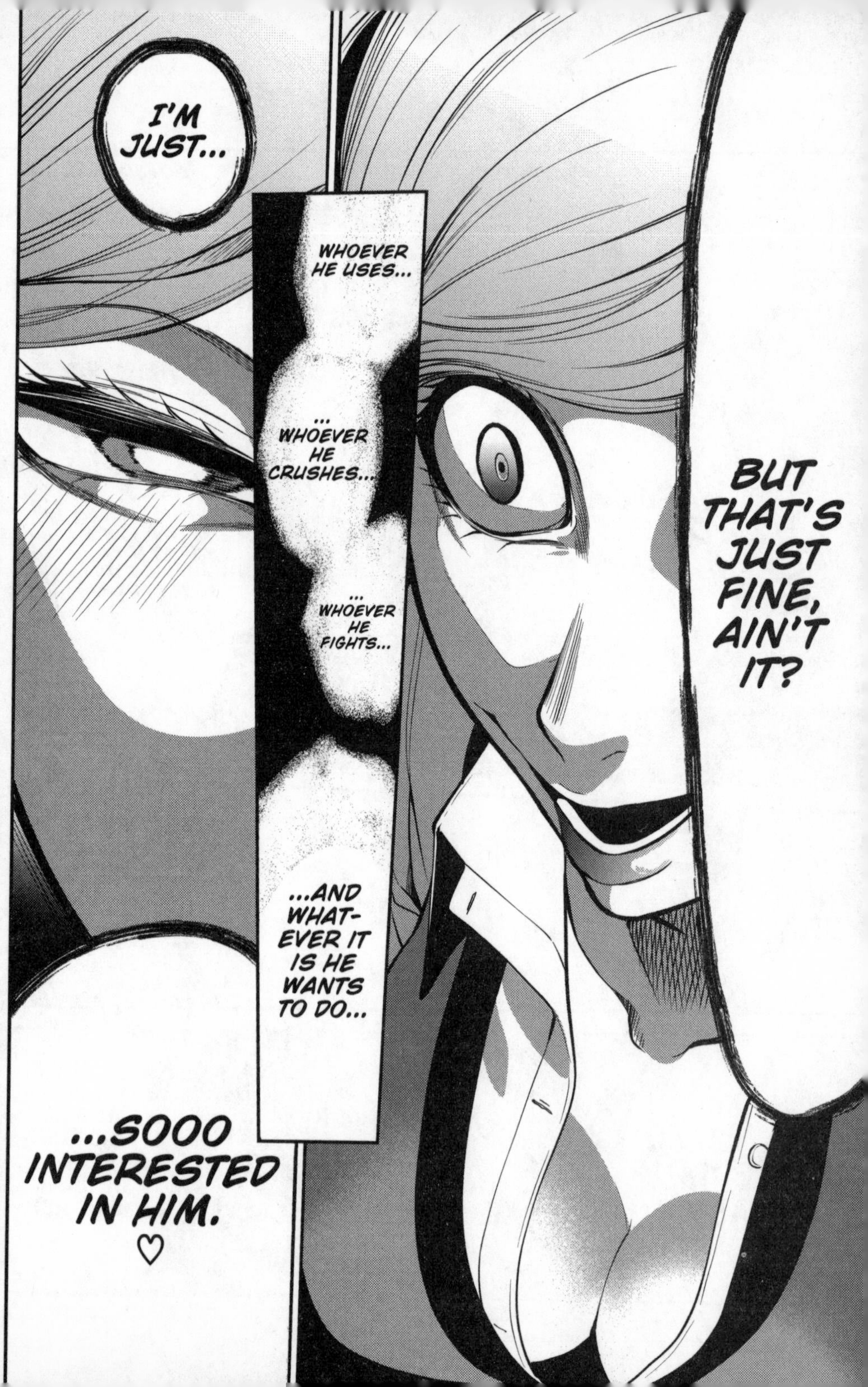
WHOEVER HE USES...
...WHOEVER HE CRUSHES...
...WHOEVER HE FIGHTS...
...AND WHAT-EVER IT IS HE WANTS TO DO...
BUT THAT'S JUST FINE, AIN'T IT?
I'M JUST...
...SOOO INTERESTED IN HIM. ♡

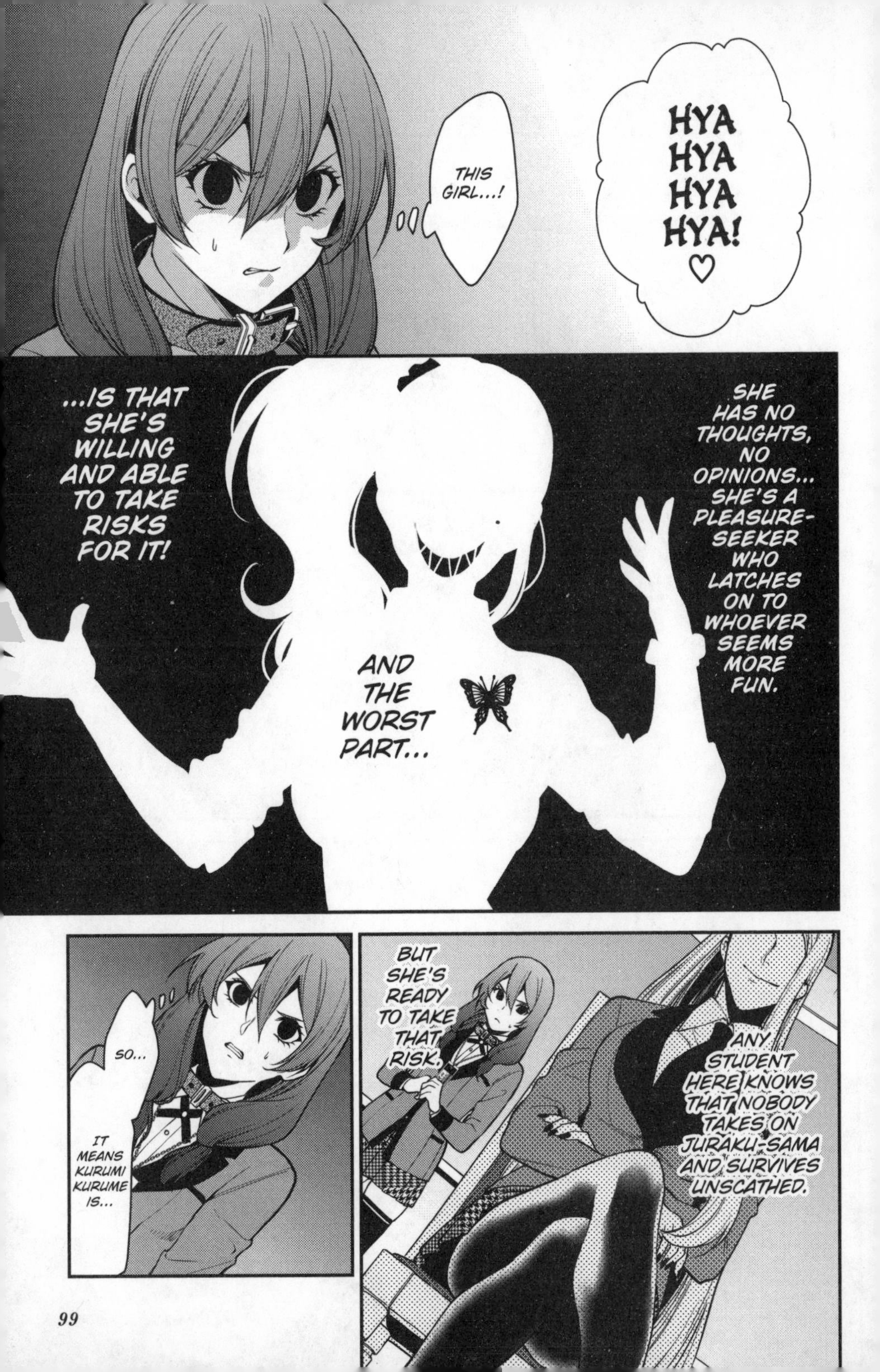
HYA HYA HYA HYA! ♡
THIS GIRL...!
SHE HAS NO THOUGHTS, NO OPINIONS... SHE'S A PLEASURE-SEEKER WHO LATCHES ON TO WHOEVER SEEMS MORE FUN.
AND THE WORST PART...
...IS THAT SHE'S WILLING AND ABLE TO TAKE RISKS FOR IT!
ANY STUDENT HERE KNOWS THAT NOBODY TAKES ON JURAKU-SAMA AND SURVIVES UNSCATHED.
BUT SHE'S READY TO TAKE THAT RISK.
SO...
IT MEANS KURUMI KURUME IS...

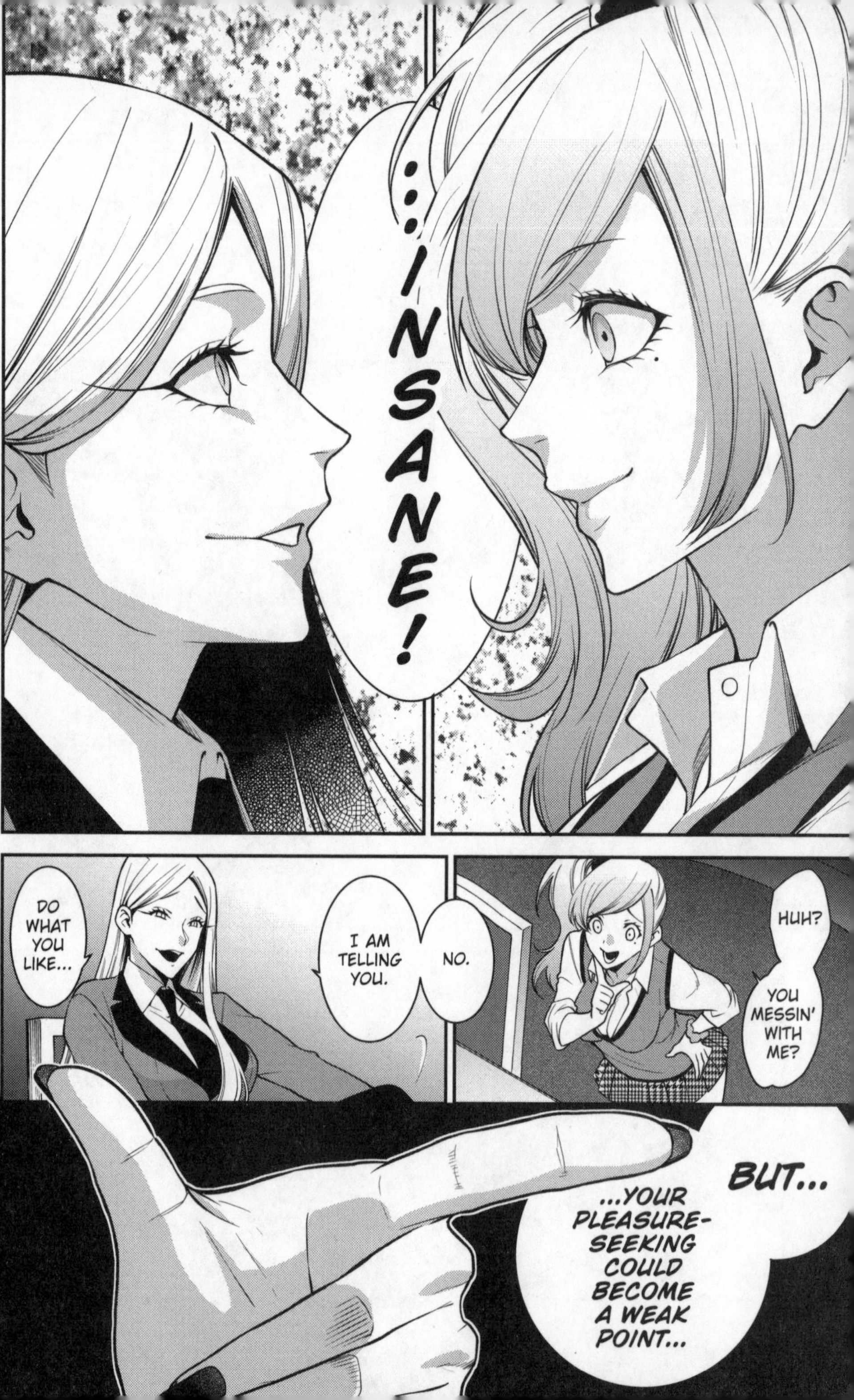
...INSANE!
HUH?
YOU MESSIN' WITH ME?
NO.
I AM TELLING YOU.
DO WHAT YOU LIKE...
BUT...
...YOUR PLEASURE-SEEKING COULD BECOME A WEAK POINT...

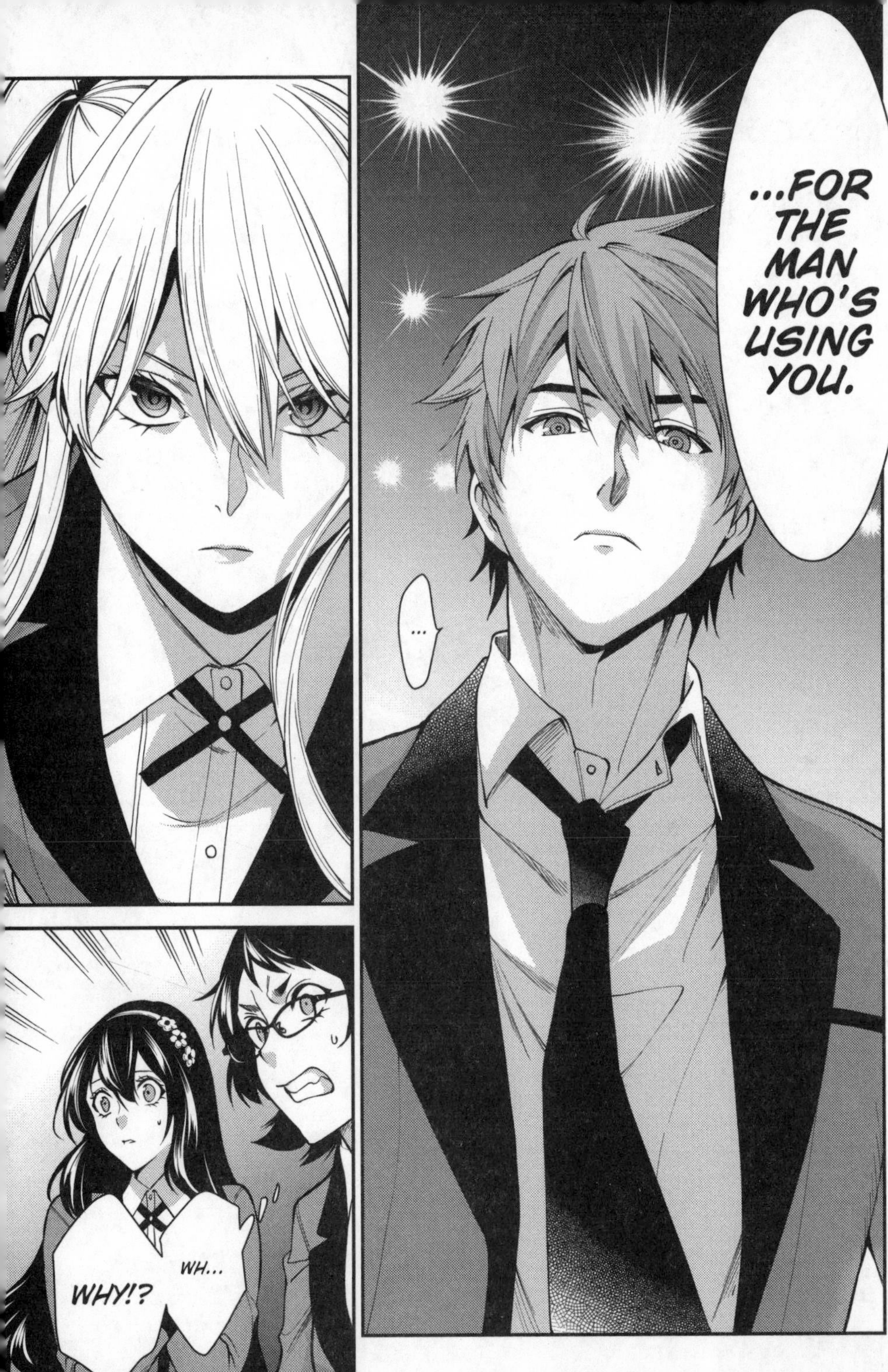
...FOR THE MAN WHO'S USING YOU.
...
WH... WHY!?

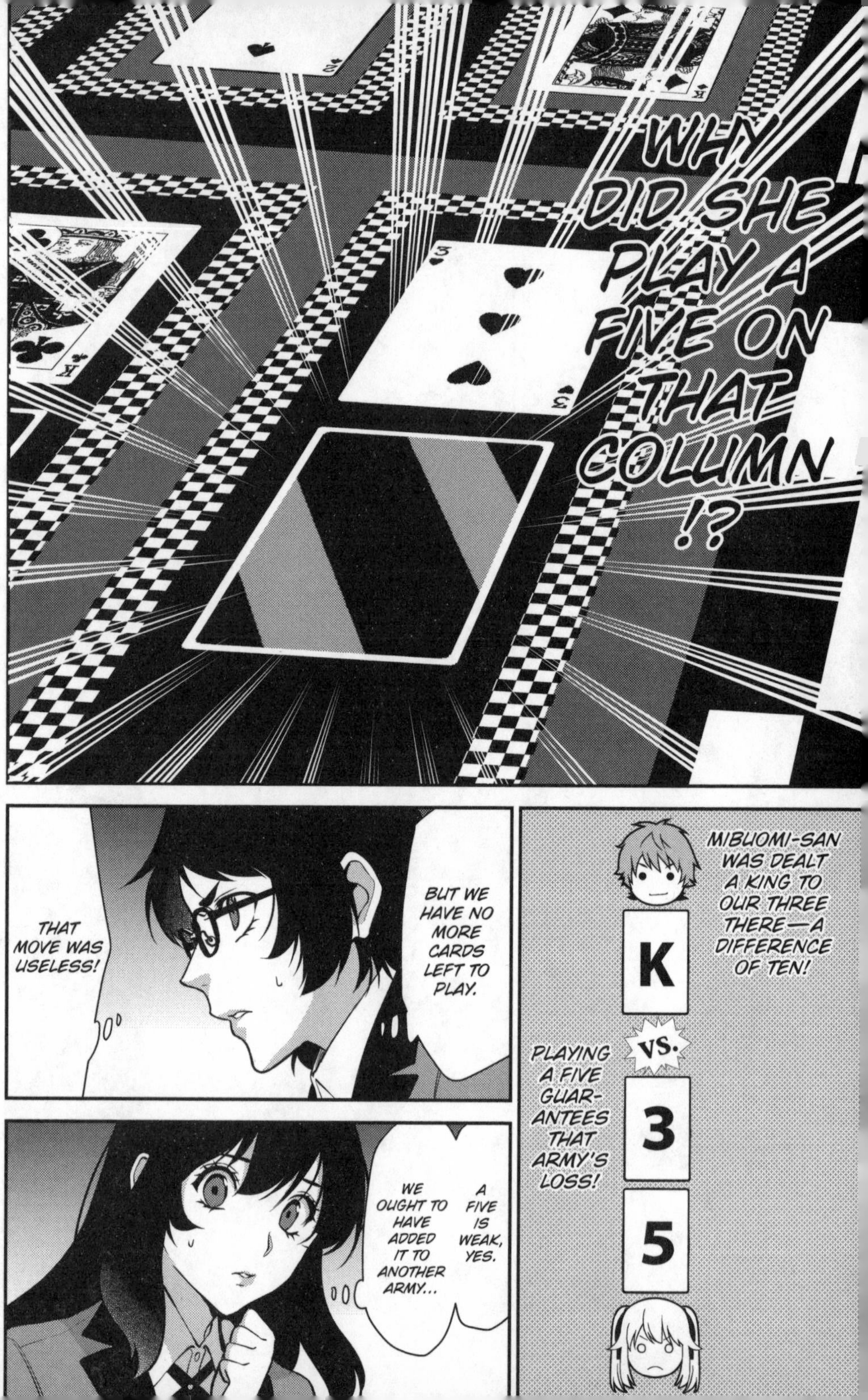
WHY DID SHE PLAY A FIVE ON THAT COLUMN !?
MIBUOMI-SAN WAS DEALT A KING TO OUR THREE THERE—A DIFFERENCE OF TEN!
K
VS.
3
5
PLAYING A FIVE GUAR-ANTEES THAT ARMY'S LOSS!
BUT WE HAVE NO MORE CARDS LEFT TO PLAY.
THAT MOVE WAS USELESS!
A FIVE IS WEAK, YES.
WE OUGHT TO HAVE ADDED IT TO ANOTHER ARMY...

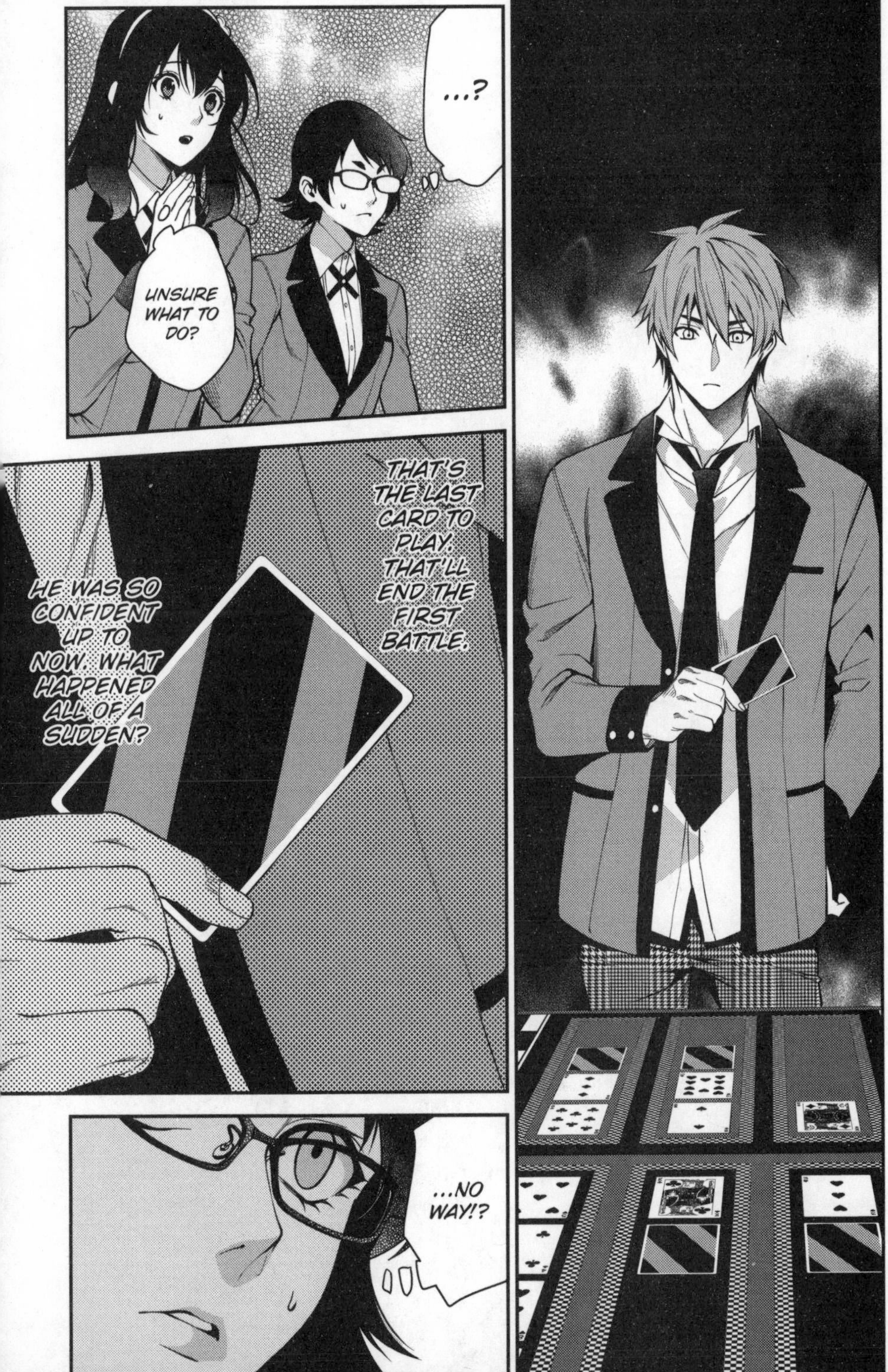
...?
UNSURE WHAT TO DO?
THAT'S THE LAST CARD TO PLAY. THAT'LL END THE FIRST BATTLE.
HE WAS SO CONFIDENT UP TO NOW. WHAT HAPPENED ALL OF A SUDDEN?
...NO WAY!?

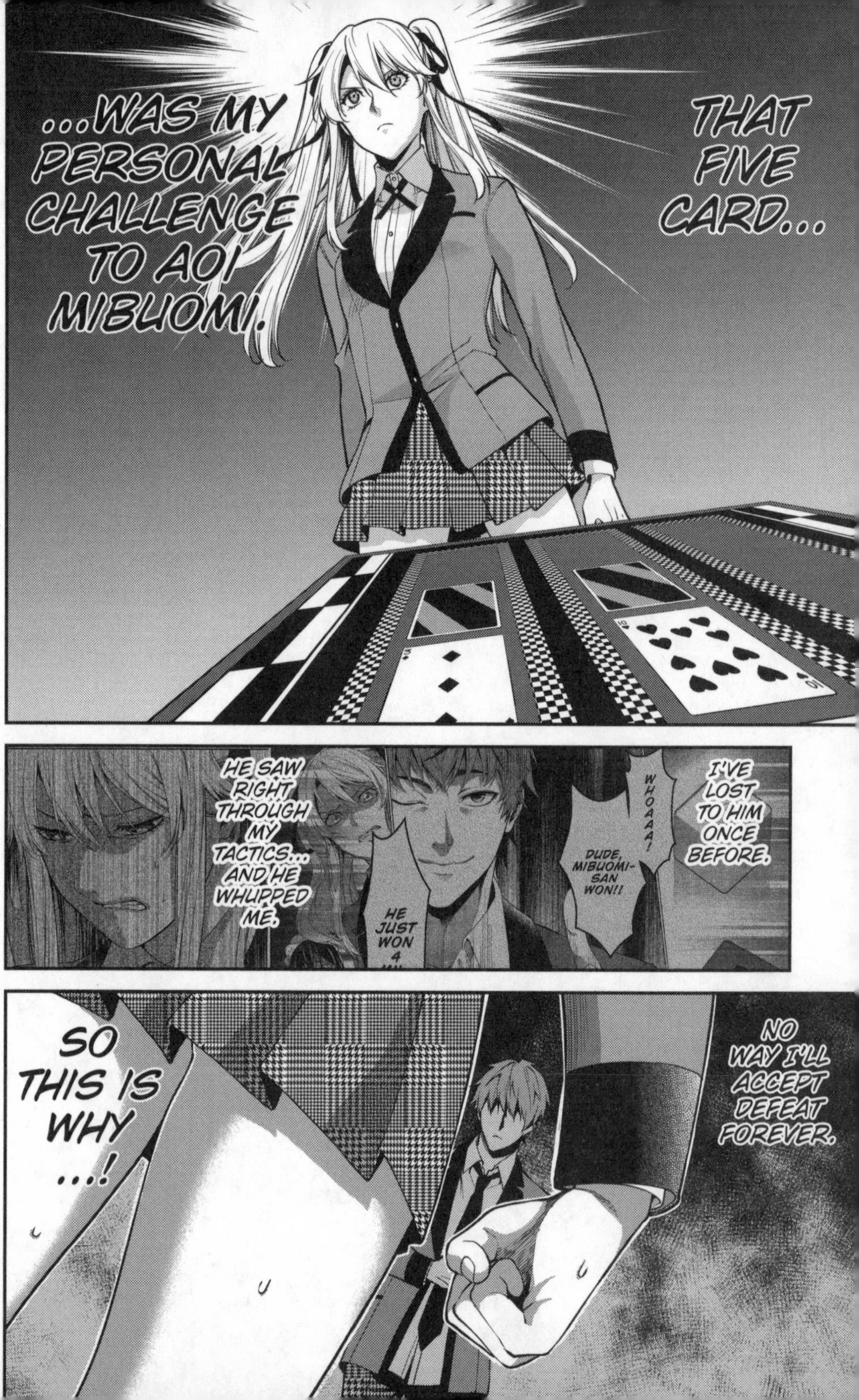
THAT FIVE CARD...
...WAS MY PERSONAL CHALLENGE TO AOI MIBUOMI.
I'VE LOST TO HIM ONCE BEFORE.
WHOAAA!
DUDE, MIBUOMI-SAN WON!!
HE JUST WON 4
HE SAW RIGHT THROUGH MY TACTICS... AND HE WHUPPED ME.
NO WAY I'LL ACCEPT DEFEAT FOREVER.
SO THIS IS WHY ...!

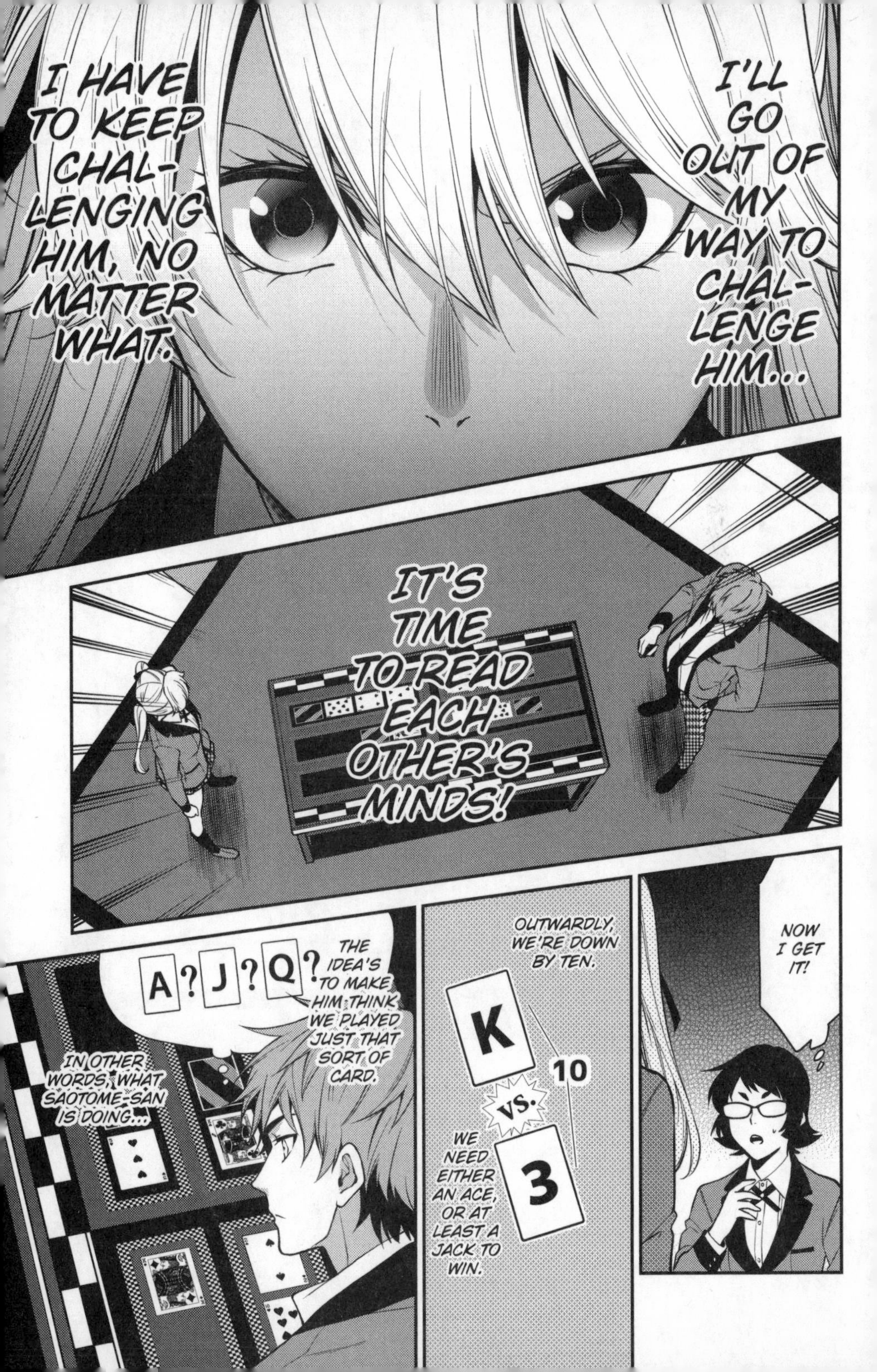
I'LL GO OUT OF MY WAY TO CHAL-LENGE HIM...
I HAVE TO KEEP CHAL-LENGING HIM, NO MATTER WHAT.
IT'S TIME TO READ EACH OTHER'S MINDS!
NOW I GET IT!
OUTWARDLY, WE'RE DOWN BY TEN.
K
10
VS.
3
WE NEED EITHER AN ACE, OR AT LEAST A JACK TO WIN.
A?J?Q?
THE IDEA'S TO MAKE HIM THINK WE PLAYED JUST THAT SORT OF CARD.
IN OTHER WORDS, WHAT SAOTOME-SAN IS DOING...

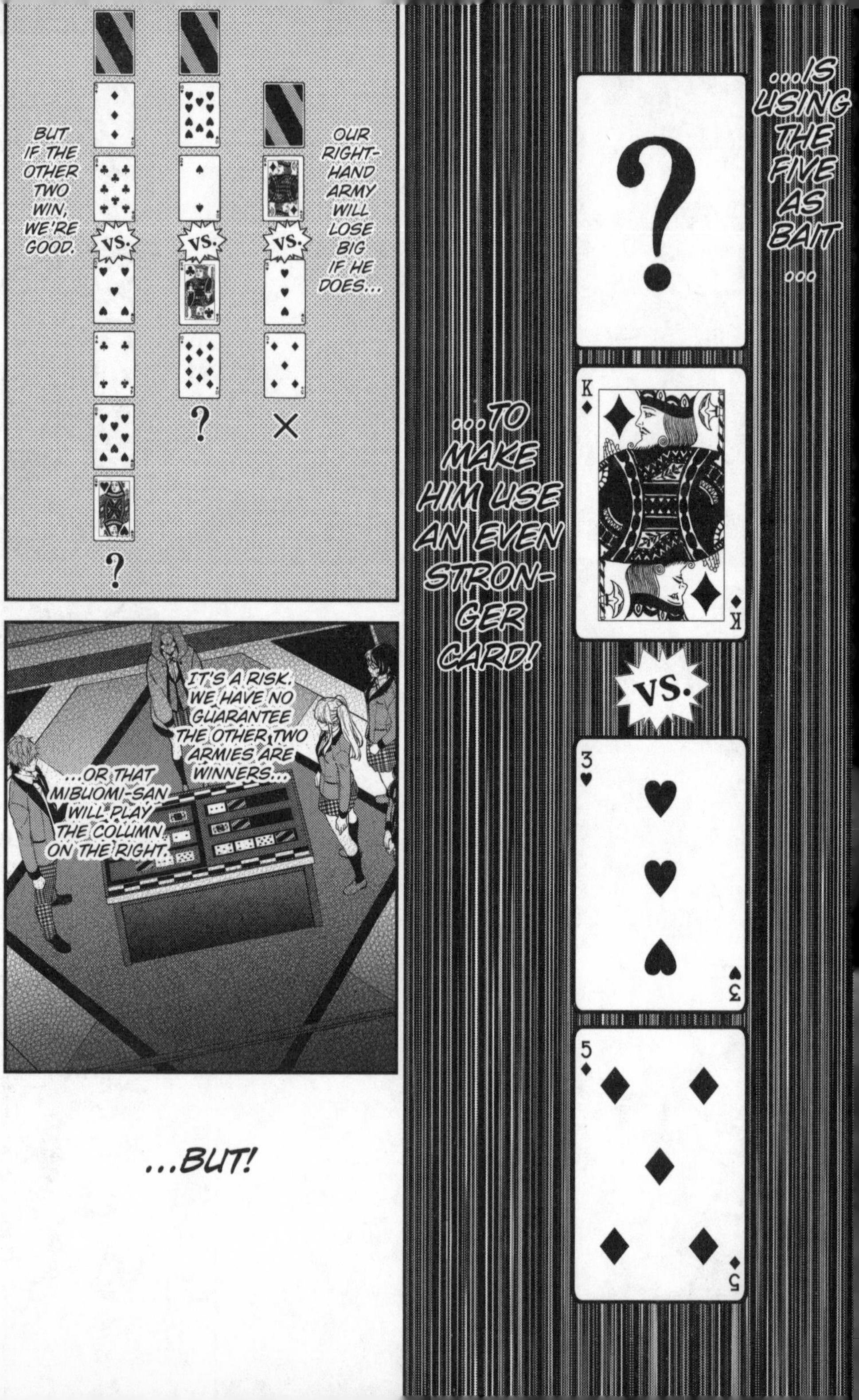
...IS USING THE FIVE AS BAIT...
...TO MAKE HIM USE AN EVEN STRONGER CARD!
VS.
OUR RIGHT-HAND ARMY WILL LOSE BIG IF HE DOES...
BUT IF THE OTHER TWO WIN, WE'RE GOOD.
VS.
VS.
VS.
IT'S A RISK. WE HAVE NO GUARANTEE THE OTHER TWO ARMIES ARE WINNERS...
...OR THAT MIBUOMI-SAN WILL PLAY THE COLUMN ON THE RIGHT.
...BUT!

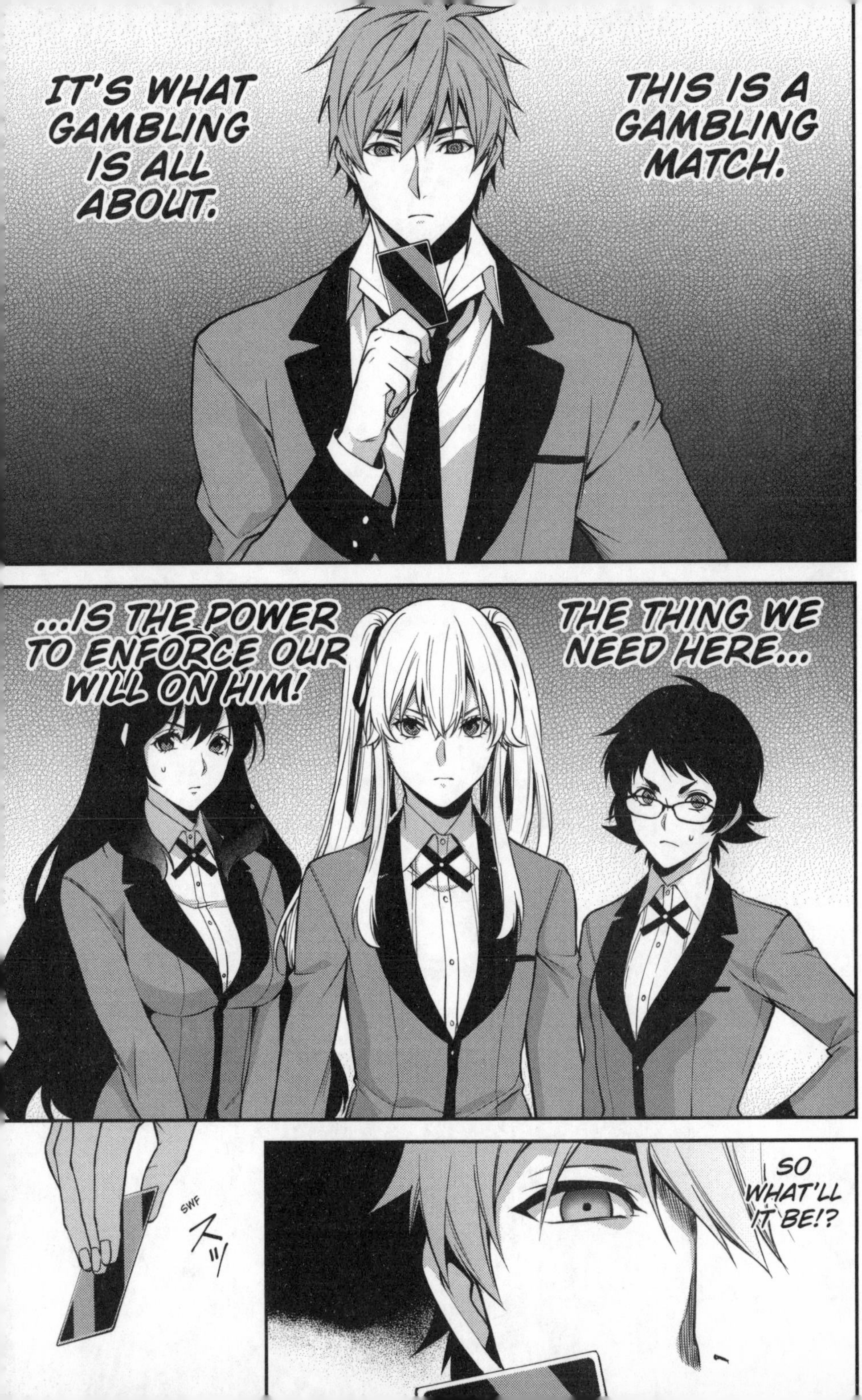
THIS IS A GAMBLING MATCH.
IT'S WHAT GAMBLING IS ALL ABOUT.
THE THING WE NEED HERE...
...IS THE POWER TO ENFORCE OUR WILL ON HIM!
SO WHAT'LL IT BE!?
SWF

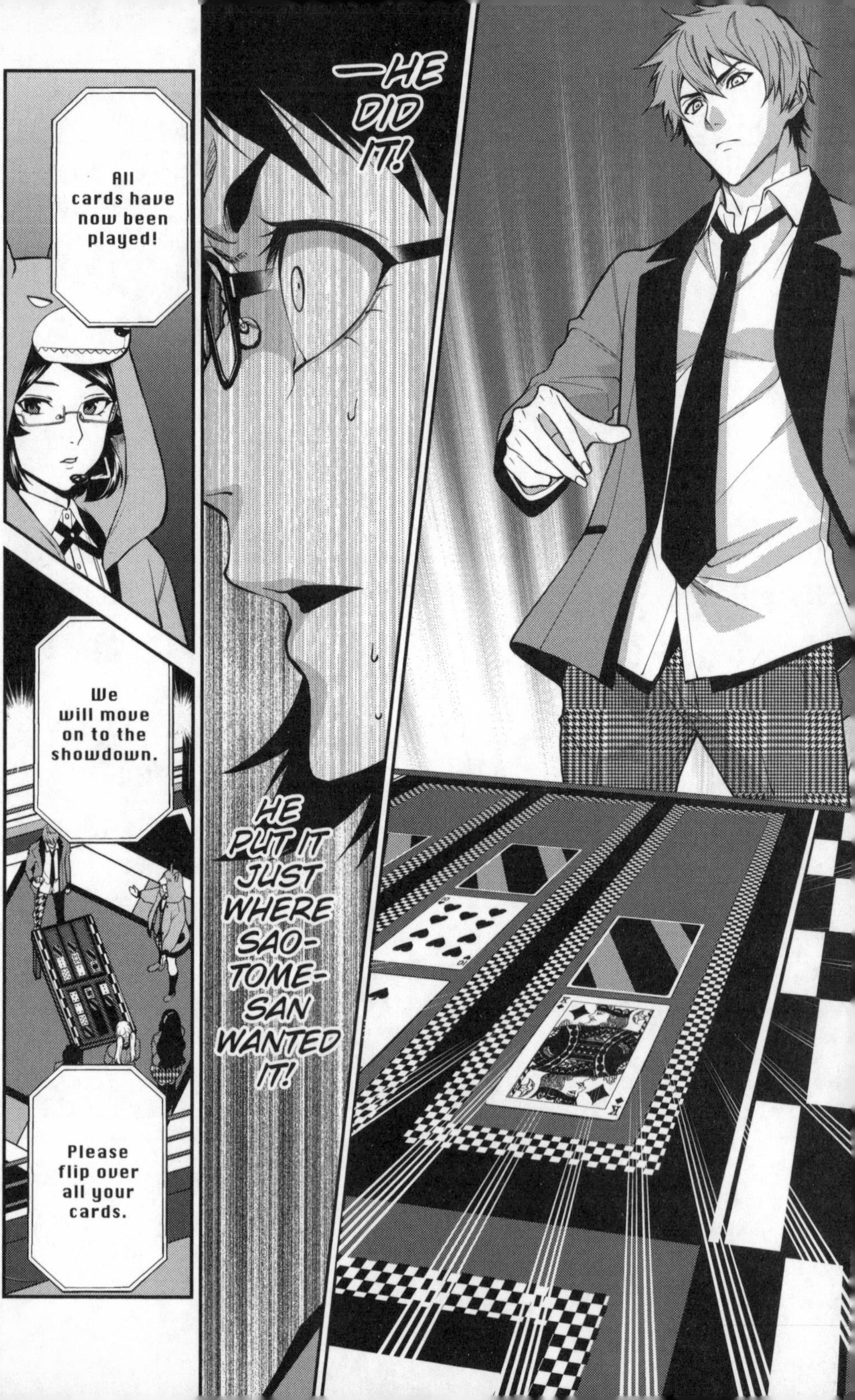
—HE DID IT!
HE PUT IT JUST WHERE SAO-TOME-SAN WANTED IT!
All cards have now been played!
We will move on to the showdown.
Please flip over all your cards.

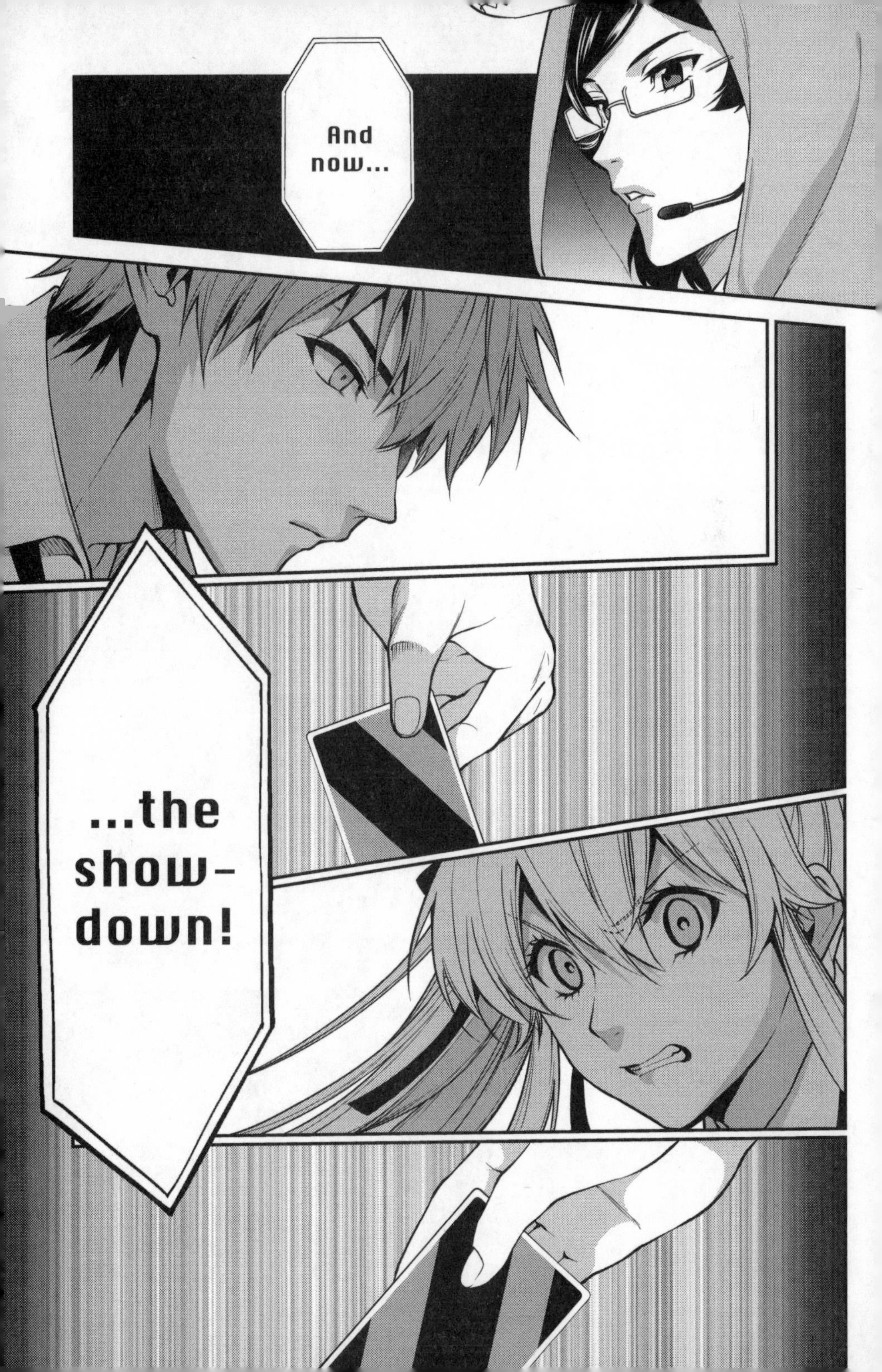
And now...
...the show-down!

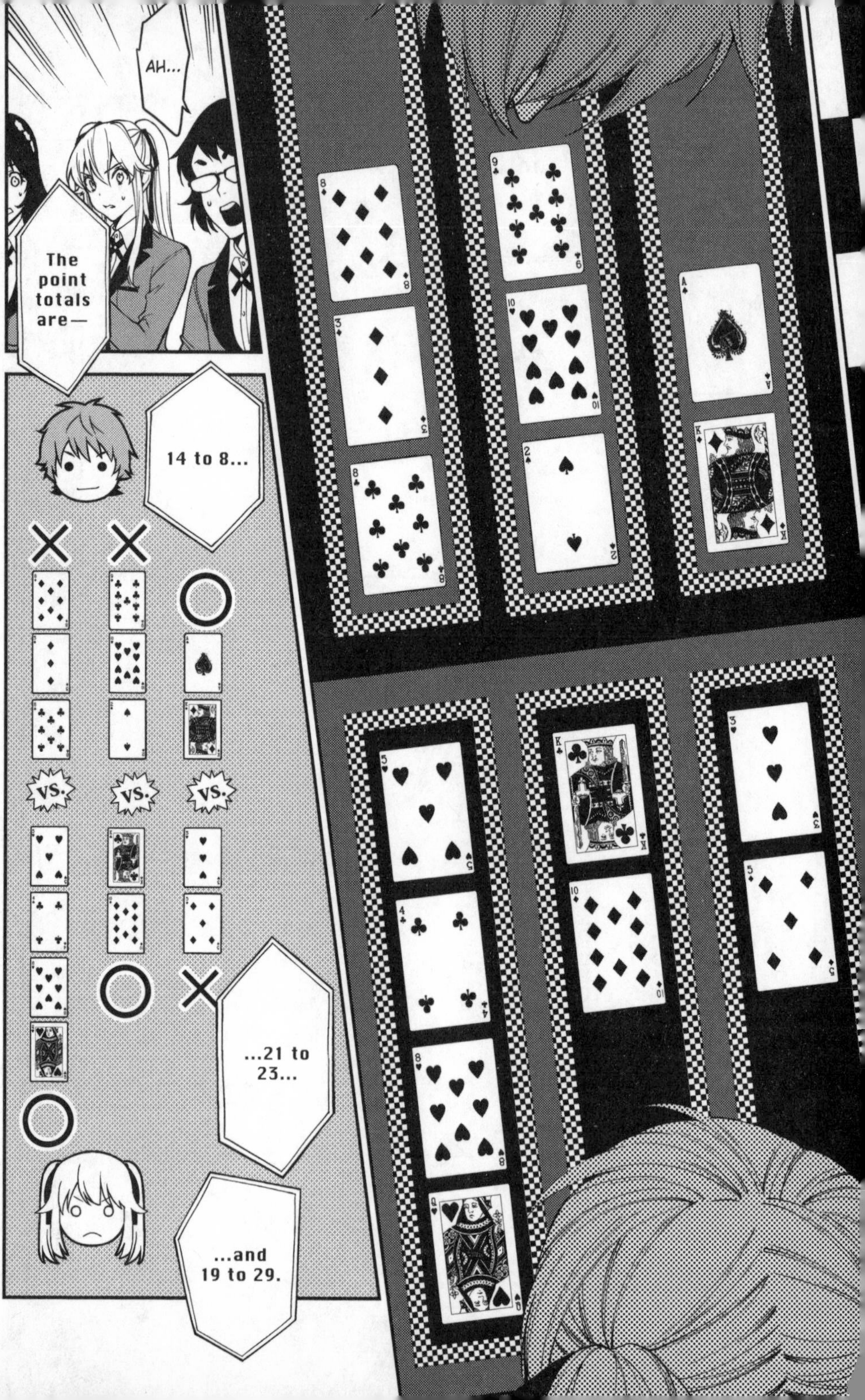
AH...
The point totals are—
14 to 8...
VS.
VS.
VS.
...21 to 23...
...and 19 to 29.

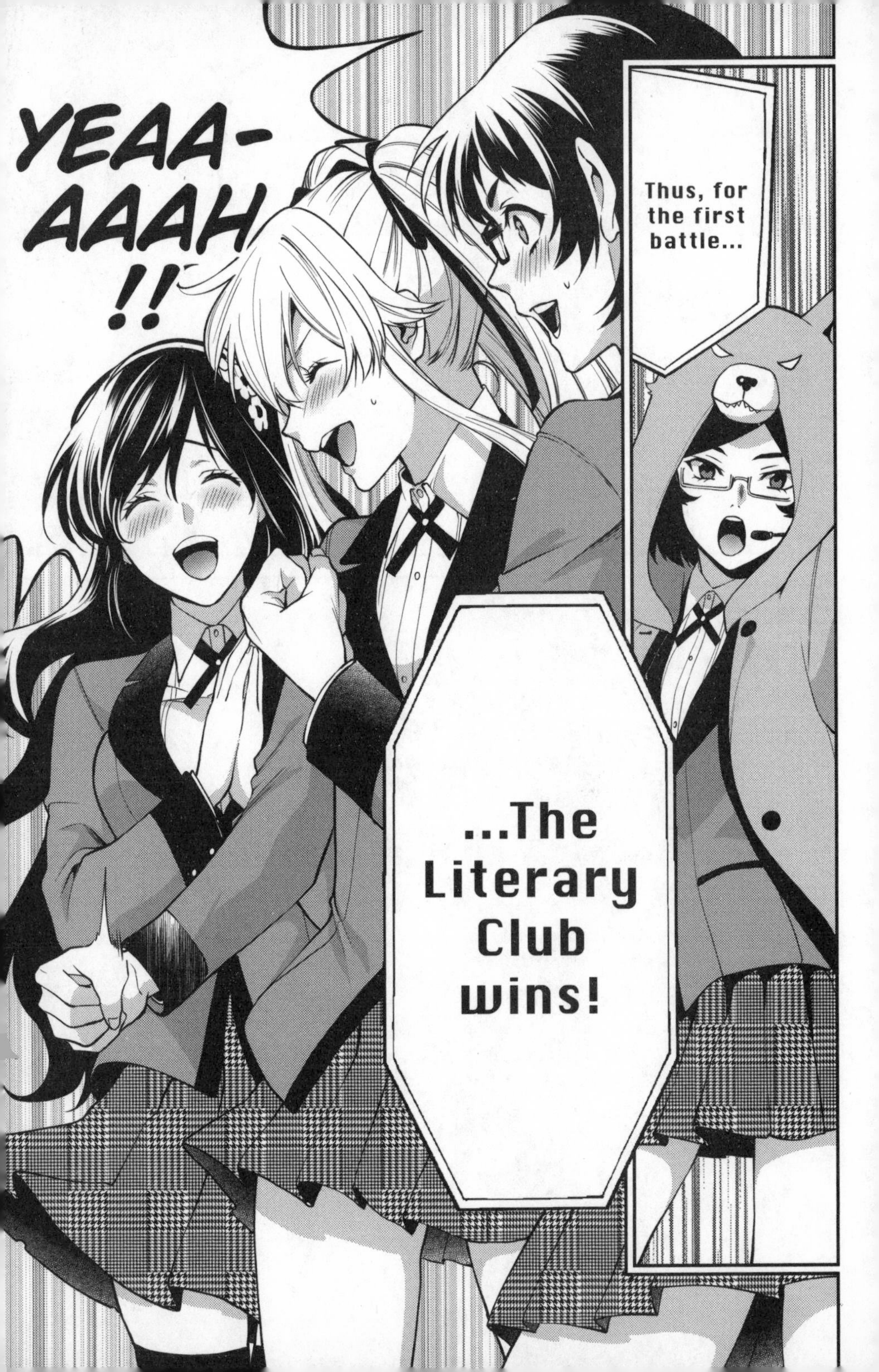
Thus, for the first battle...
...The Literary Club wins!
YEAA-AAAH!!

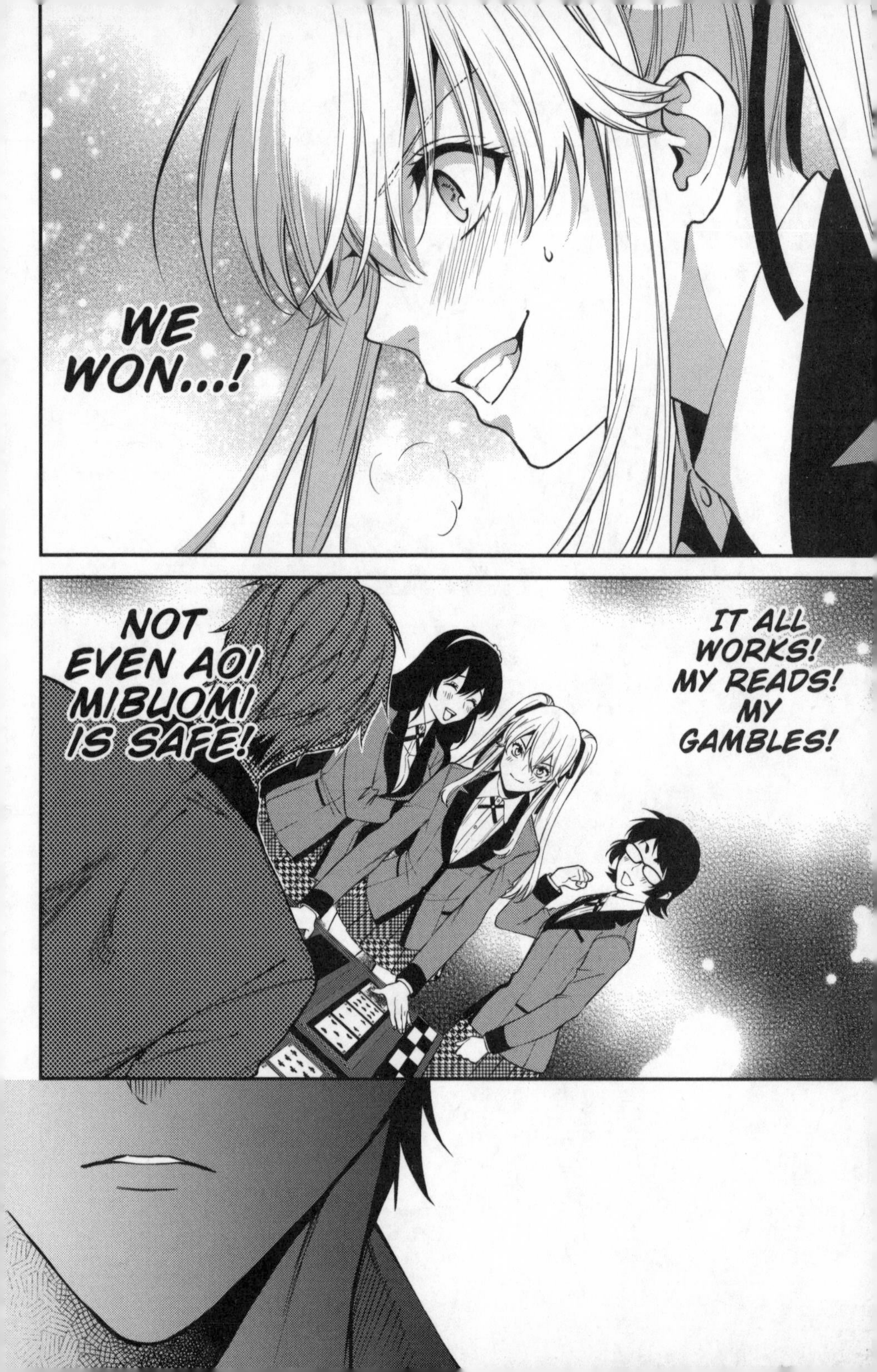
WE WON...!
IT ALL WORKS! MY READS! MY GAMBLES!
NOT EVEN AOI MIBUOMI IS SAFE!

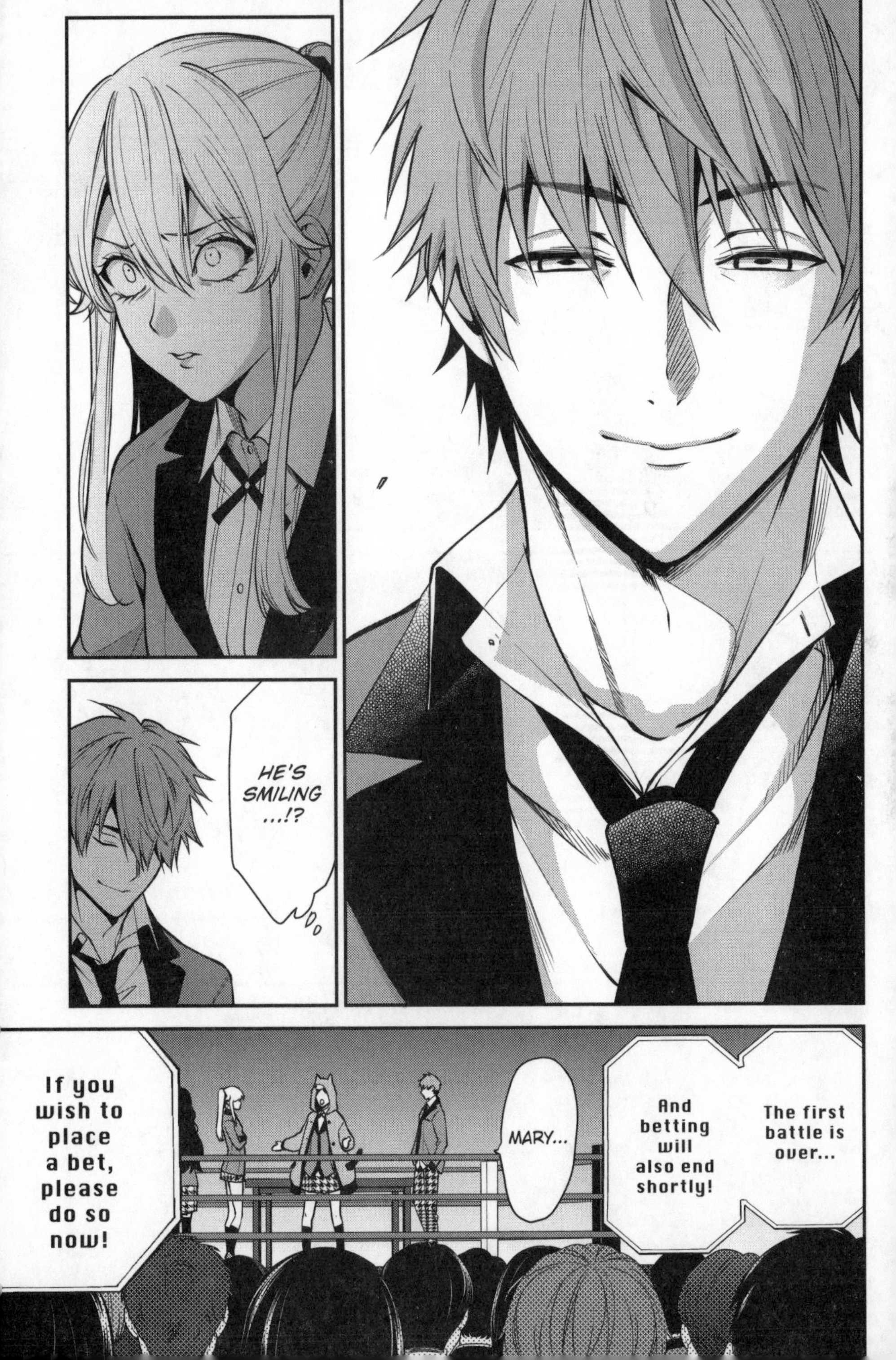
HE'S SMILING ...!?
The first battle is over...
And betting will also end shortly!
MARY...
If you wish to place a bet, please do so now!

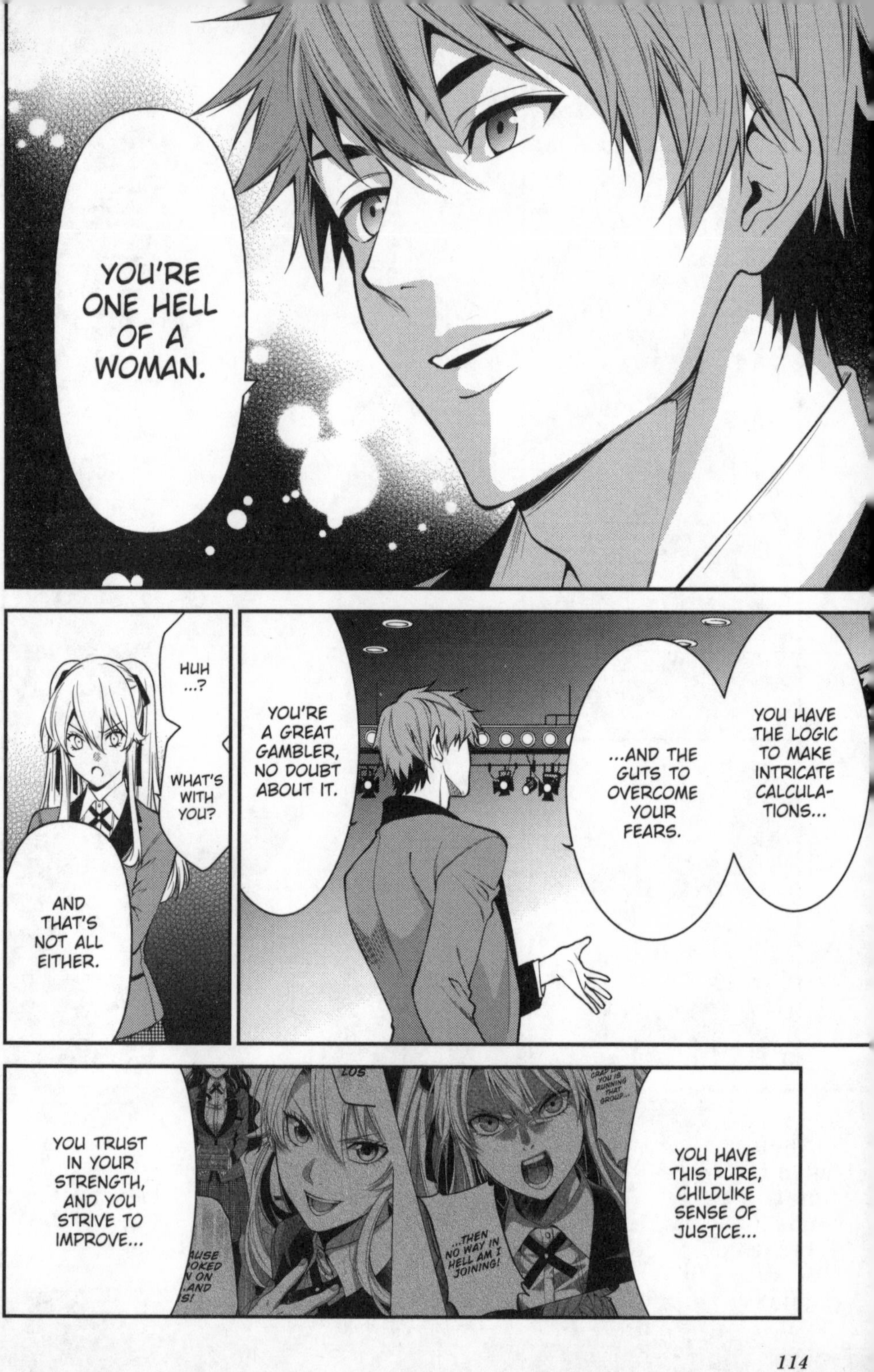
YOU'RE ONE HELL OF A WOMAN.
YOU HAVE THE LOGIC TO MAKE INTRICATE CALCULATIONS...
...AND THE GUTS TO OVERCOME YOUR FEARS.
YOU'RE A GREAT GAMBLER, NO DOUBT ABOUT IT.
HUH ...?
WHAT'S WITH YOU?
AND THAT'S NOT ALL EITHER.
YOU HAVE THIS PURE, CHILDLIKE SENSE OF JUSTICE...
YOU IS RUNNING THAT GROUP...
...THEN NO WAY IN HELL AM I JOINING!
YOU TRUST IN YOUR STRENGTH, AND YOU STRIVE TO IMPROVE...

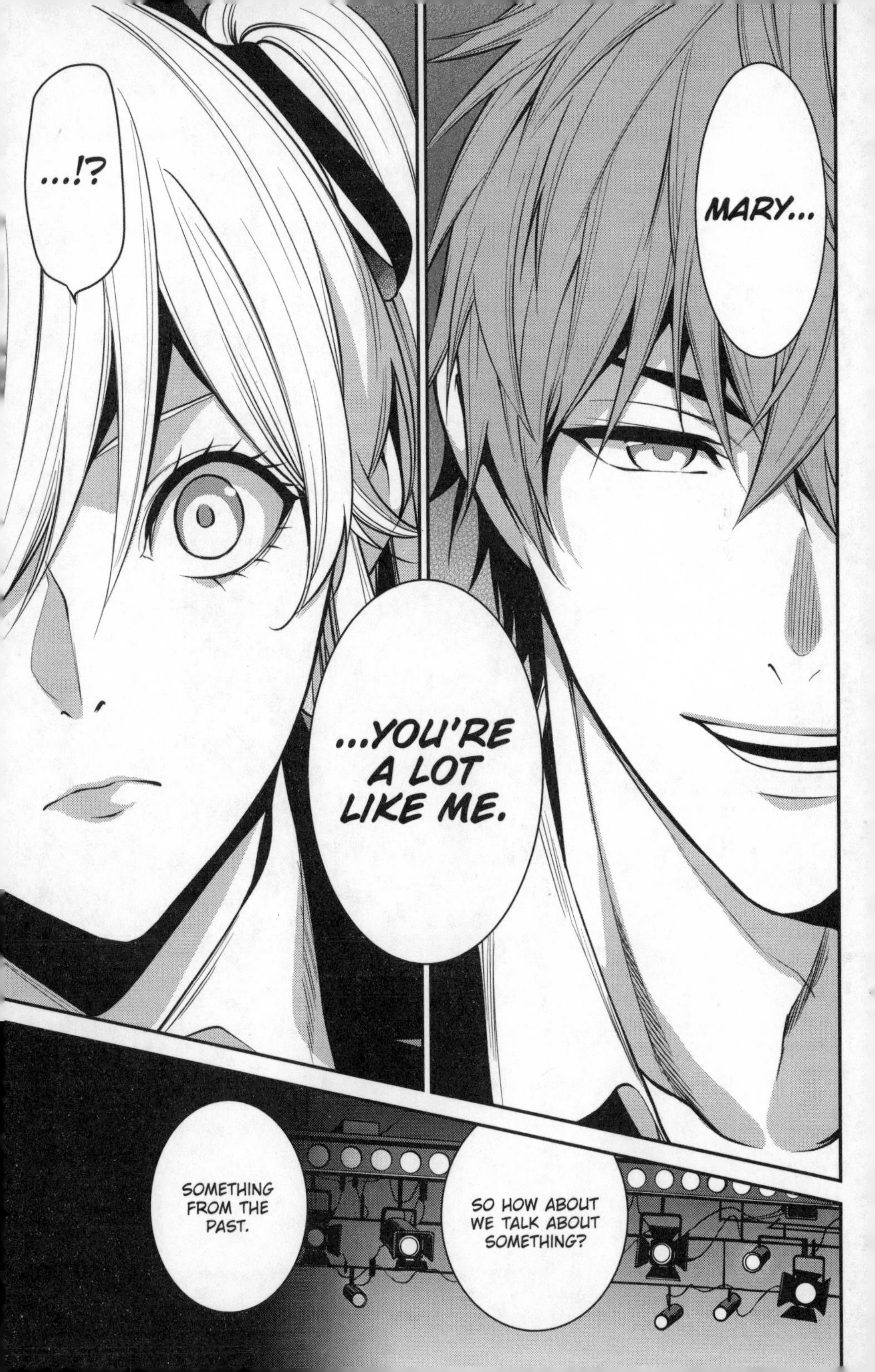
MARY...
...YOU'RE A LOT LIKE ME.
...!?
SO HOW ABOUT WE TALK ABOUT SOMETHING?
SOMETHING FROM THE PAST.

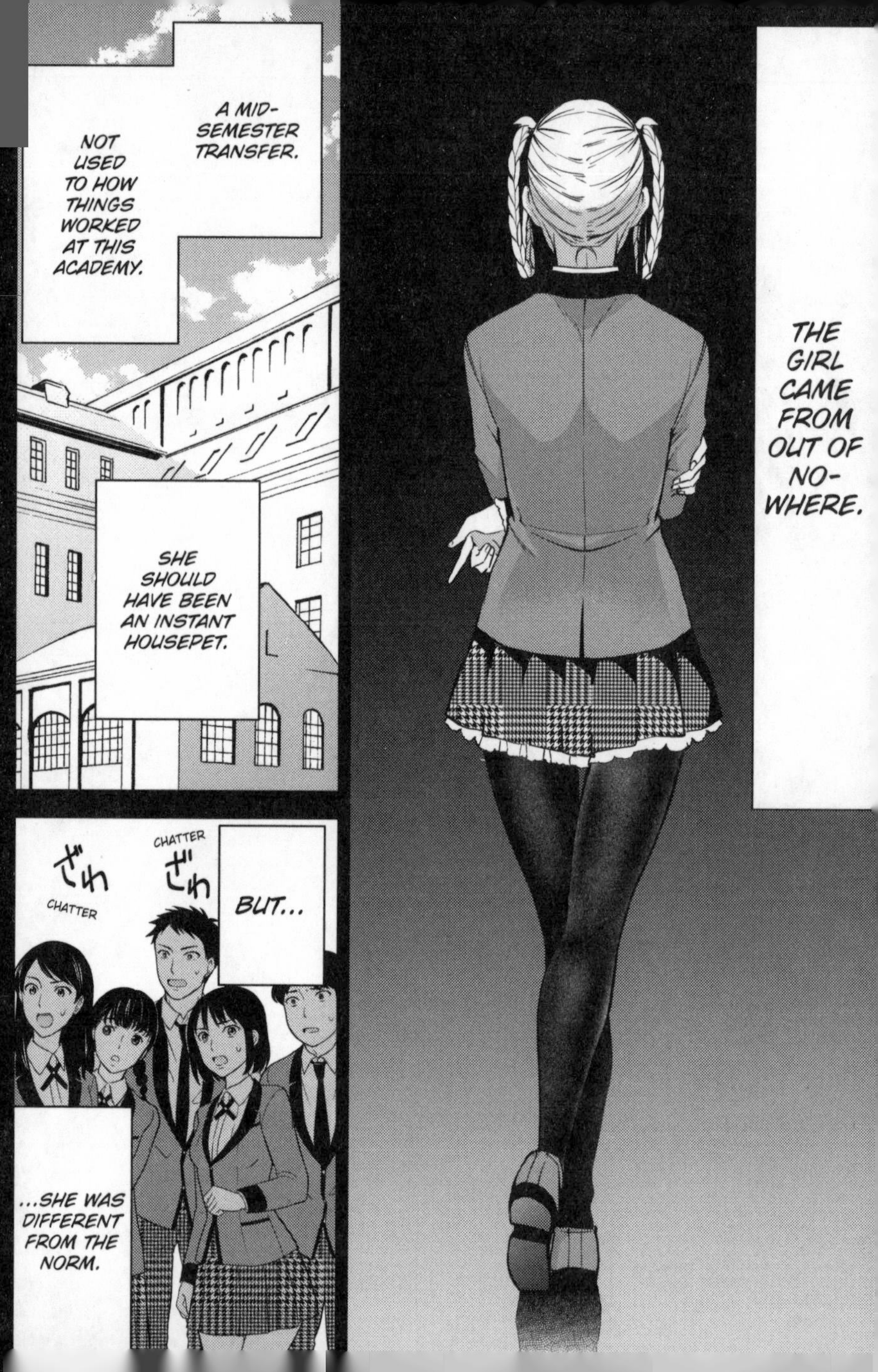
THE GIRL CAME FROM OUT OF NO-WHERE.
A MID-SEMESTER TRANSFER.
NOT USED TO HOW THINGS WORKED AT THIS ACADEMY.
SHE SHOULD HAVE BEEN AN INSTANT HOUSEPET.
BUT...
ざわ
CHATTER
ざわ
CHATTER
...SHE WAS DIFFERENT FROM THE NORM.

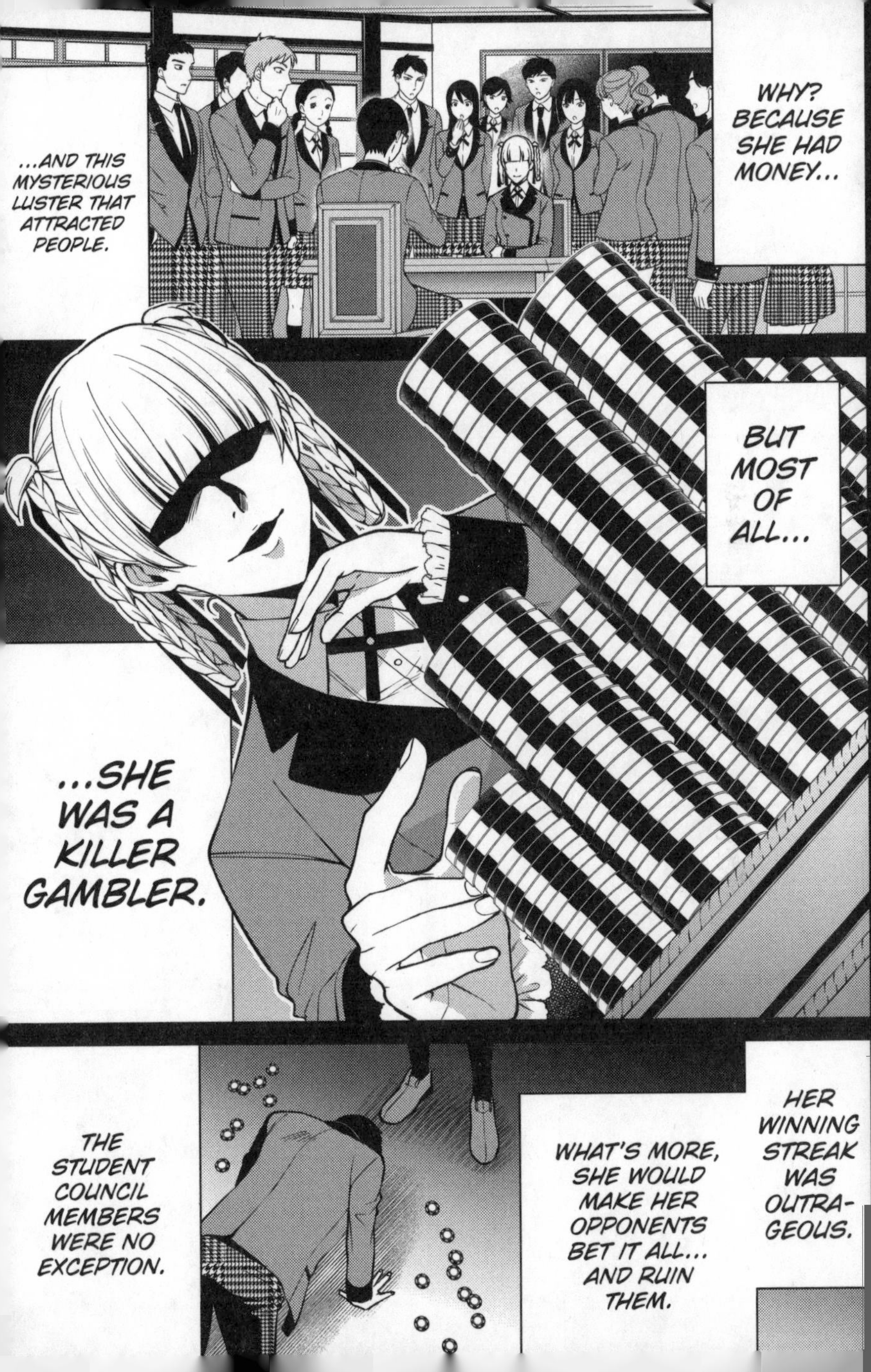
WHY? BECAUSE SHE HAD MONEY...
...AND THIS MYSTERIOUS LUSTER THAT ATTRACTED PEOPLE.
BUT MOST OF ALL...
...SHE WAS A KILLER GAMBLER.
HER WINNING STREAK WAS OUTRA-GEOUS.
WHAT'S MORE, SHE WOULD MAKE HER OPPONENTS BET IT ALL... AND RUIN THEM.
THE STUDENT COUNCIL MEMBERS WERE NO EXCEPTION.

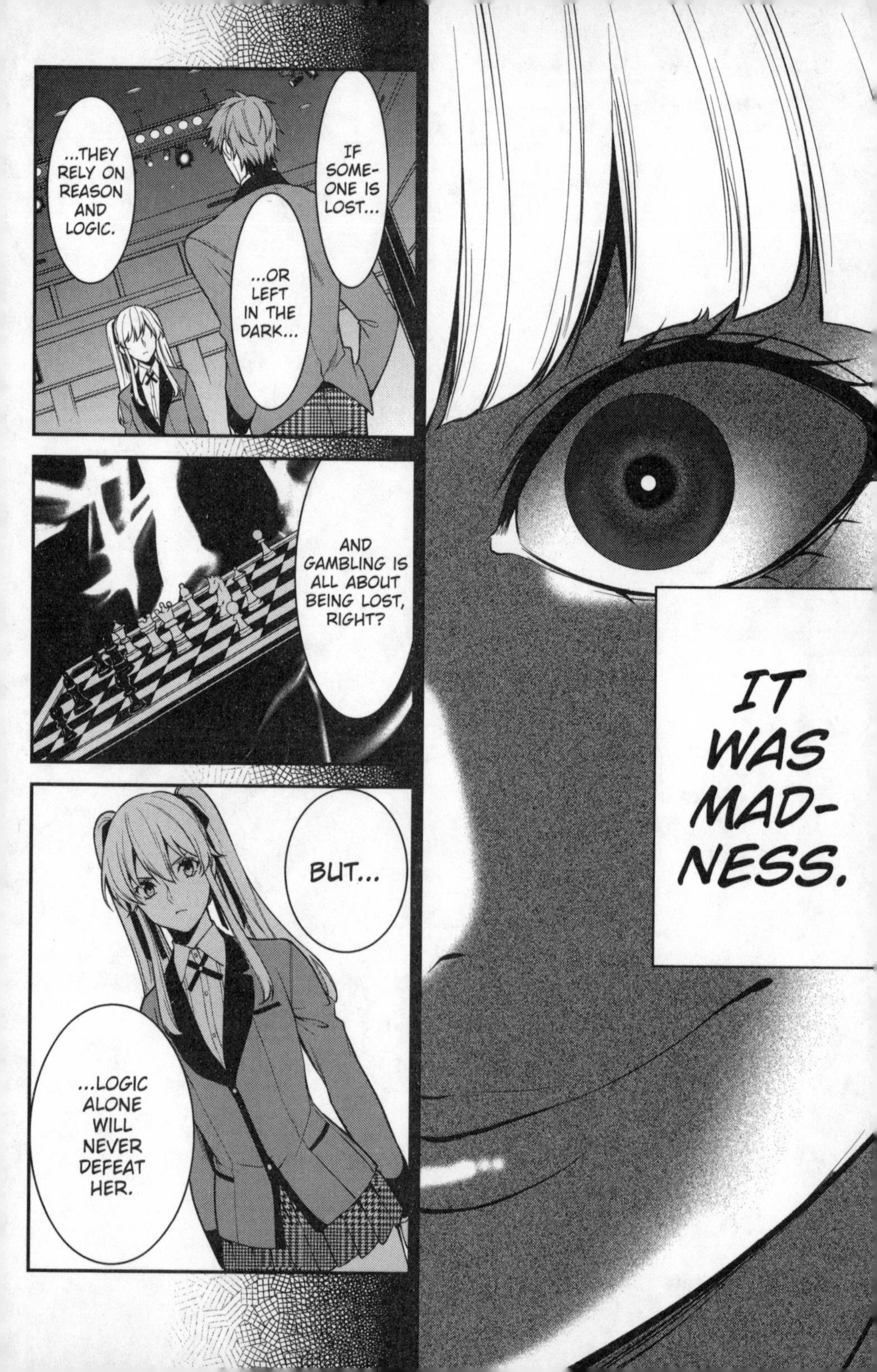
IT WAS MADNESS.
IF SOMEONE IS LOST...
...OR LEFT IN THE DARK...
...THEY RELY ON REASON AND LOGIC.
AND GAMBLING IS ALL ABOUT BEING LOST, RIGHT?
BUT...
...LOGIC ALONE WILL NEVER DEFEAT HER.

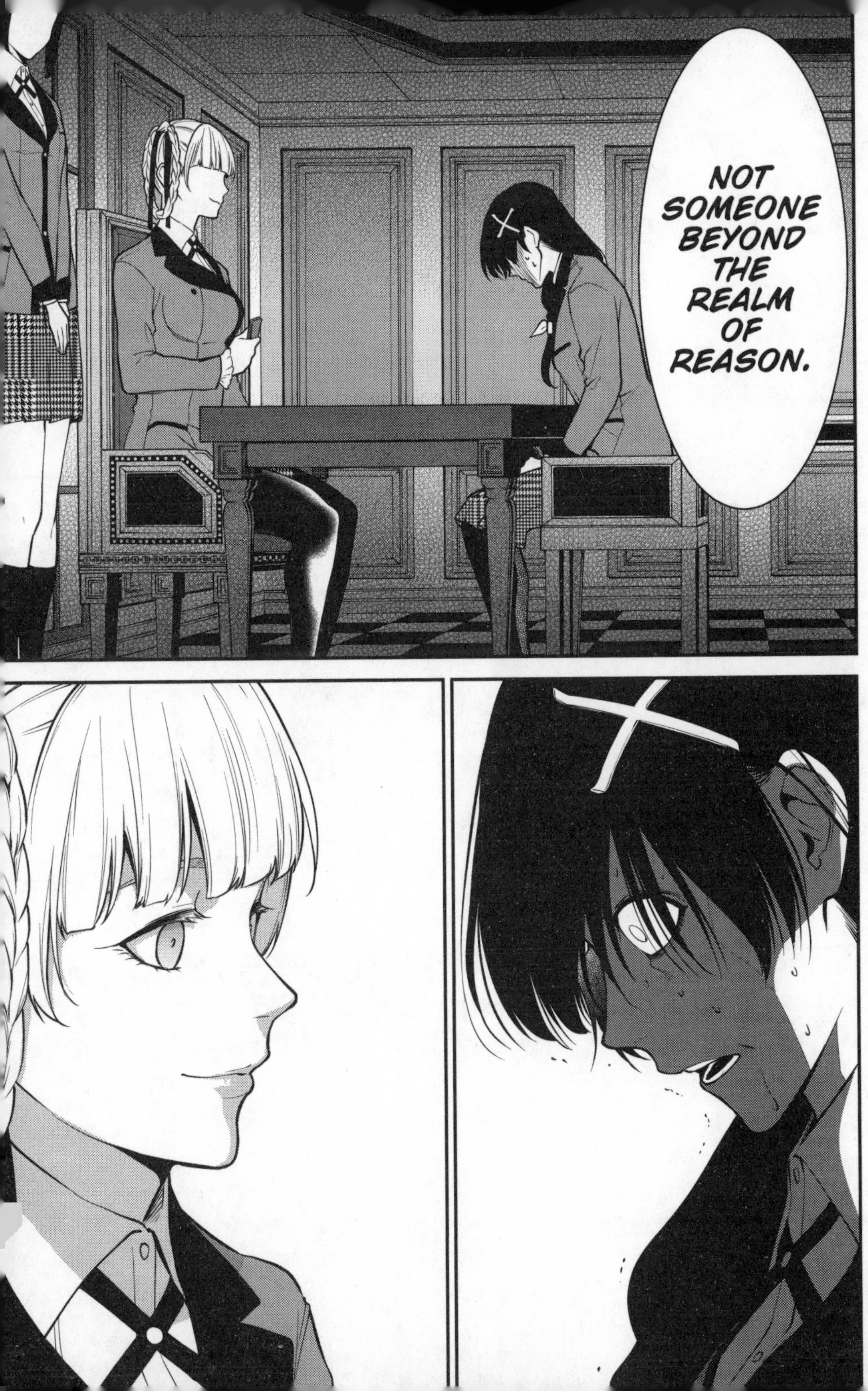
NOT SOMEONE BEYOND THE REALM OF REASON.

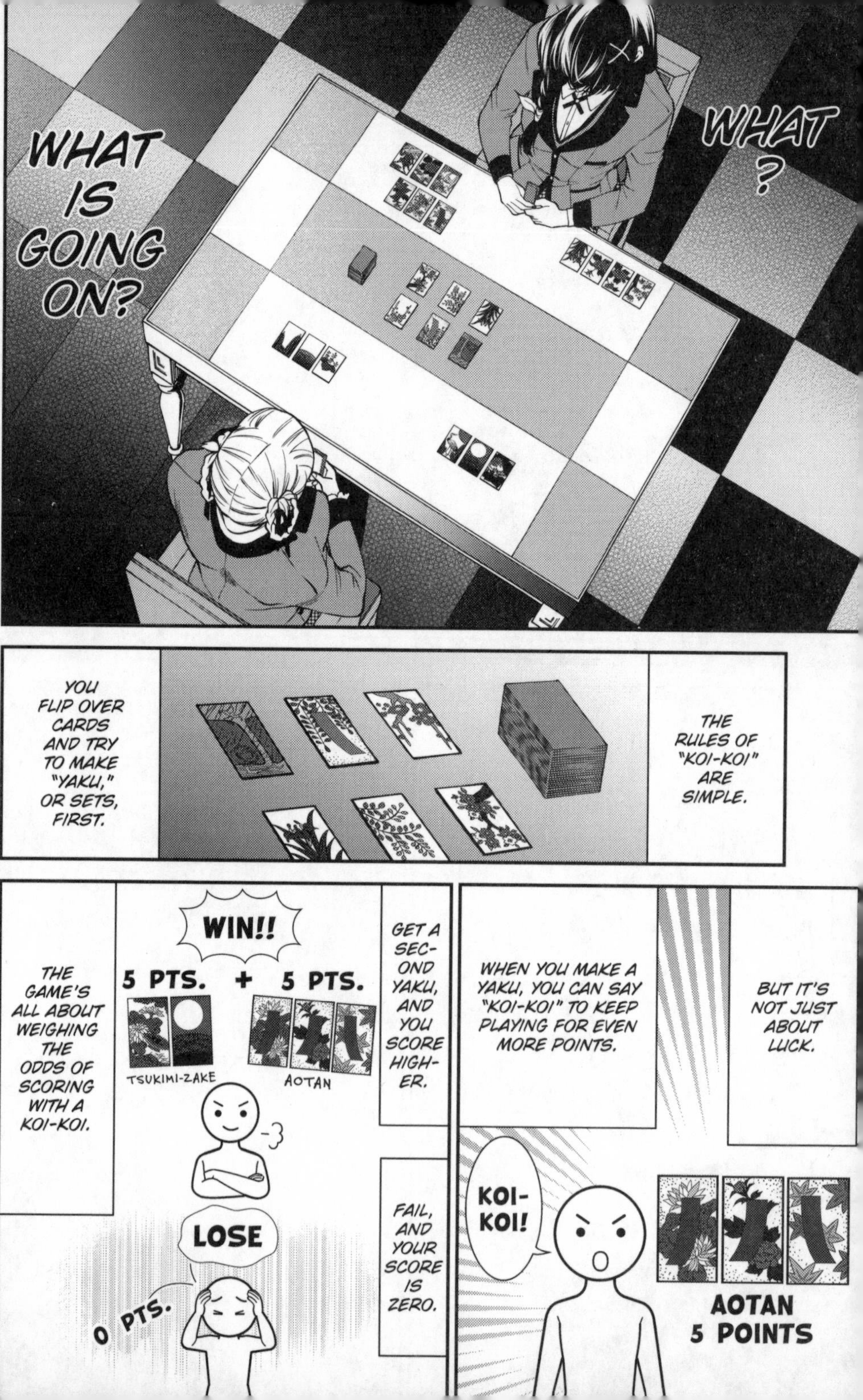
WHAT ?
WHAT IS GOING ON?
THE RULES OF "KOI-KOI" ARE SIMPLE.
YOU FLIP OVER CARDS AND TRY TO MAKE "YAKU," OR SETS, FIRST.
BUT IT'S NOT JUST ABOUT LUCK.
WHEN YOU MAKE A YAKU, YOU CAN SAY "KOI-KOI" TO KEEP PLAYING FOR EVEN MORE POINTS.
AOTAN 5 POINTS
KOI-KOI!
GET A SEC-OND YAKU, AND YOU SCORE HIGH-ER.
WIN!!
5 PTS. + 5 PTS.
TSUKIMI-ZAKE
AOTAN
THE GAME'S ALL ABOUT WEIGHING THE ODDS OF SCORING WITH A KOI-KOI.
FAIL, AND YOUR SCORE IS ZERO.
LOSE
0 PTS.

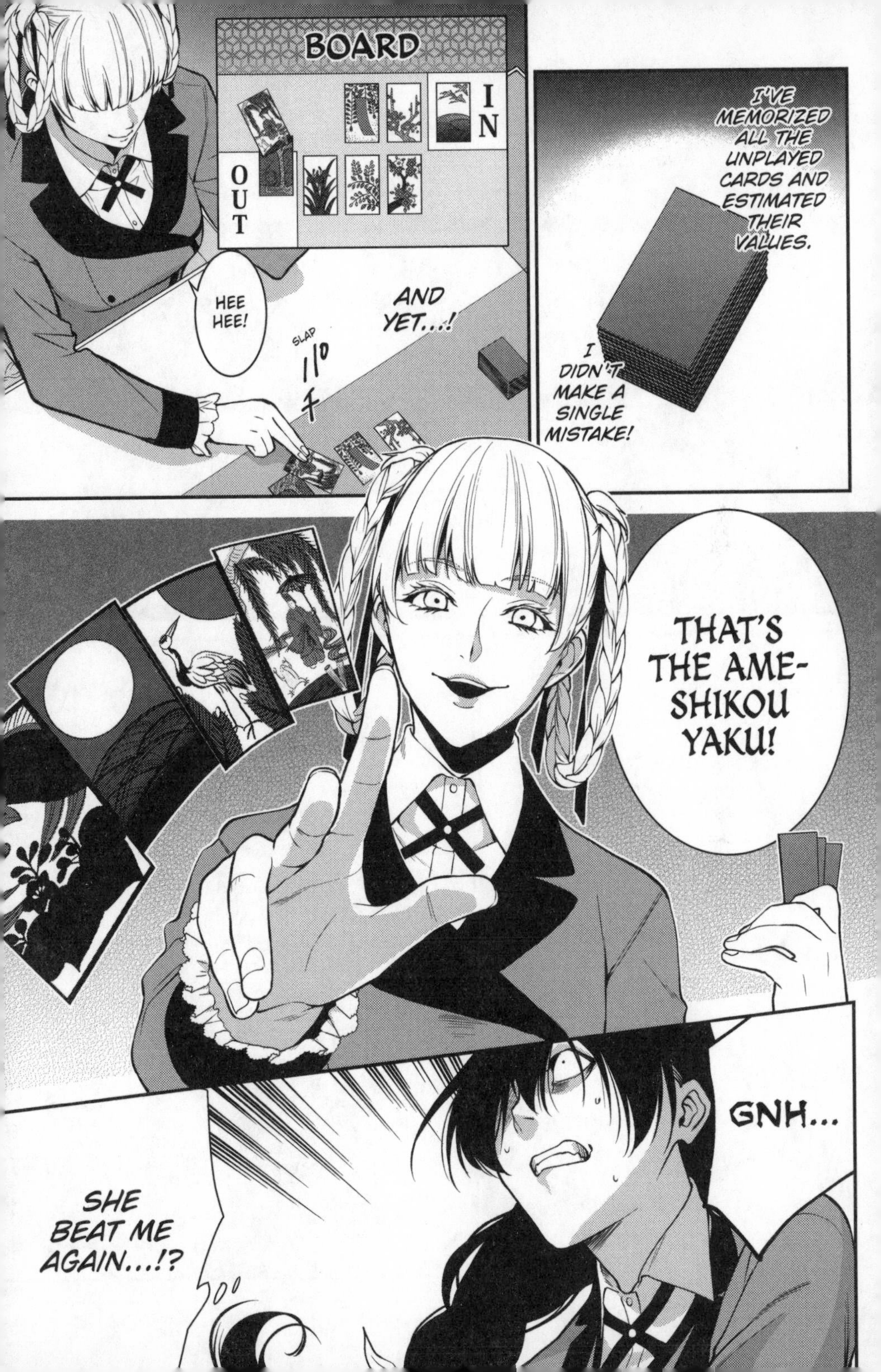
I'VE MEMORIZED ALL THE UNPLAYED CARDS AND ESTIMATED THEIR VALUES.
I DIDN'T MAKE A SINGLE MISTAKE!
BOARD
IN
OUT
HEE HEE!
AND YET...!
SLAP
THAT'S THE AME-SHIKOU YAKU!
GNH...
SHE BEAT ME AGAIN...!?

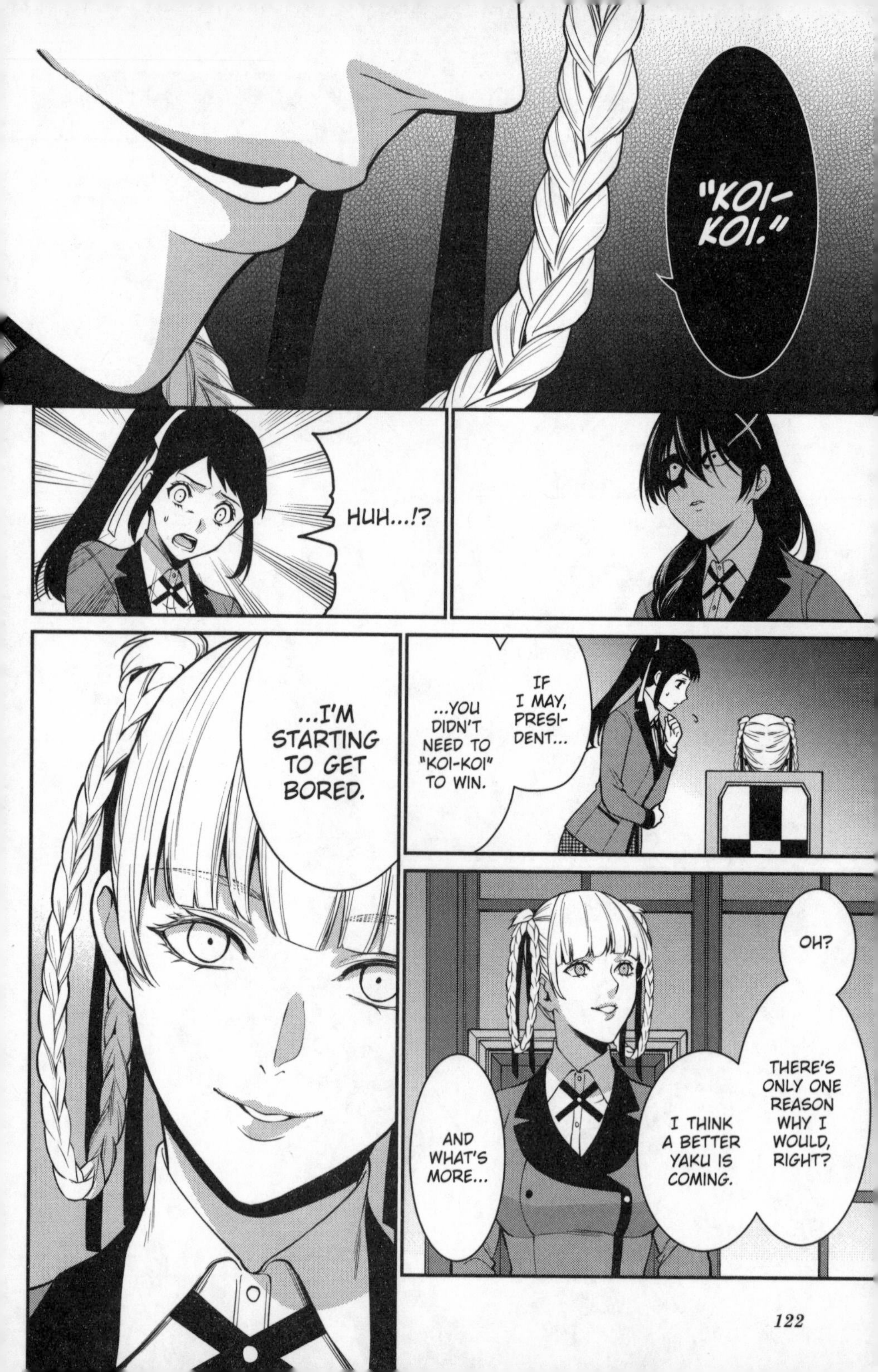
"KOI-KOI."
HUH...!?
IF I MAY, PRESIDENT...
...YOU DIDN'T NEED TO "KOI-KOI" TO WIN.
OH?
THERE'S ONLY ONE REASON WHY I WOULD, RIGHT?
I THINK A BETTER YAKU IS COMING.
AND WHAT'S MORE...
...I'M STARTING TO GET BORED.

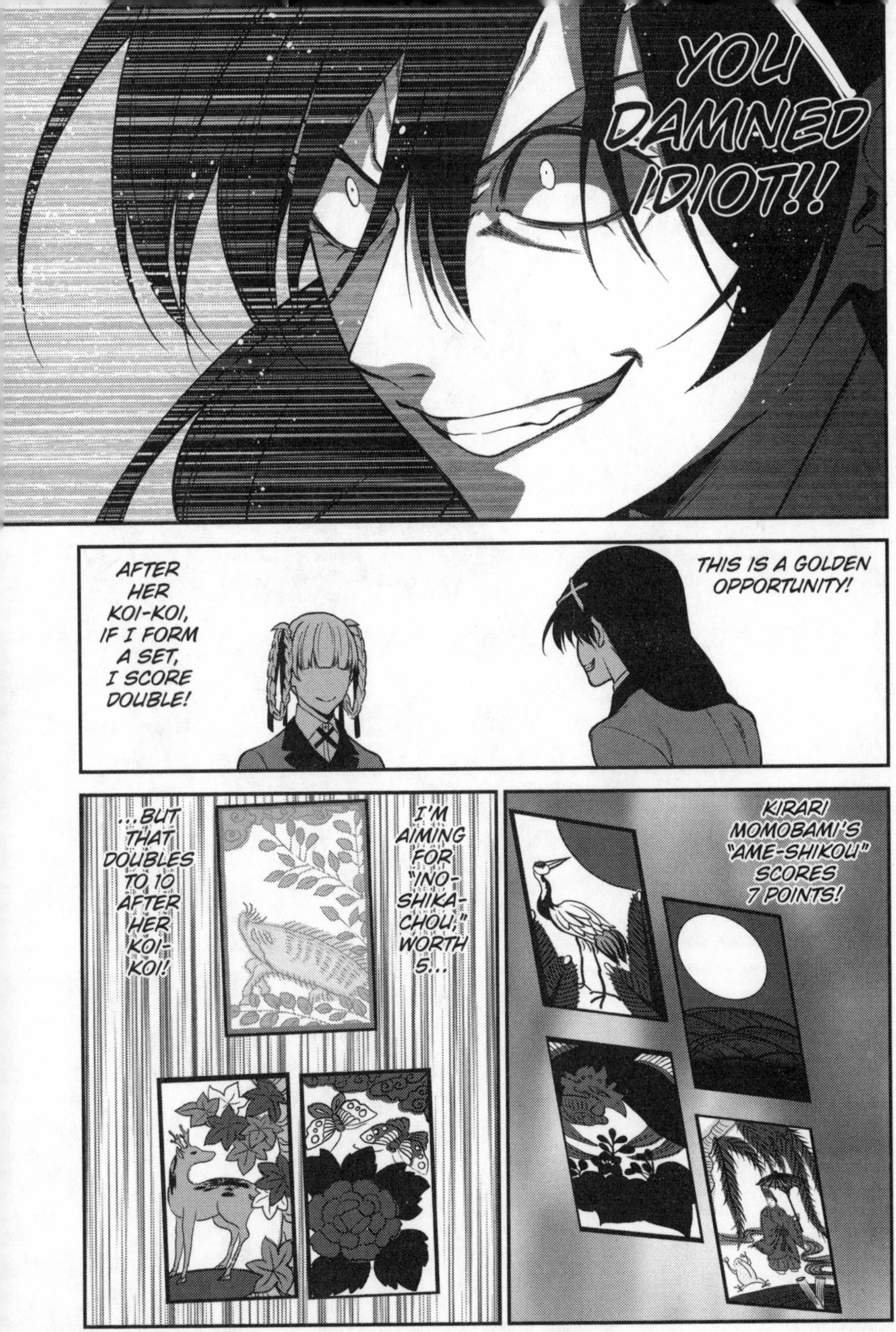
YOU DAMNED IDIOT!!
THIS IS A GOLDEN OPPORTUNITY!
AFTER HER KOI-KOI, IF I FORM A SET, I SCORE DOUBLE!
KIRARI MOMOBAMI'S "AME-SHIKOU" SCORES 7 POINTS!
I'M AIMING FOR "INO-SHIKA-CHOU," WORTH 5...
...BUT THAT DOUBLES TO 10 AFTER HER KOI-KOI!

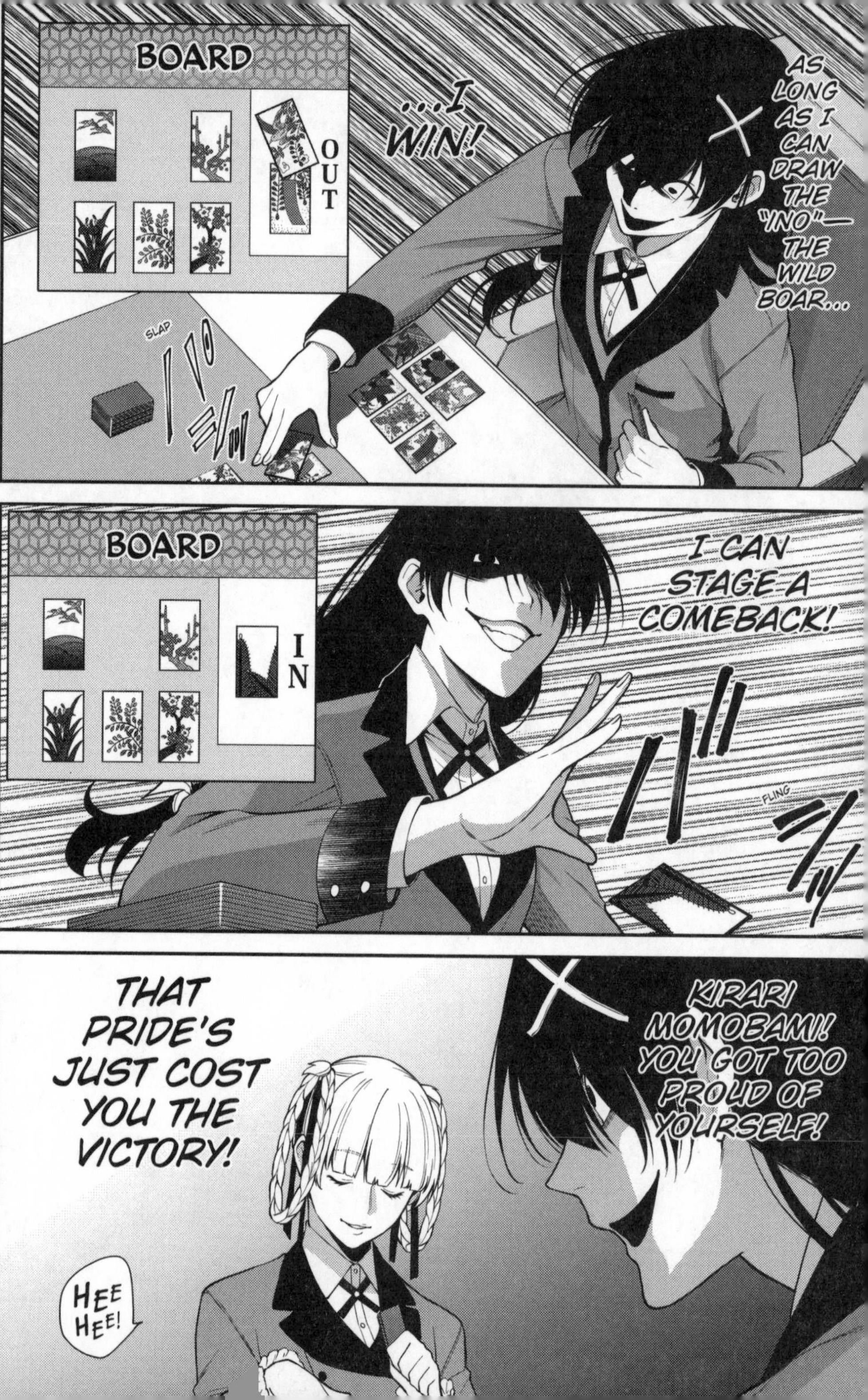
AS LONG AS I CAN DRAW THE "INO"—THE WILD BOAR...
...I WIN!
BOARD
OUT
SLAP
BOARD
IN
I CAN STAGE A COMEBACK!
FLING
KIRARI MOMOBAMI! YOU GOT TOO PROUD OF YOURSELF!
THAT PRIDE'S JUST COST YOU THE VICTORY!
HEE HEE!

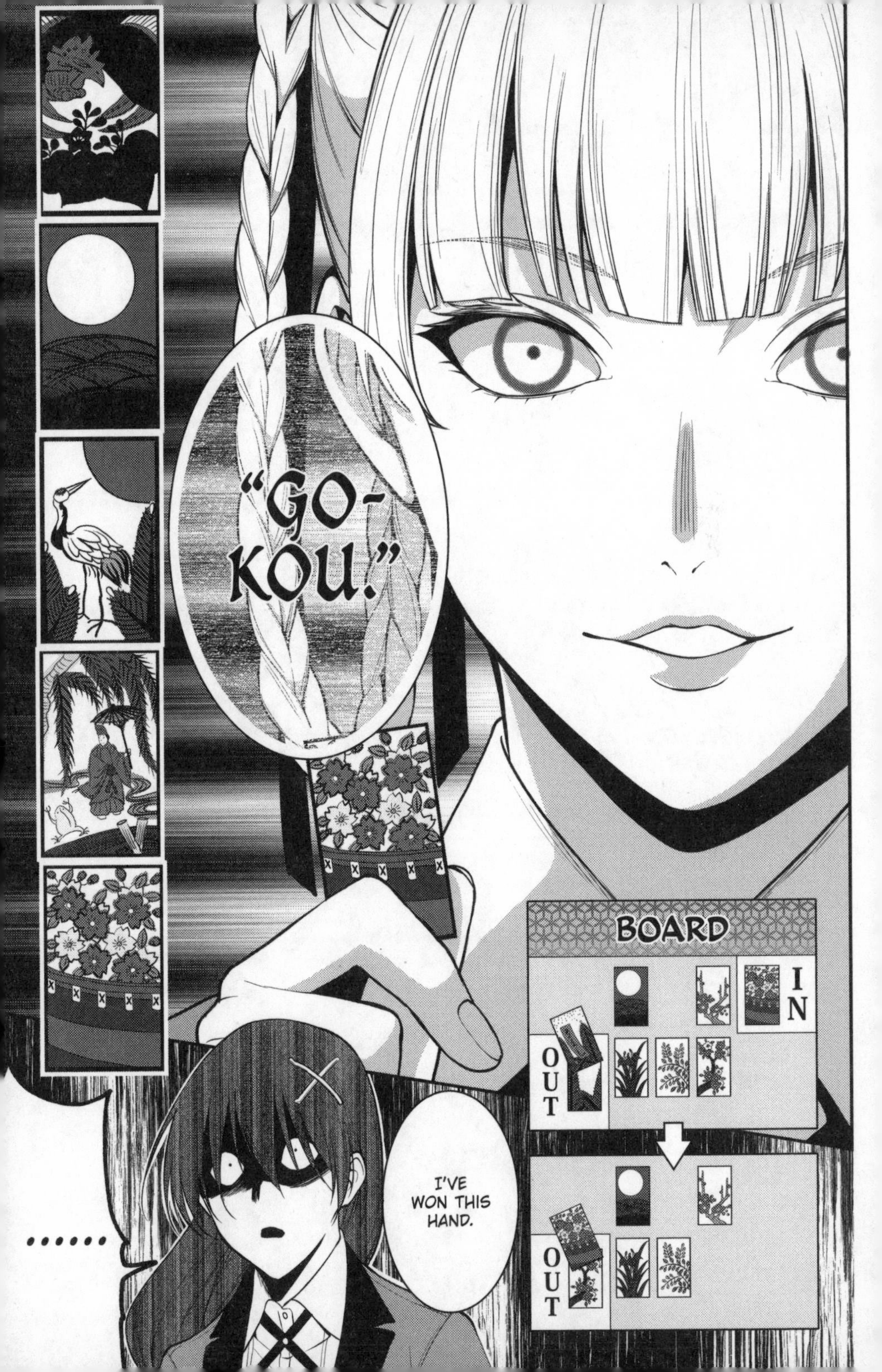
"GO-KOU."
BOARD
IN
OUT
OUT
I'VE WON THIS HAND.
......

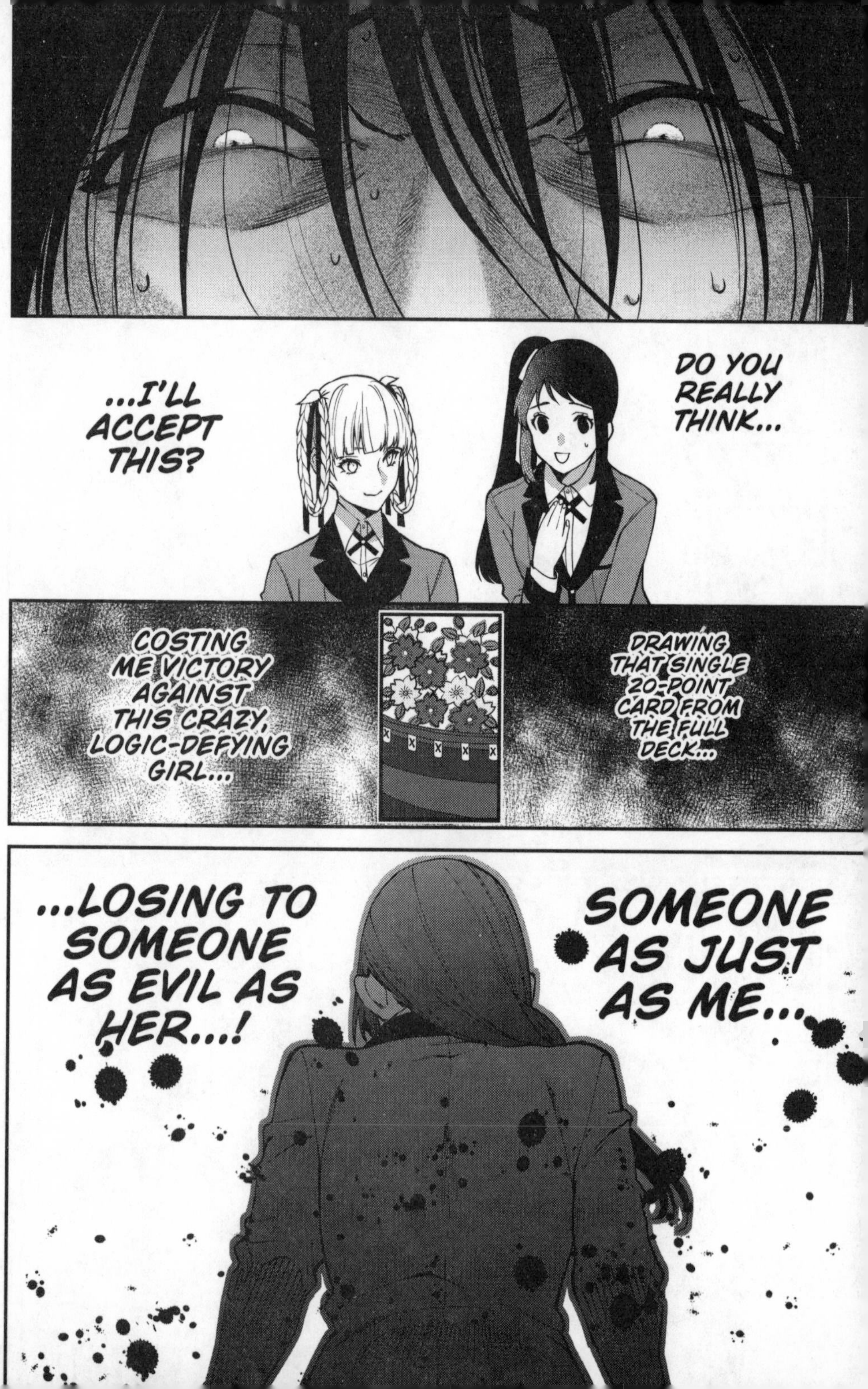
DO YOU REALLY THINK...
...I'LL ACCEPT THIS?
DRAWING THAT SINGLE 20-POINT CARD FROM THE FULL DECK...
COSTING ME VICTORY AGAINST THIS CRAZY, LOGIC-DEFYING GIRL...
SOMEONE AS JUST AS ME...
...LOSING TO SOMEONE AS EVIL AS HER...!

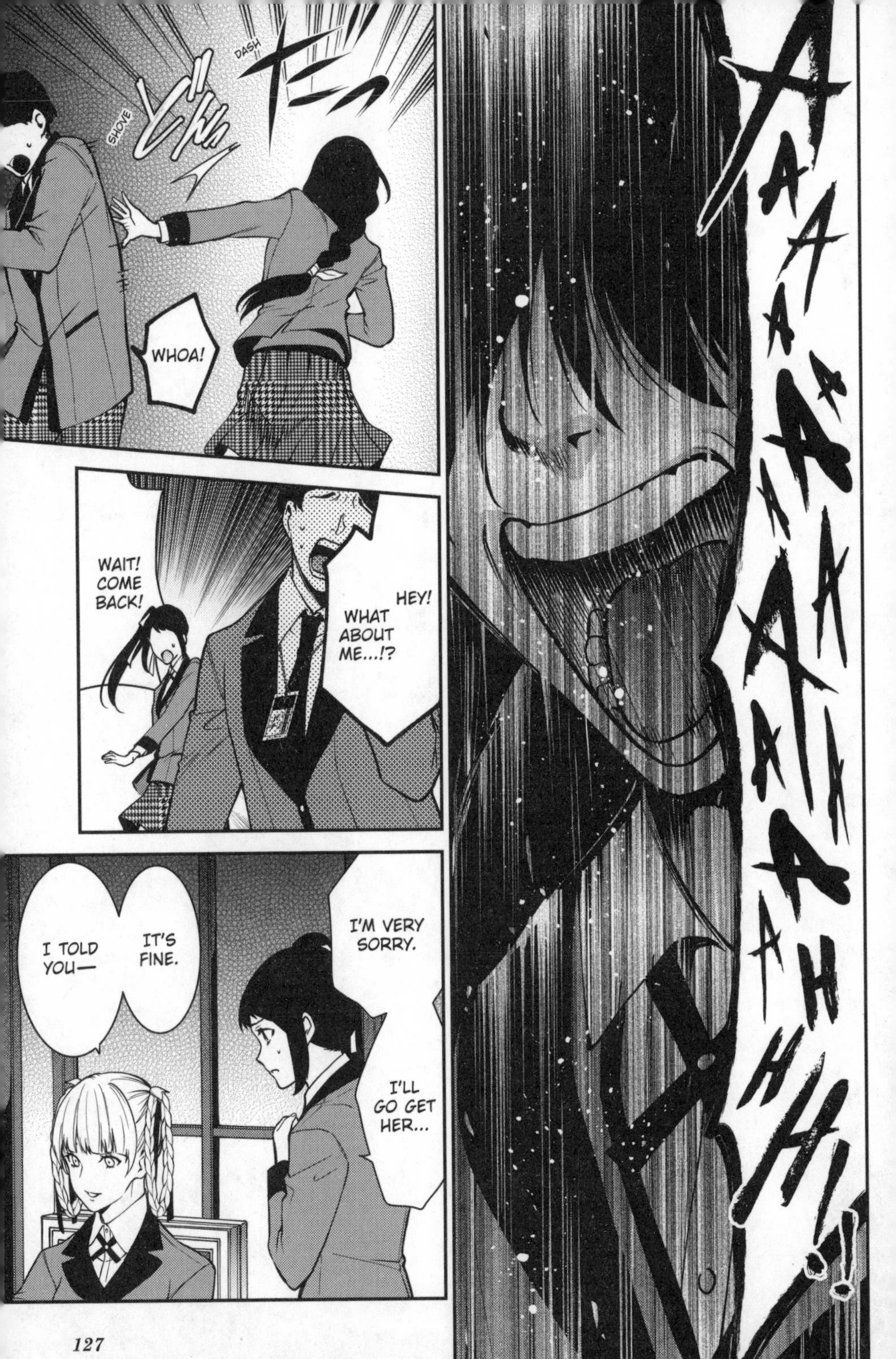
AAAAAAAAAAAAAAAAAAAAAAH!!
DASH
SHOVE
WHOA!
HEY! WHAT ABOUT ME...!?
WAIT! COME BACK!
I'M VERY SORRY.
I'LL GO GET HER...
I TOLD YOU—
IT'S FINE.

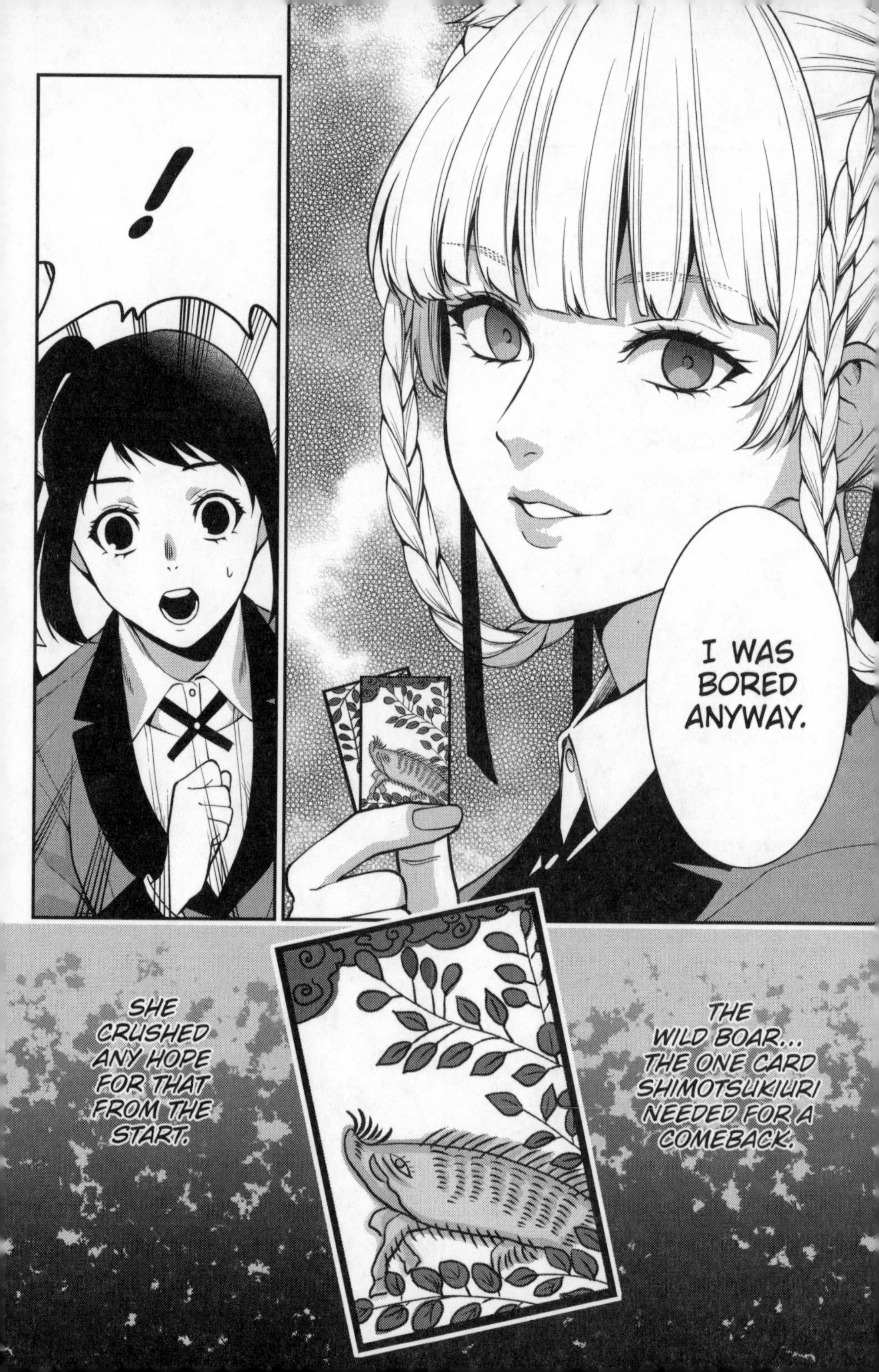
I WAS BORED ANYWAY.
!
THE WILD BOAR... THE ONE CARD SHIMOTSUKIURI NEEDED FOR A COMEBACK.
SHE CRUSHED ANY HOPE FOR THAT FROM THE START.

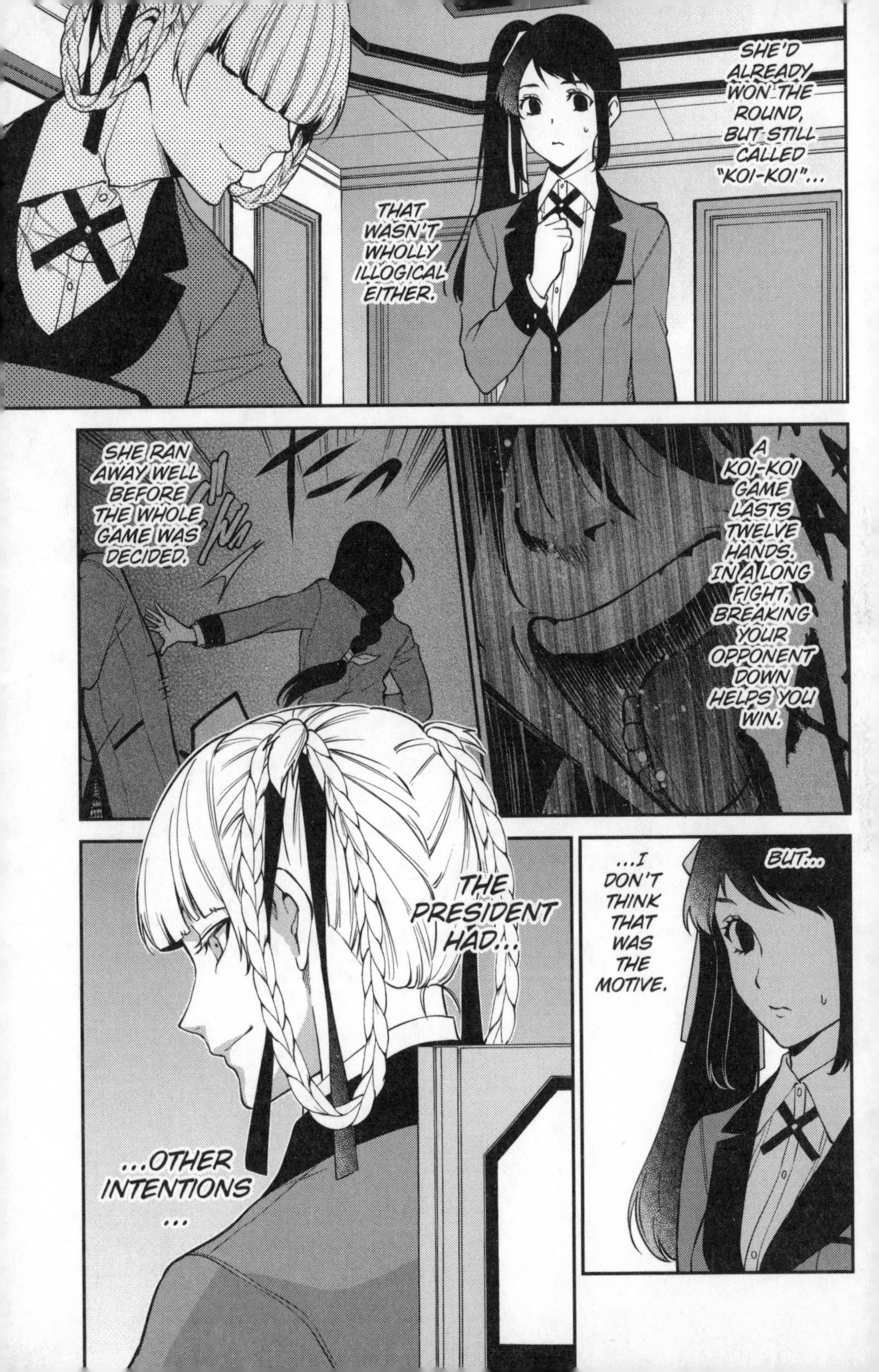
SHE'D ALREADY WON THE ROUND, BUT STILL CALLED "KOI-KOI"...
THAT WASN'T WHOLLY ILLOGICAL EITHER.
A KOI-KOI GAME LASTS TWELVE HANDS. IN A LONG FIGHT, BREAKING YOUR OPPONENT DOWN HELPS YOU WIN.
SHE RAN AWAY WELL BEFORE THE WHOLE GAME WAS DECIDED.
BUT...
...I DON'T THINK THAT WAS THE MOTIVE.
THE PRESIDENT HAD...
...OTHER INTENTIONS...

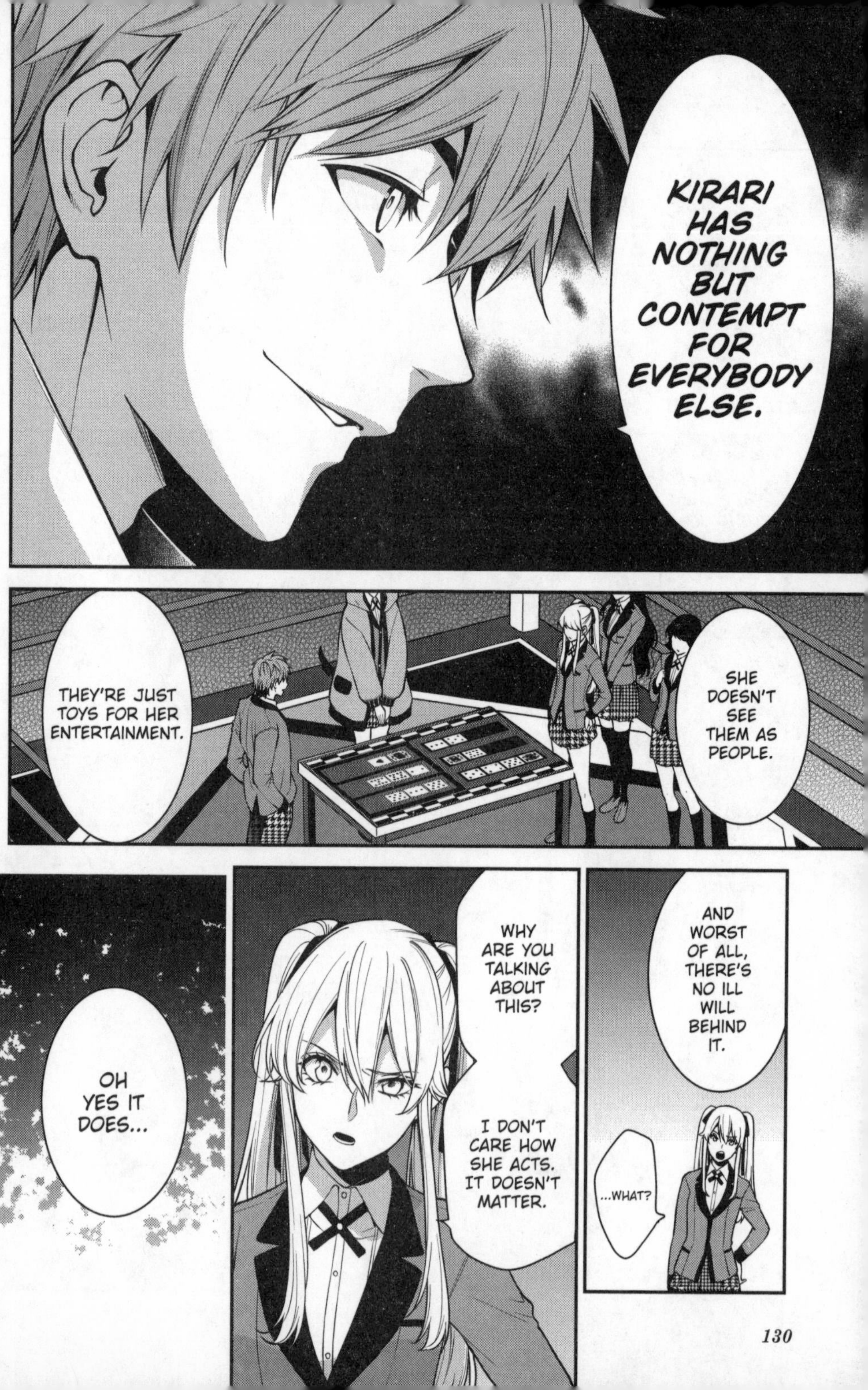
KIRARI HAS NOTHING BUT CONTEMPT FOR EVERYBODY ELSE.
SHE DOESN'T SEE THEM AS PEOPLE.
THEY'RE JUST TOYS FOR HER ENTERTAINMENT.
AND WORST OF ALL, THERE'S NO ILL WILL BEHIND IT.
...WHAT?
WHY ARE YOU TALKING ABOUT THIS?
I DON'T CARE HOW SHE ACTS. IT DOESN'T MATTER.
OH YES IT DOES...

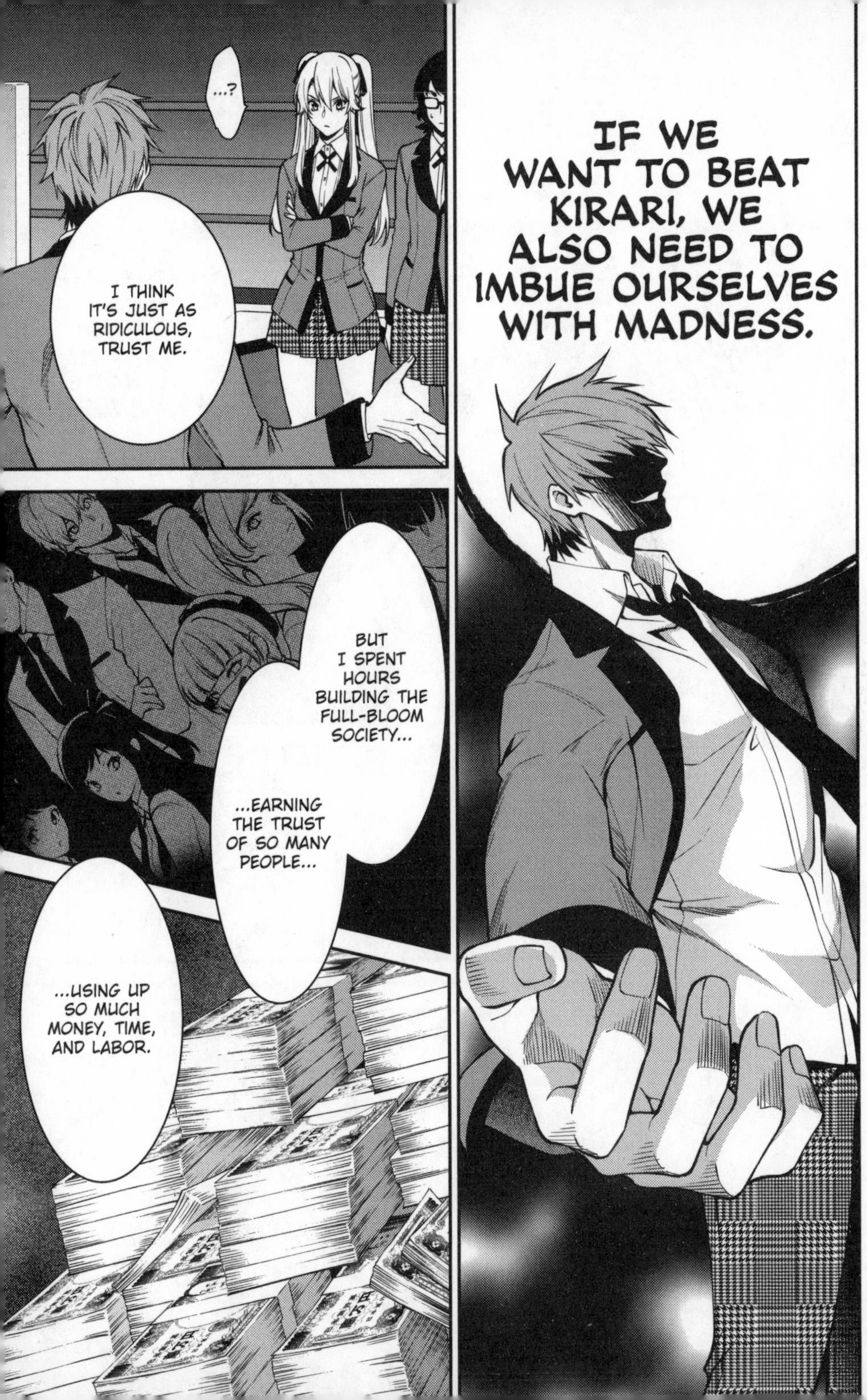

IF WE WANT TO BEAT KIRARI, WE ALSO NEED TO IMBUE OURSELVES WITH MADNESS.
...?
I THINK IT'S JUST AS RIDICULOUS, TRUST ME.
BUT I SPENT HOURS BUILDING THE FULL-BLOOM SOCIETY...
...EARNING THE TRUST OF SO MANY PEOPLE...
...USING UP SO MUCH MONEY, TIME, AND LABOR.

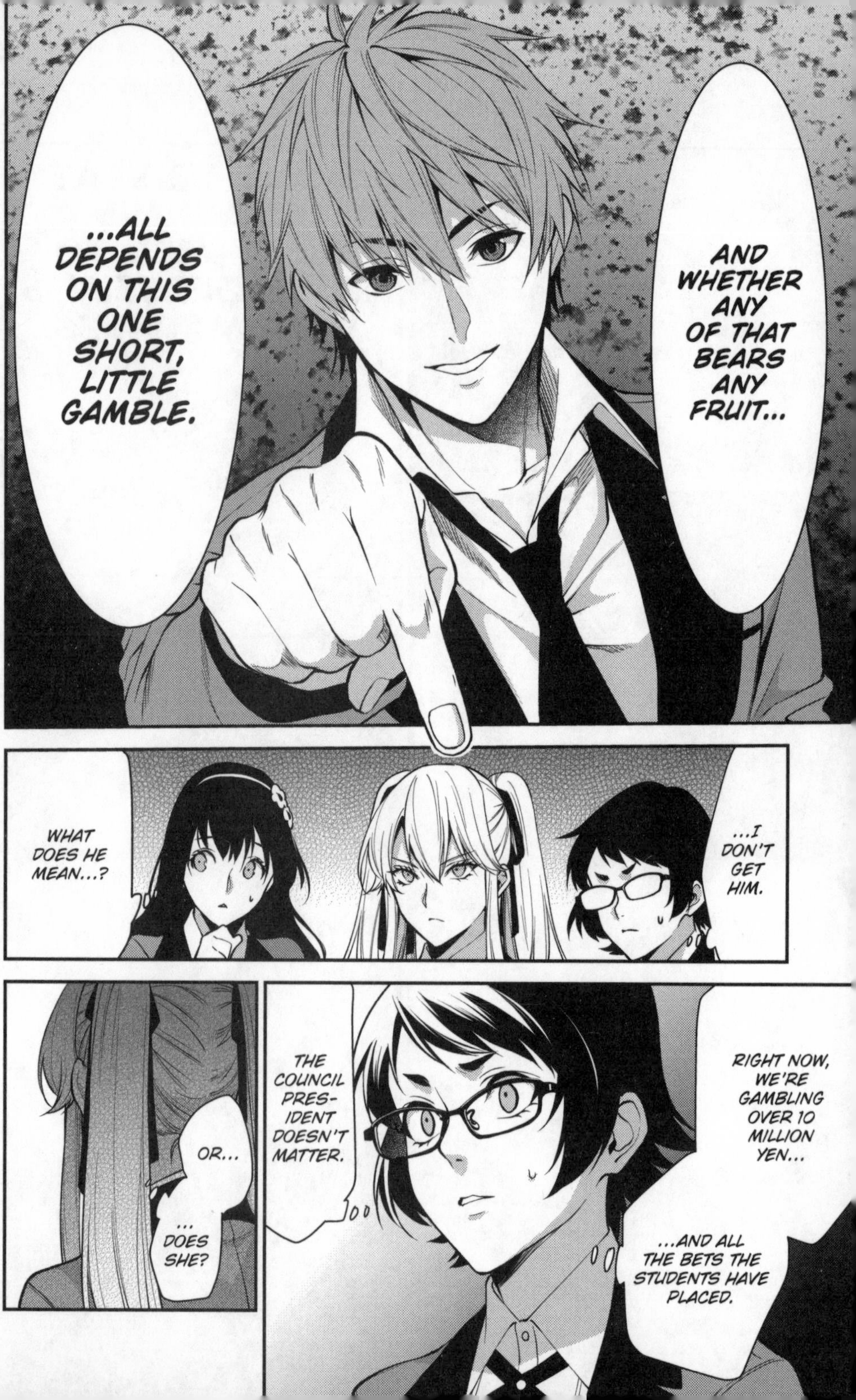
AND WHETHER ANY OF THAT BEARS ANY FRUIT...
...ALL DEPENDS ON THIS ONE SHORT, LITTLE GAMBLE.
...I DON'T GET HIM.
WHAT DOES HE MEAN...?
RIGHT NOW, WE'RE GAMBLING OVER 10 MILLION YEN...
...AND ALL THE BETS THE STUDENTS HAVE PLACED.
THE COUNCIL PRES-IDENT DOESN'T MATTER.
OR...
...DOES SHE?

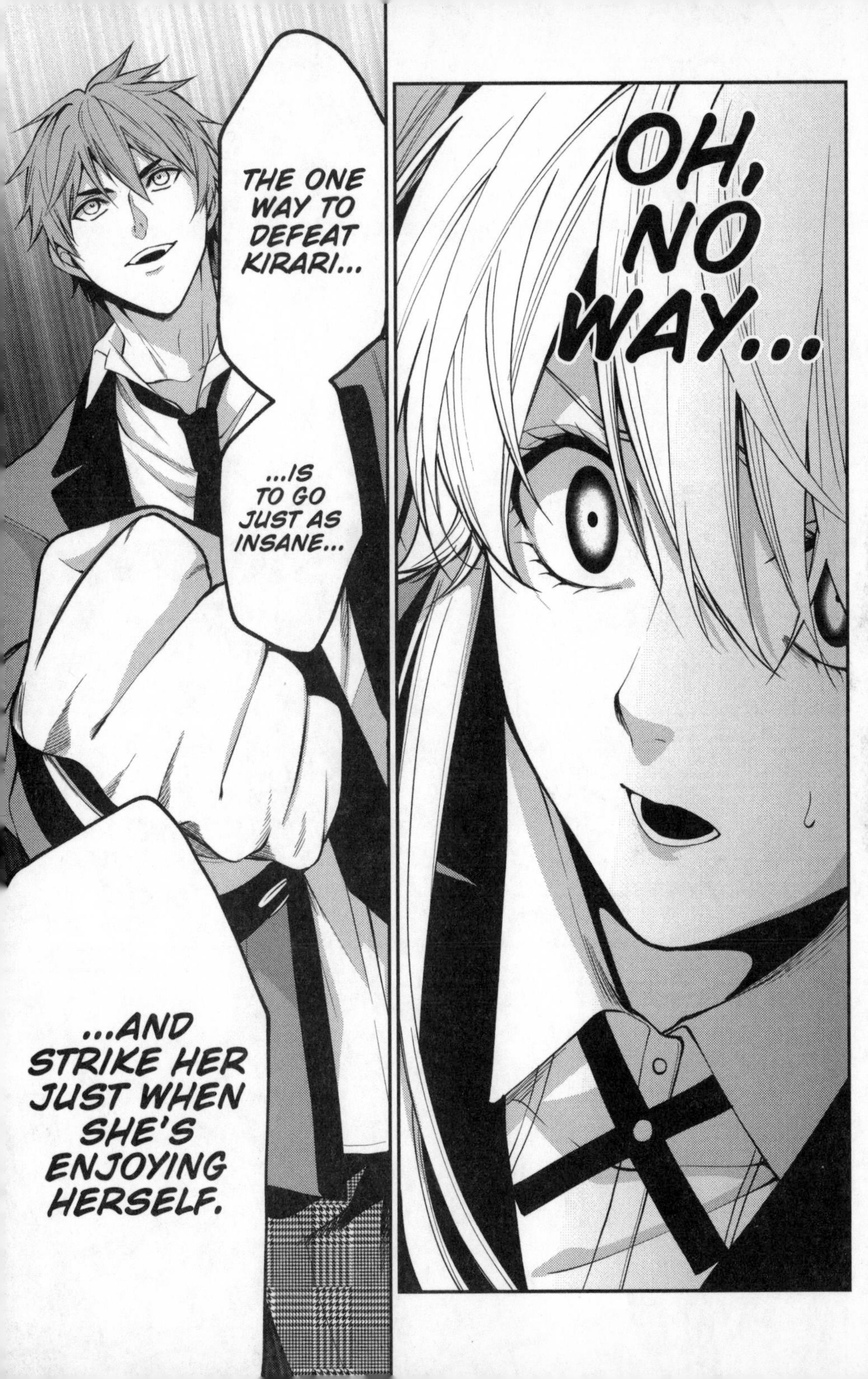
OH, NO WAY...
THE ONE WAY TO DEFEAT KIRARI...
...IS TO GO JUST AS INSANE...
...AND STRIKE HER JUST WHEN SHE'S ENJOYING HERSELF.

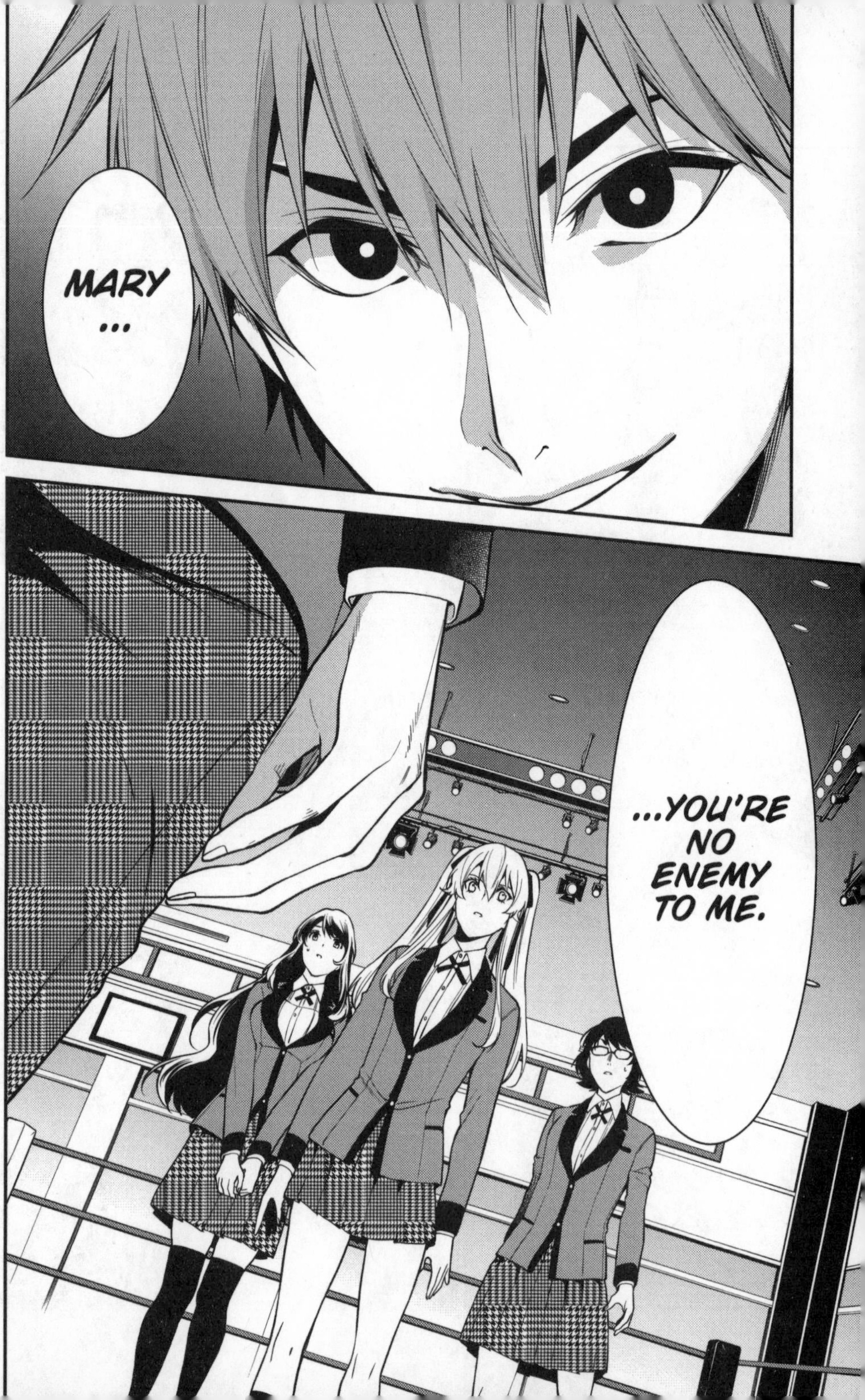
MARY ...
...YOU'RE NO ENEMY TO ME.

CHAPTER FIFTY-ONE
THE FRUSTRATED GIRL

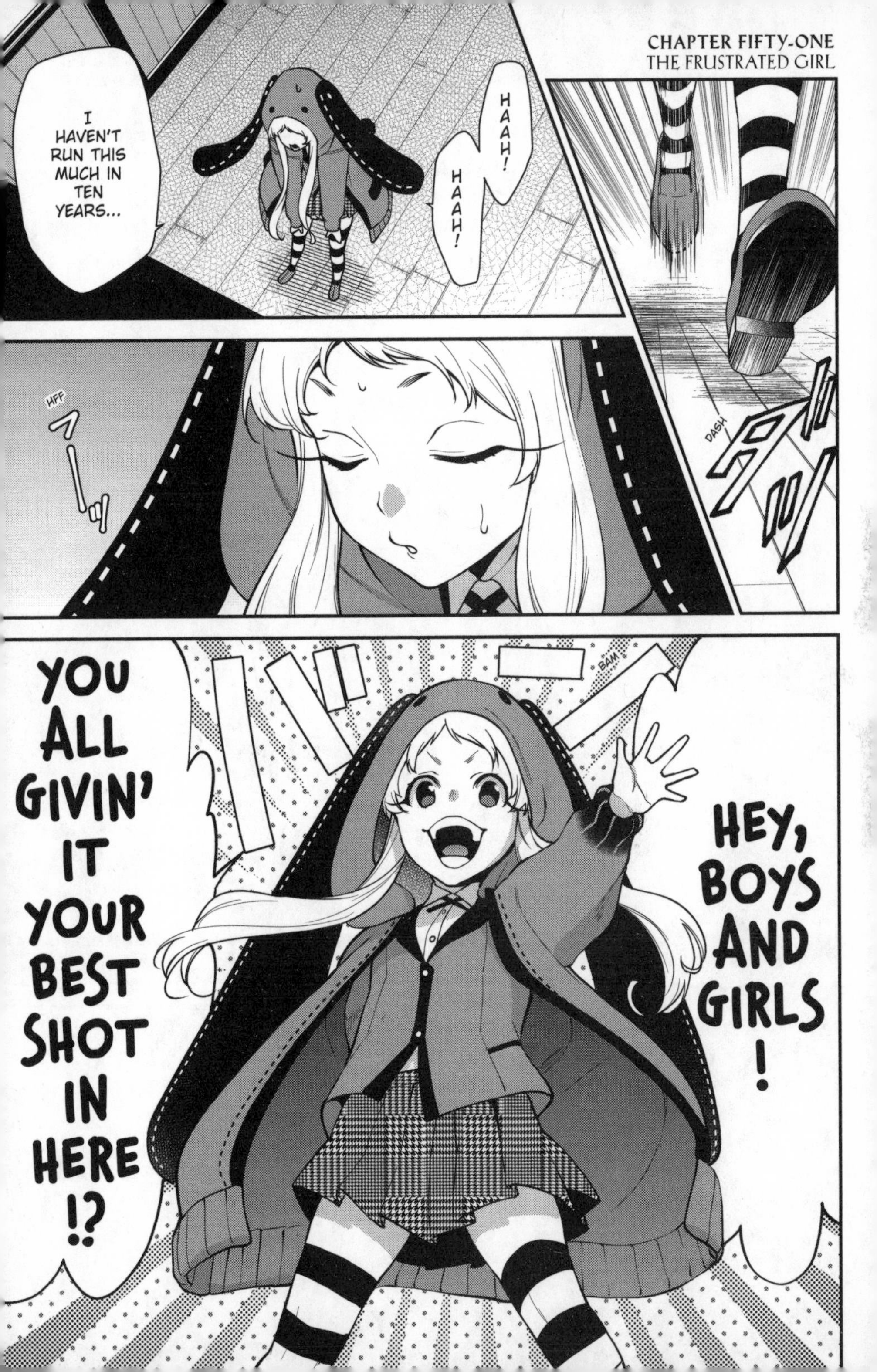
DASH
HAAAH! HAAAH!
I HAVEN'T RUN THIS MUCH IN TEN YEARS...
HFF
BAM
HEY, BOYS AND GIRLS!
YOU ALL GIVIN' IT YOUR BEST SHOT IN HERE!?

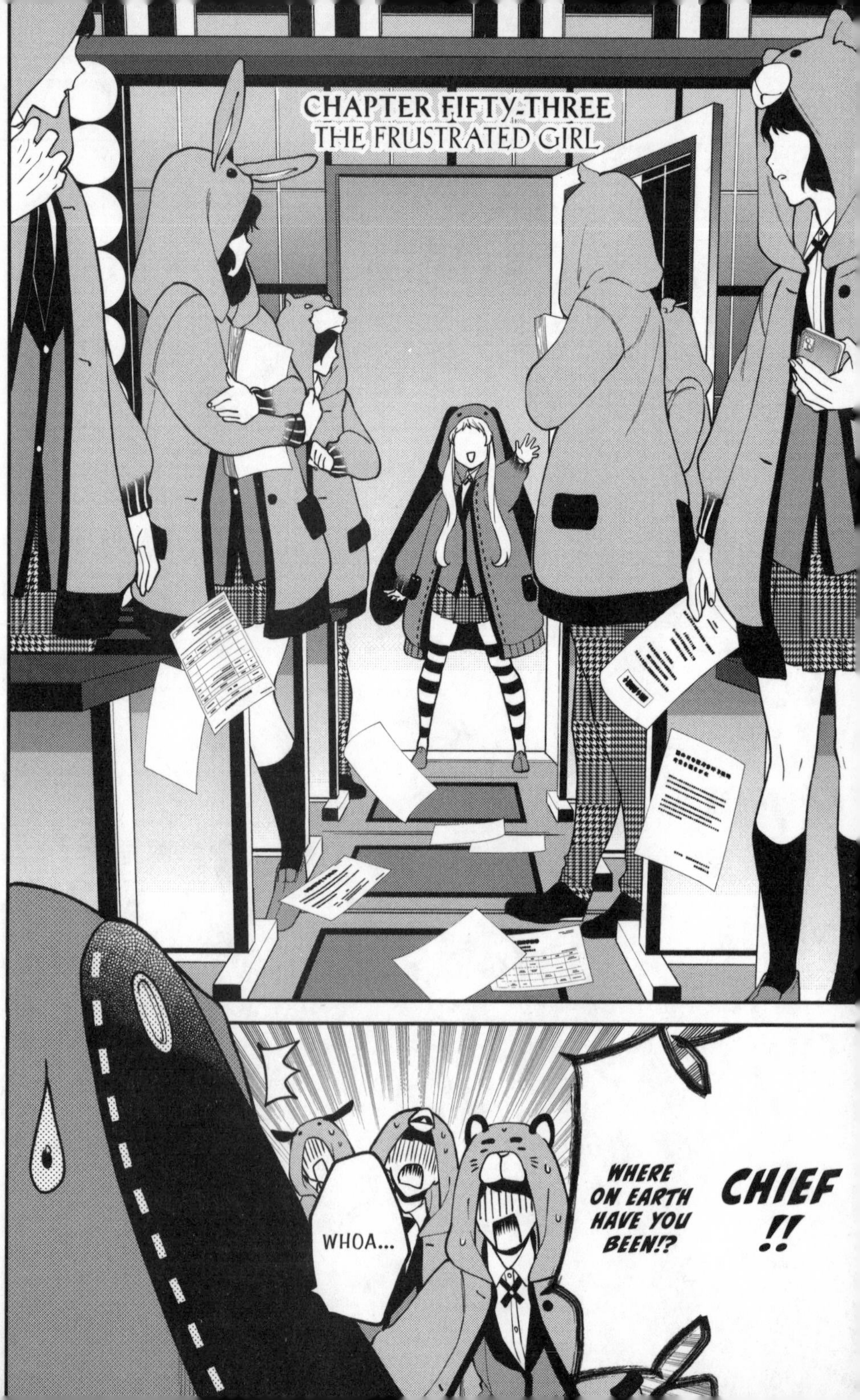
CHAPTER FIFTY-THREE
THE FRUSTRATED GIRL
CHIEF!!
WHERE ON EARTH HAVE YOU BEEN!?
WHOA...

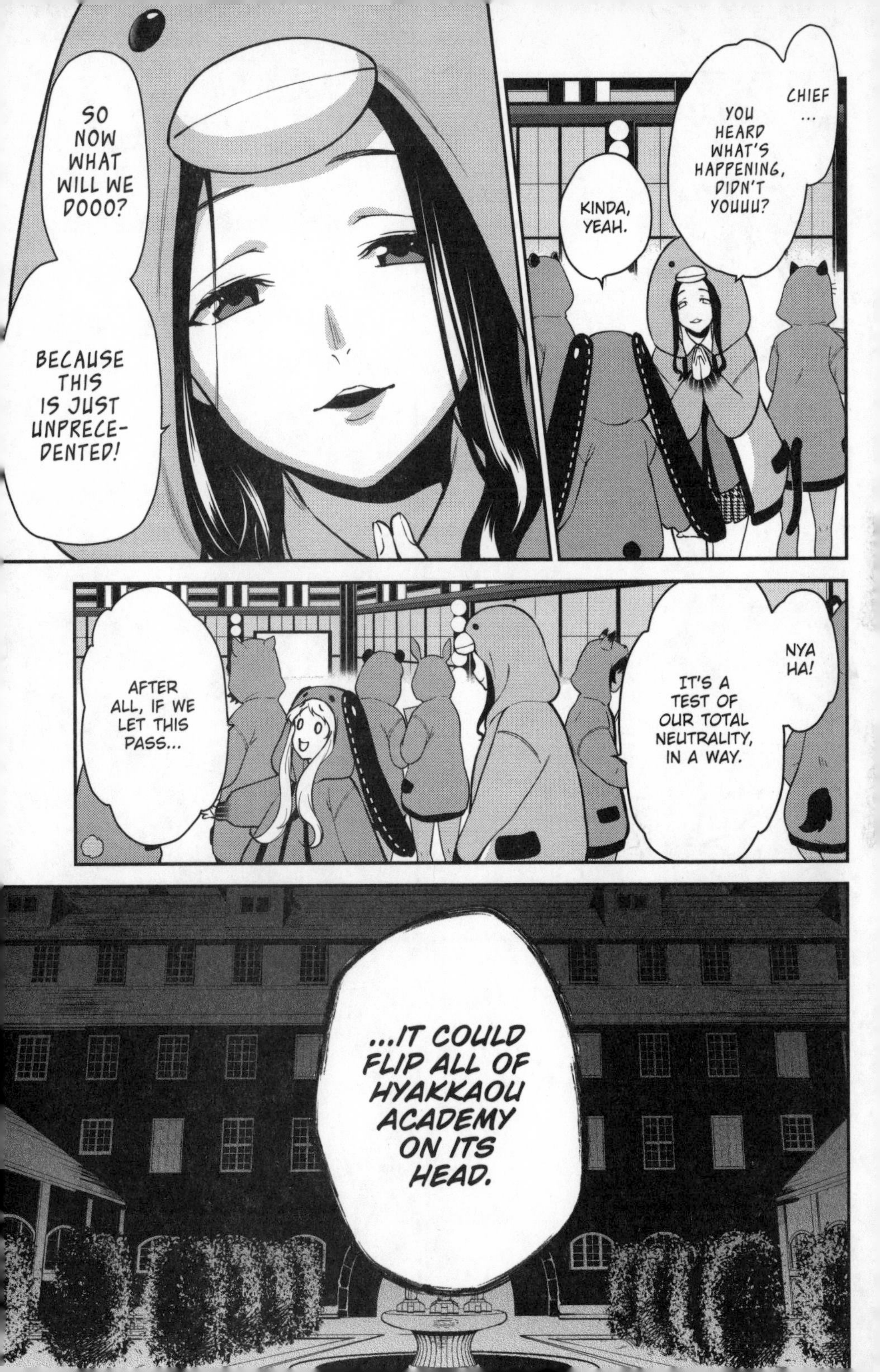
CHIEF ...
YOU HEARD WHAT'S HAPPENING, DIDN'T YOUUU?
KINDA, YEAH.
SO NOW WHAT WILL WE DOOO?
BECAUSE THIS IS JUST UNPRECE-DENTED!
NYA HA!
IT'S A TEST OF OUR TOTAL NEUTRALITY, IN A WAY.
AFTER ALL, IF WE LET THIS PASS...
...IT COULD FLIP ALL OF HYAKKAOU ACADEMY ON ITS HEAD.

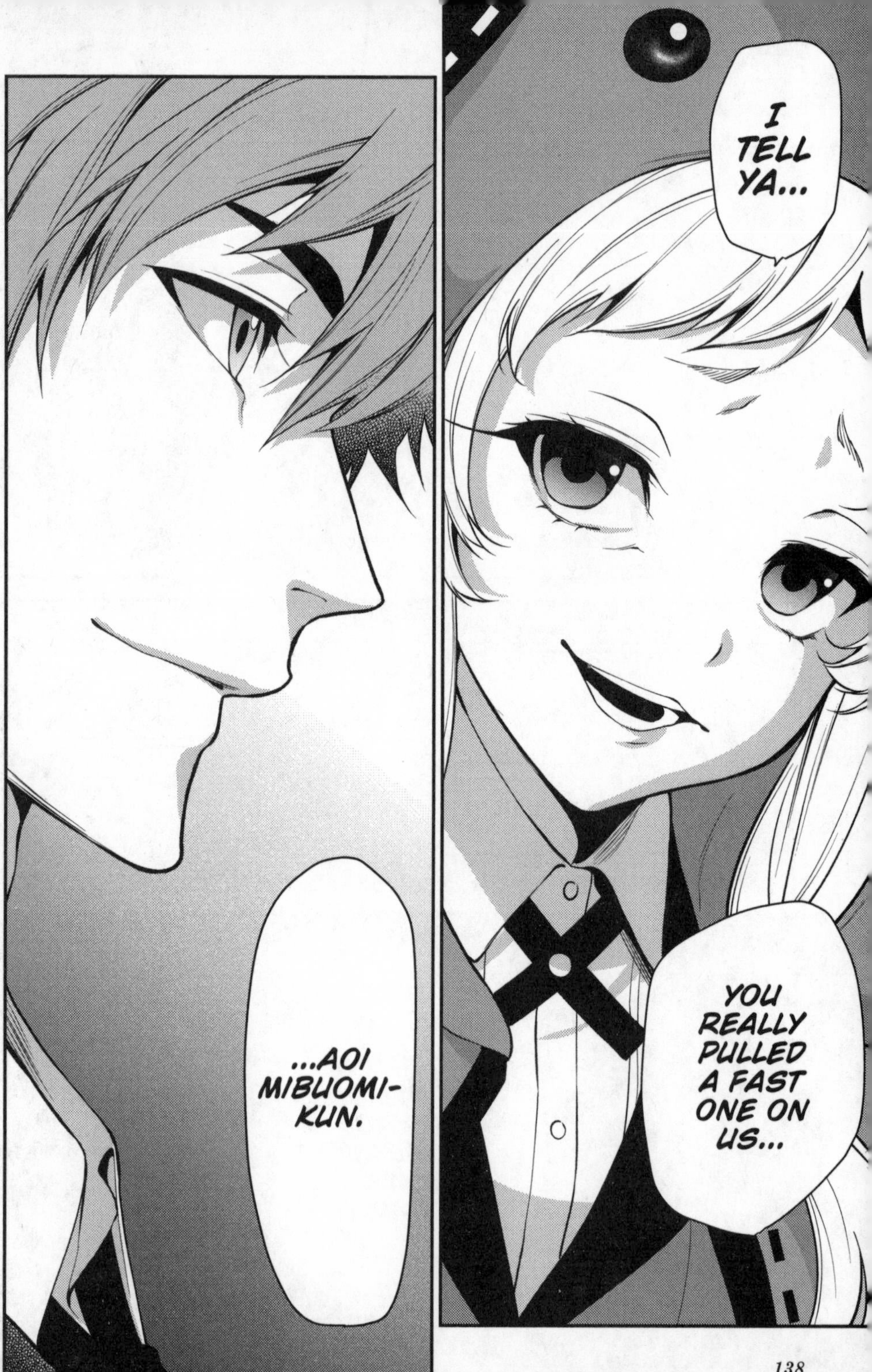
I TELL YA...
YOU REALLY PULLED A FAST ONE ON US...
...AOI MIBUOMI-KUN.

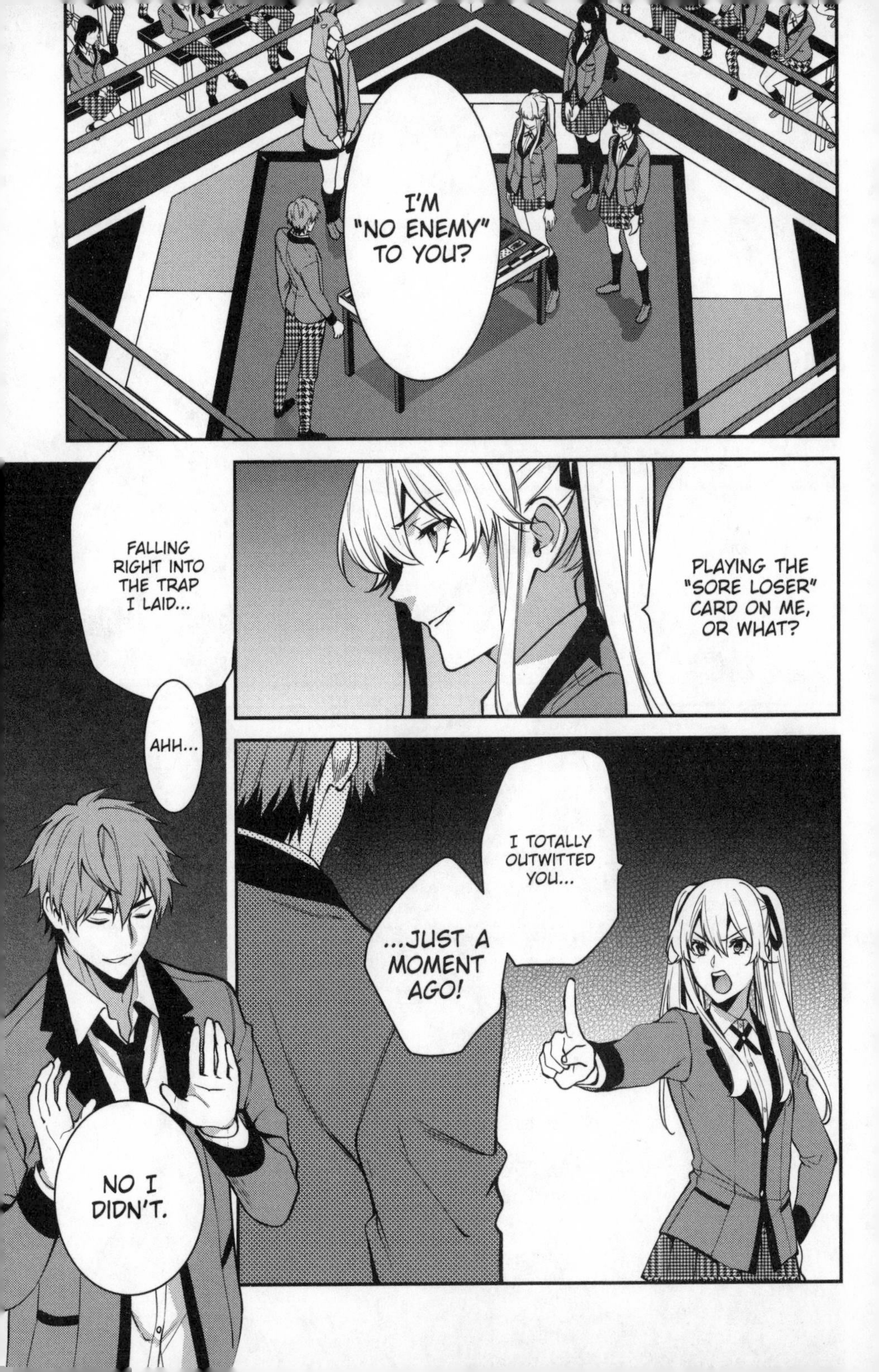
I'M "NO ENEMY" TO YOU?
PLAYING THE "SORE LOSER" CARD ON ME, OR WHAT?
FALLING RIGHT INTO THE TRAP I LAID...
AHH...
I TOTALLY OUTWITTED YOU...
...JUST A MOMENT AGO!
NO I DIDN'T.

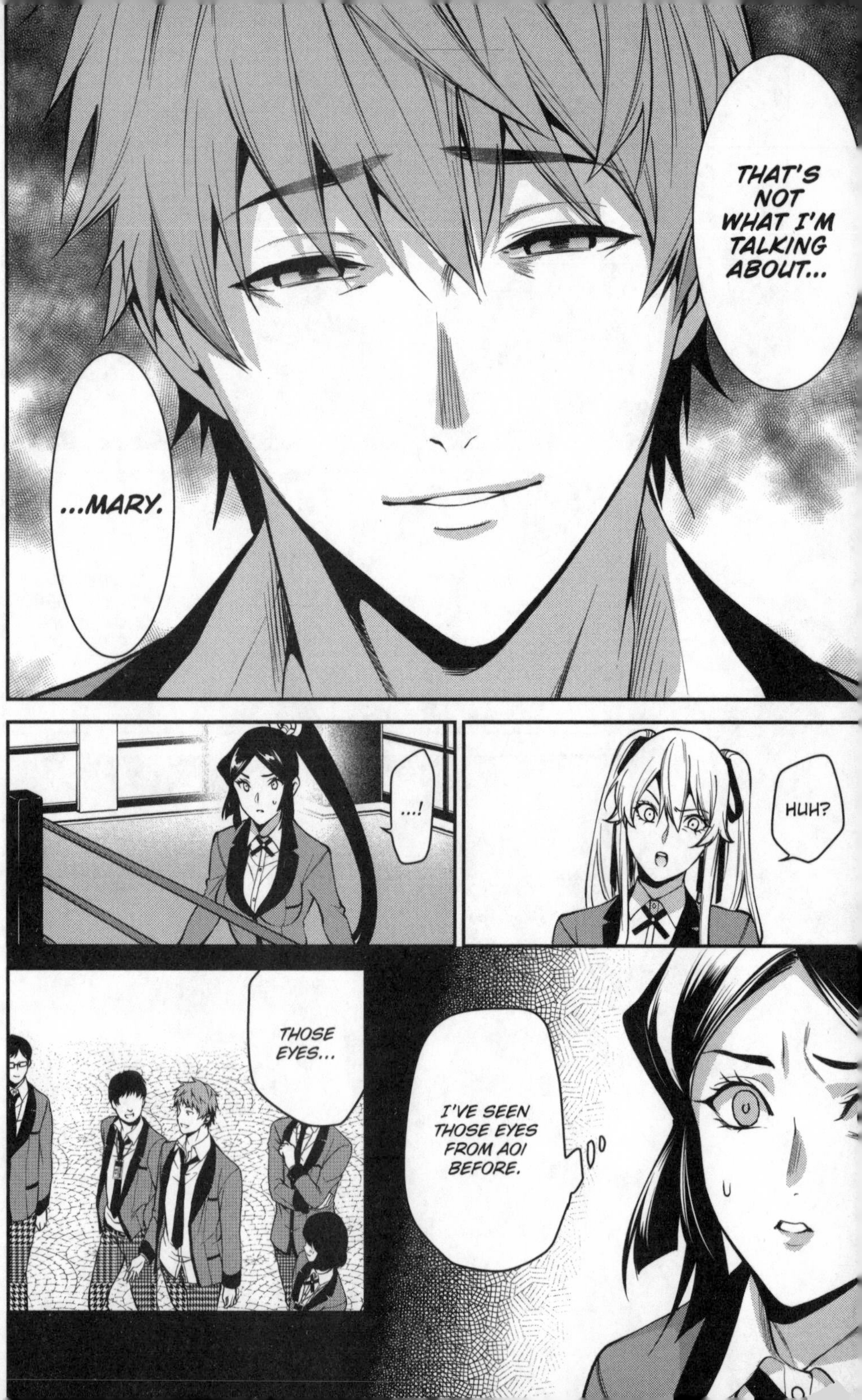
THAT'S NOT WHAT I'M TALKING ABOUT...
...MARY.
HUH?
...!
I'VE SEEN THOSE EYES FROM AOI BEFORE.
THOSE EYES...

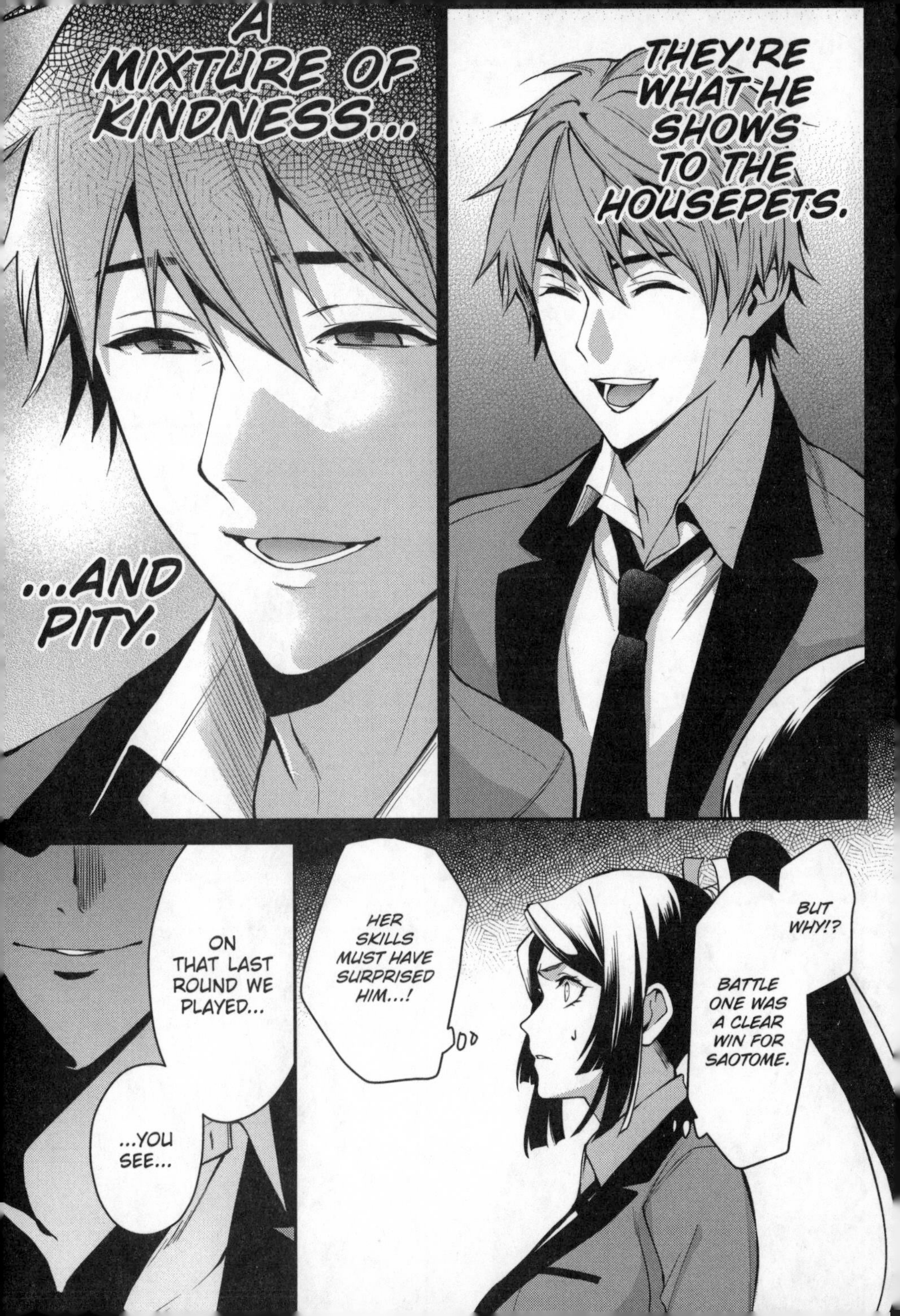
THEY'RE WHAT HE SHOWS TO THE HOUSEPETS.
A MIXTURE OF KINDNESS...
...AND PITY.
BUT WHY!?
BATTLE ONE WAS A CLEAR WIN FOR SAOTOME.
HER SKILLS MUST HAVE SURPRISED HIM...!
ON THAT LAST ROUND WE PLAYED...
...YOU SEE...

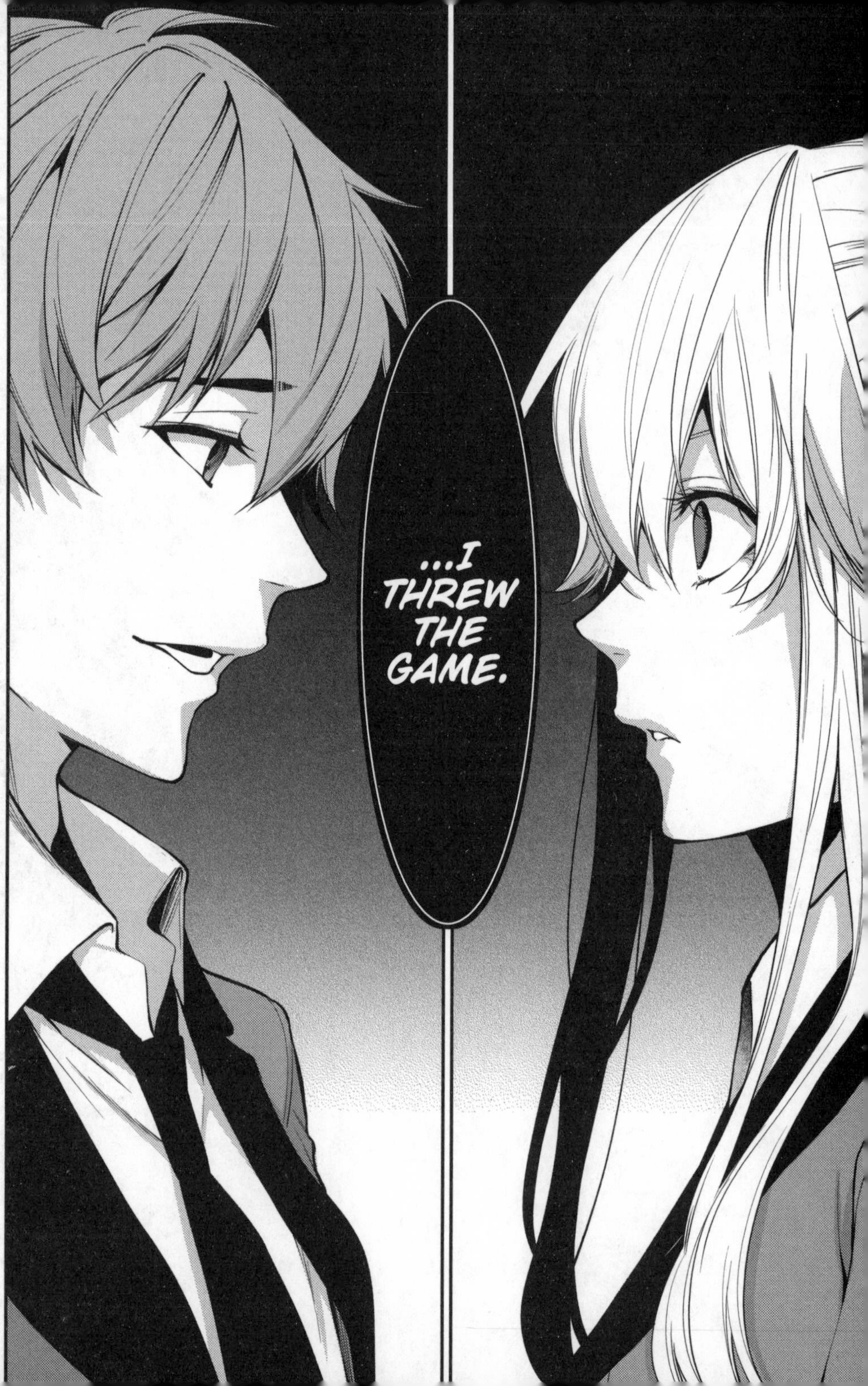
...I THREW THE GAME.

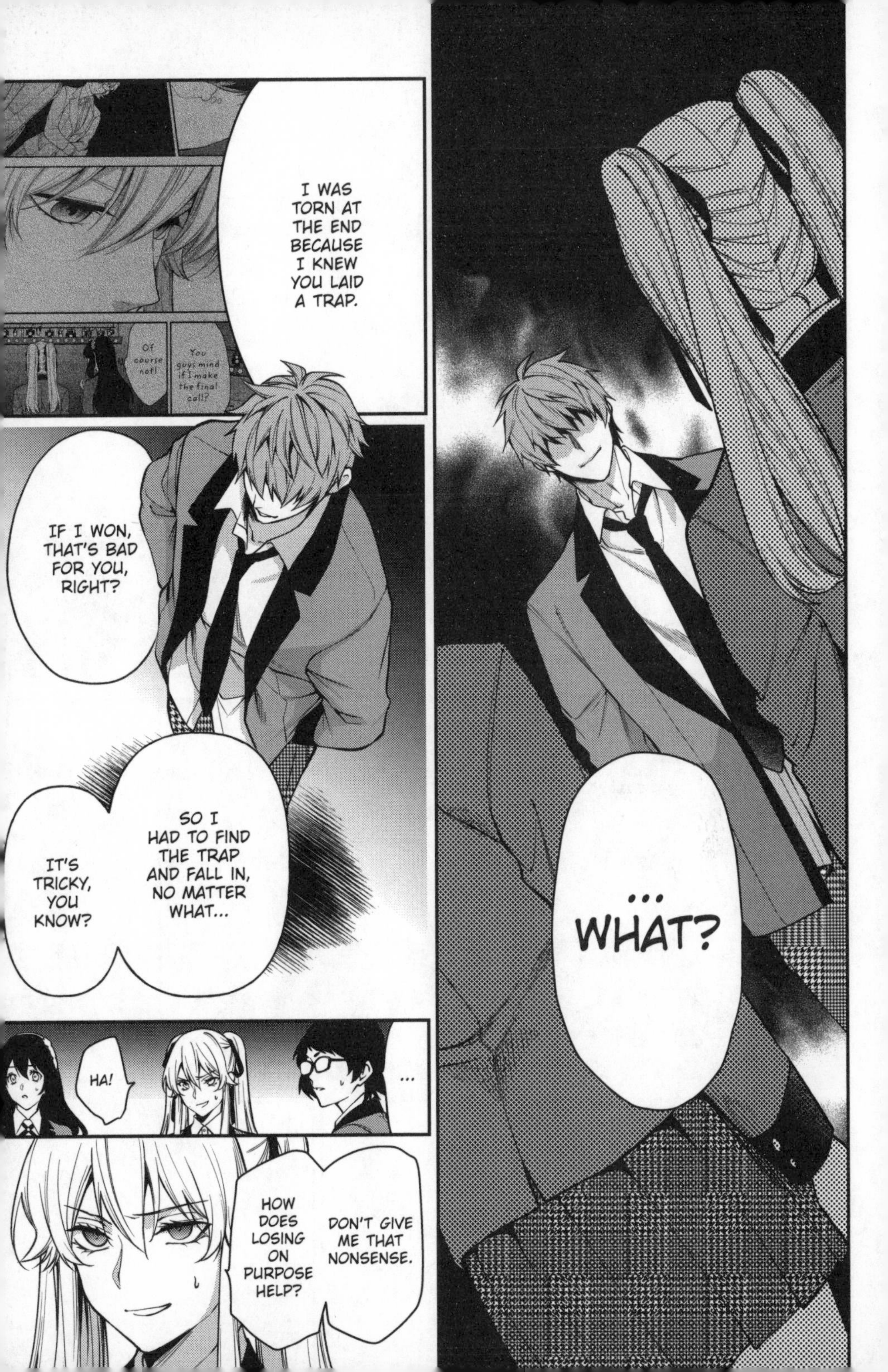
...WHAT?
I WAS TORN AT THE END BECAUSE I KNEW YOU LAID A TRAP.
You guys mind if I make the final call?
Of course not!
IF I WON, THAT'S BAD FOR YOU, RIGHT?
SO I HAD TO FIND THE TRAP AND FALL IN, NO MATTER WHAT...
IT'S TRICKY, YOU KNOW?
...
HA!
DON'T GIVE ME THAT NONSENSE.
HOW DOES LOSING ON PURPOSE HELP?

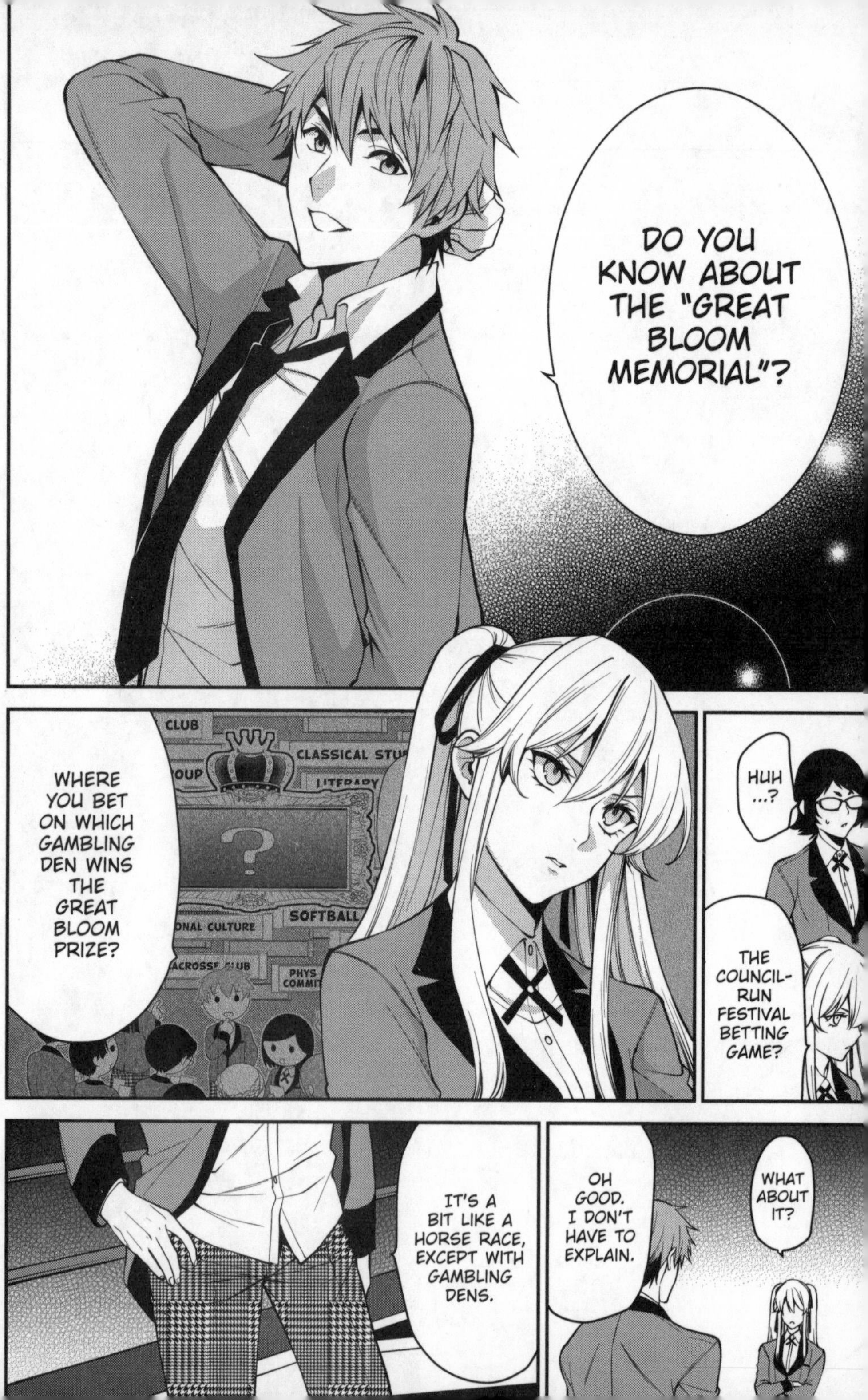
DO YOU KNOW ABOUT THE "GREAT BLOOM MEMORIAL"?
HUH ...?
THE COUNCIL-RUN FESTIVAL BETTING GAME?
CLUB
SOFTBALL
WHERE YOU BET ON WHICH GAMBLING DEN WINS THE GREAT BLOOM PRIZE?
WHAT ABOUT IT?
OH GOOD. I DON'T HAVE TO EXPLAIN.
IT'S A BIT LIKE A HORSE RACE, EXCEPT WITH GAMBLING DENS.

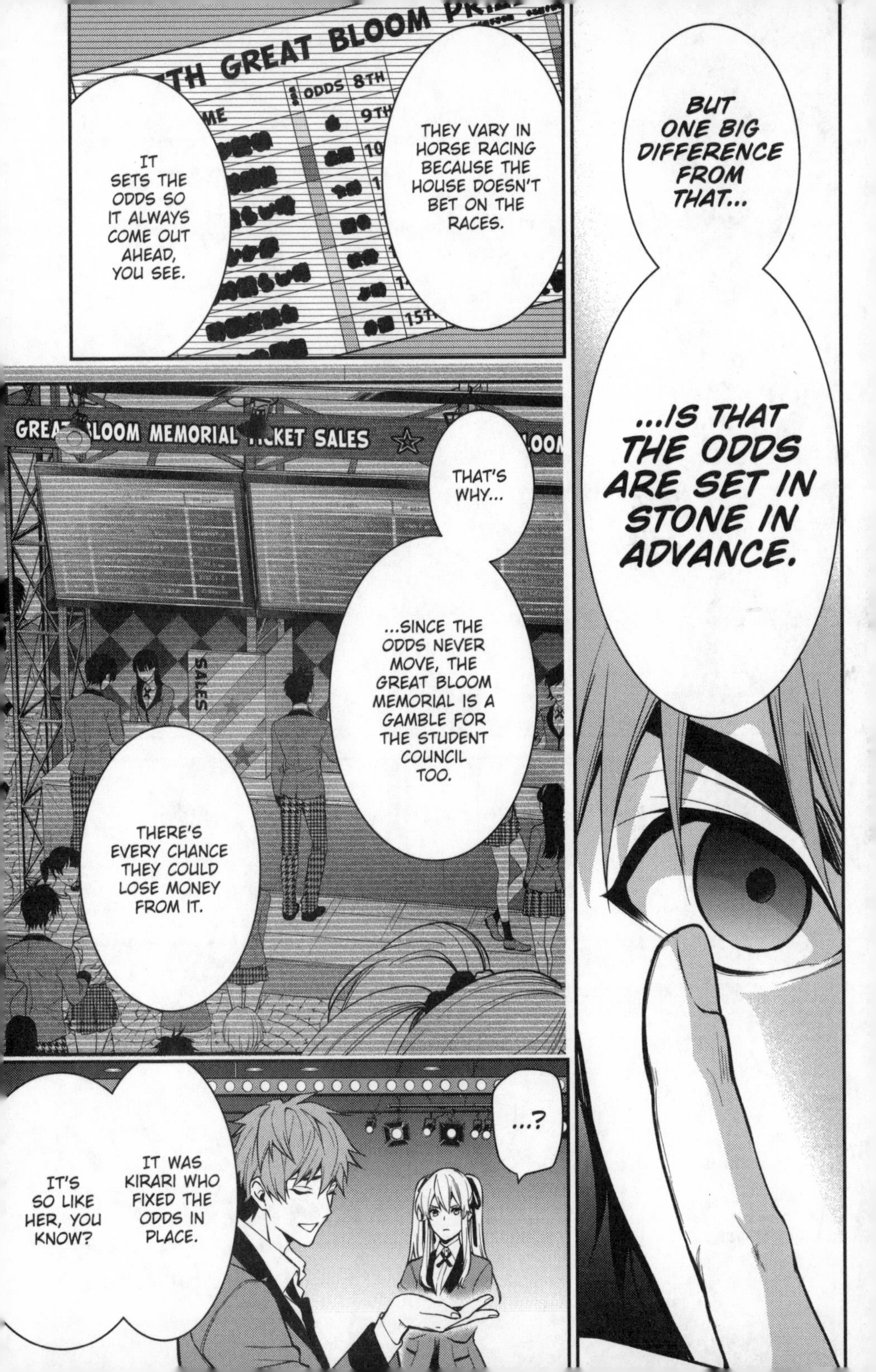
BUT ONE BIG DIFFERENCE FROM THAT...
...IS THAT THE ODDS ARE SET IN STONE IN ADVANCE.
THEY VARY IN HORSE RACING BECAUSE THE HOUSE DOESN'T BET ON THE RACES.
IT SETS THE ODDS SO IT ALWAYS COME OUT AHEAD, YOU SEE.
THAT'S WHY...
...SINCE THE ODDS NEVER MOVE, THE GREAT BLOOM MEMORIAL IS A GAMBLE FOR THE STUDENT COUNCIL TOO.
THERE'S EVERY CHANCE THEY COULD LOSE MONEY FROM IT.
SALES
...?
IT WAS KIRARI WHO FIXED THE ODDS IN PLACE.
IT'S SO LIKE HER, YOU KNOW?

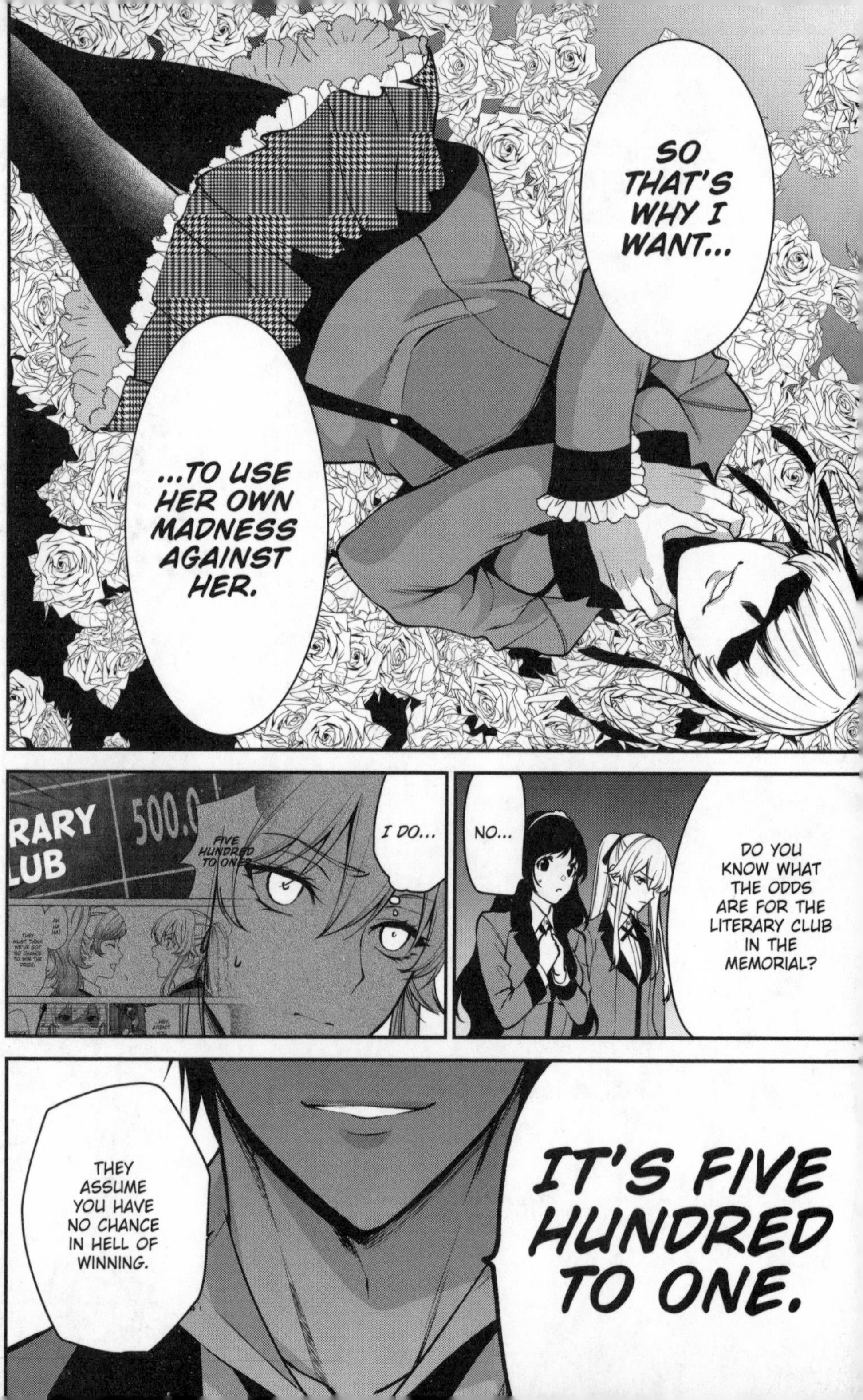
SO THAT'S WHY I WANT...
...TO USE HER OWN MADNESS AGAINST HER.
DO YOU KNOW WHAT THE ODDS ARE FOR THE LITERARY CLUB IN THE MEMORIAL?
NO...
I DO...
RARY
LUB
500.0
FIVE HUNDRED TO ONE
IT'S FIVE HUNDRED TO ONE.
THEY ASSUME YOU HAVE NO CHANCE IN HELL OF WINNING.

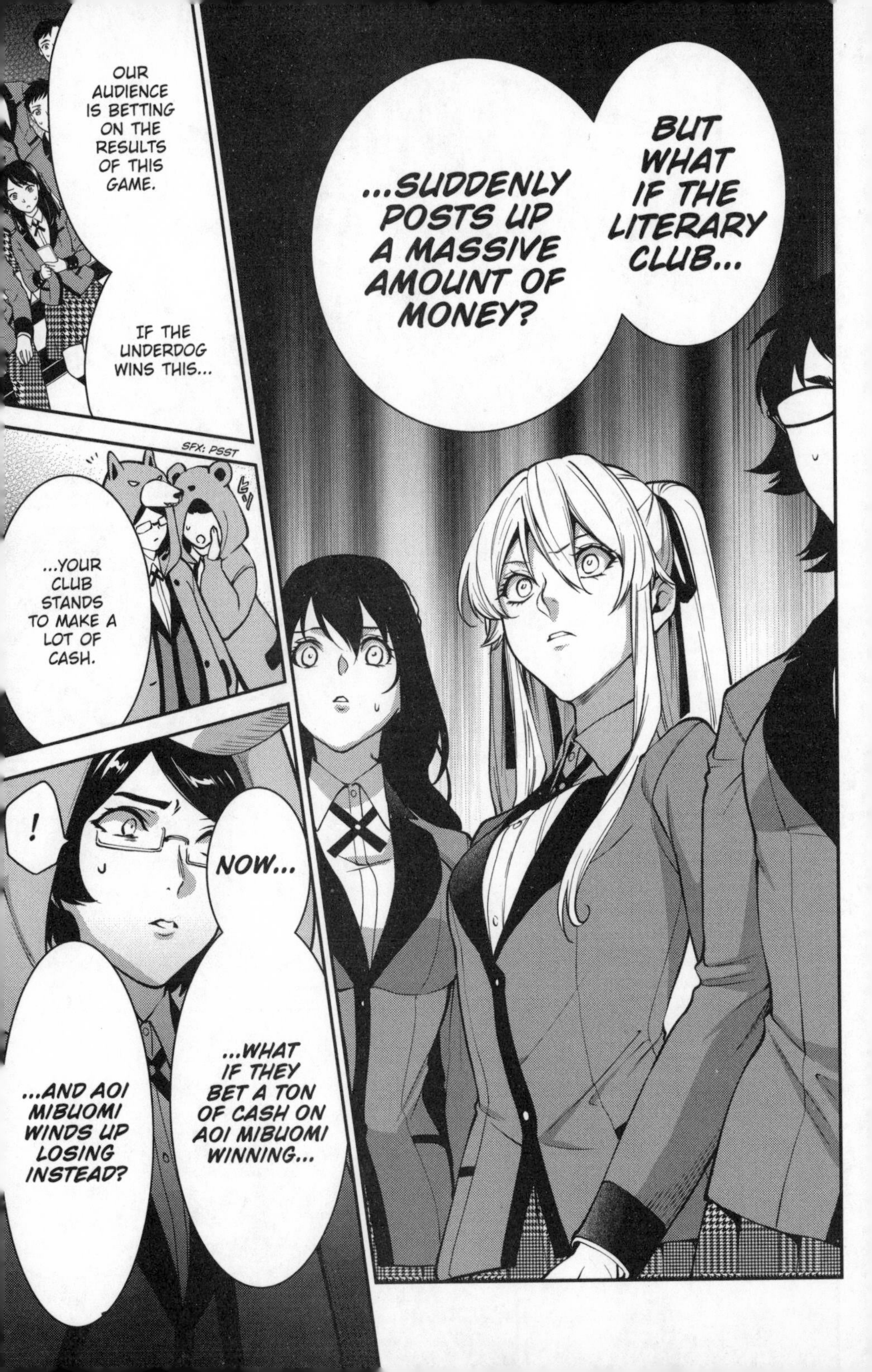
BUT WHAT IF THE LITERARY CLUB...
...SUDDENLY POSTS UP A MASSIVE AMOUNT OF MONEY?
OUR AUDIENCE IS BETTING ON THE RESULTS OF THIS GAME.
IF THE UNDERDOG WINS THIS...
SFX: PSST
...YOUR CLUB STANDS TO MAKE A LOT OF CASH.
!
NOW...
...WHAT IF THEY BET A TON OF CASH ON AOI MIBUOMI WINNING...
...AND AOI MIBUOMI WINDS UP LOSING INSTEAD?

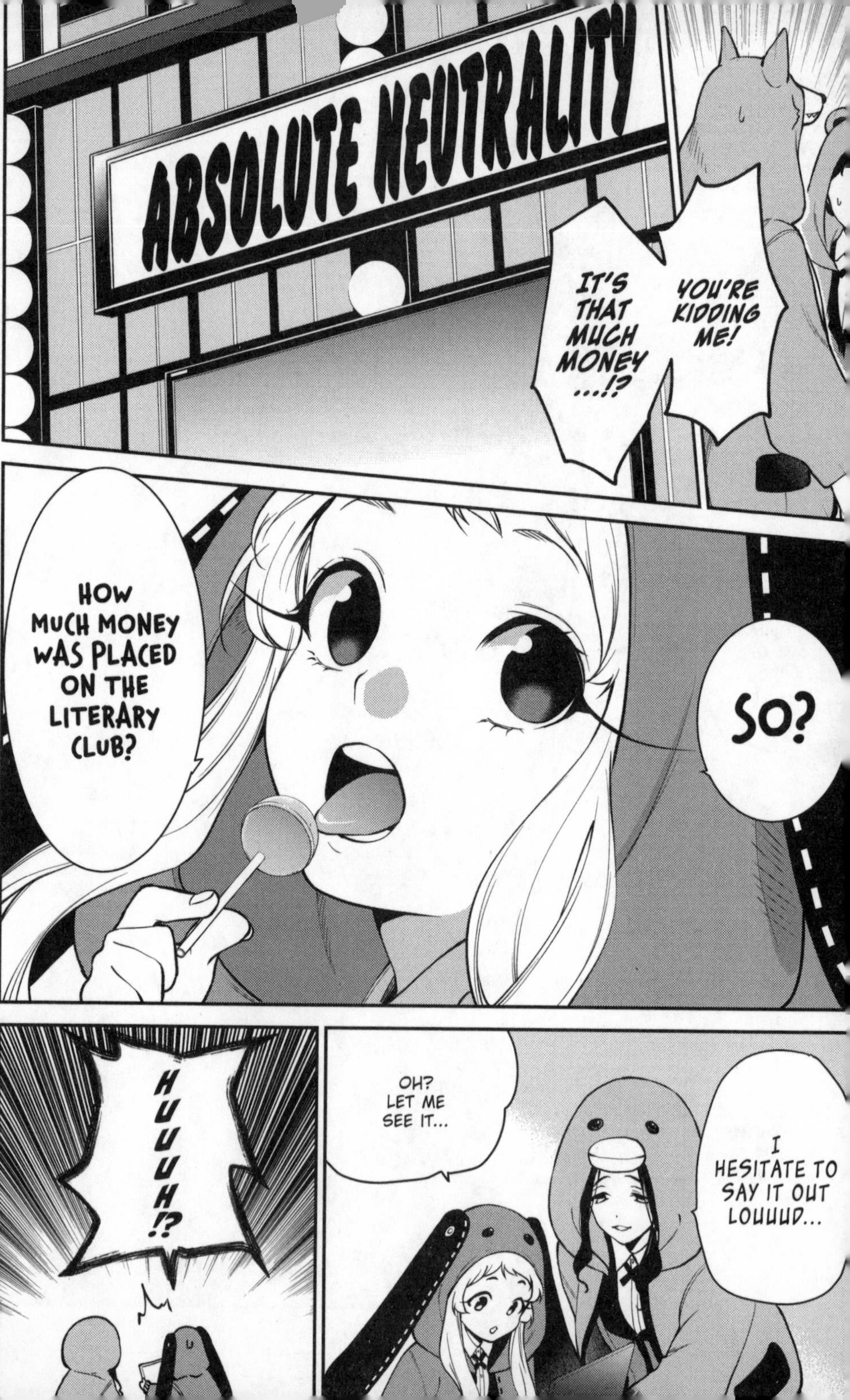
ABSOLUTE NEUTRALITY
YOU'RE KIDDING ME!
IT'S THAT MUCH MONEY ...!?
SO?
HOW MUCH MONEY WAS PLACED ON THE LITERARY CLUB?
I HESITATE TO SAY IT OUT LOUUUD...
OH? LET ME SEE IT...
HUUUUH!?

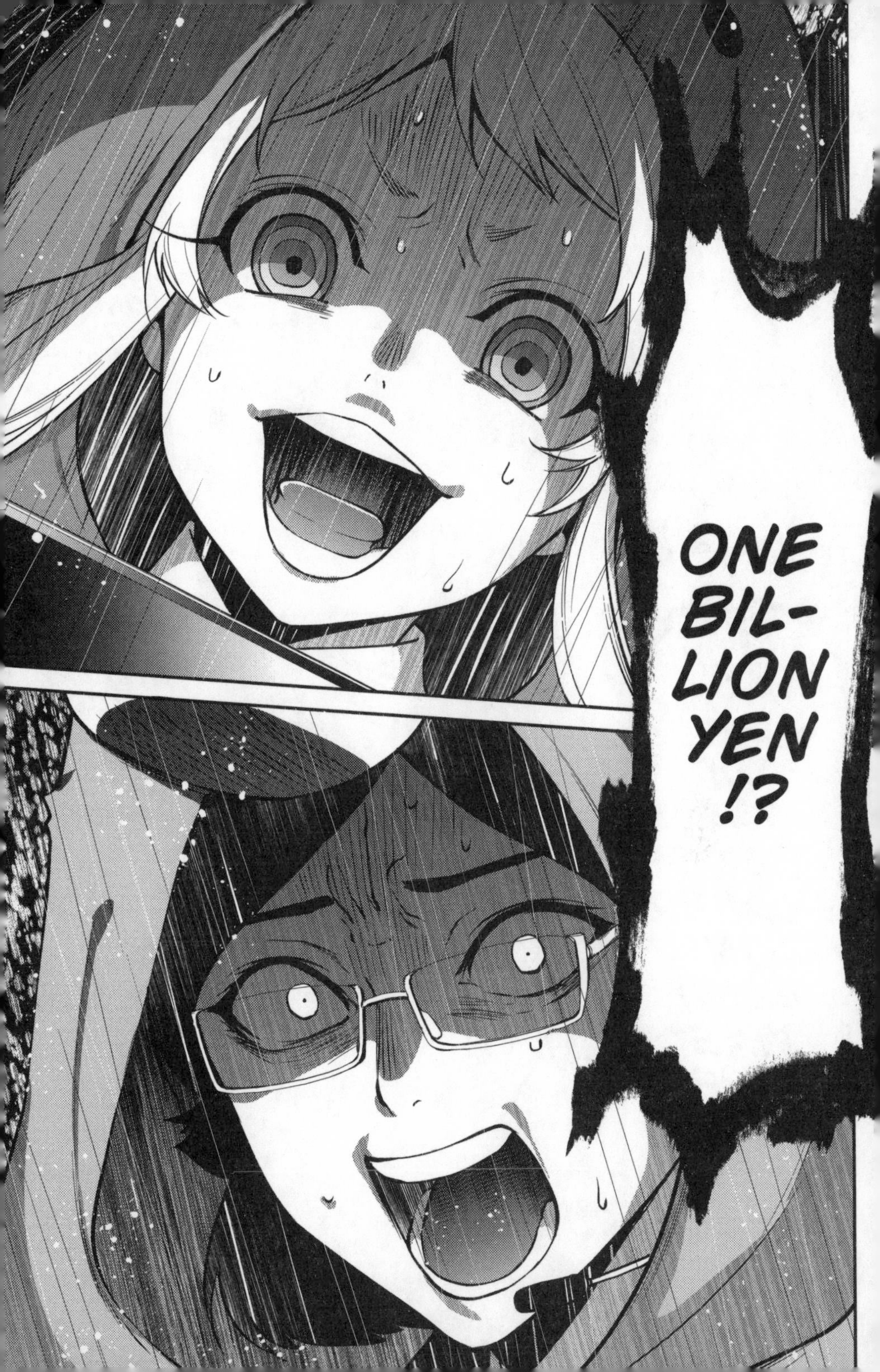
ONE BIL-LION YEN !?

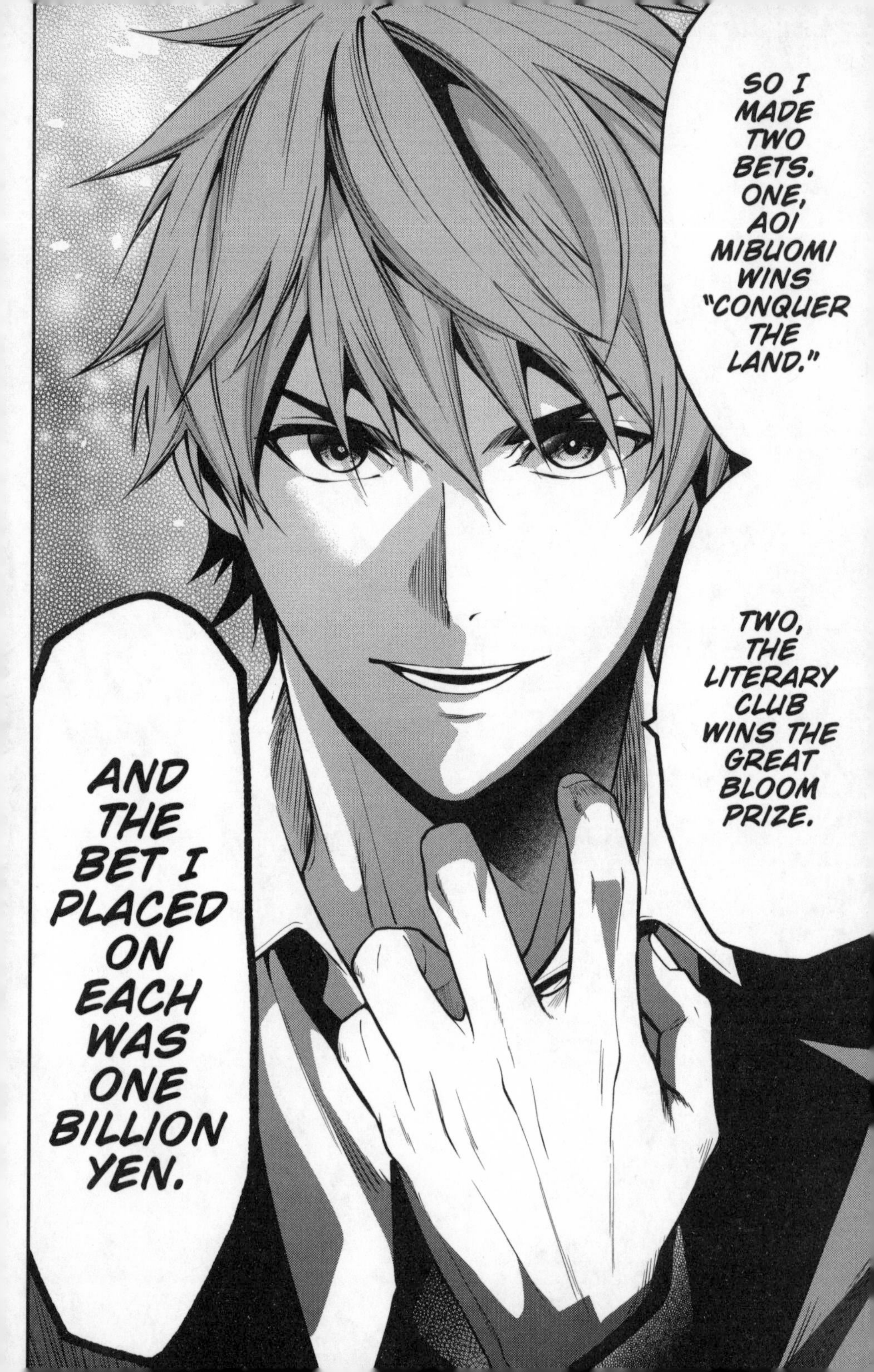
SO I MADE TWO BETS. ONE, AOI MIBUOMI WINS "CONQUER THE LAND."
TWO, THE LITERARY CLUB WINS THE GREAT BLOOM PRIZE.
AND THE BET I PLACED ON EACH WAS ONE BILLION YEN.

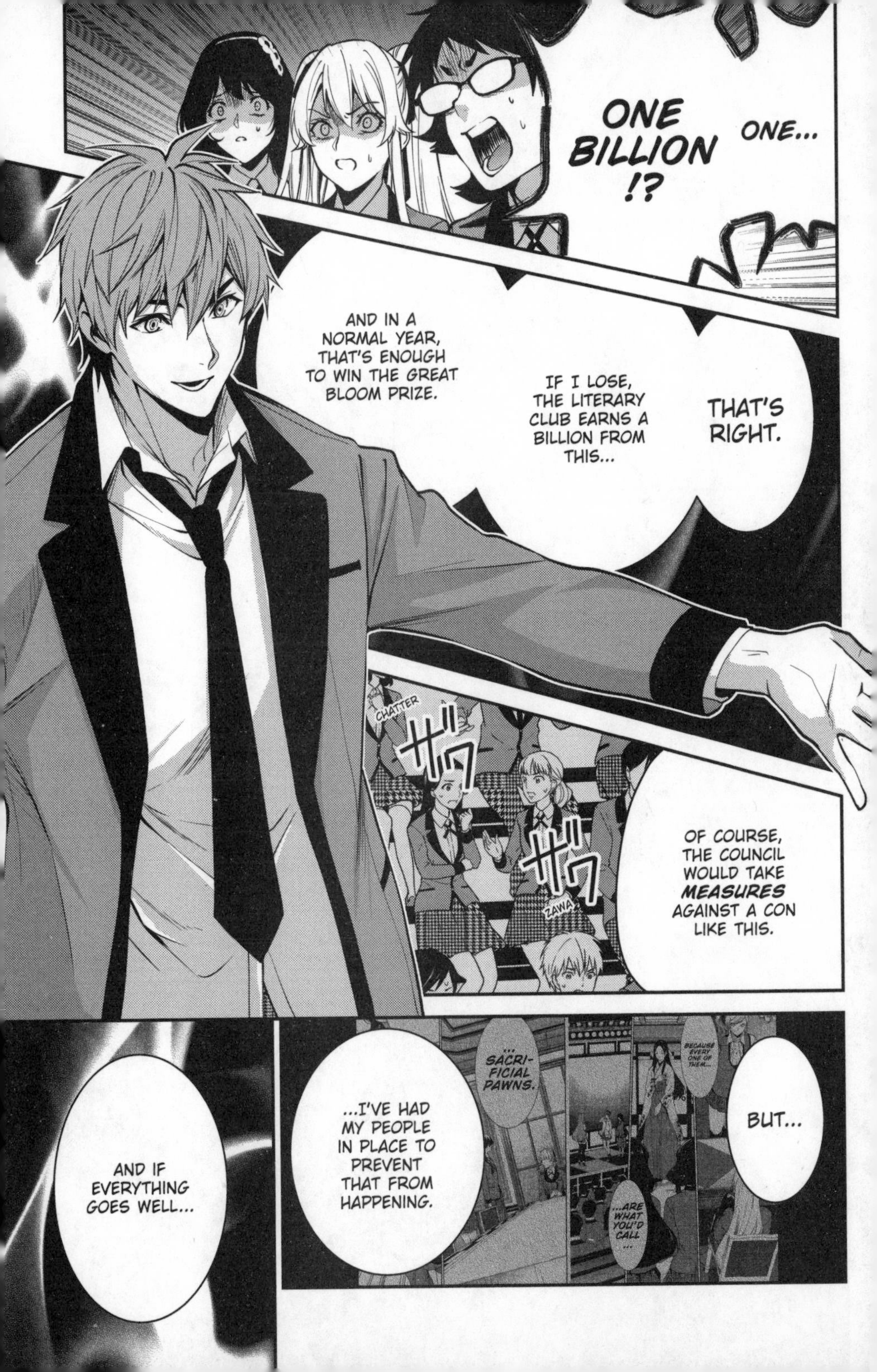
ONE...
ONE BILLION !?
THAT'S RIGHT.
IF I LOSE, THE LITERARY CLUB EARNS A BILLION FROM THIS...
AND IN A NORMAL YEAR, THAT'S ENOUGH TO WIN THE GREAT BLOOM PRIZE.
OF COURSE, THE COUNCIL WOULD TAKE *MEASURES* AGAINST A CON LIKE THIS.
ザワ
ZAWA
ザワ
CHATTER
BUT...
BECAUSE EVERY ONE OF THEM...
...ARE WHAT YOU'D CALL...
...SACRIFICIAL PAWNS.
...I'VE HAD MY PEOPLE IN PLACE TO PREVENT THAT FROM HAPPENING.
AND IF EVERYTHING GOES WELL...

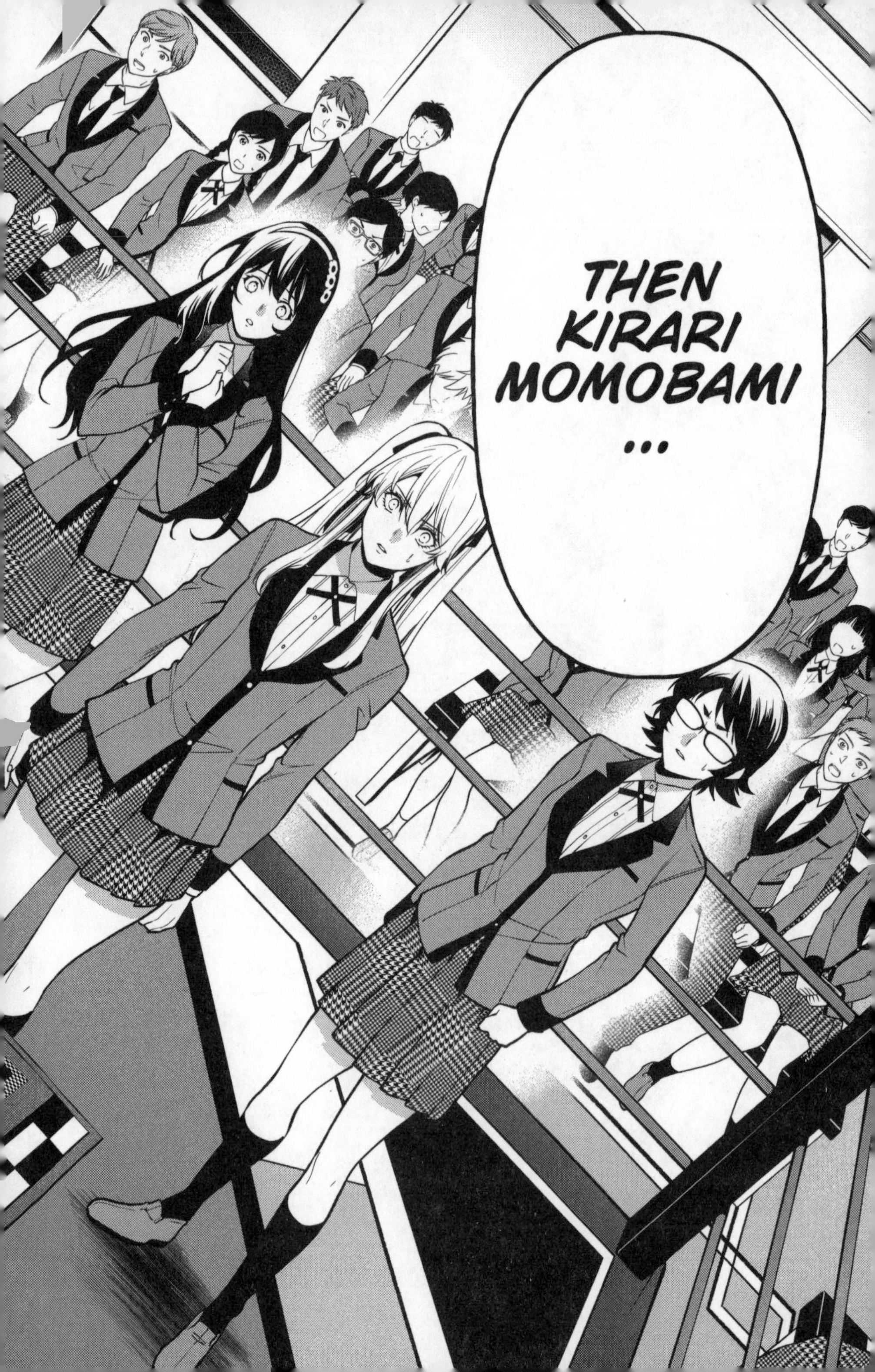
THEN KIRARI MOMOBAMI ...

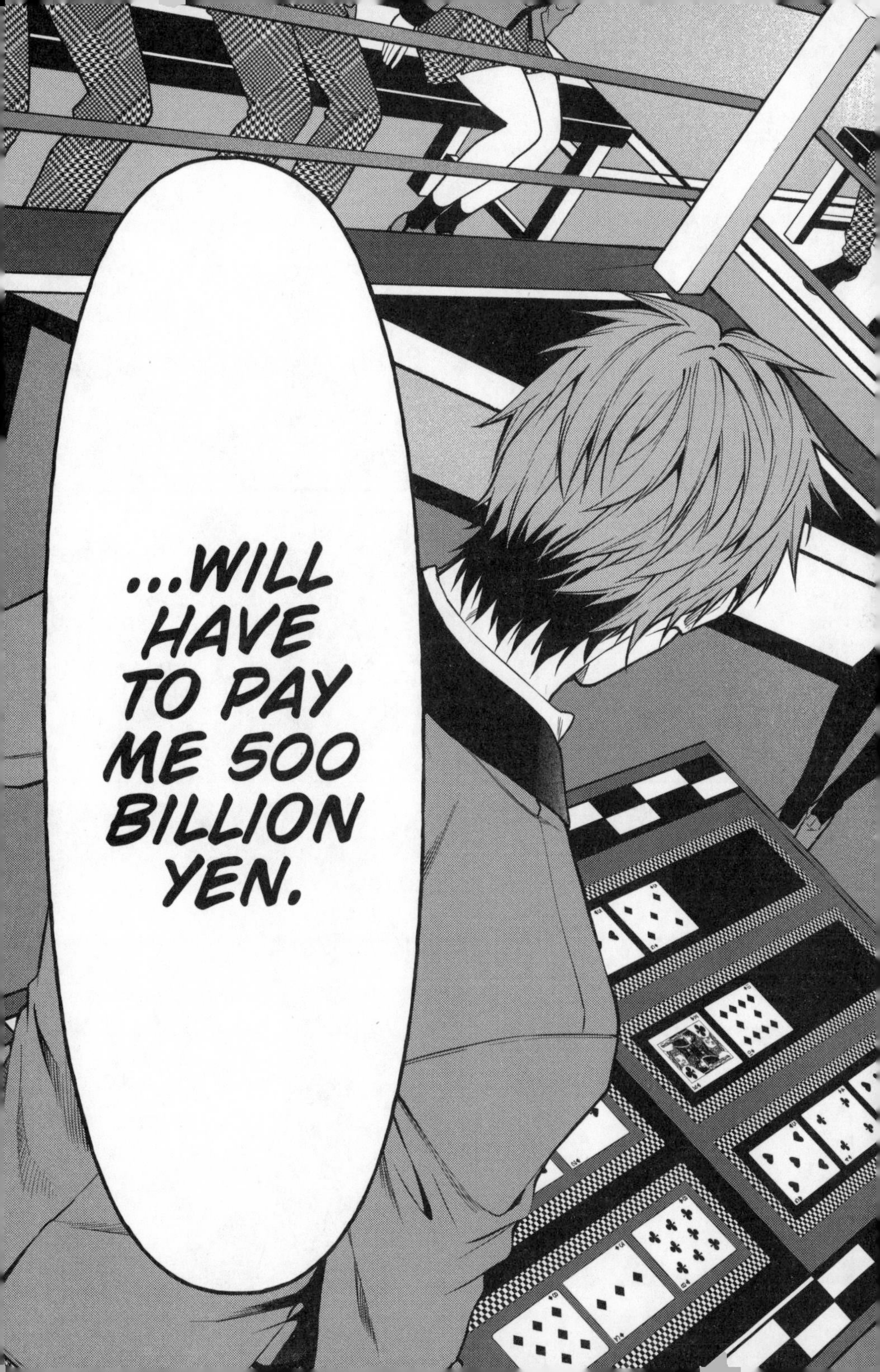
...WILL HAVE TO PAY ME 500 BILLION YEN.

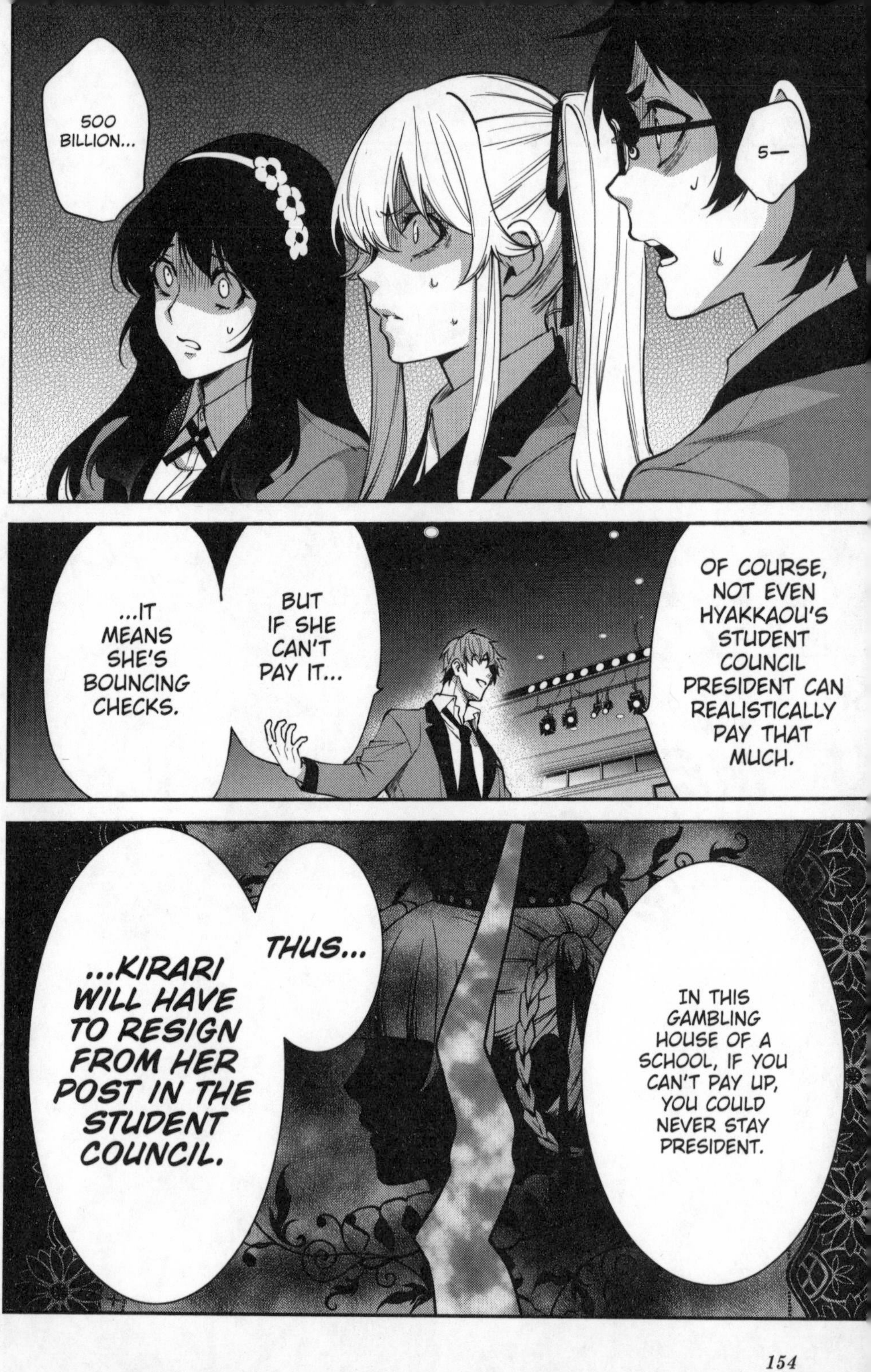
S—
500 BILLION...
OF COURSE, NOT EVEN HYAKKAOU'S STUDENT COUNCIL PRESIDENT CAN REALISTICALLY PAY THAT MUCH.
BUT IF SHE CAN'T PAY IT...
...IT MEANS SHE'S BOUNCING CHECKS.
IN THIS GAMBLING HOUSE OF A SCHOOL, IF YOU CAN'T PAY UP, YOU COULD NEVER STAY PRESIDENT.
THUS...
...KIRARI WILL HAVE TO RESIGN FROM HER POST IN THE STUDENT COUNCIL.

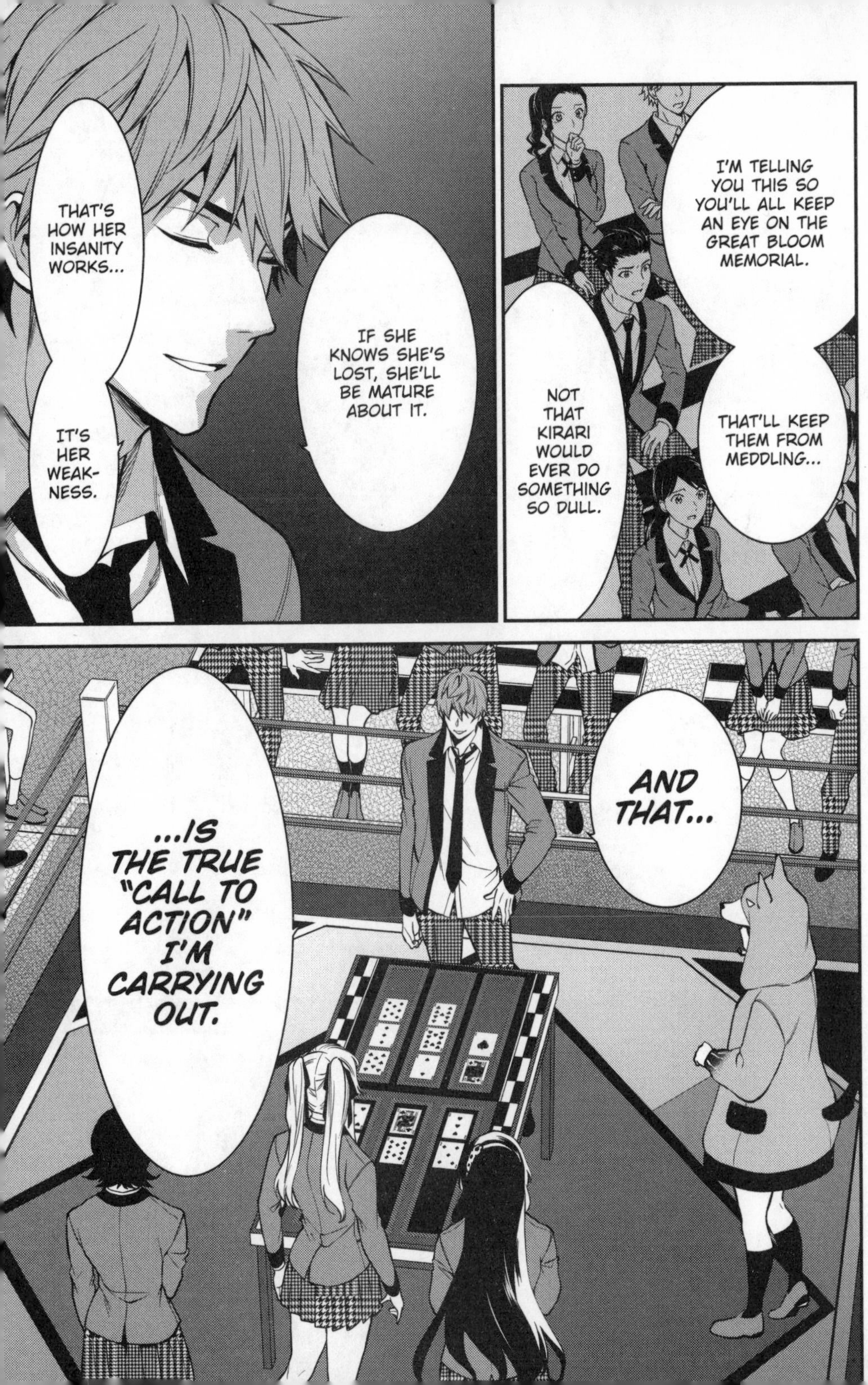
I'M TELLING YOU THIS SO YOU'LL ALL KEEP AN EYE ON THE GREAT BLOOM MEMORIAL.
THAT'LL KEEP THEM FROM MEDDLING...
NOT THAT KIRARI WOULD EVER DO SOMETHING SO DULL.
IF SHE KNOWS SHE'S LOST, SHE'LL BE MATURE ABOUT IT.
THAT'S HOW HER INSANITY WORKS...
IT'S HER WEAK-NESS.
AND THAT...
...IS THE TRUE "CALL TO ACTION" I'M CARRYING OUT.

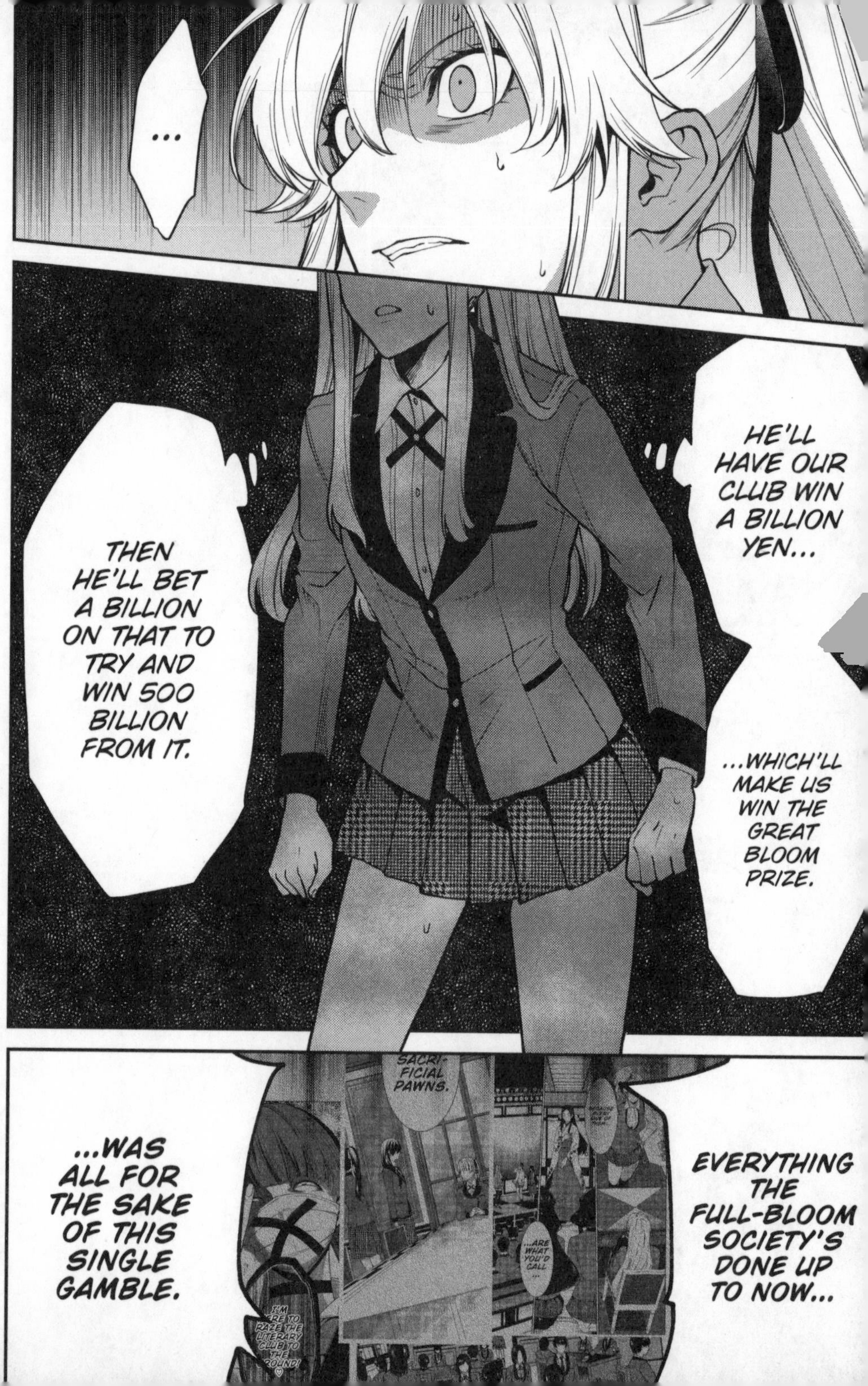
...
HE'LL HAVE OUR CLUB WIN A BILLION YEN...
...WHICH'LL MAKE US WIN THE GREAT BLOOM PRIZE.
THEN HE'LL BET A BILLION ON THAT TO TRY AND WIN 500 BILLION FROM IT.
EVERYTHING THE FULL-BLOOM SOCIETY'S DONE UP TO NOW...
...ARE WHAT YOU'D CALL...
SACRIFICIAL PAWNS.
...WAS ALL FOR THE SAKE OF THIS SINGLE GAMBLE.

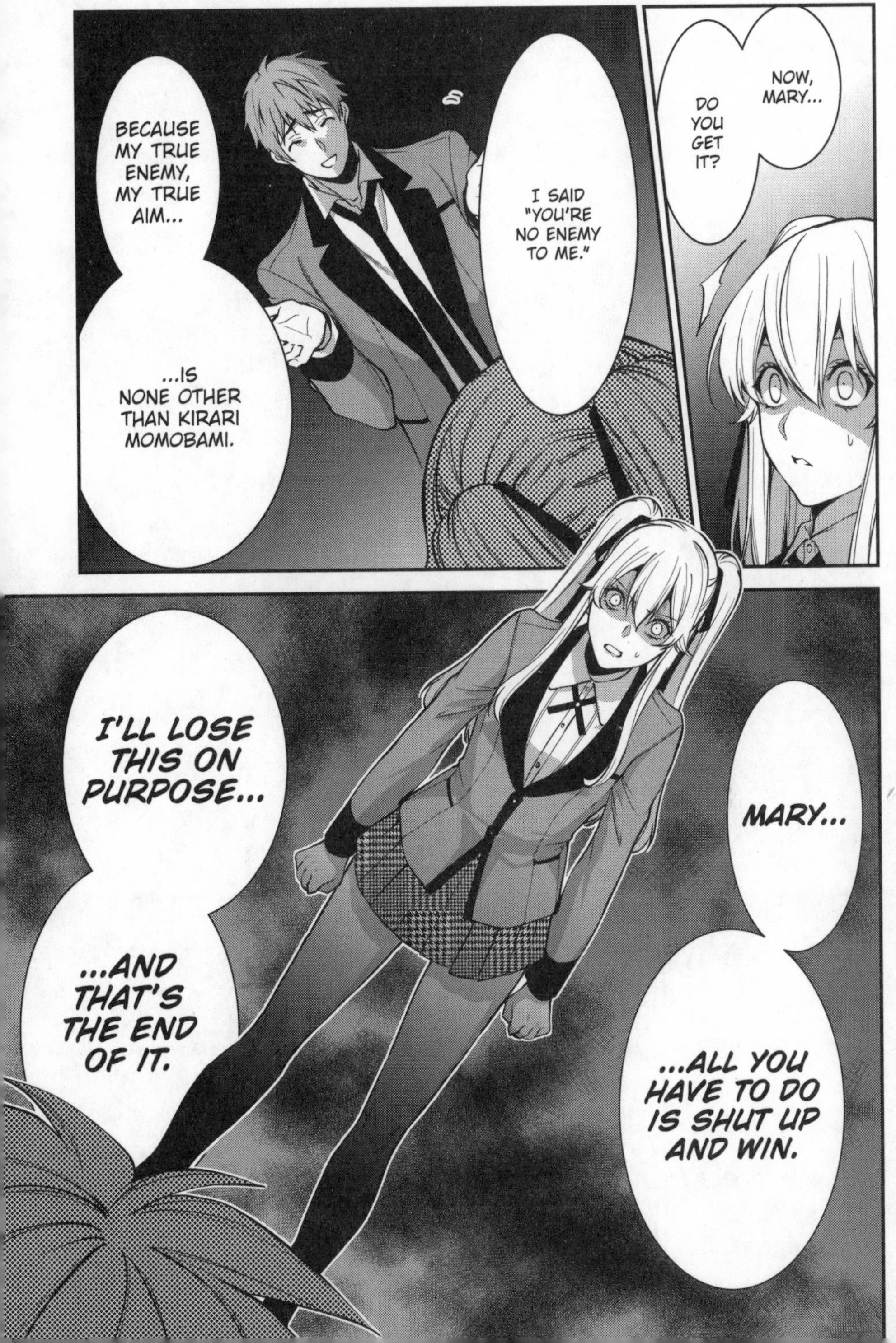
NOW, MARY...
DO YOU GET IT?
I SAID "YOU'RE NO ENEMY TO ME."
BECAUSE MY TRUE ENEMY, MY TRUE AIM...
...IS NONE OTHER THAN KIRARI MOMOBAMI.
MARY...
...ALL YOU HAVE TO DO IS SHUT UP AND WIN.
I'LL LOSE THIS ON PURPOSE...
...AND THAT'S THE END OF IT.

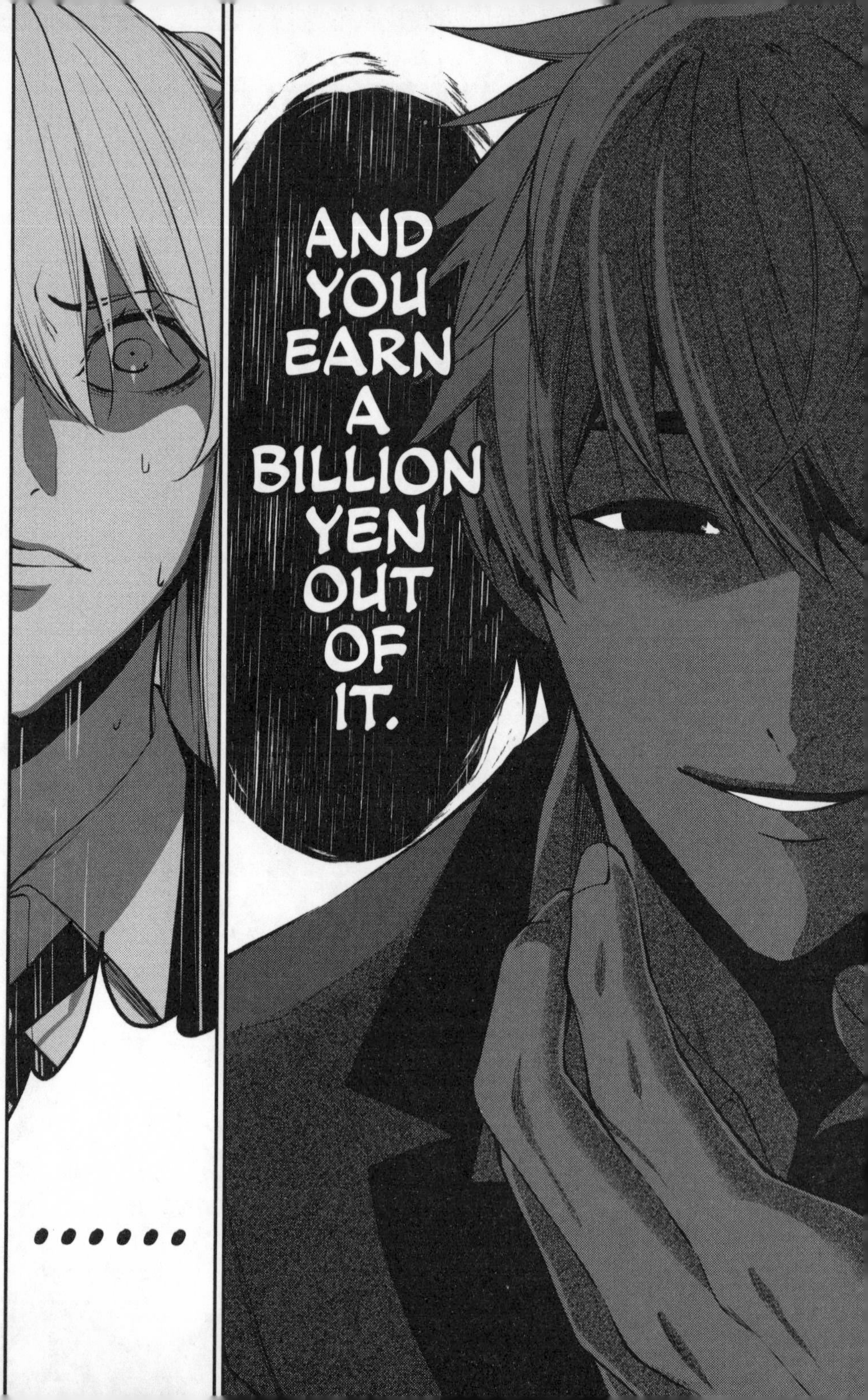
AND YOU EARN A BILLION YEN OUT OF IT.
......

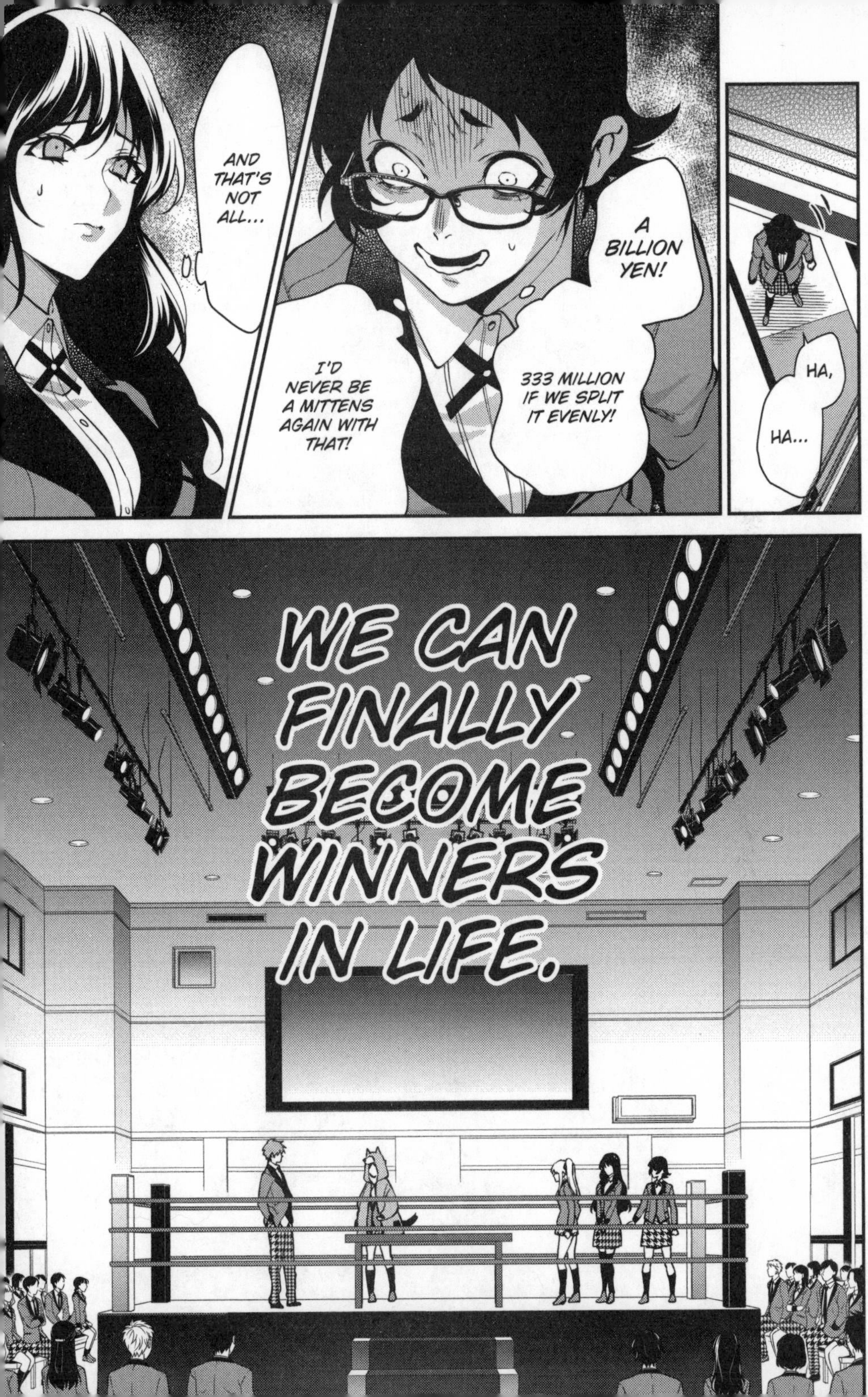
HA,
HA...
A BILLION YEN!
333 MILLION IF WE SPLIT IT EVENLY!
I'D NEVER BE A MITTENS AGAIN WITH THAT!
AND THAT'S NOT ALL...
WE CAN FINALLY BECOME WINNERS IN LIFE.

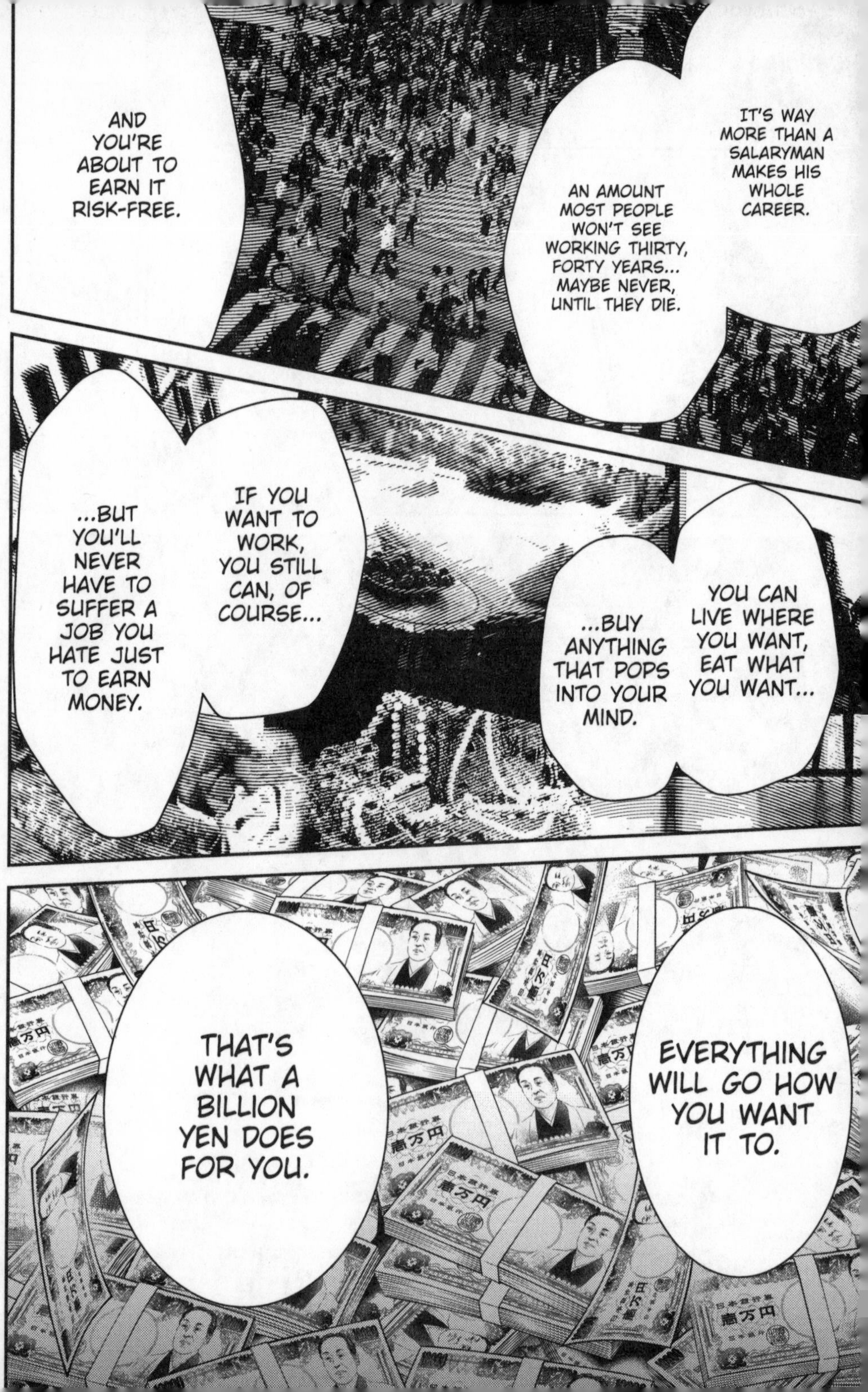
IT'S WAY MORE THAN A SALARYMAN MAKES HIS WHOLE CAREER.
AN AMOUNT MOST PEOPLE WON'T SEE WORKING THIRTY, FORTY YEARS... MAYBE NEVER, UNTIL THEY DIE.
AND YOU'RE ABOUT TO EARN IT RISK-FREE.
YOU CAN LIVE WHERE YOU WANT, EAT WHAT YOU WANT...
...BUY ANYTHING THAT POPS INTO YOUR MIND.
IF YOU WANT TO WORK, YOU STILL CAN, OF COURSE...
...BUT YOU'LL NEVER HAVE TO SUFFER A JOB YOU HATE JUST TO EARN MONEY.
EVERYTHING WILL GO HOW YOU WANT IT TO.
THAT'S WHAT A BILLION YEN DOES FOR YOU.

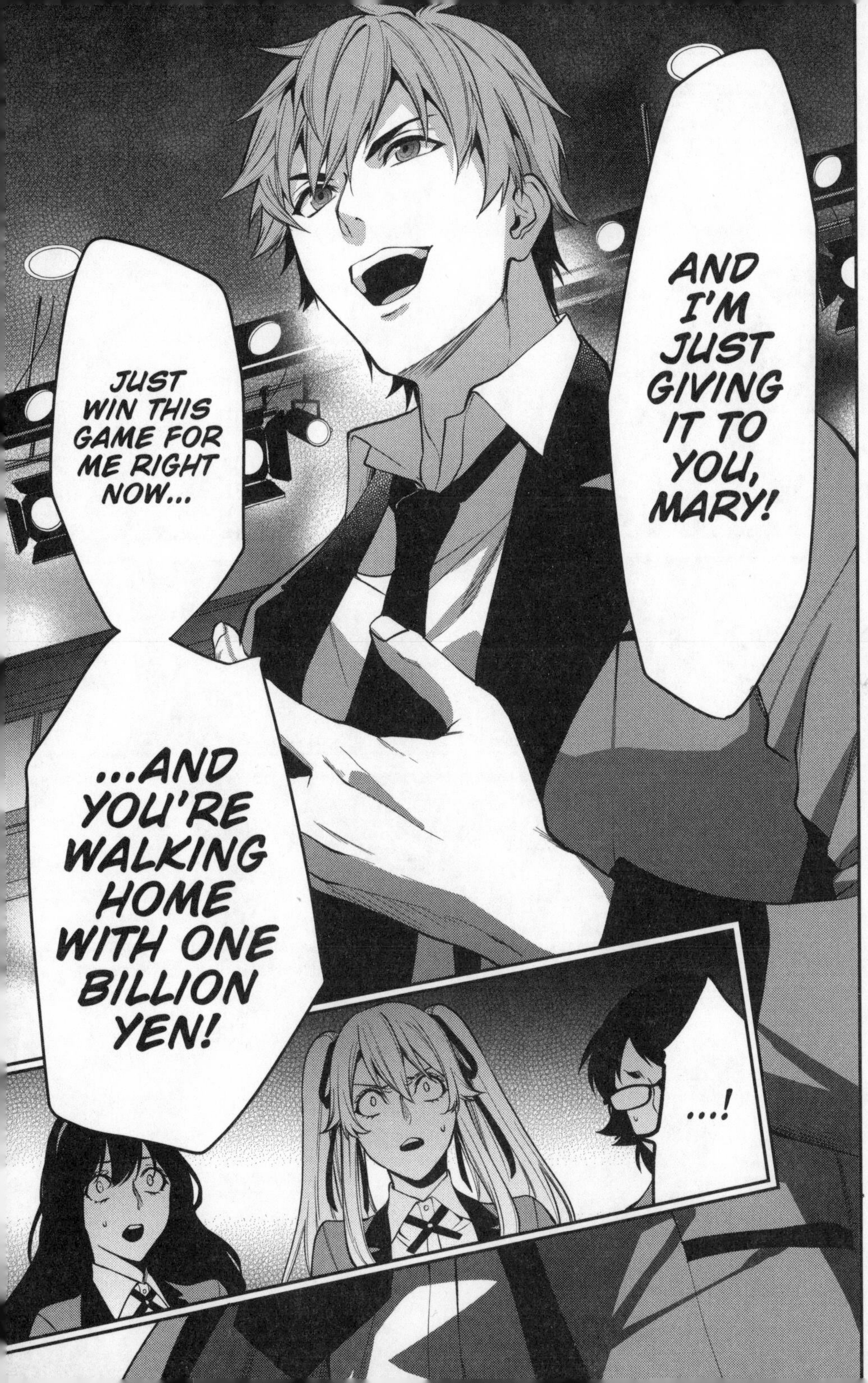
AND I'M JUST GIVING IT TO YOU, MARY!
JUST WIN THIS GAME FOR ME RIGHT NOW...
...AND YOU'RE WALKING HOME WITH ONE BILLION YEN!
...!

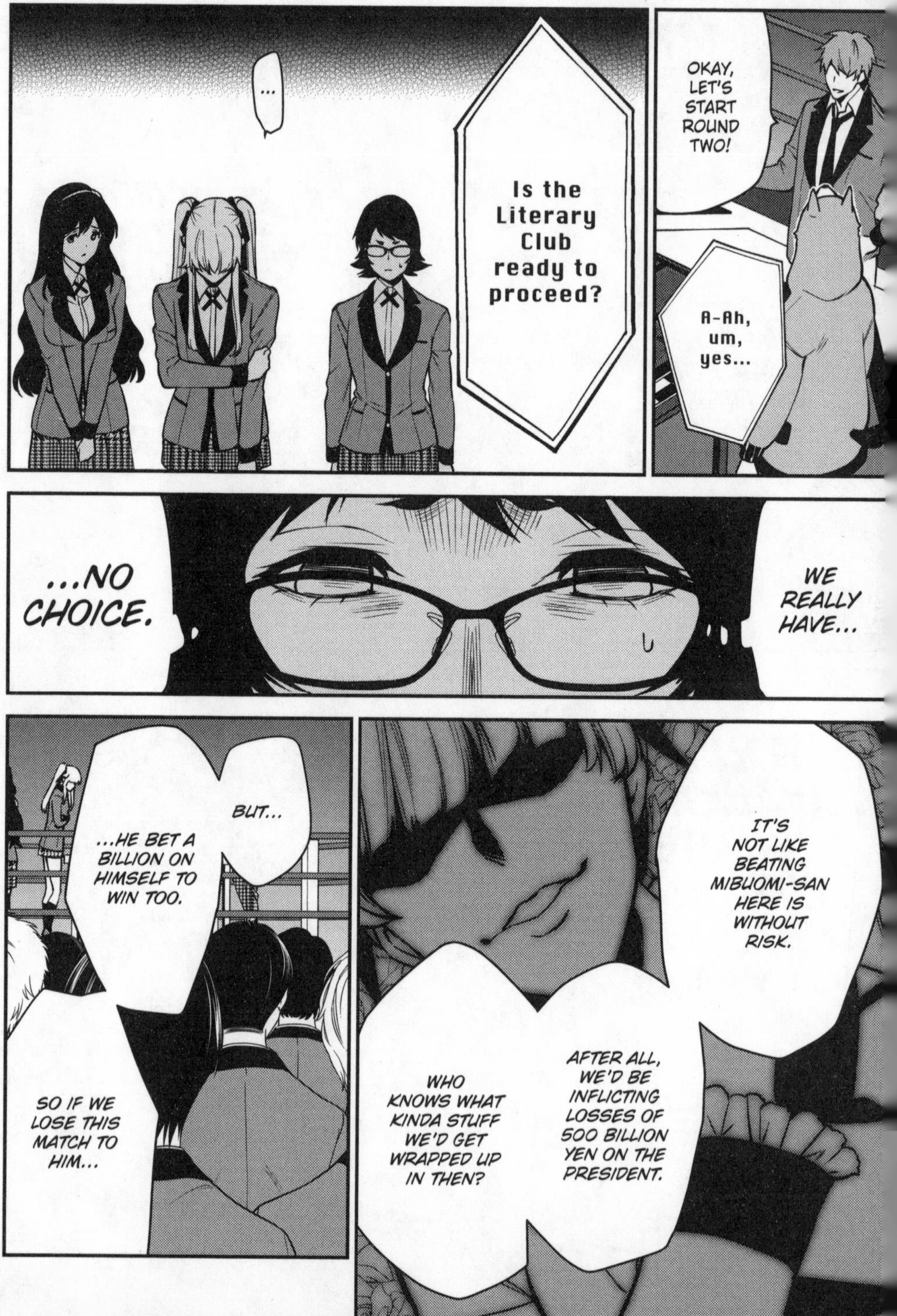
OKAY, LET'S START ROUND TWO!
A-Ah, um, yes...
Is the Literary Club ready to proceed?
...
WE REALLY HAVE...
...NO CHOICE.
IT'S NOT LIKE BEATING MIBUOMI-SAN HERE IS WITHOUT RISK.
AFTER ALL, WE'D BE INFLICTING LOSSES OF 500 BILLION YEN ON THE PRESIDENT.
WHO KNOWS WHAT KINDA STUFF WE'D GET WRAPPED UP IN THEN?
BUT...
...HE BET A BILLION ON HIMSELF TO WIN TOO.
SO IF WE LOSE THIS MATCH TO HIM...

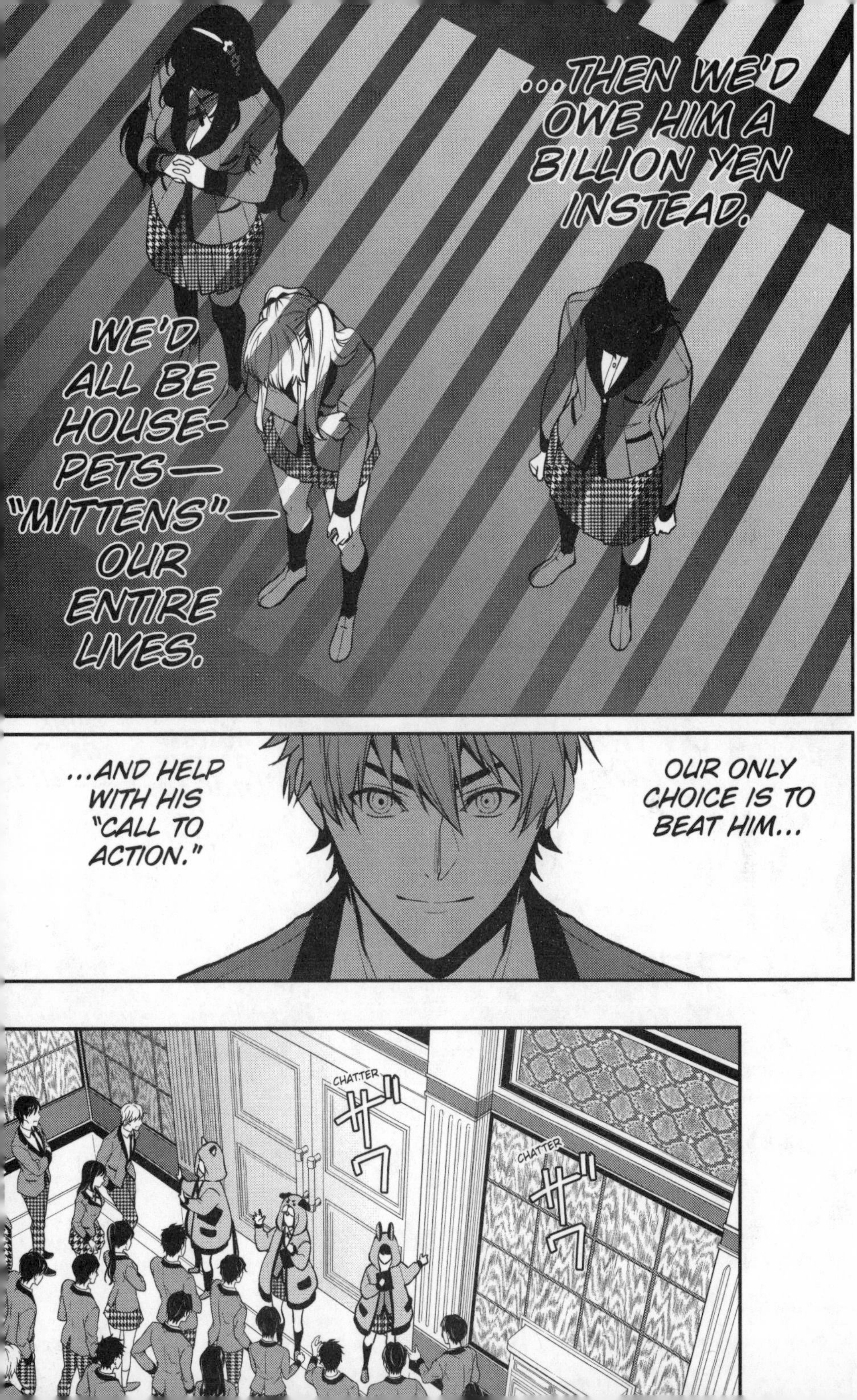
...THEN WE'D OWE HIM A BILLION YEN INSTEAD.
WE'D ALL BE HOUSE-PETS—"MITTENS"—OUR ENTIRE LIVES.
OUR ONLY CHOICE IS TO BEAT HIM...
...AND HELP WITH HIS "CALL TO ACTION."
CHATTER
ザワ
CHATTER
ザワ

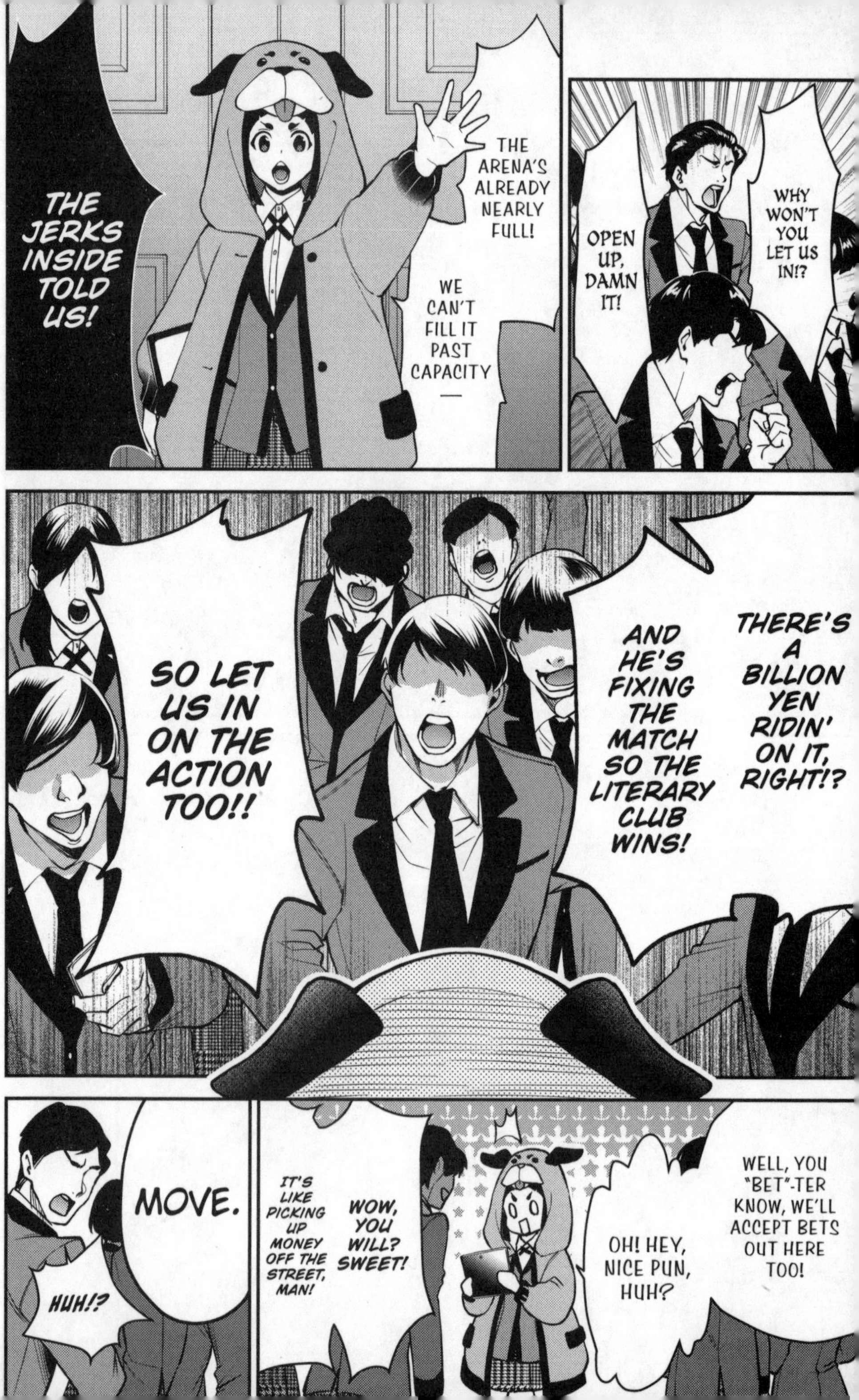
WHY WON'T YOU LET US IN!?
OPEN UP, DAMN IT!
THE ARENA'S ALREADY NEARLY FULL!
WE CAN'T FILL IT PAST CAPACITY —
THE JERKS INSIDE TOLD US!
THERE'S A BILLION YEN RIDIN' ON IT, RIGHT!?
AND HE'S FIXING THE MATCH SO THE LITERARY CLUB WINS!
SO LET US IN ON THE ACTION TOO!!
WELL, YOU "BET"-TER KNOW, WE'LL ACCEPT BETS OUT HERE TOO!
OH! HEY, NICE PUN, HUH?
WOW, YOU WILL? SWEET!
IT'S LIKE PICKING UP MONEY OFF THE STREET, MAN!
MOVE.
HUH!?

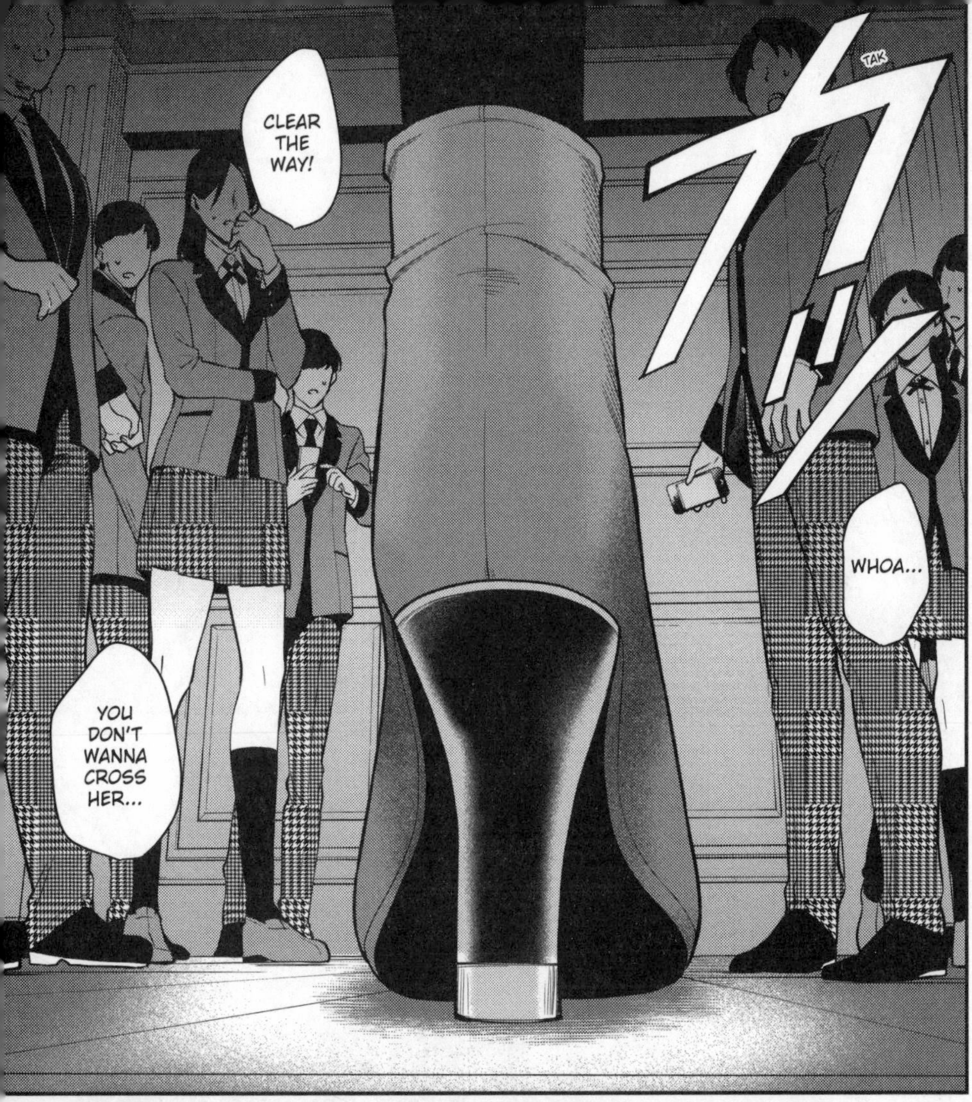
TAK
CLEAR THE WAY!
WHOA...
YOU DON'T WANNA CROSS HER...
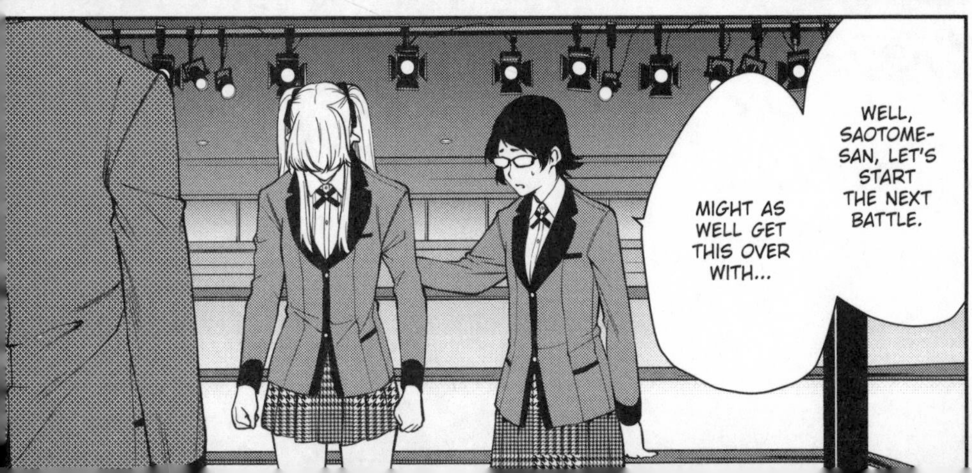
WELL, SAOTOME-SAN, LET'S START THE NEXT BATTLE.
MIGHT AS WELL GET THIS OVER WITH...

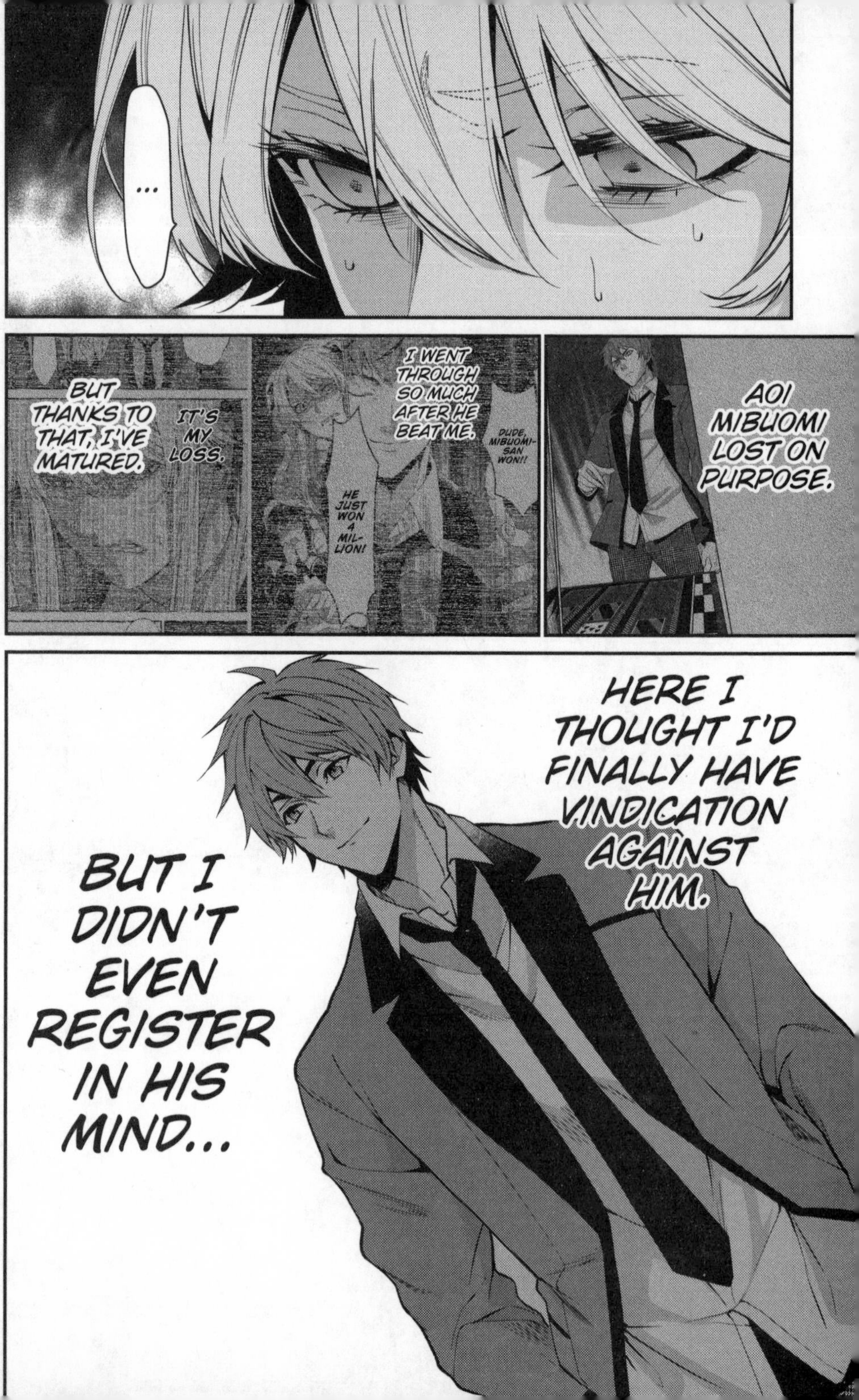
...
AOI MIBUOMI LOST ON PURPOSE.
I WENT THROUGH SO MUCH AFTER HE BEAT ME.
DUDE, MIBUOMI-SAN WON!!
HE JUST WON 4 MILLION!
IT'S MY LOSS.
BUT THANKS TO THAT, I'VE MATURED.
HERE I THOUGHT I'D FINALLY HAVE VINDICATION AGAINST HIM.
BUT I DIDN'T EVEN REGISTER IN HIS MIND...

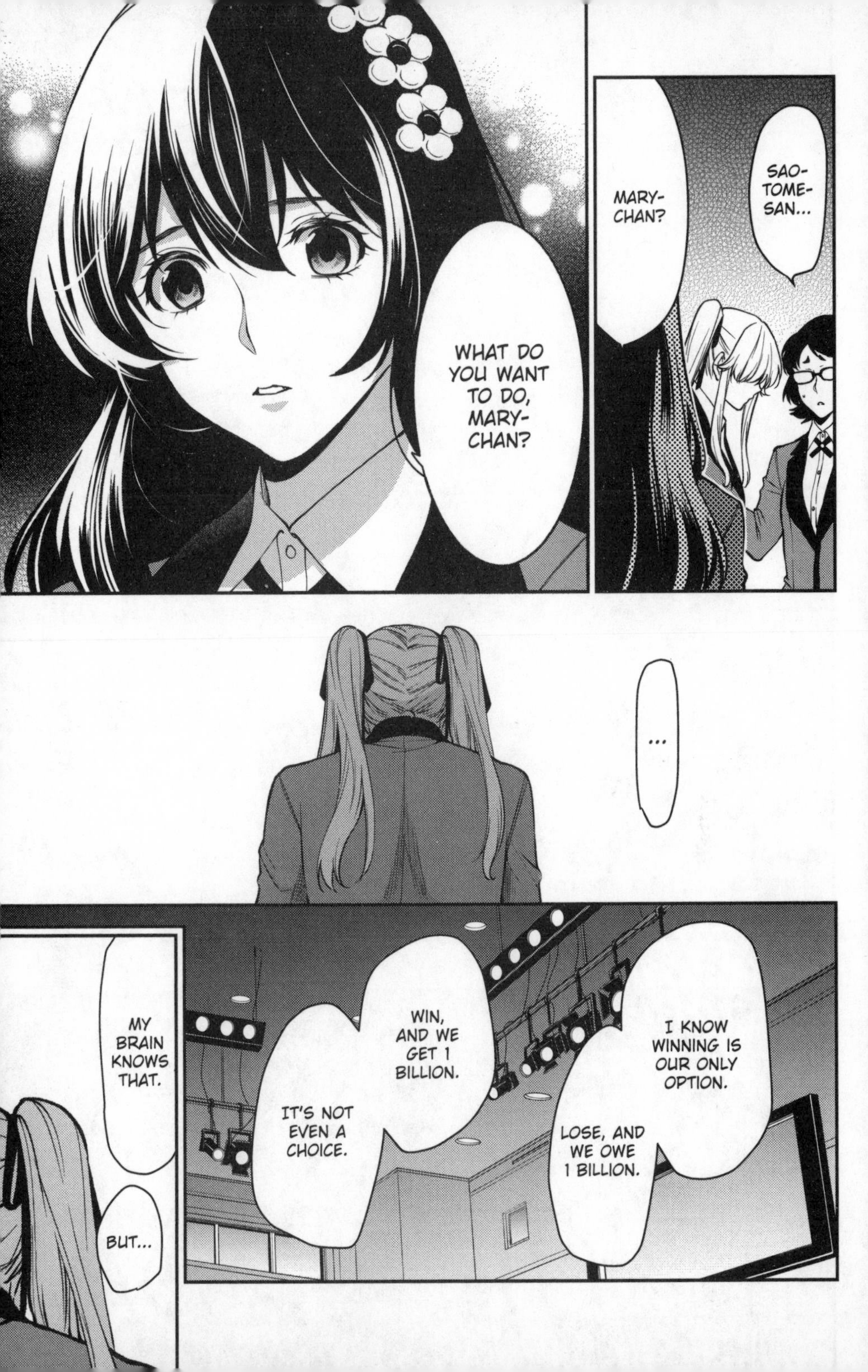
SAO-TOME-SAN...
MARY-CHAN?
WHAT DO YOU WANT TO DO, MARY-CHAN?
...
I KNOW WINNING IS OUR ONLY OPTION.
LOSE, AND WE OWE 1 BILLION.
WIN, AND WE GET 1 BILLION.
IT'S NOT EVEN A CHOICE.
MY BRAIN KNOWS THAT.
BUT...

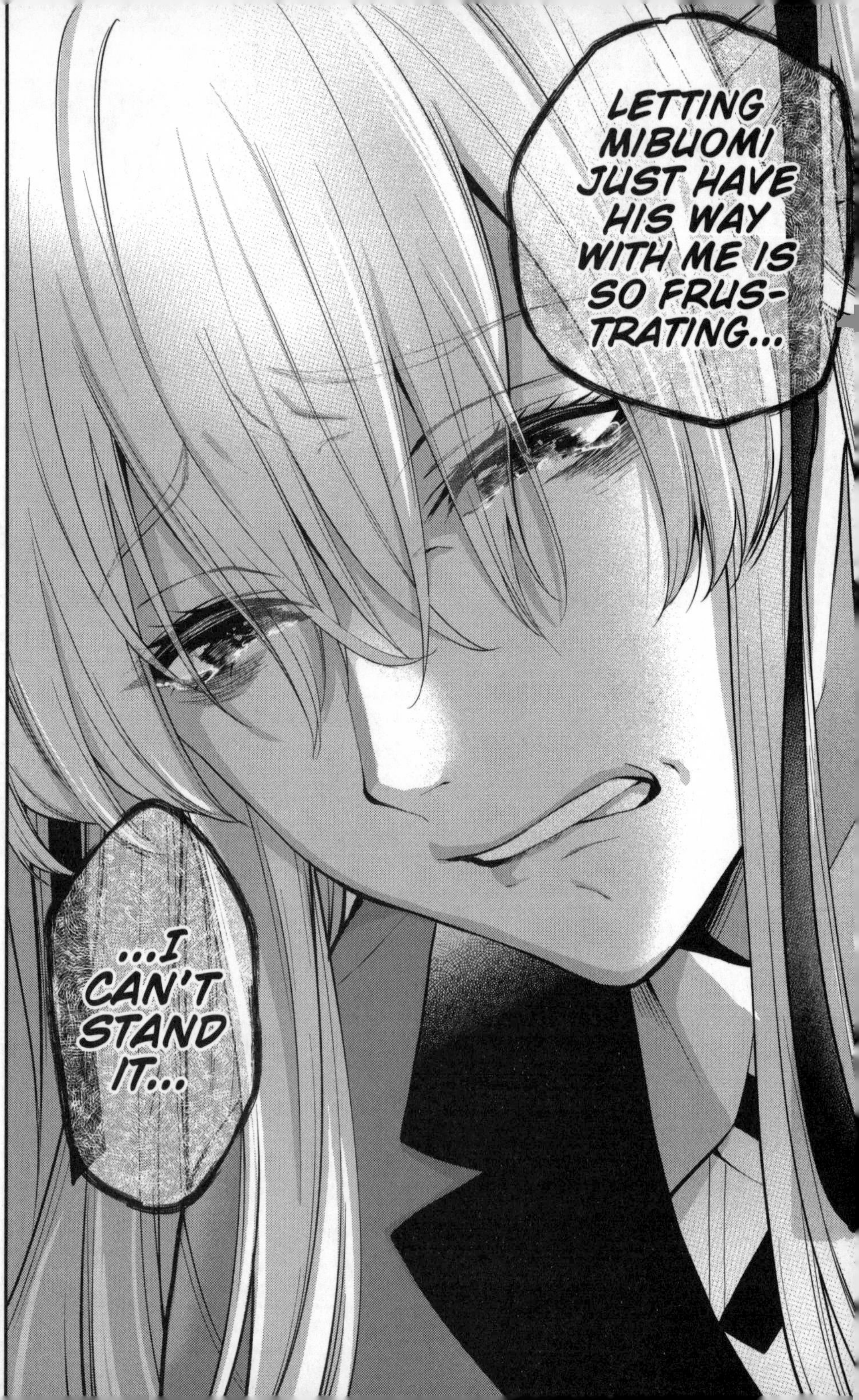
LETTING MIBUOMI JUST HAVE HIS WAY WITH ME IS SO FRUS-TRATING...
...I CAN'T STAND IT...

Kakegurui Twin

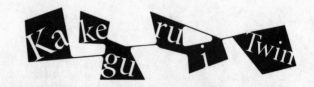

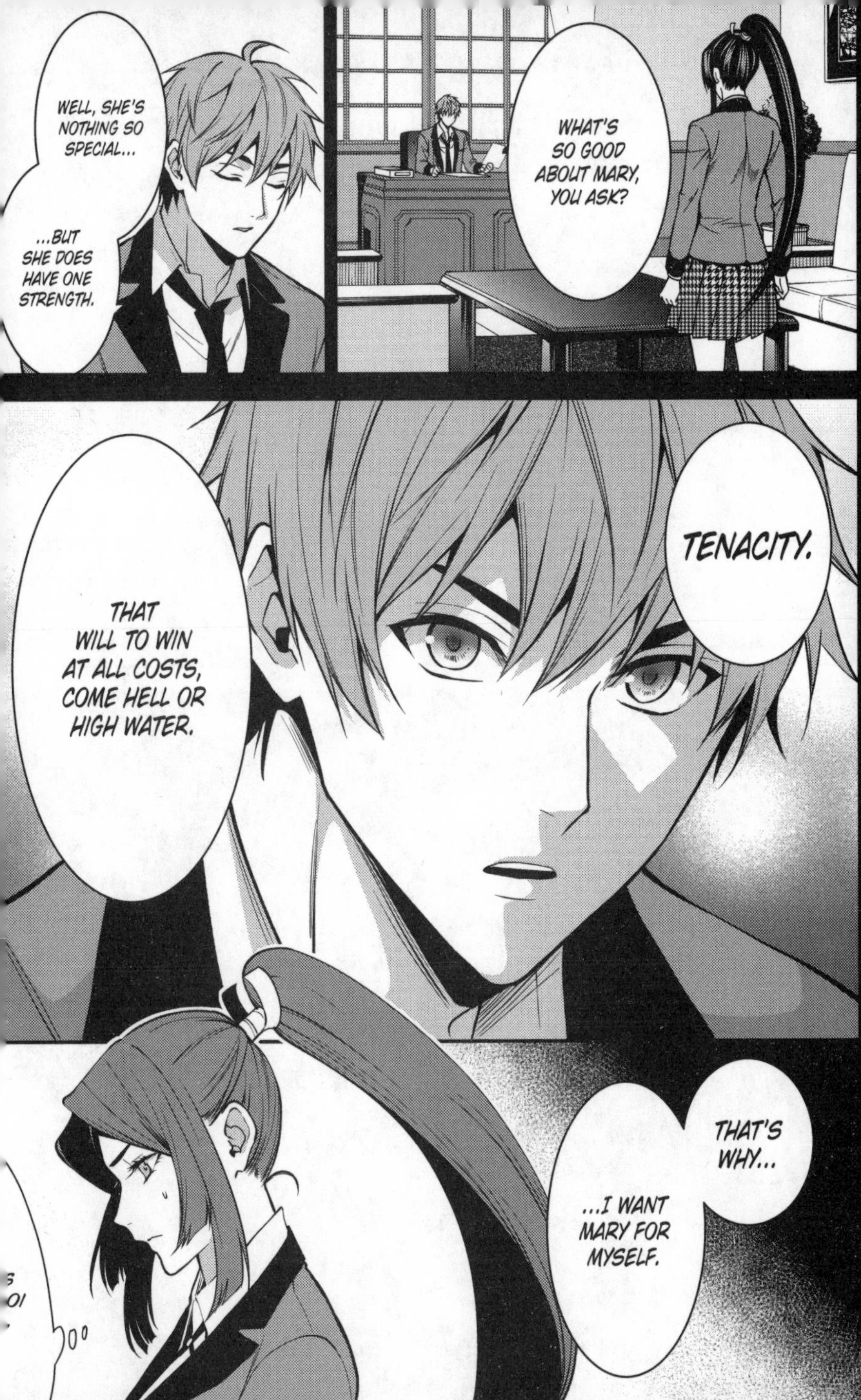
WHAT'S SO GOOD ABOUT MARY, YOU ASK?
WELL, SHE'S NOTHING SO SPECIAL...
...BUT SHE DOES HAVE ONE STRENGTH.
TENACITY.
THAT WILL TO WIN AT ALL COSTS, COME HELL OR HIGH WATER.
THAT'S WHY...
...I WANT MARY FOR MYSELF.

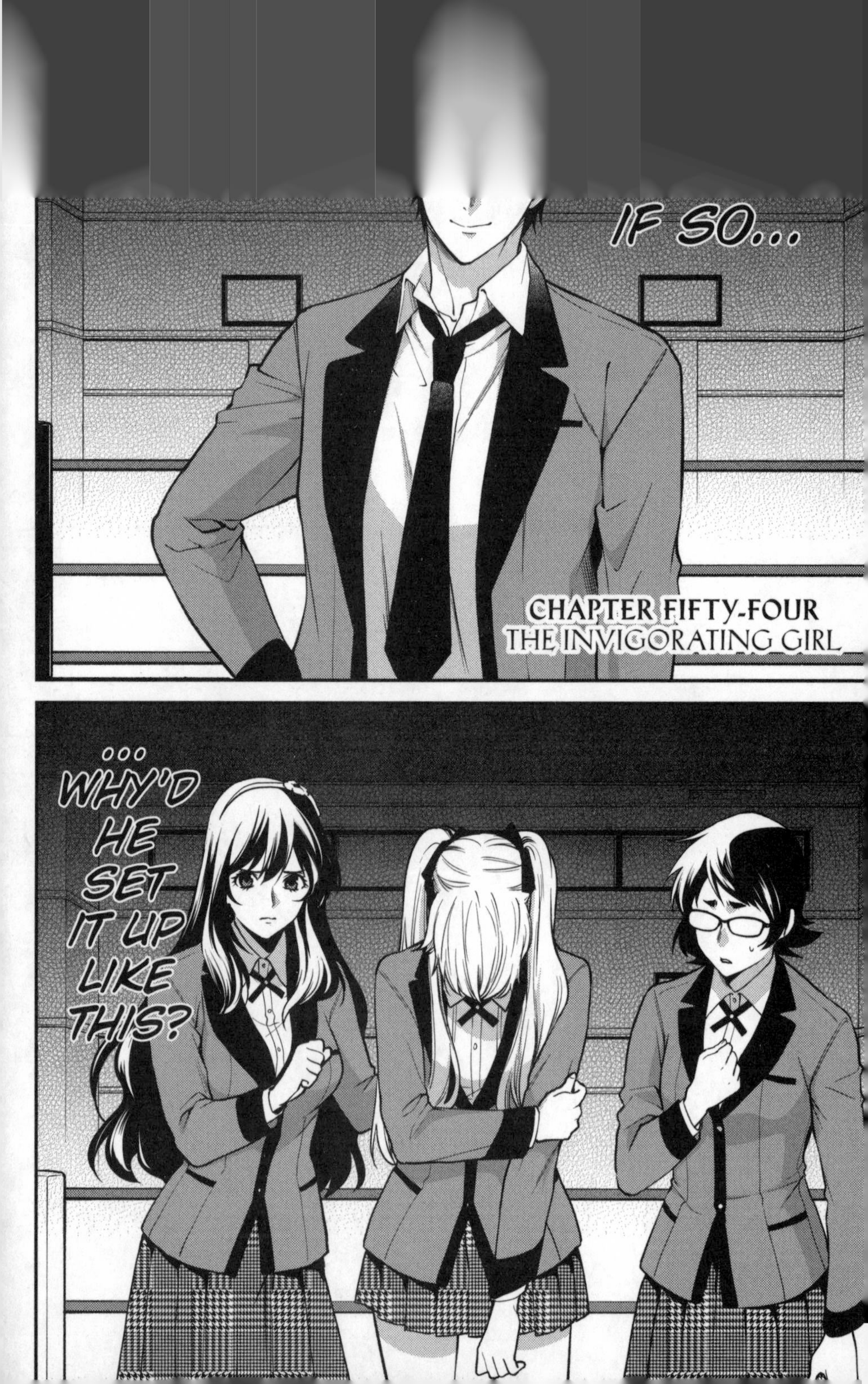
IF SO...
CHAPTER FIFTY-FOUR
THE INVIGORATING GIRL
...WHY'D HE SET IT UP LIKE THIS?

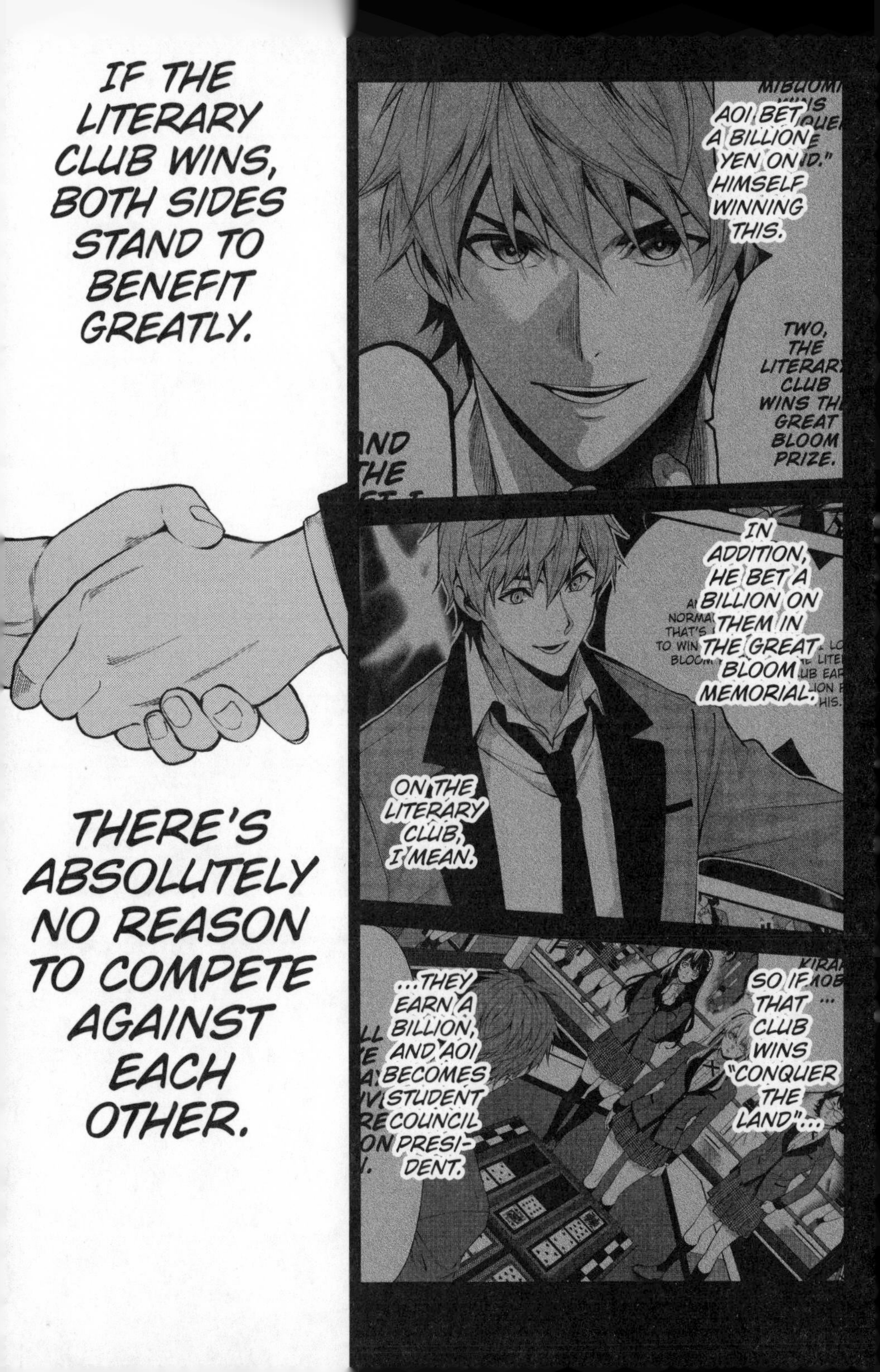
AOI BET A BILLION YEN ON HIMSELF WINNING THIS.
TWO, THE LITERARY CLUB WINS THE GREAT BLOOM PRIZE.
IN ADDITION, HE BET A BILLION ON THEM IN THE GREAT BLOOM MEMORIAL.
ON THE LITERARY CLUB, I MEAN.
SO IF THAT CLUB WINS "CONQUER THE LAND"...
...THEY EARN A BILLION, AND AOI BECOMES STUDENT COUNCIL PRESI-DENT.
IF THE LITERARY CLUB WINS, BOTH SIDES STAND TO BENEFIT GREATLY.
THERE'S ABSOLUTELY NO REASON TO COMPETE AGAINST EACH OTHER.

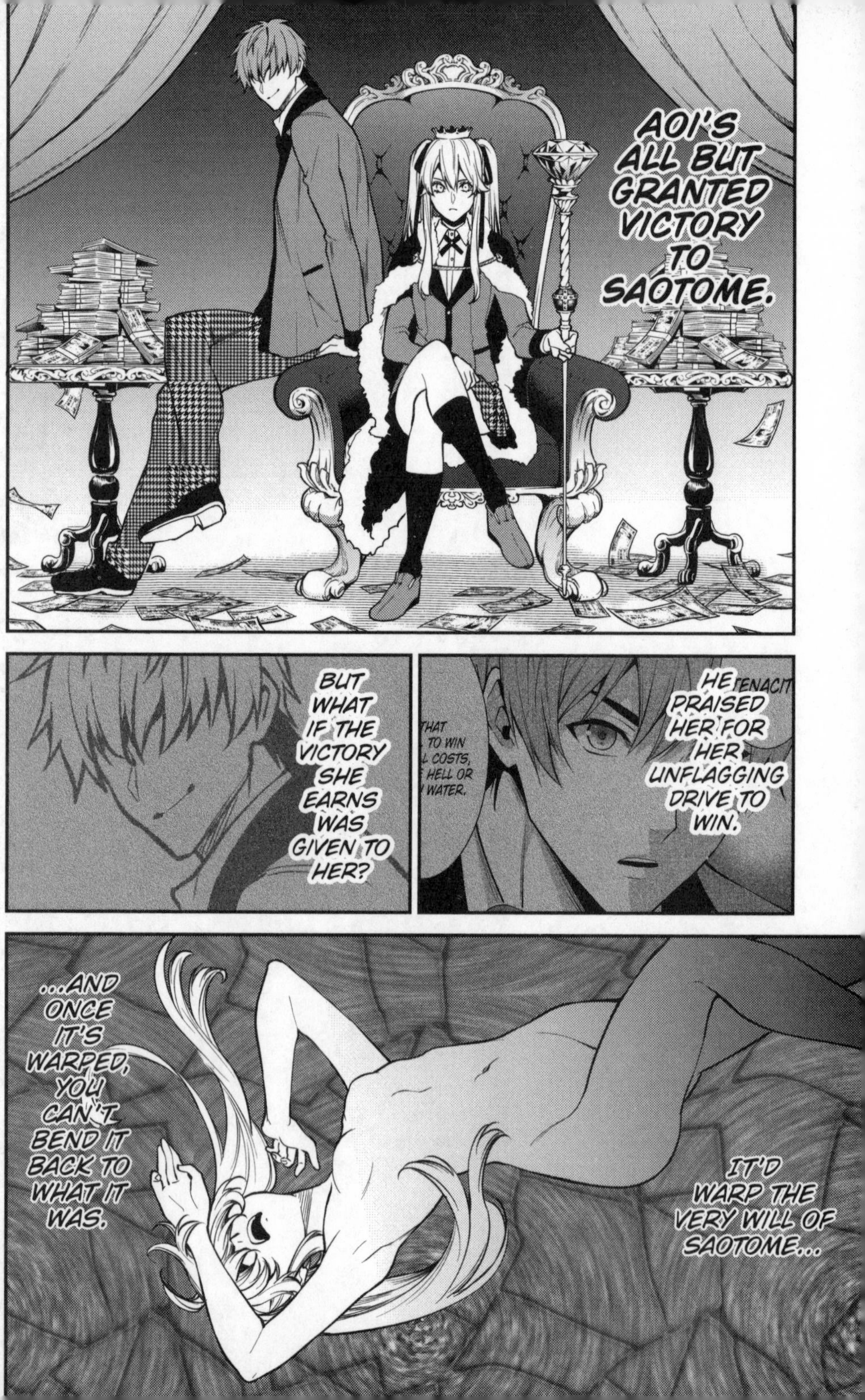
AOI'S ALL BUT GRANTED VICTORY TO SAOTOME.
HE PRAISED HER FOR HER UNFLAGGING DRIVE TO WIN.
BUT WHAT IF THE VICTORY SHE EARNS WAS GIVEN TO HER?
IT'D WARP THE VERY WILL OF SAOTOME...
...AND ONCE IT'S WARPED, YOU CAN'T BEND IT BACK TO WHAT IT WAS.

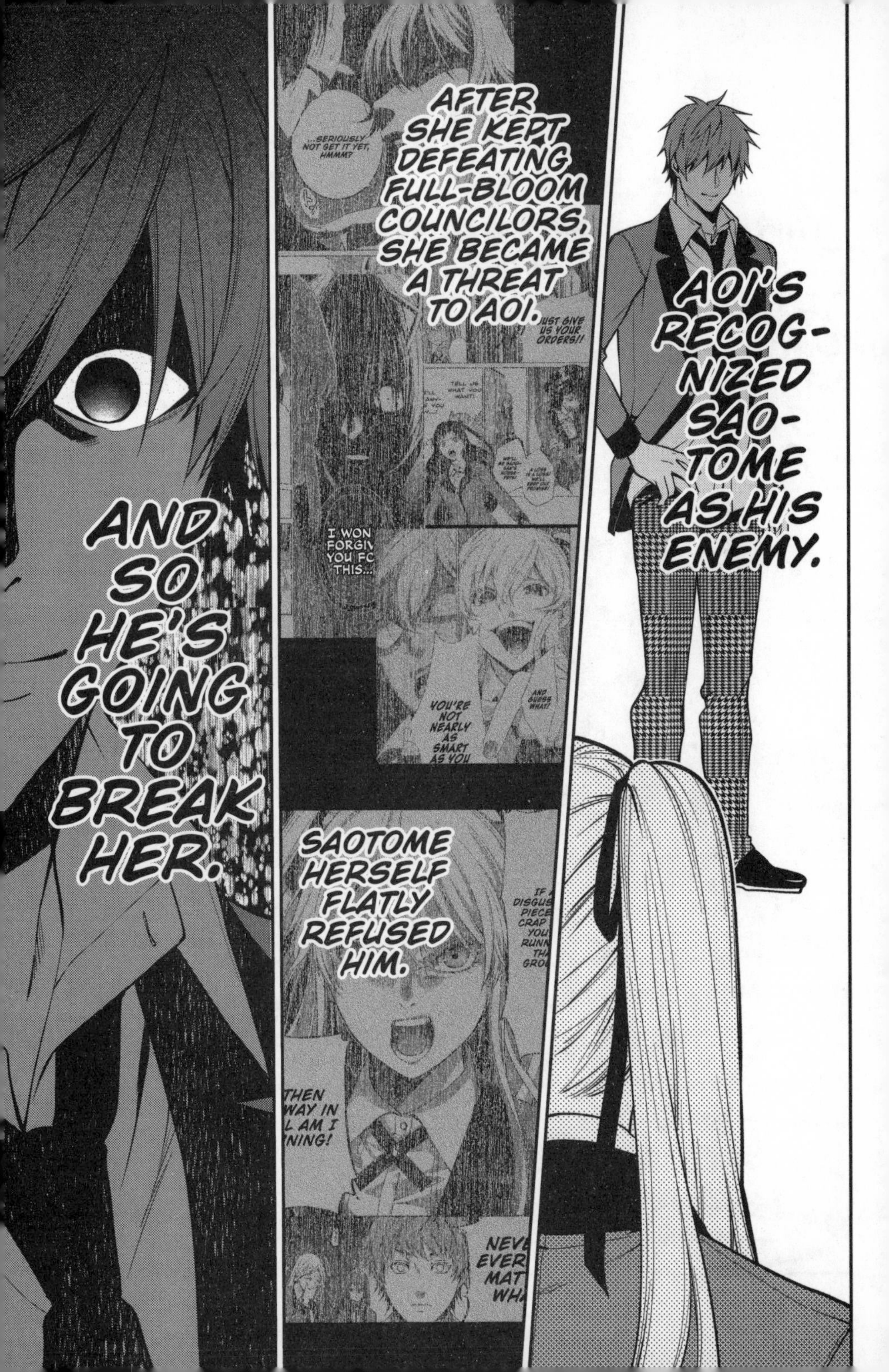
AOI'S RECOGNIZED SAOTOME AS HIS ENEMY.
AFTER SHE KEPT DEFEATING FULL-BLOOM COUNCILORS, SHE BECAME A THREAT TO AOI.
...SERIOUSLY NOT GET IT YET, HMMM?
JUST GIVE US YOUR ORDERS!!
AND GUESS WHAT!
YOU'RE NOT NEARLY AS SMART AS YOU
SAOTOME HERSELF FLATLY REFUSED HIM.
AND SO HE'S GOING TO BREAK HER.

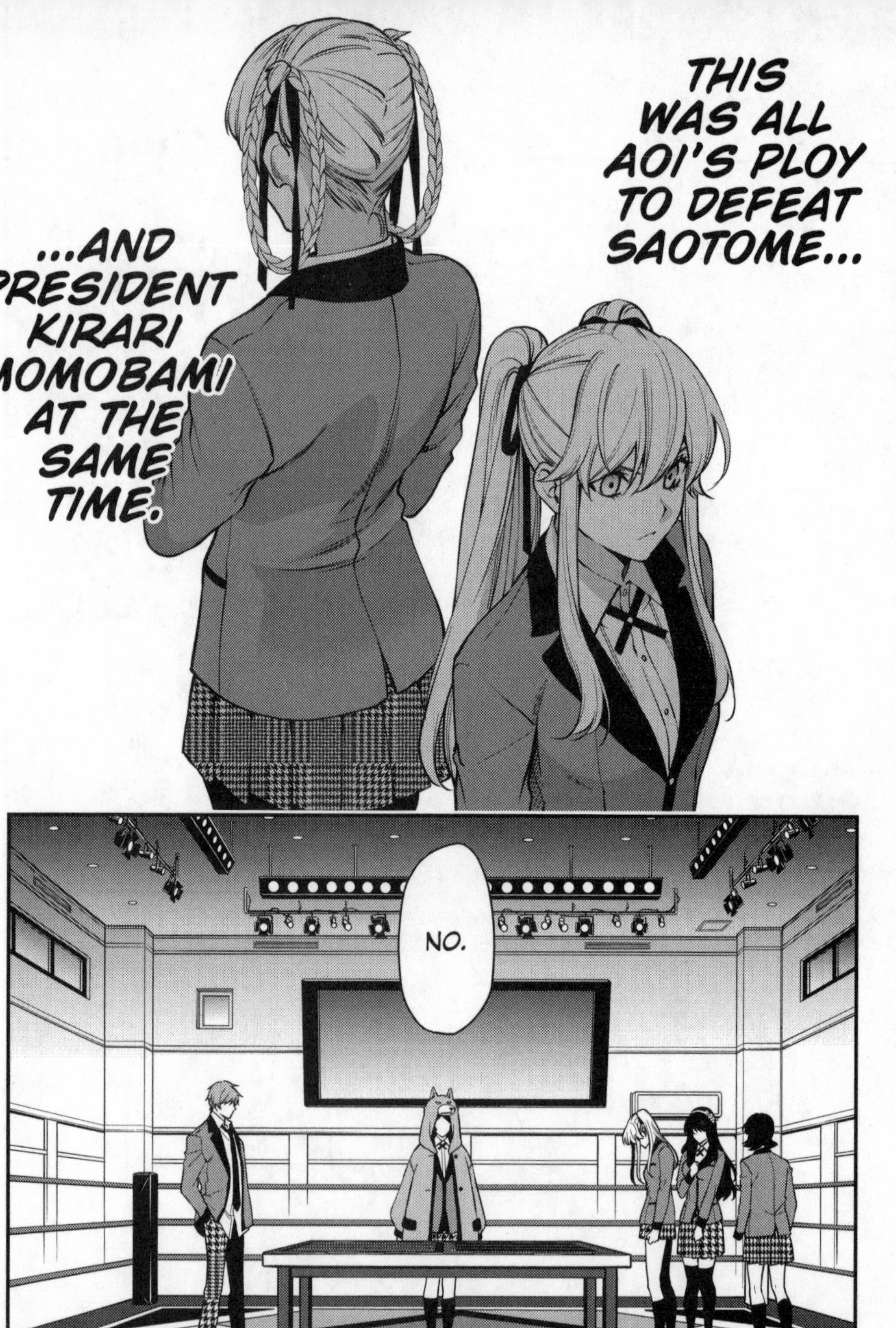
THIS WAS ALL AOI'S PLOY TO DEFEAT SAOTOME...
...AND PRESIDENT KIRARI MOMOBAMI AT THE SAME TIME.
NO.

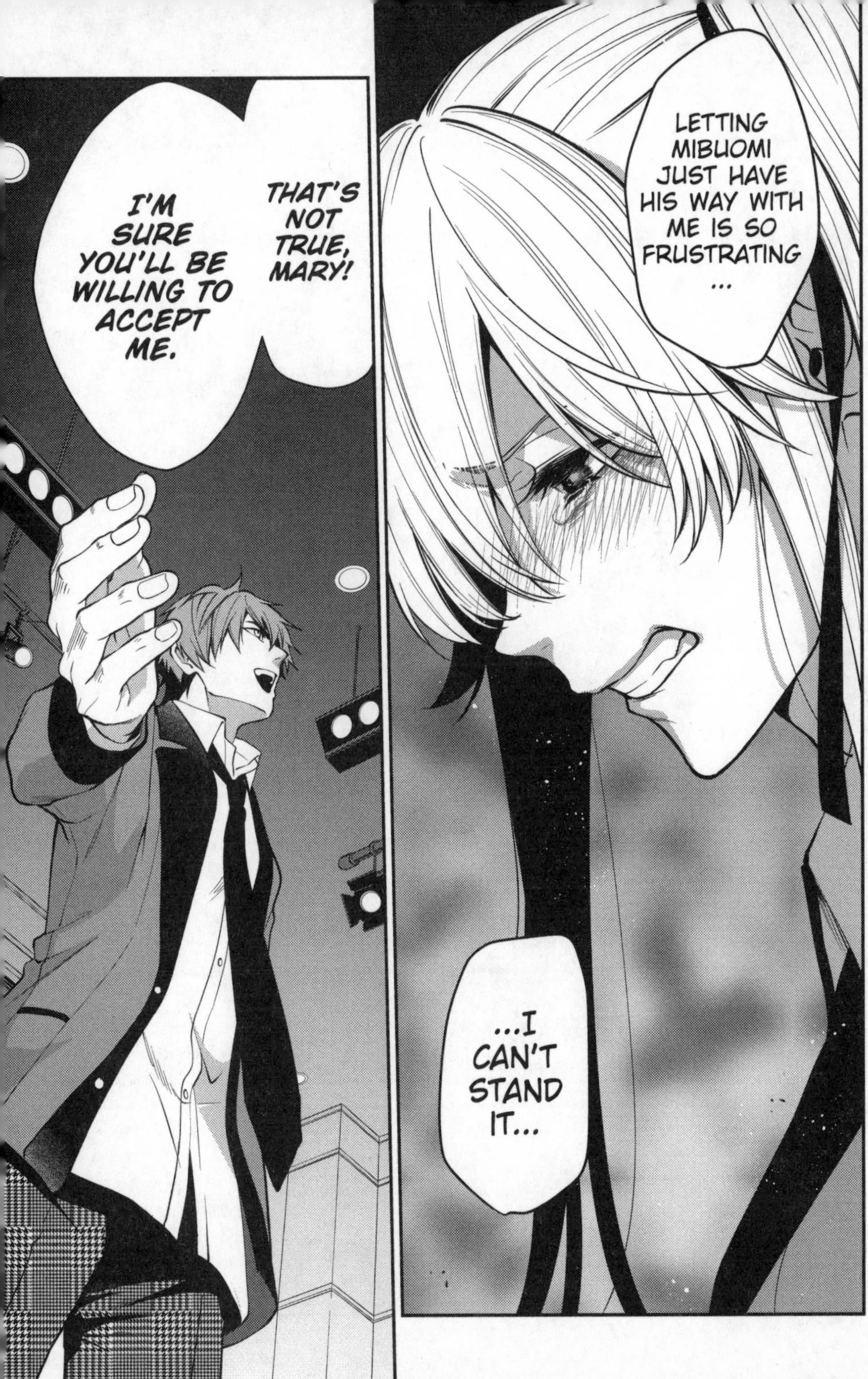
LETTING MIBUOMI JUST HAVE HIS WAY WITH ME IS SO FRUSTRATING ...
...I CAN'T STAND IT...
THAT'S NOT TRUE, MARY!
I'M SURE YOU'LL BE WILLING TO ACCEPT ME.

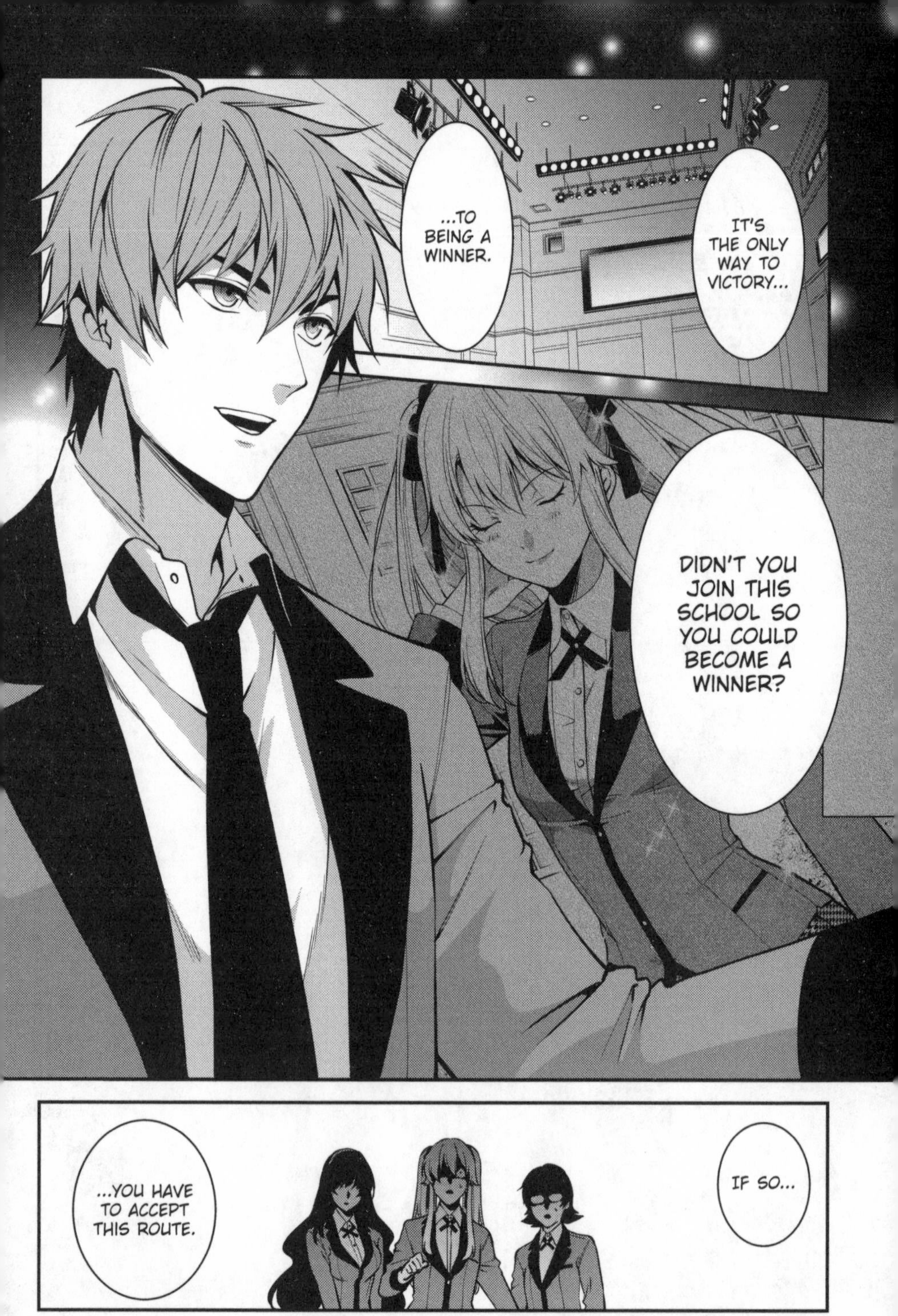
IT'S THE ONLY WAY TO VICTORY...
...TO BEING A WINNER.
DIDN'T YOU JOIN THIS SCHOOL SO YOU COULD BECOME A WINNER?
IF SO...
...YOU HAVE TO ACCEPT THIS ROUTE.

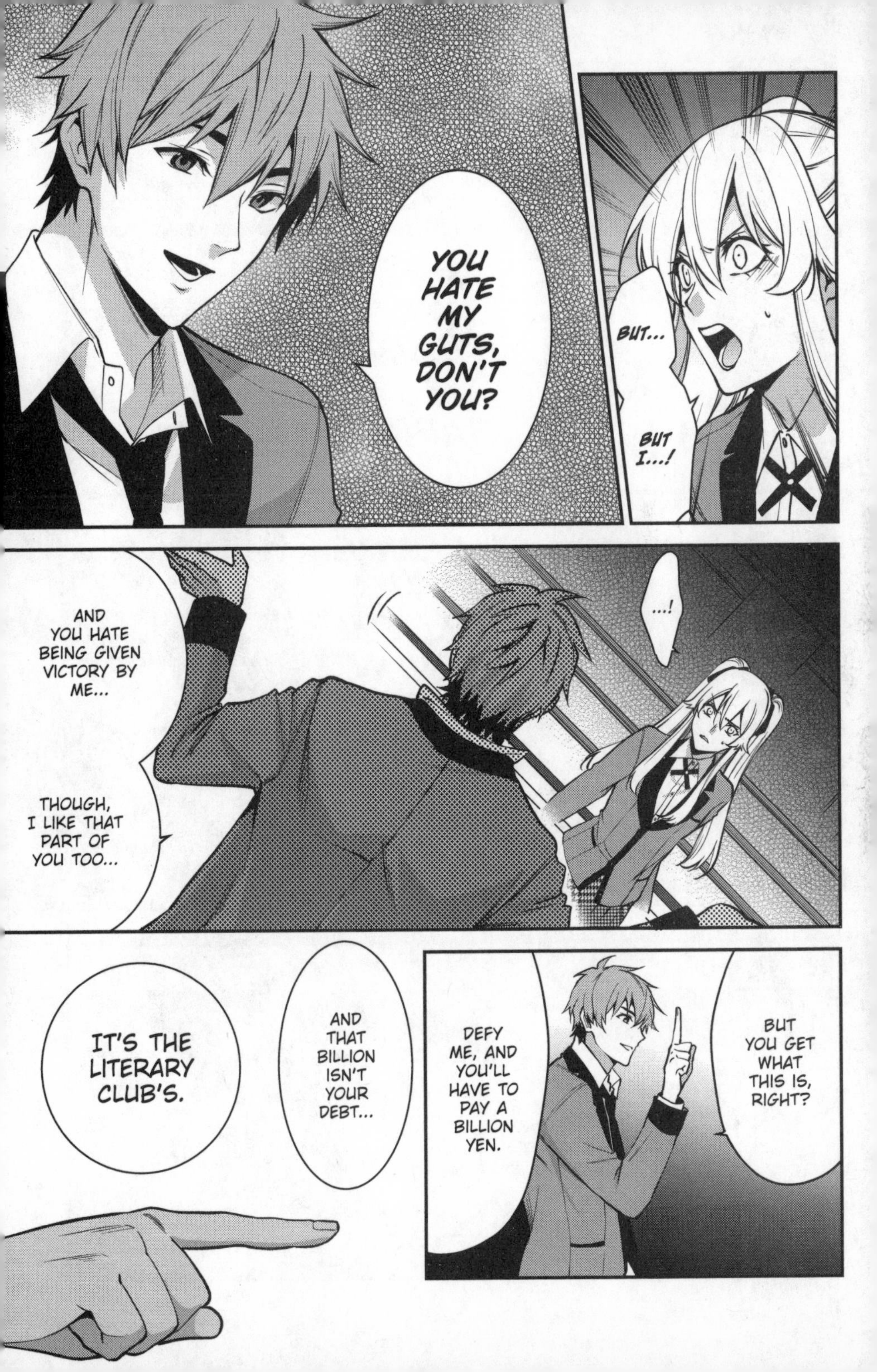
BUT...
BUT I...!
YOU HATE MY GUTS, DON'T YOU?
...!
AND YOU HATE BEING GIVEN VICTORY BY ME...
THOUGH, I LIKE THAT PART OF YOU TOO...
BUT YOU GET WHAT THIS IS, RIGHT?
DEFY ME, AND YOU'LL HAVE TO PAY A BILLION YEN.
AND THAT BILLION ISN'T YOUR DEBT...
IT'S THE LITERARY CLUB'S.

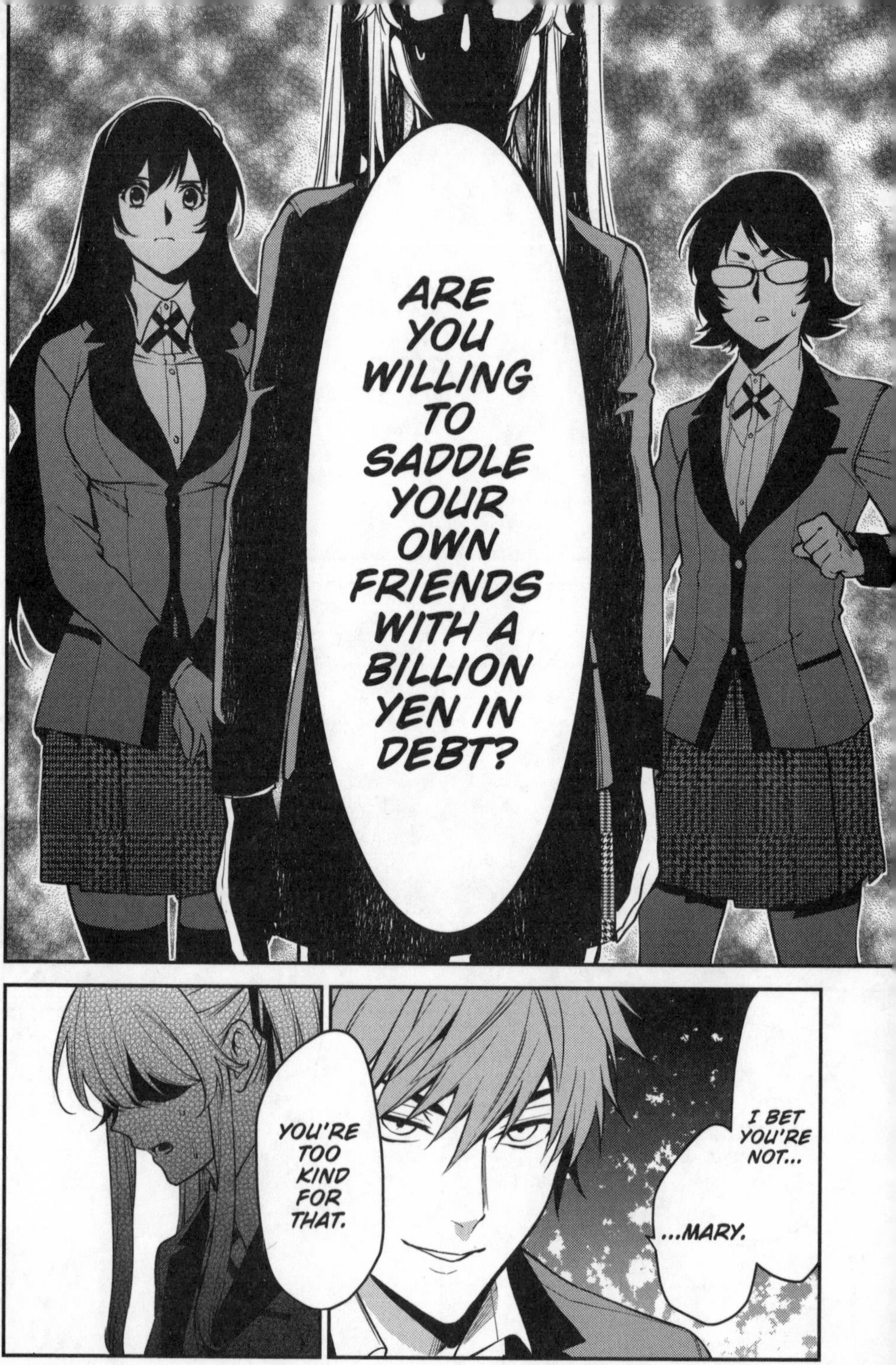
ARE YOU WILLING TO SADDLE YOUR OWN FRIENDS WITH A BILLION YEN IN DEBT?
I BET YOU'RE NOT...
...MARY.
YOU'RE TOO KIND FOR THAT.

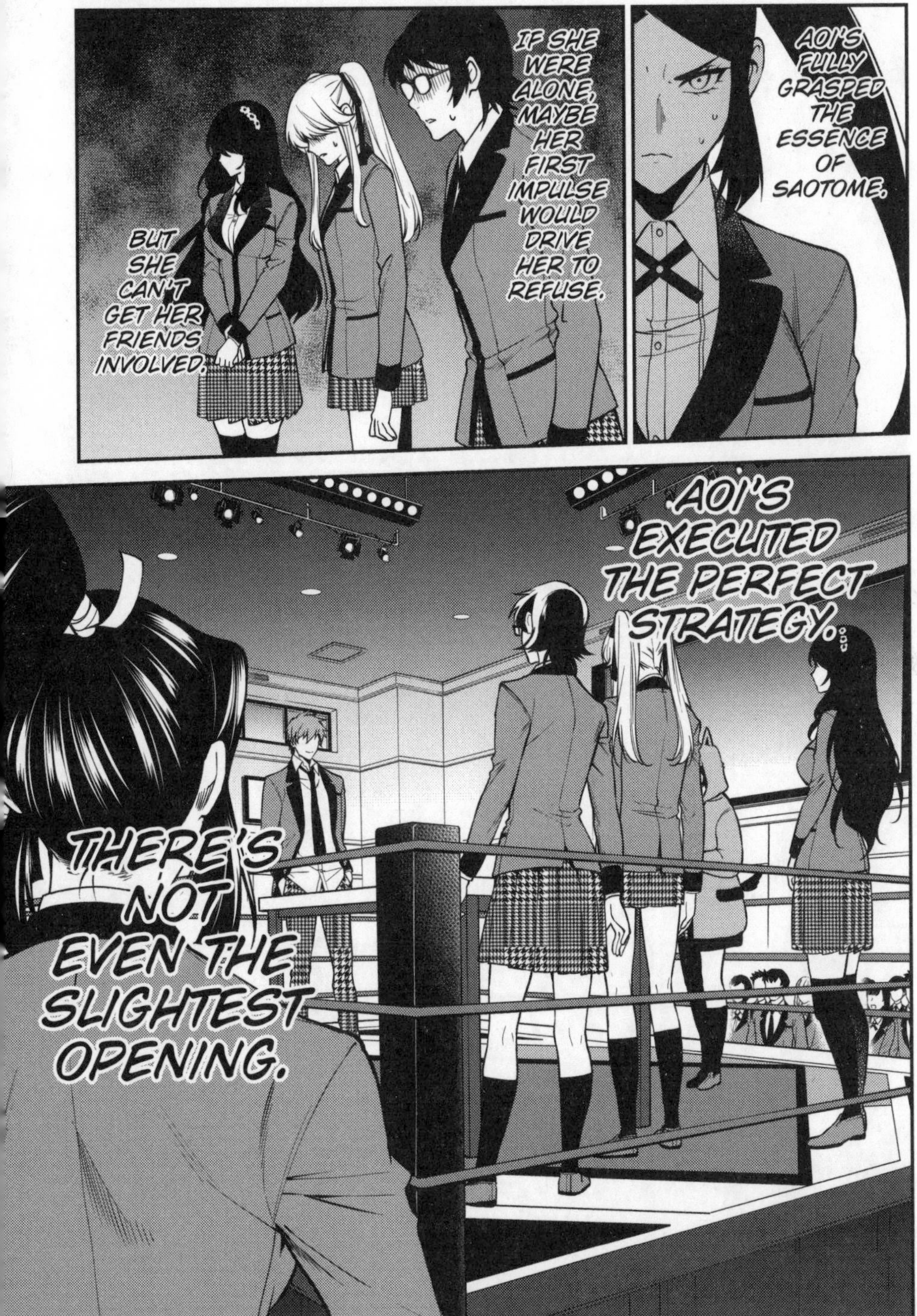
AOI'S FULLY GRASPED THE ESSENCE OF SAOTOME.
IF SHE WERE ALONE, MAYBE HER FIRST IMPULSE WOULD DRIVE HER TO REFUSE.
BUT SHE CAN'T GET HER FRIENDS INVOLVED.
AOI'S EXECUTED THE PERFECT STRATEGY.
THERE'S NOT EVEN THE SLIGHTEST OPENING.

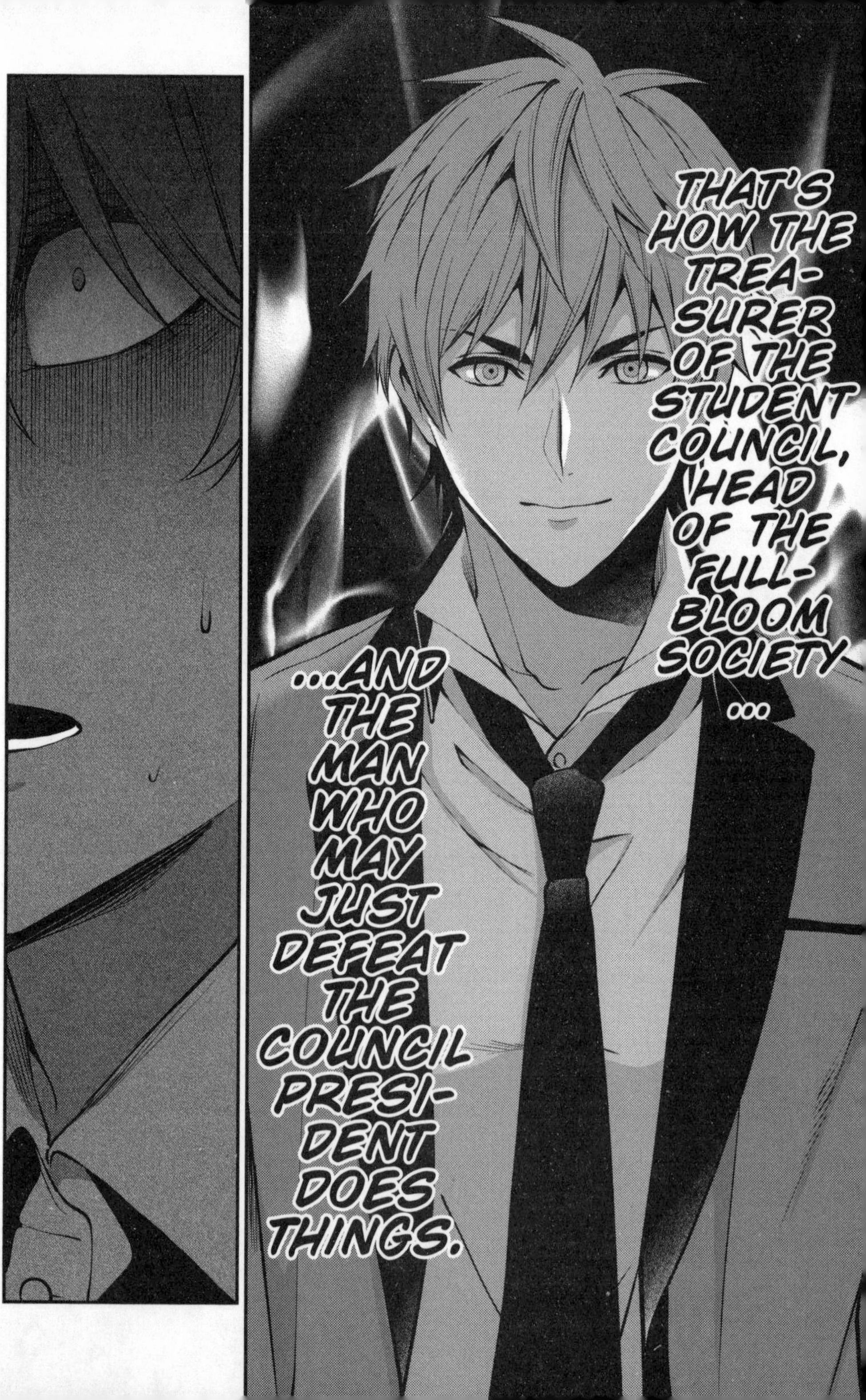
THAT'S HOW THE TREA-SURER OF THE STUDENT COUNCIL, HEAD OF THE FULL-BLOOM SOCIETY...
...AND THE MAN WHO MAY JUST DEFEAT THE COUNCIL PRESI-DENT DOES THINGS.

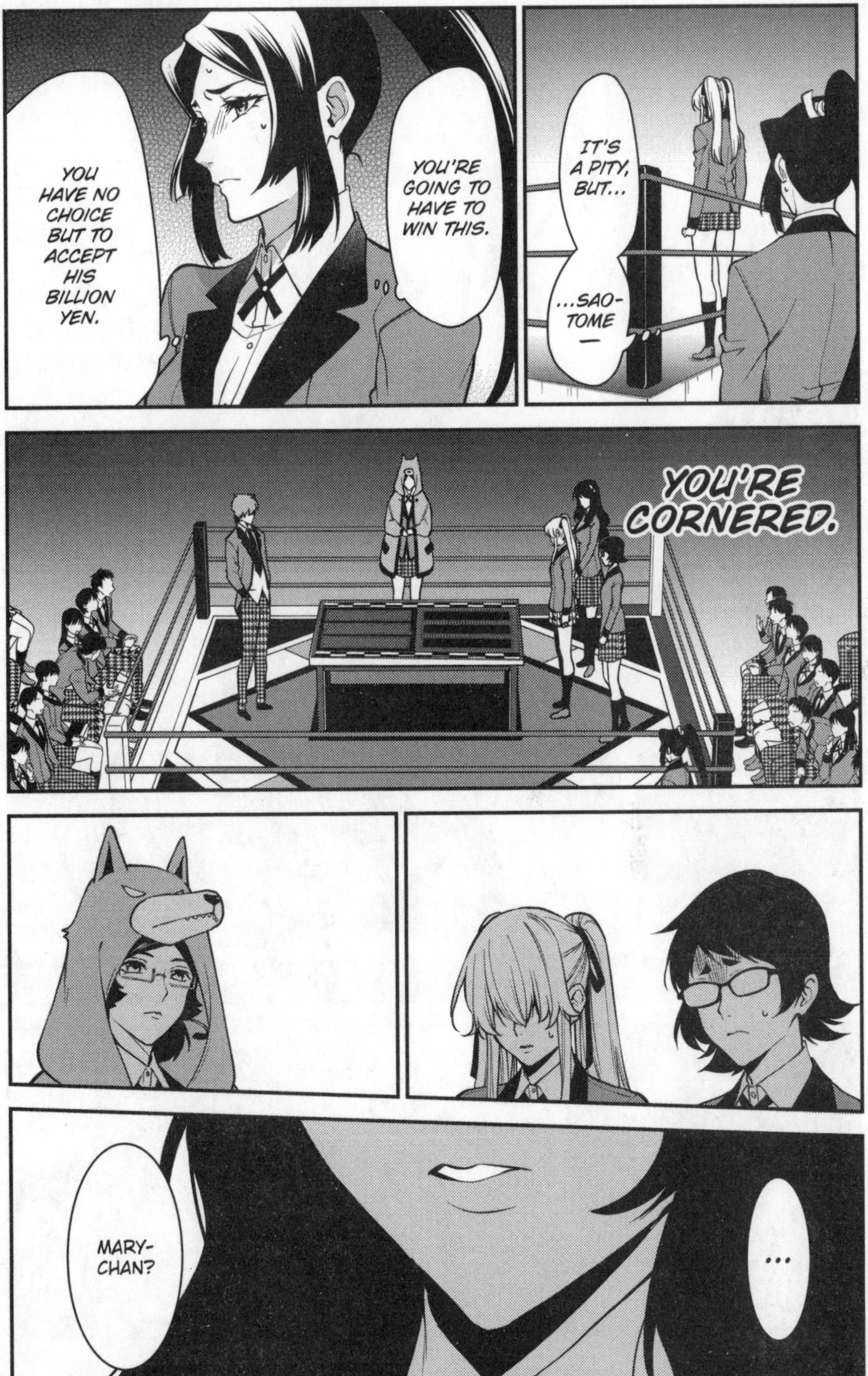
IT'S A PITY, BUT...
...SAO-TOME —
YOU'RE GOING TO HAVE TO WIN THIS.
YOU HAVE NO CHOICE BUT TO ACCEPT HIS BILLION YEN.
YOU'RE CORNERED.
...
MARY-CHAN?

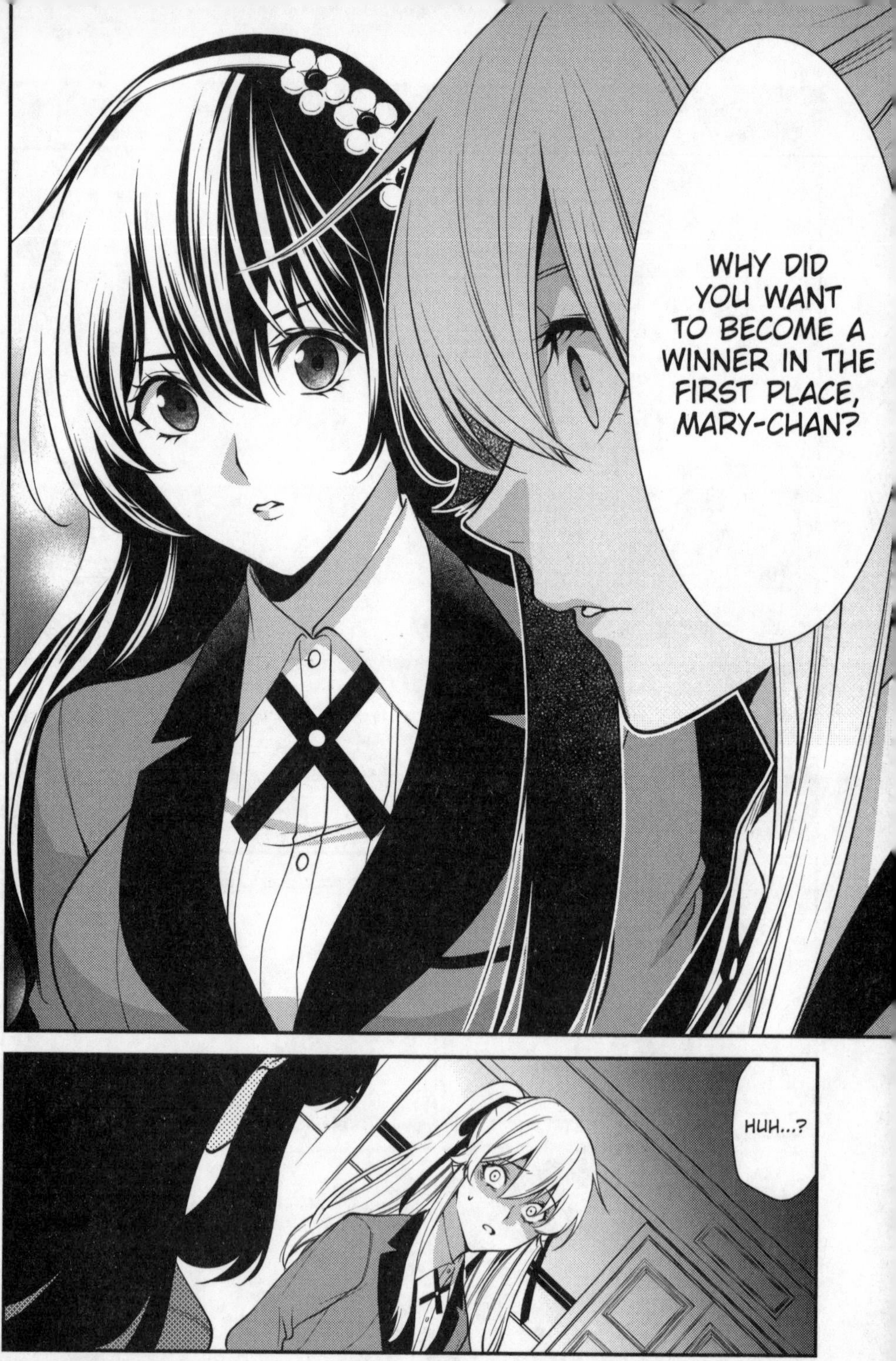
WHY DID YOU WANT TO BECOME A WINNER IN THE FIRST PLACE, MARY-CHAN?
HUH...?

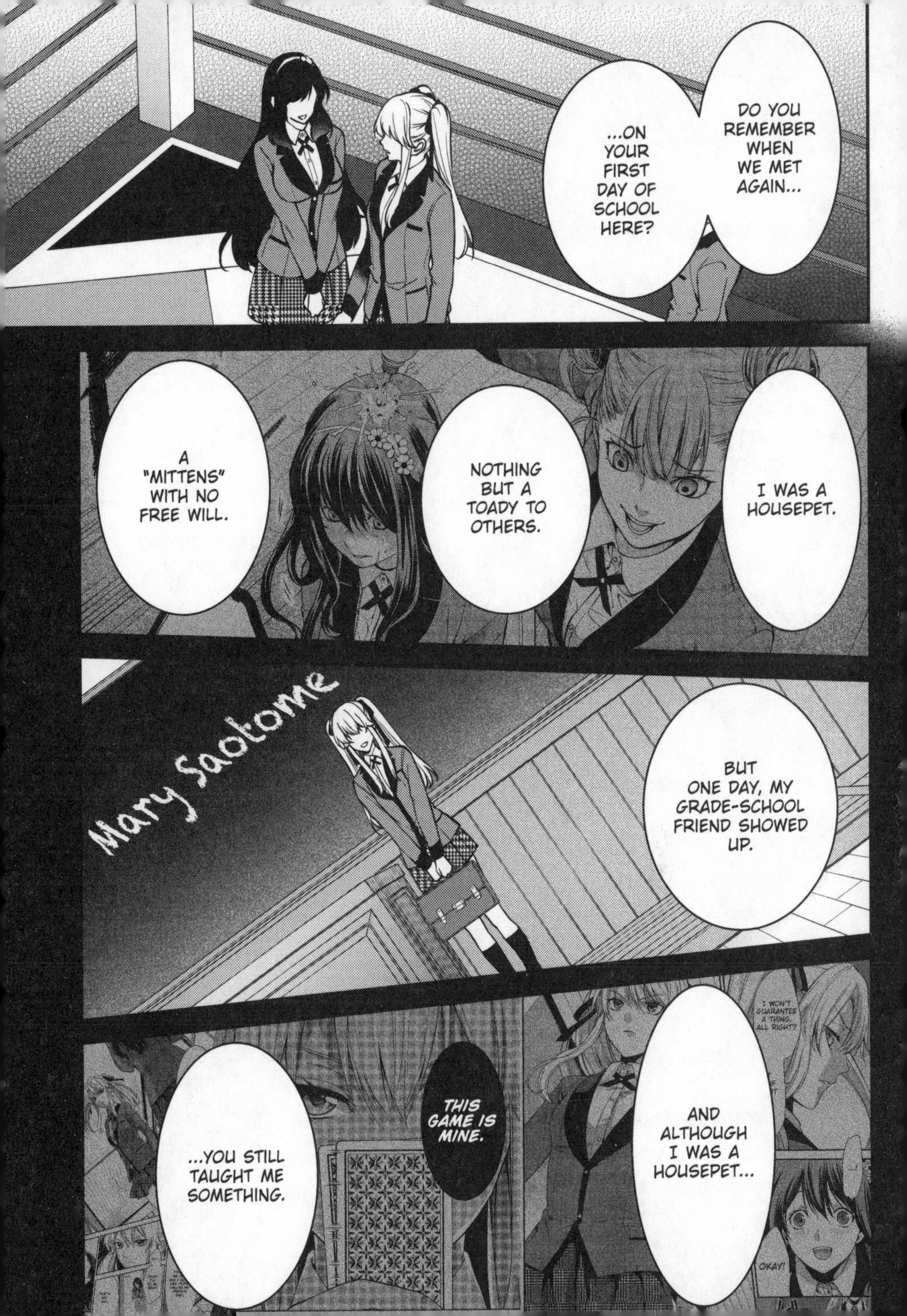
DO YOU REMEMBER WHEN WE MET AGAIN...
...ON YOUR FIRST DAY OF SCHOOL HERE?
I WAS A HOUSEPET.
NOTHING BUT A TOADY TO OTHERS.
A "MITTENS" WITH NO FREE WILL.
Mary Saotome
BUT ONE DAY, MY GRADE-SCHOOL FRIEND SHOWED UP.
I WON'T GUARANTEE A THING, ALL RIGHT?
AND ALTHOUGH I WAS A HOUSEPET...
...!
OKAY!
THIS GAME IS MINE.
...YOU STILL TAUGHT ME SOMETHING.

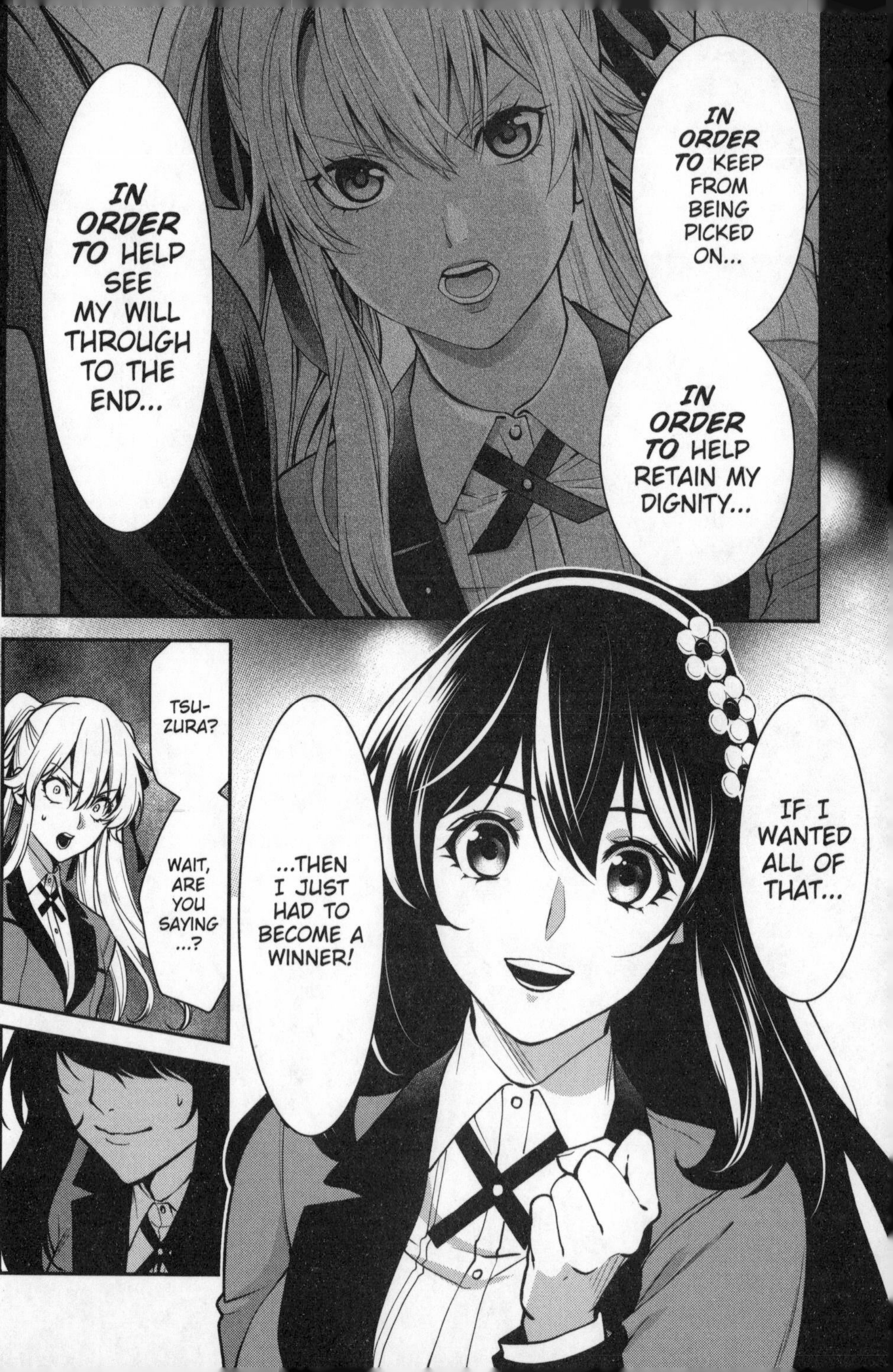
IN ORDER TO KEEP FROM BEING PICKED ON...
IN ORDER TO HELP RETAIN MY DIGNITY...
IN ORDER TO HELP SEE MY WILL THROUGH TO THE END...
IF I WANTED ALL OF THAT...
...THEN I JUST HAD TO BECOME A WINNER!
TSU-ZURA?
WAIT, ARE YOU SAYING ...?

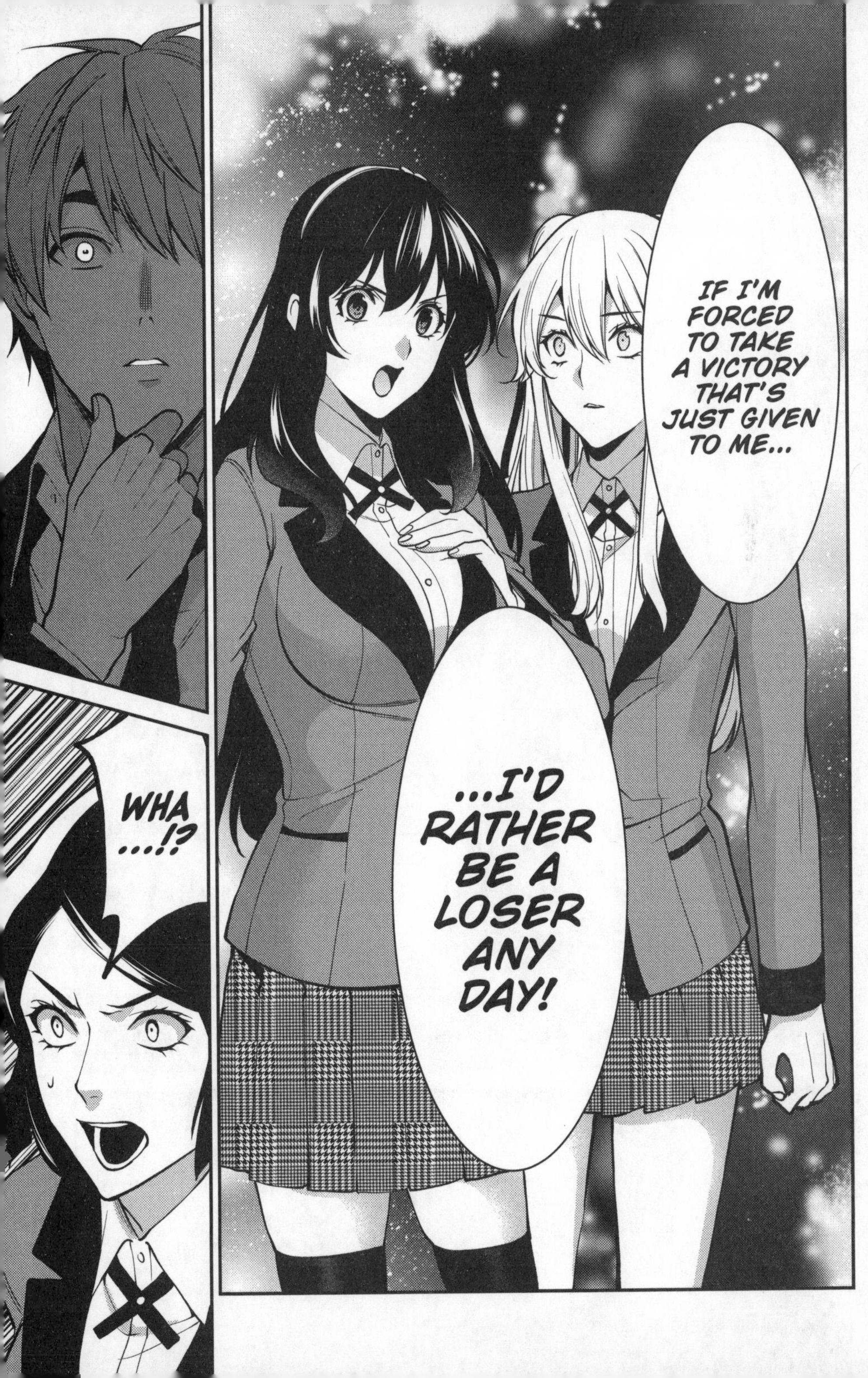
IF I'M FORCED TO TAKE A VICTORY THAT'S JUST GIVEN TO ME...
...I'D RATHER BE A LOSER ANY DAY!
WHA ...!?

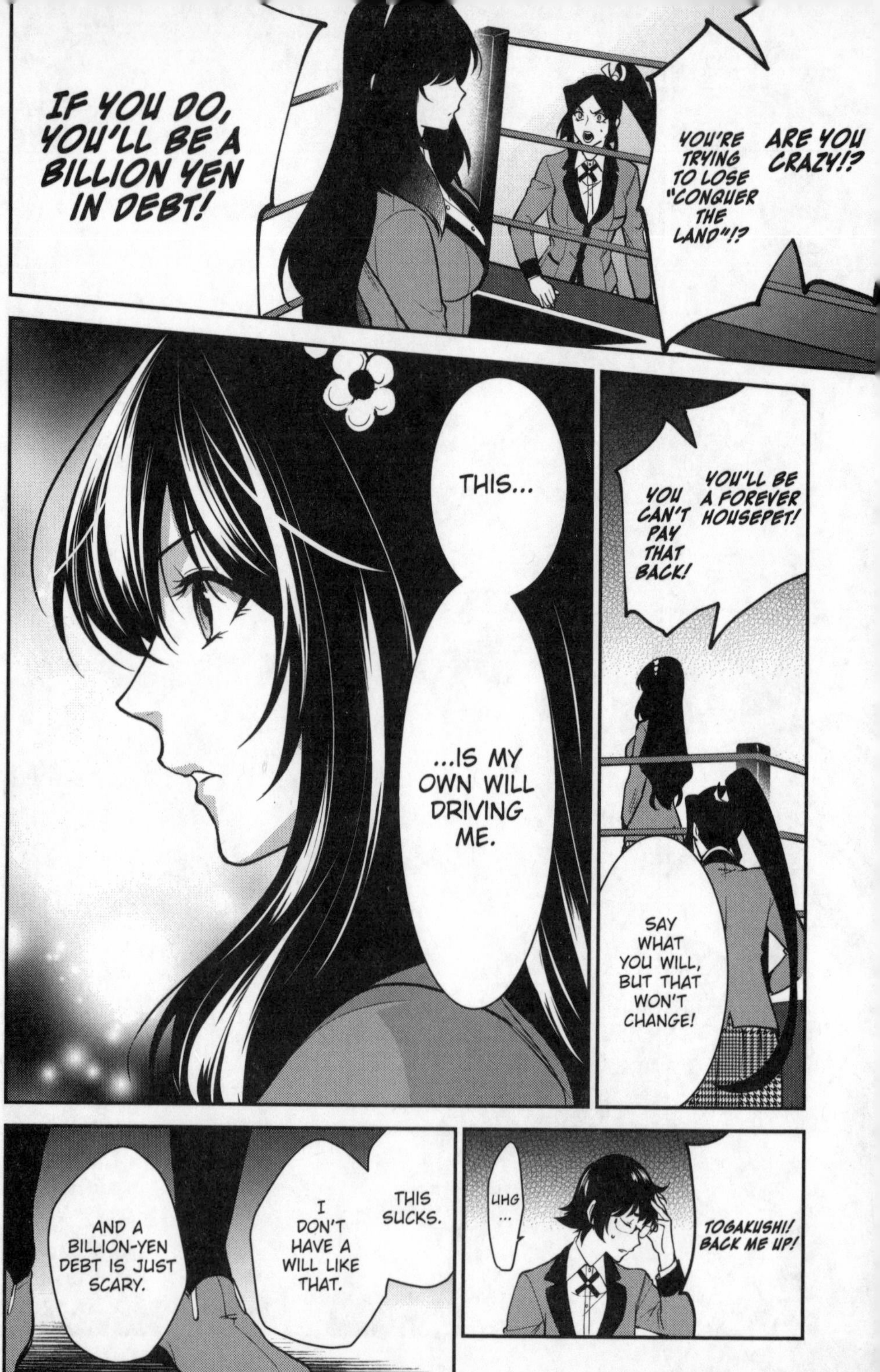
ARE YOU CRAZY!?
YOU'RE TRYING TO LOSE "CONQUER THE LAND"!?
IF YOU DO, YOU'LL BE A BILLION YEN IN DEBT!
YOU'LL BE A FOREVER HOUSEPET!
YOU CAN'T PAY THAT BACK!
SAY WHAT YOU WILL, BUT THAT WON'T CHANGE!
THIS...
...IS MY OWN WILL DRIVING ME.
TOGAKUSHI! BACK ME UP!
UHG...
THIS SUCKS.
I DON'T HAVE A WILL LIKE THAT.
AND A BILLION-YEN DEBT IS JUST SCARY.

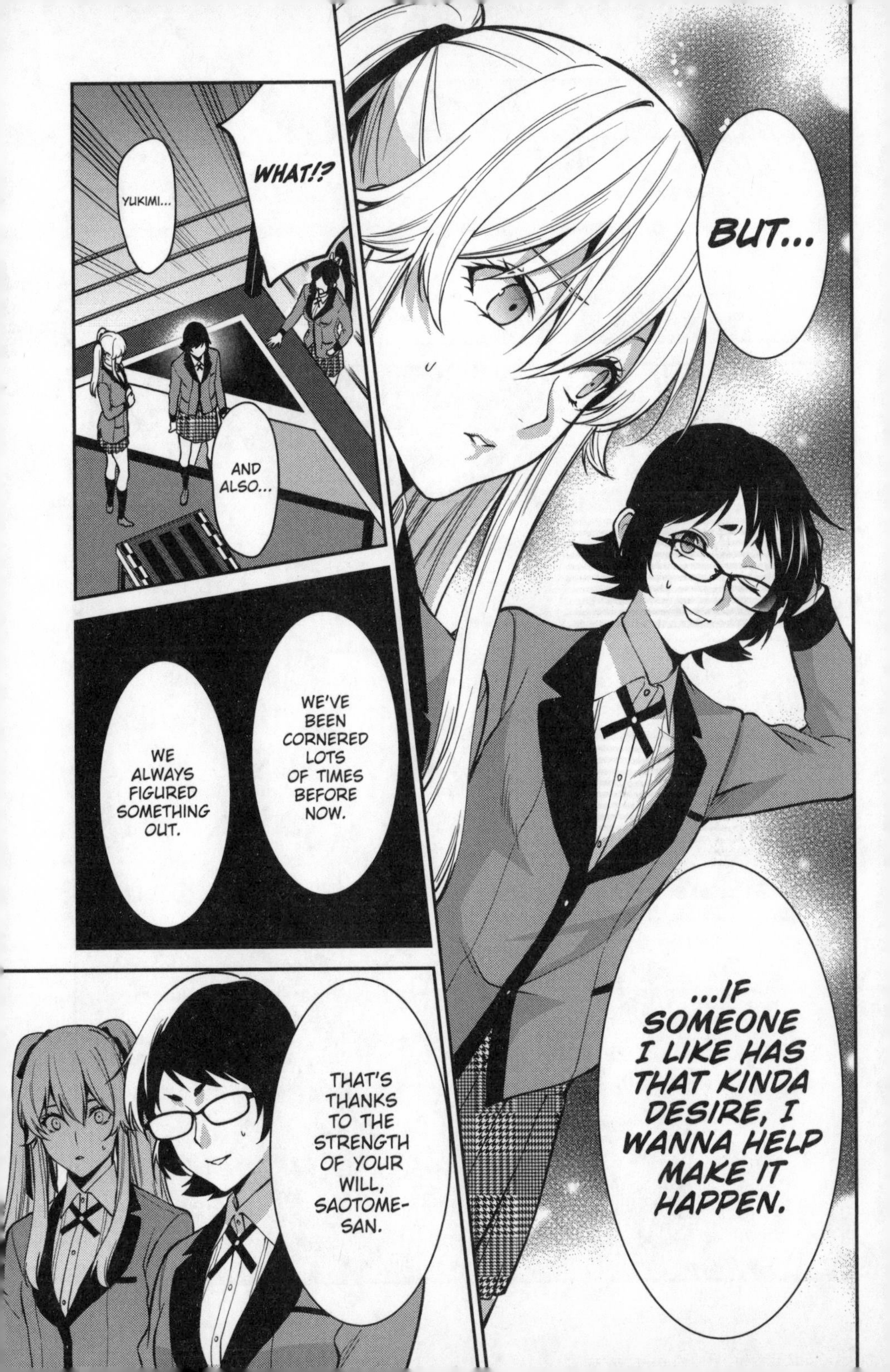
BUT...
...IF SOMEONE I LIKE HAS THAT KINDA DESIRE, I WANNA HELP MAKE IT HAPPEN.
WHAT!?
YUKIMI...
AND ALSO...
WE'VE BEEN CORNERED LOTS OF TIMES BEFORE NOW.
WE ALWAYS FIGURED SOMETHING OUT.
THAT'S THANKS TO THE STRENGTH OF YOUR WILL, SAOTOME-SAN.

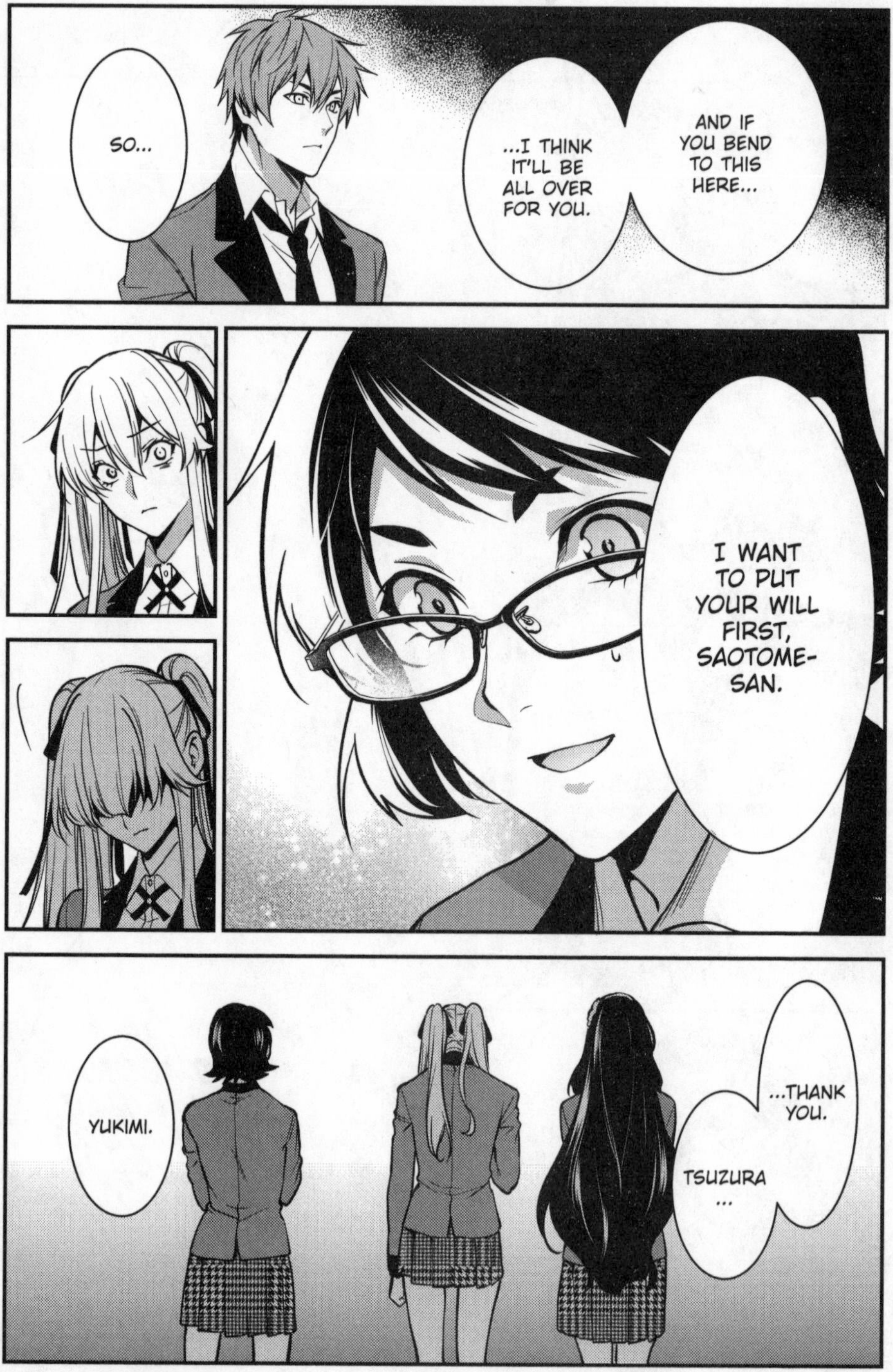
AND IF YOU BEND TO THIS HERE...
...I THINK IT'LL BE ALL OVER FOR YOU.
SO...
I WANT TO PUT YOUR WILL FIRST, SAOTOME-SAN.
...THANK YOU.
TSUZURA ...
YUKIMI.

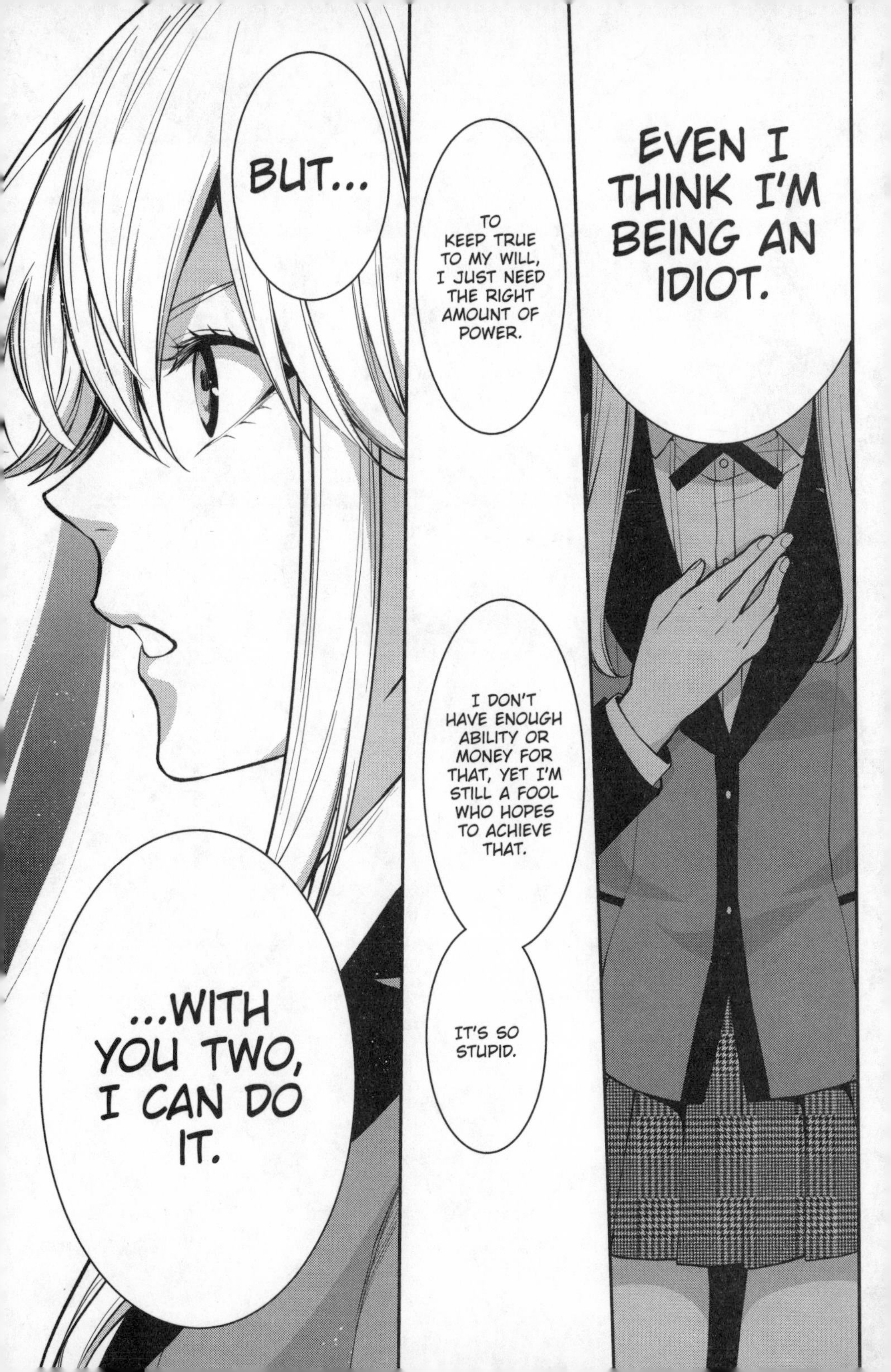
EVEN I THINK I'M BEING AN IDIOT.
TO KEEP TRUE TO MY WILL, I JUST NEED THE RIGHT AMOUNT OF POWER.
I DON'T HAVE ENOUGH ABILITY OR MONEY FOR THAT, YET I'M STILL A FOOL WHO HOPES TO ACHIEVE THAT.
IT'S SO STUPID.
BUT...
...WITH YOU TWO, I CAN DO IT.

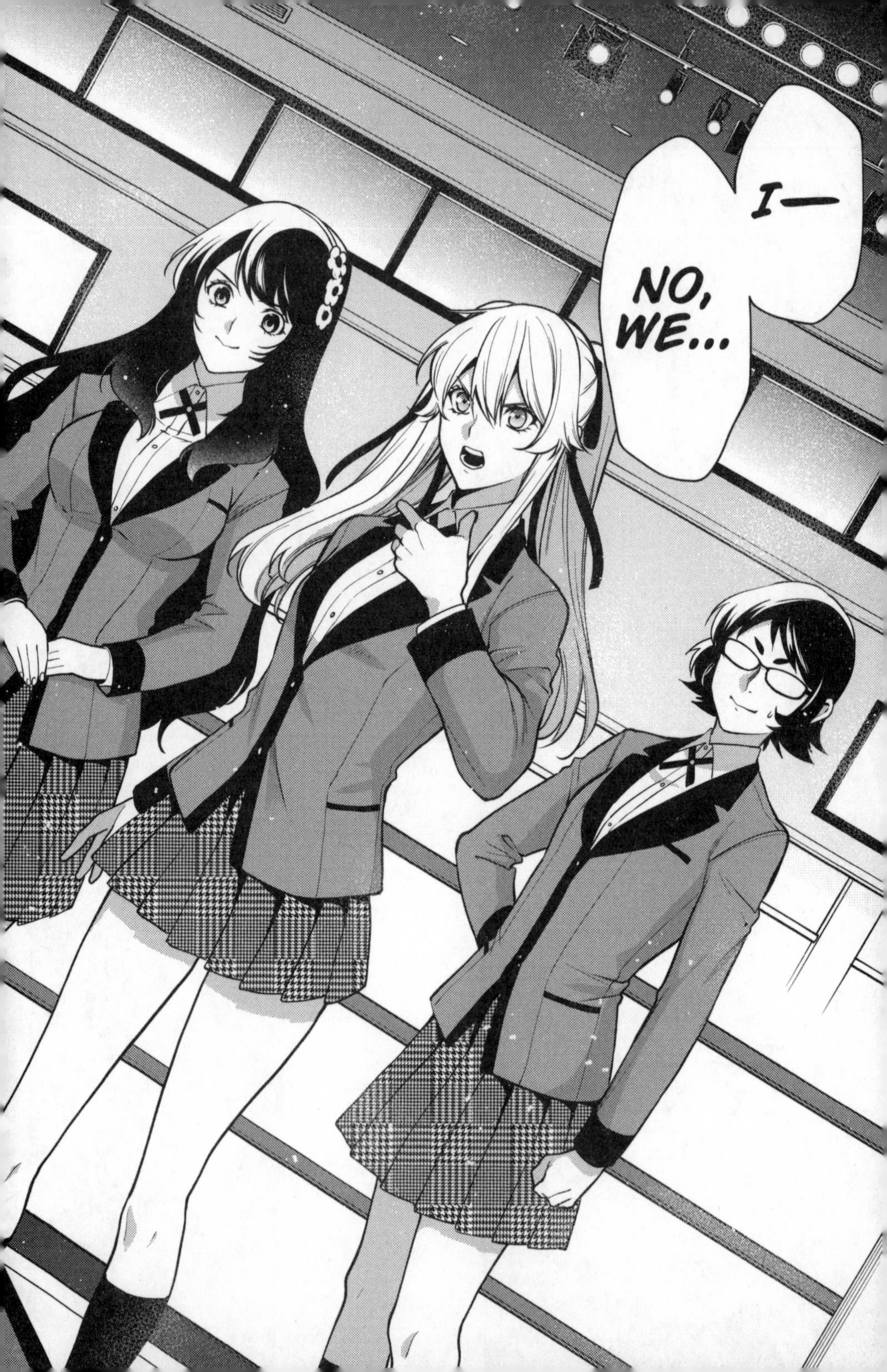
I— NO, WE...

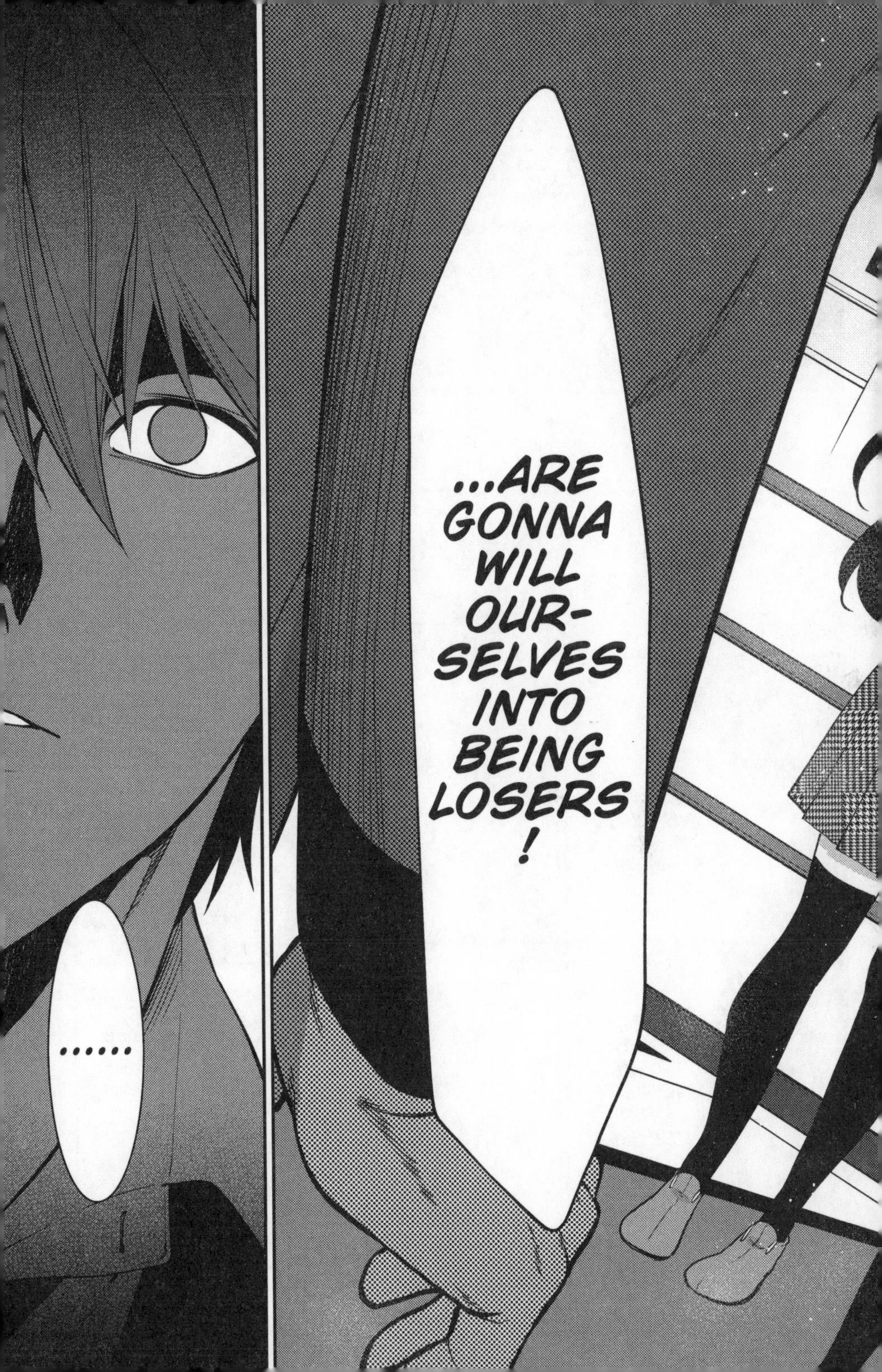
...ARE GONNA WILL OUR-SELVES INTO BEING LOSERS!
......

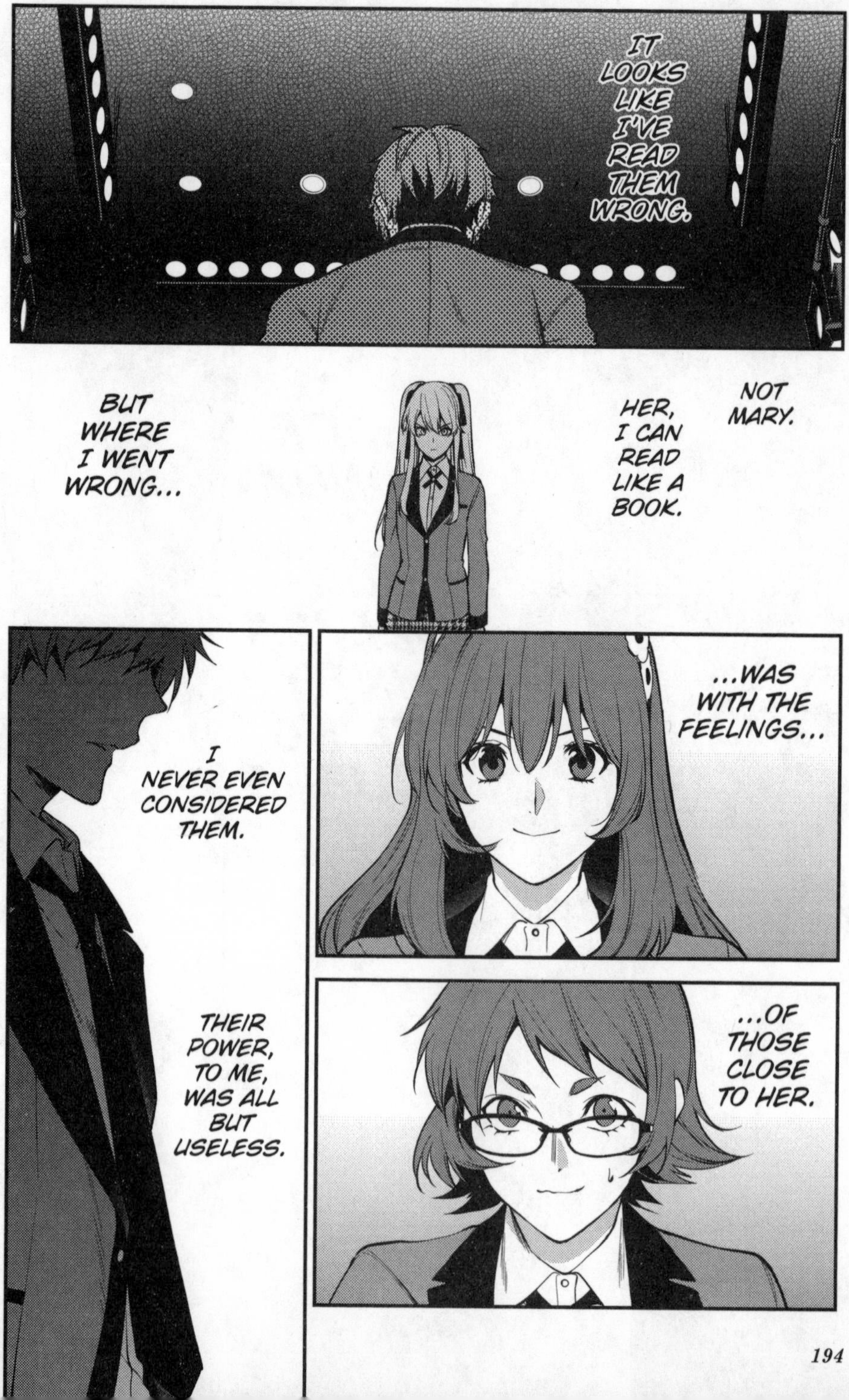
IT LOOKS LIKE I'VE READ THEM WRONG.
NOT MARY.
HER, I CAN READ LIKE A BOOK.
BUT WHERE I WENT WRONG...
...WAS WITH THE FEELINGS...
...OF THOSE CLOSE TO HER.
I NEVER EVEN CONSIDERED THEM.
THEIR POWER, TO ME, WAS ALL BUT USELESS.

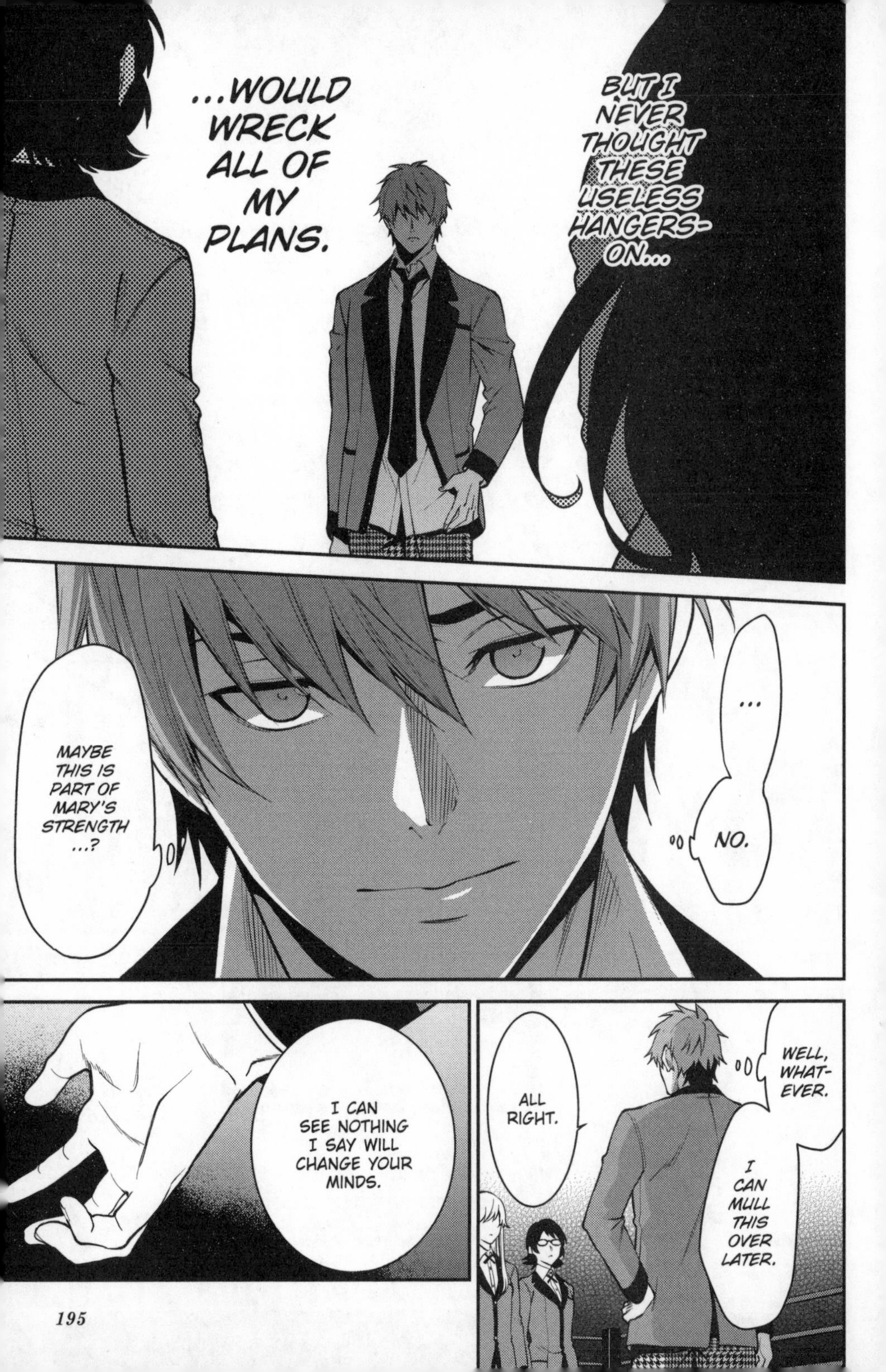
BUT I NEVER THOUGHT THESE USELESS HANGERS-ON...
...WOULD WRECK ALL OF MY PLANS.
...
NO.
MAYBE THIS IS PART OF MARY'S STRENGTH...?
WELL, WHAT-EVER.
I CAN MULL THIS OVER LATER.
ALL RIGHT.
I CAN SEE NOTHING I SAY WILL CHANGE YOUR MINDS.

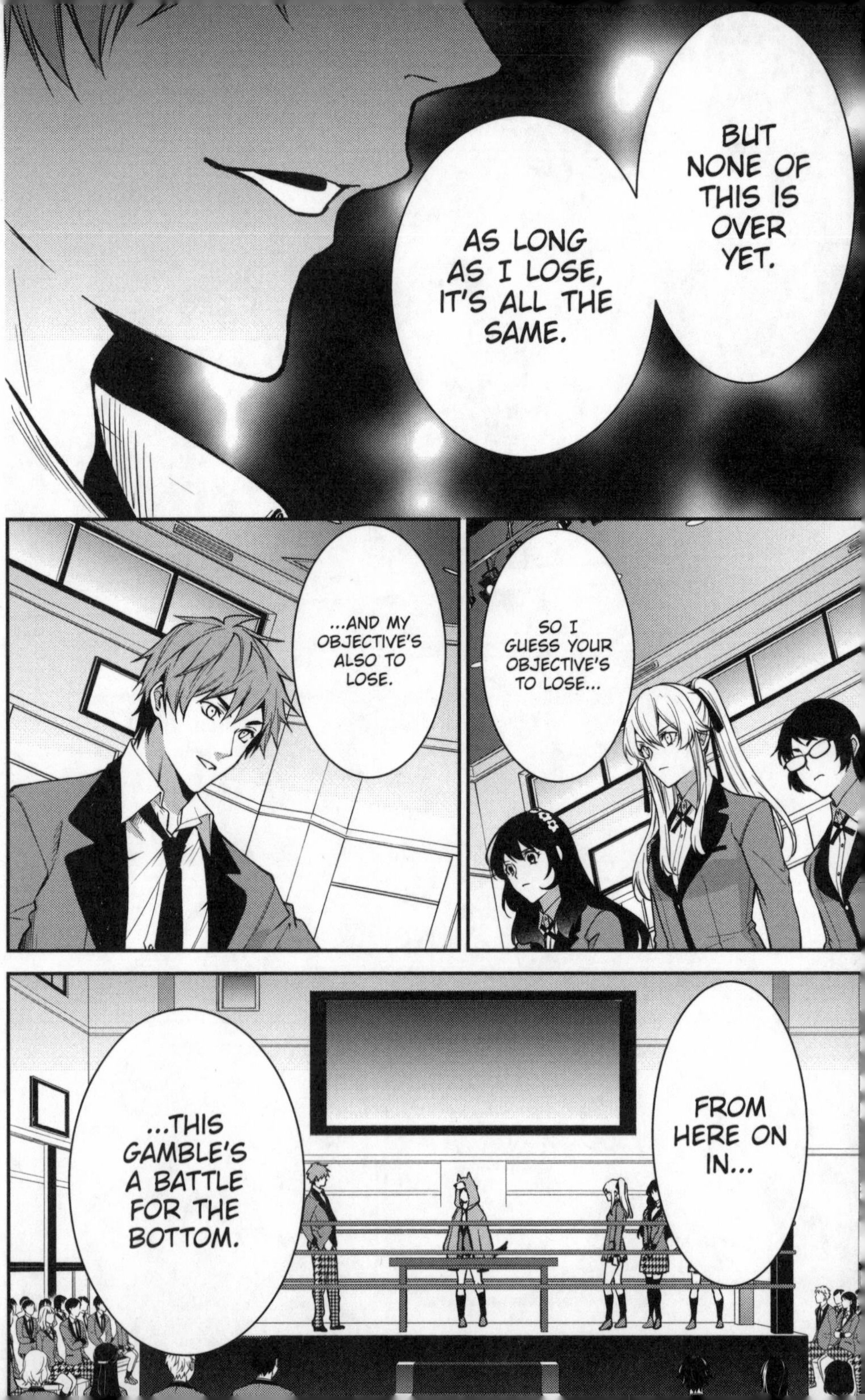
BUT NONE OF THIS IS OVER YET.
AS LONG AS I LOSE, IT'S ALL THE SAME.
SO I GUESS YOUR OBJECTIVE'S TO LOSE...
...AND MY OBJECTIVE'S ALSO TO LOSE.
FROM HERE ON IN...
...THIS GAMBLE'S A BATTLE FOR THE BOTTOM.

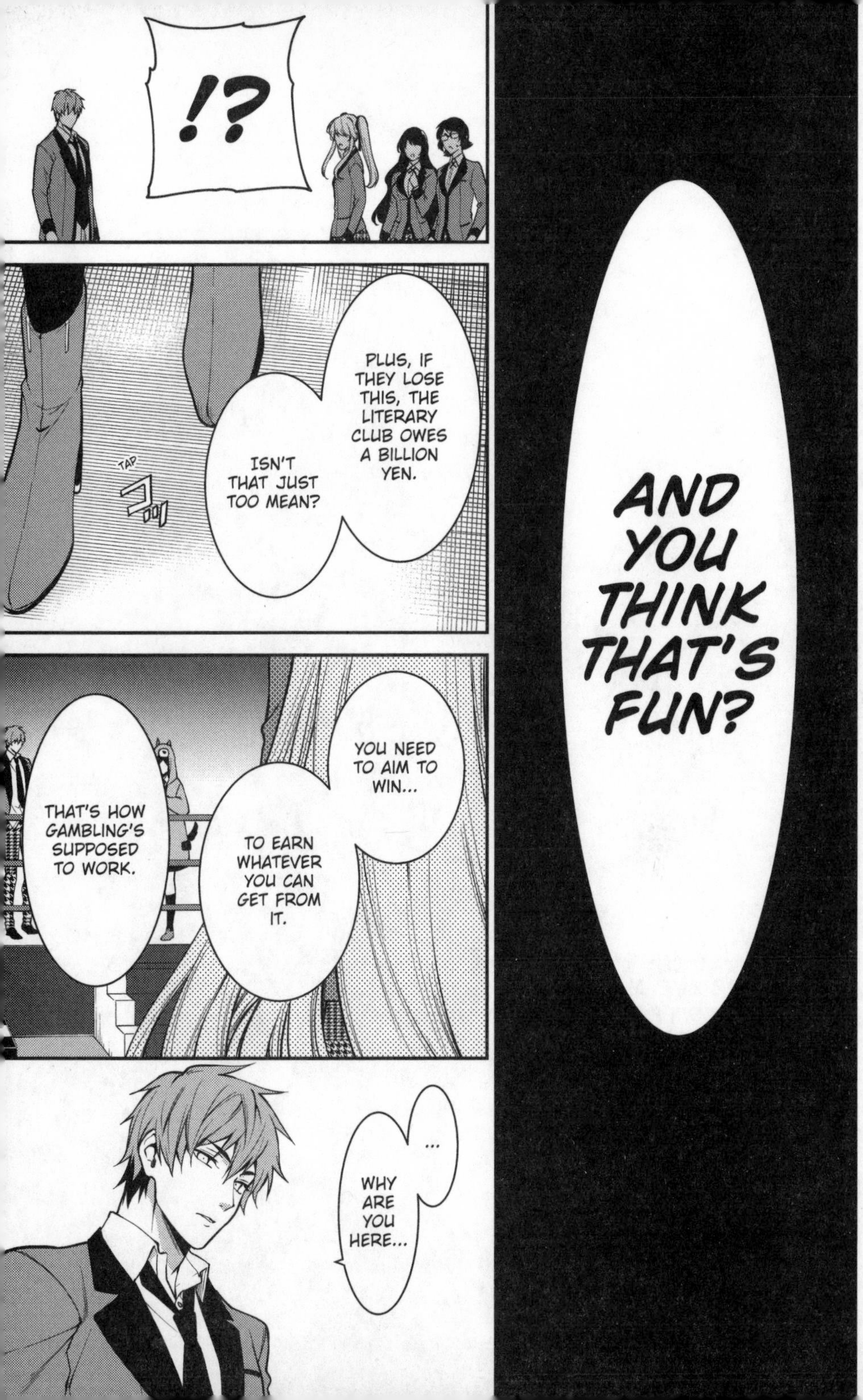
AND YOU THINK THAT'S FUN?
!?
PLUS, IF THEY LOSE THIS, THE LITERARY CLUB OWES A BILLION YEN.
ISN'T THAT JUST TOO MEAN?
TAP
YOU NEED TO AIM TO WIN...
TO EARN WHATEVER YOU CAN GET FROM IT.
THAT'S HOW GAMBLING'S SUPPOSED TO WORK.
...
WHY ARE YOU HERE...

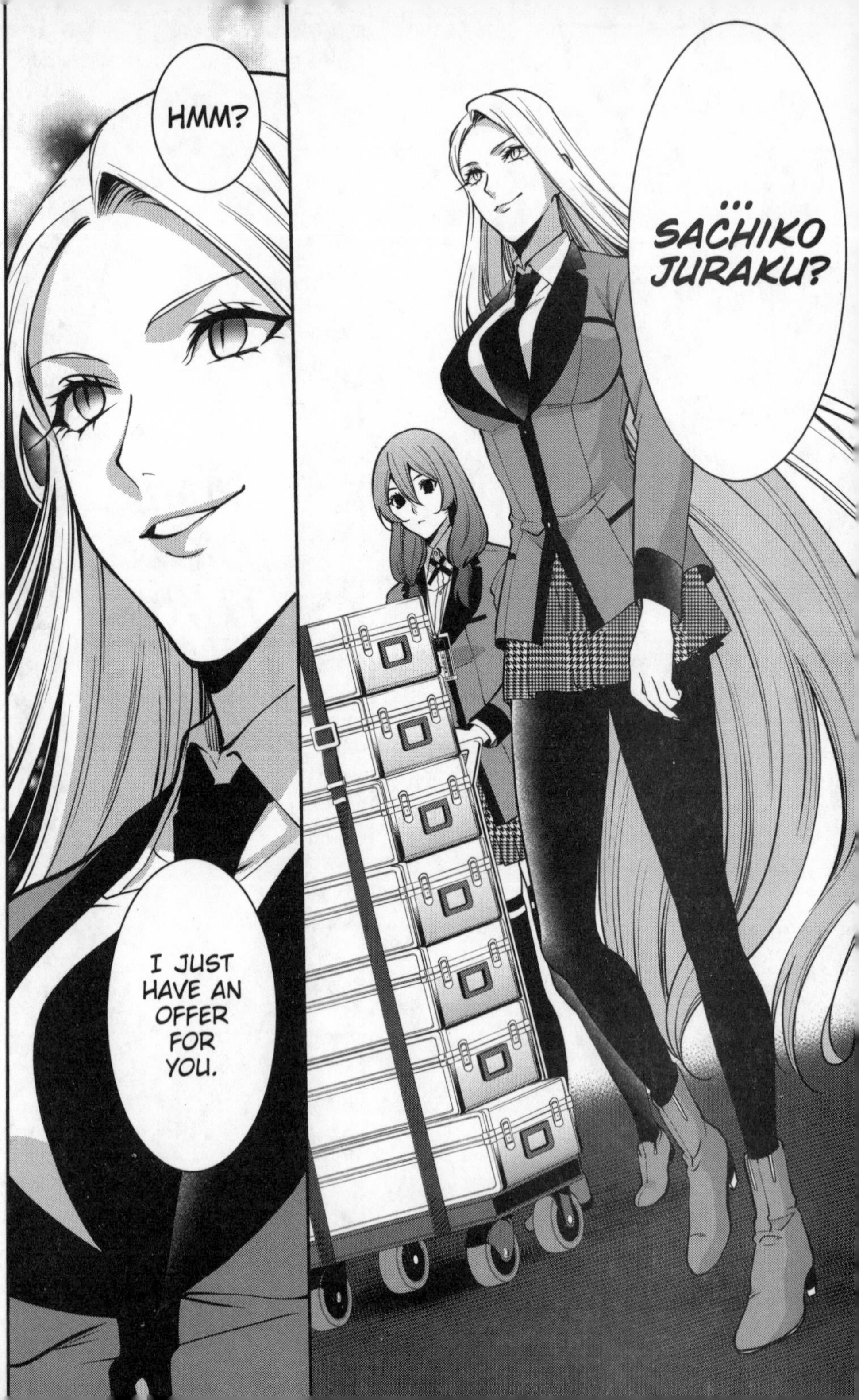
...SAČHIKO JURAKU?
HMM?
I JUST HAVE AN OFFER FOR YOU.

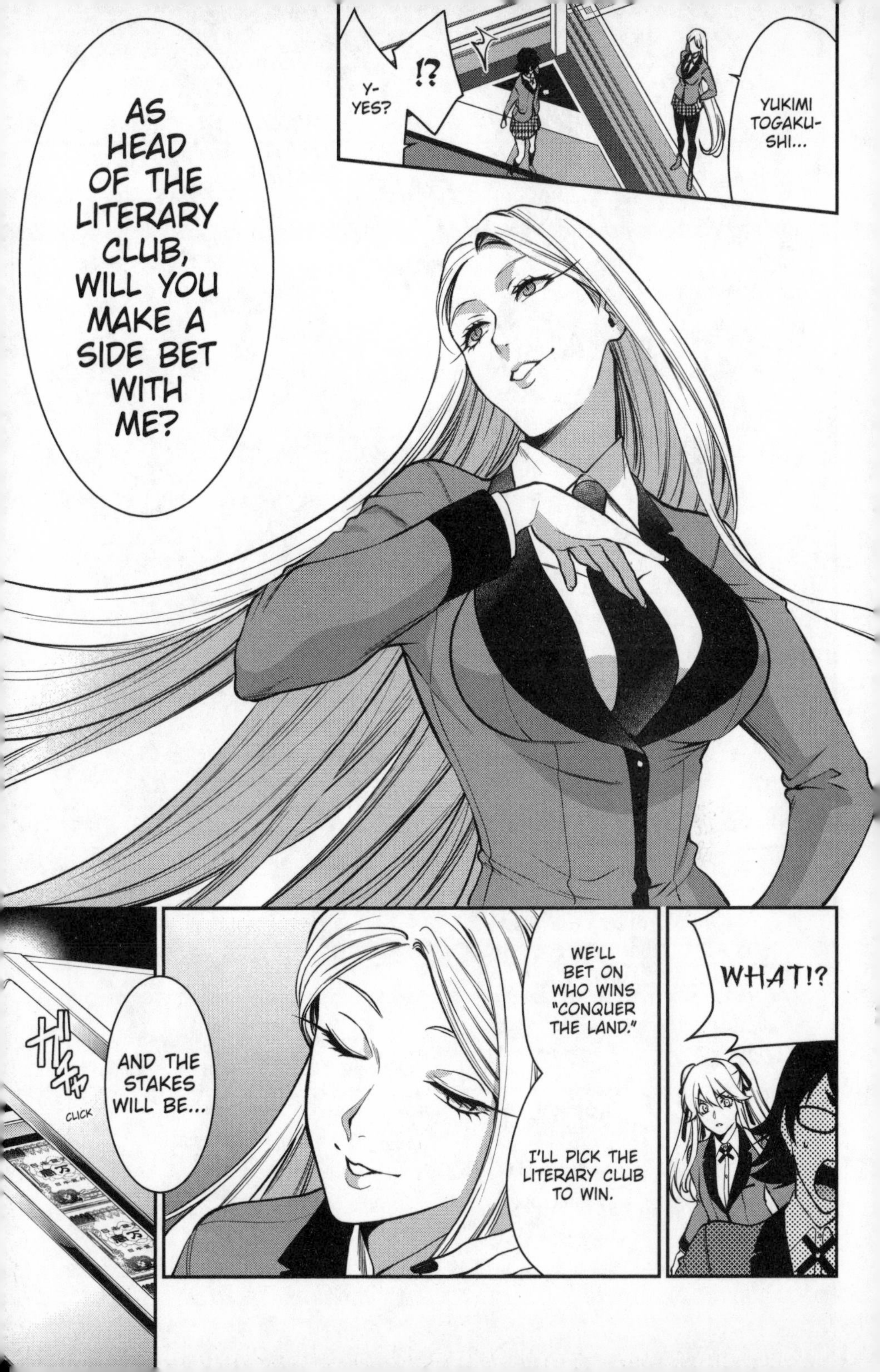
YUKIMI TOGAKUSHI...
!?
Y-YES?
AS HEAD OF THE LITERARY CLUB, WILL YOU MAKE A SIDE BET WITH ME?
WHAT!?
WE'LL BET ON WHO WINS "CONQUER THE LAND."
I'LL PICK THE LITERARY CLUB TO WIN.
AND THE STAKES WILL BE...
CLICK

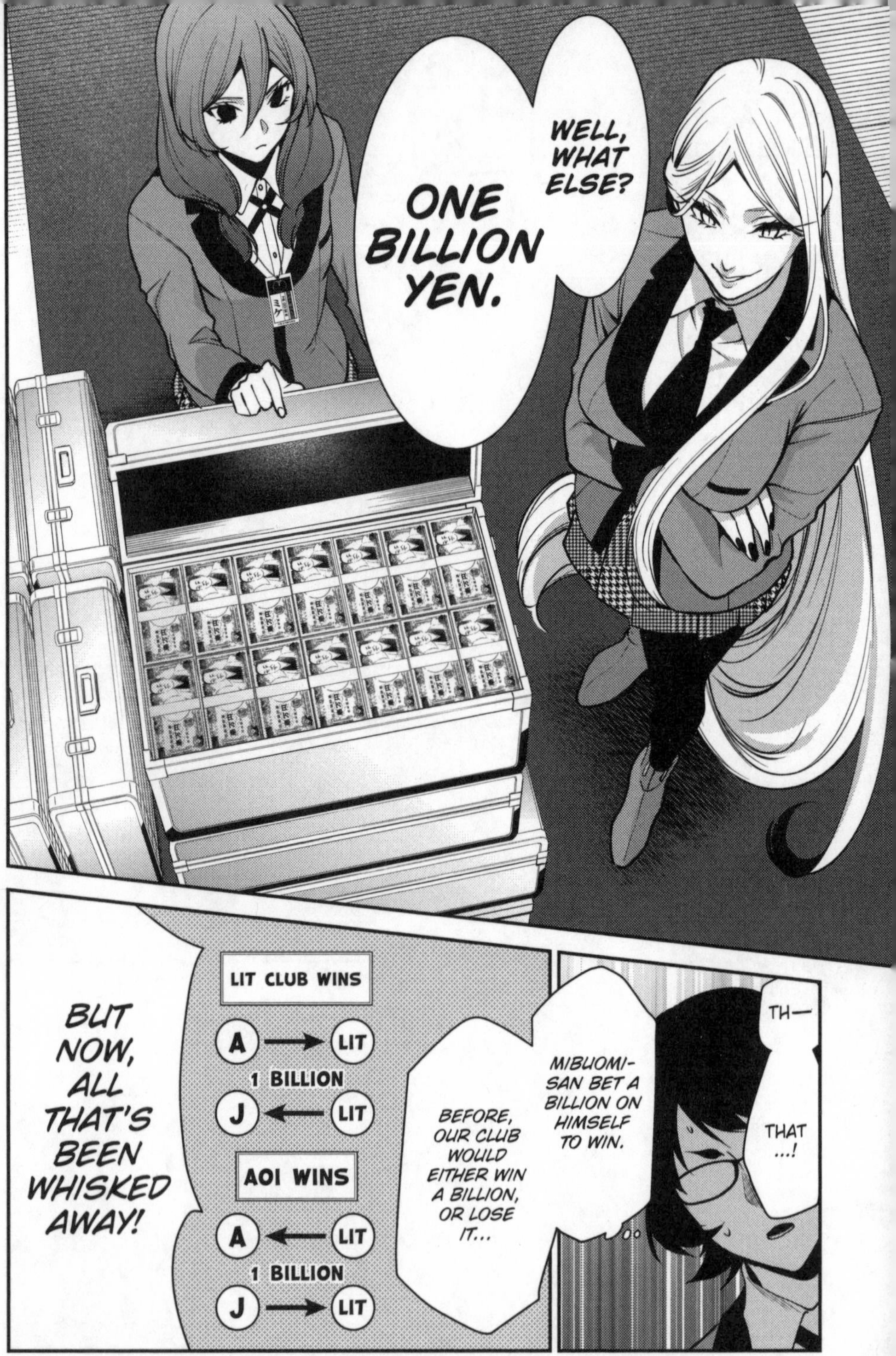
WELL, WHAT ELSE?
ONE BILLION YEN.
TH—
THAT...!
MIBUOMI-SAN BET A BILLION ON HIMSELF TO WIN.
BEFORE, OUR CLUB WOULD EITHER WIN A BILLION, OR LOSE IT...
LIT CLUB WINS
A → LIT
1 BILLION
J ← LIT
AOI WINS
A ← LIT
1 BILLION
J → LIT
BUT NOW, ALL THAT'S BEEN WHISKED AWAY!

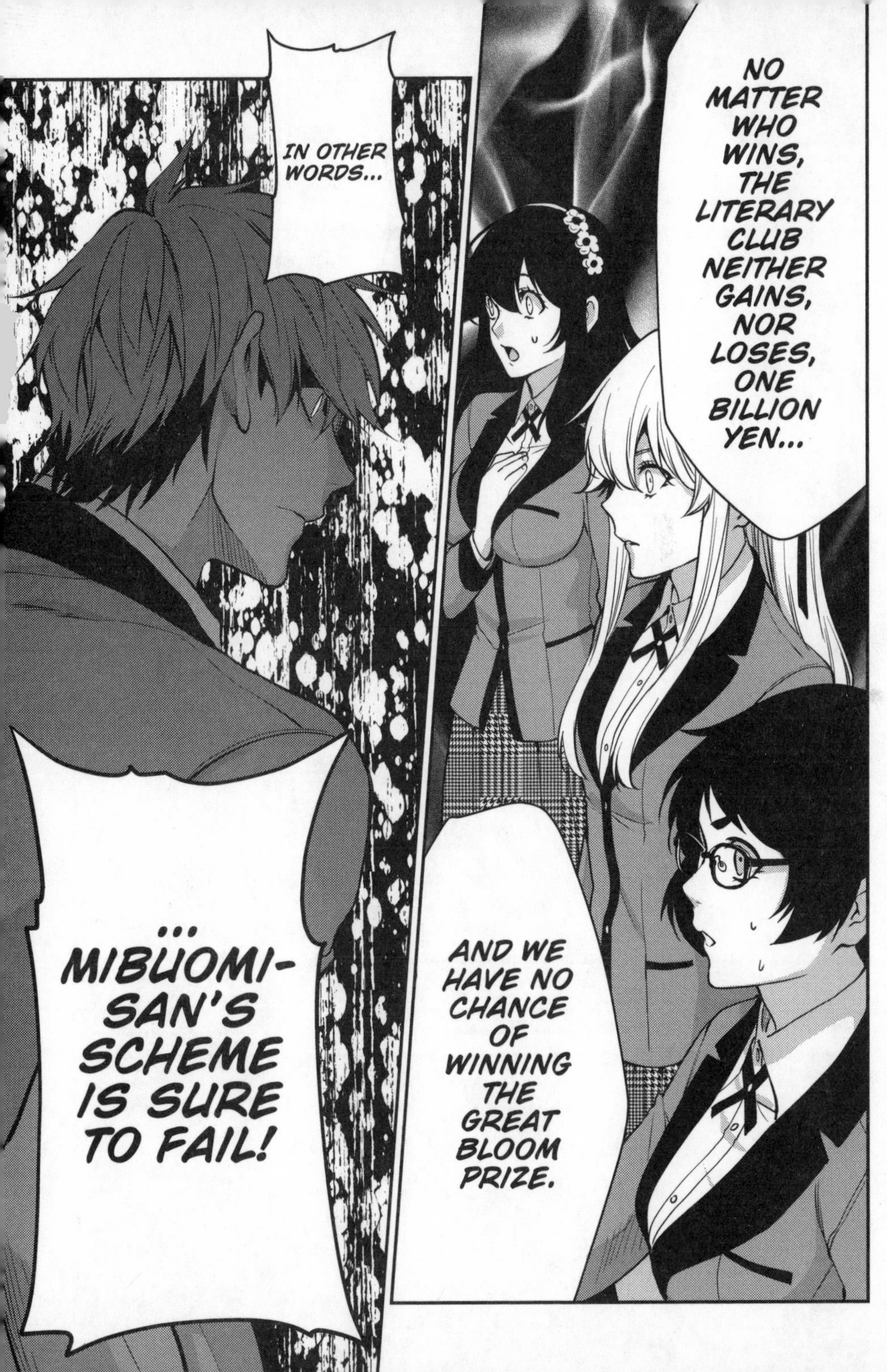
NO MATTER WHO WINS, THE LITERARY CLUB NEITHER GAINS, NOR LOSES, ONE BILLION YEN...
AND WE HAVE NO CHANCE OF WINNING THE GREAT BLOOM PRIZE.
IN OTHER WORDS...
...MIBÜOMI-SAN'S SCHEME IS SURE TO FAIL!

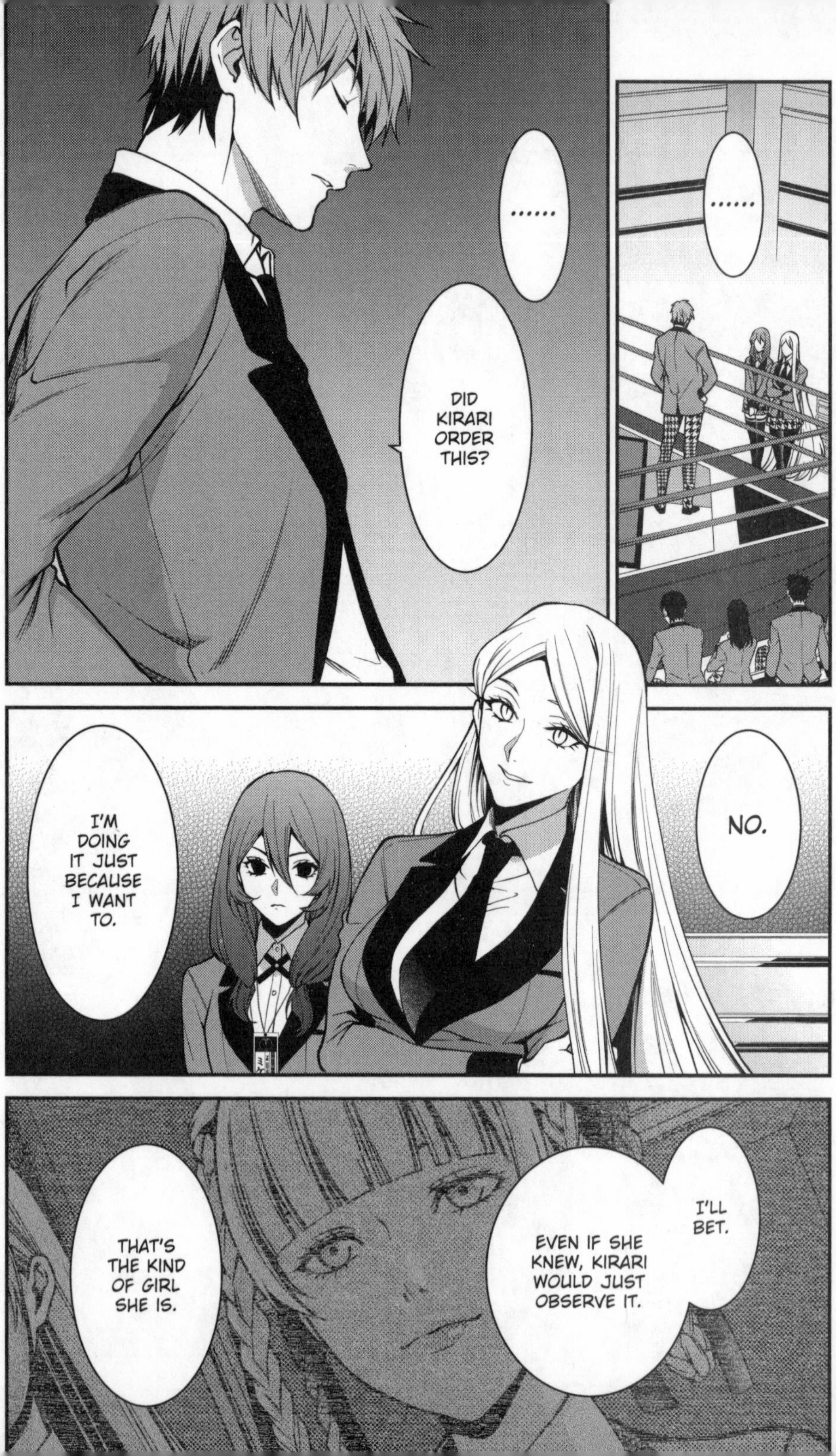

......
......
DID KIRARI ORDER THIS?
NO.
I'M DOING IT JUST BECAUSE I WANT TO.
I'LL BET.
EVEN IF SHE KNEW, KIRARI WOULD JUST OBSERVE IT.
THAT'S THE KIND OF GIRL SHE IS.

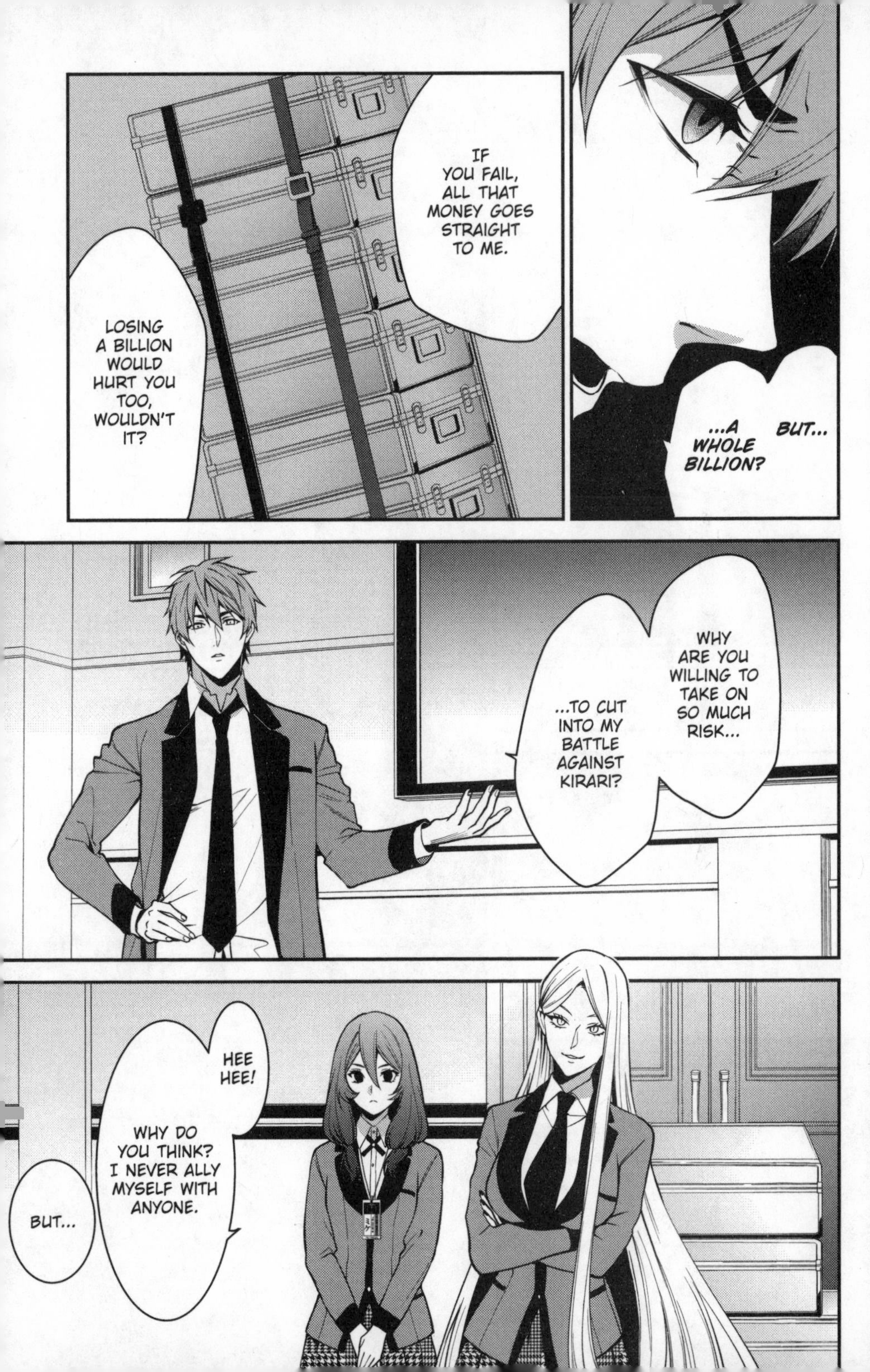
BUT...
...A WHOLE BILLION?
IF YOU FAIL, ALL THAT MONEY GOES STRAIGHT TO ME.
LOSING A BILLION WOULD HURT YOU TOO, WOULDN'T IT?
WHY ARE YOU WILLING TO TAKE ON SO MUCH RISK...
...TO CUT INTO MY BATTLE AGAINST KIRARI?
HEE HEE!
WHY DO YOU THINK? I NEVER ALLY MYSELF WITH ANYONE.
BUT...

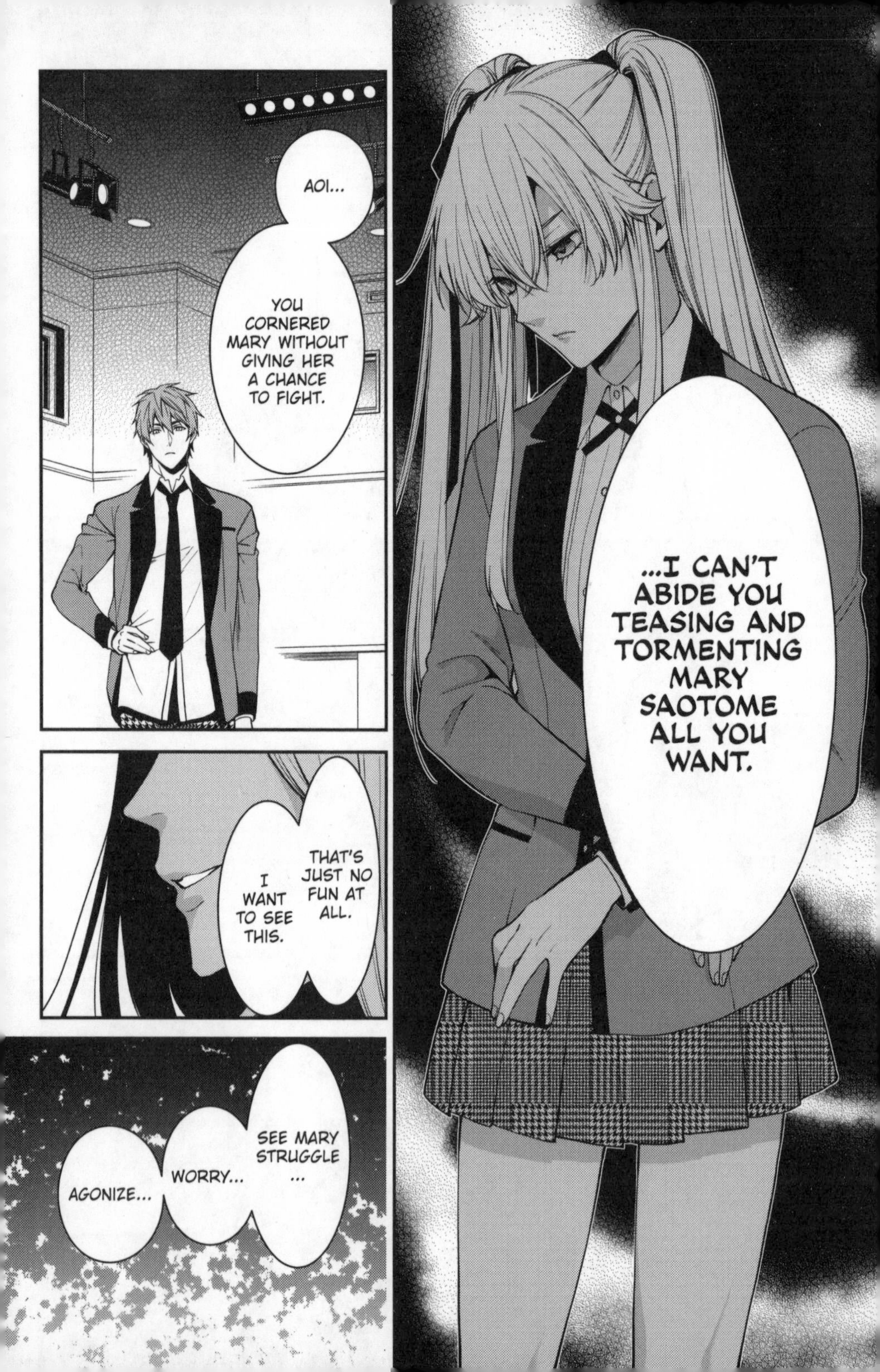
...I CAN'T ABIDE YOU TEASING AND TORMENTING MARY SAOTOME ALL YOU WANT.
AOI...
YOU CORNERED MARY WITHOUT GIVING HER A CHANCE TO FIGHT.
THAT'S JUST NO FUN AT ALL.
I WANT TO SEE THIS.
SEE MARY STRUGGLE...
WORRY...
AGONIZE...

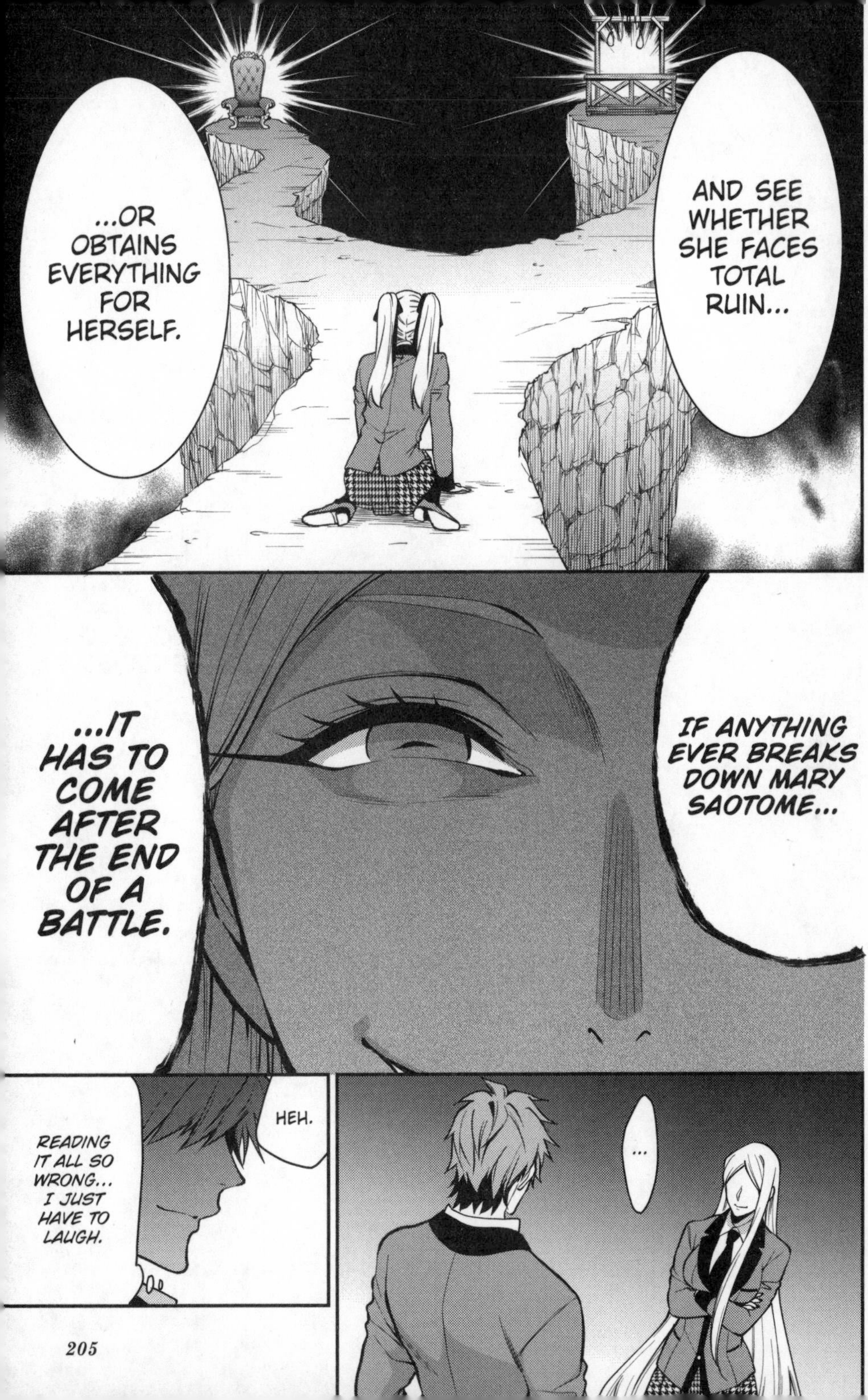
AND SEE WHETHER SHE FACES TOTAL RUIN...
...OR OBTAINS EVERYTHING FOR HERSELF.
IF ANYTHING EVER BREAKS DOWN MARY SAOTOME...
...IT HAS TO COME AFTER THE END OF A BATTLE.
...
HEH.
READING IT ALL SO WRONG... I JUST HAVE TO LAUGH.

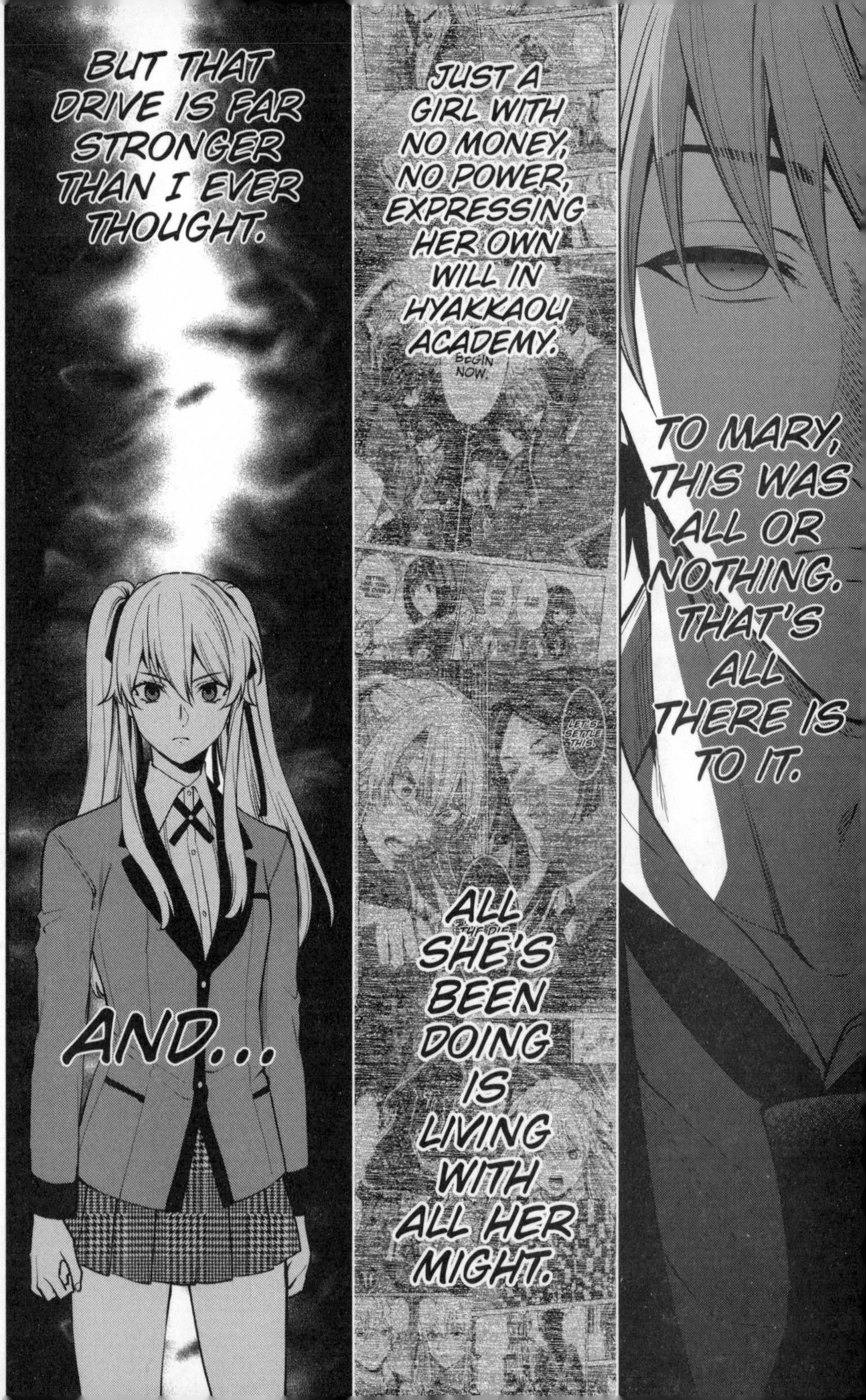
TO MARY, THIS WAS ALL OR NOTHING. THAT'S ALL THERE IS TO IT.
JUST A GIRL WITH NO MONEY, NO POWER, EXPRESSING HER OWN WILL IN HYAKKAOU ACADEMY.
BEGIN NOW.
LET'S SETTLE THIS.
ALL SHE'S BEEN DOING IS LIVING WITH ALL HER MIGHT.
BUT THAT DRIVE IS FAR STRONGER THAN I EVER THOUGHT.
AND...

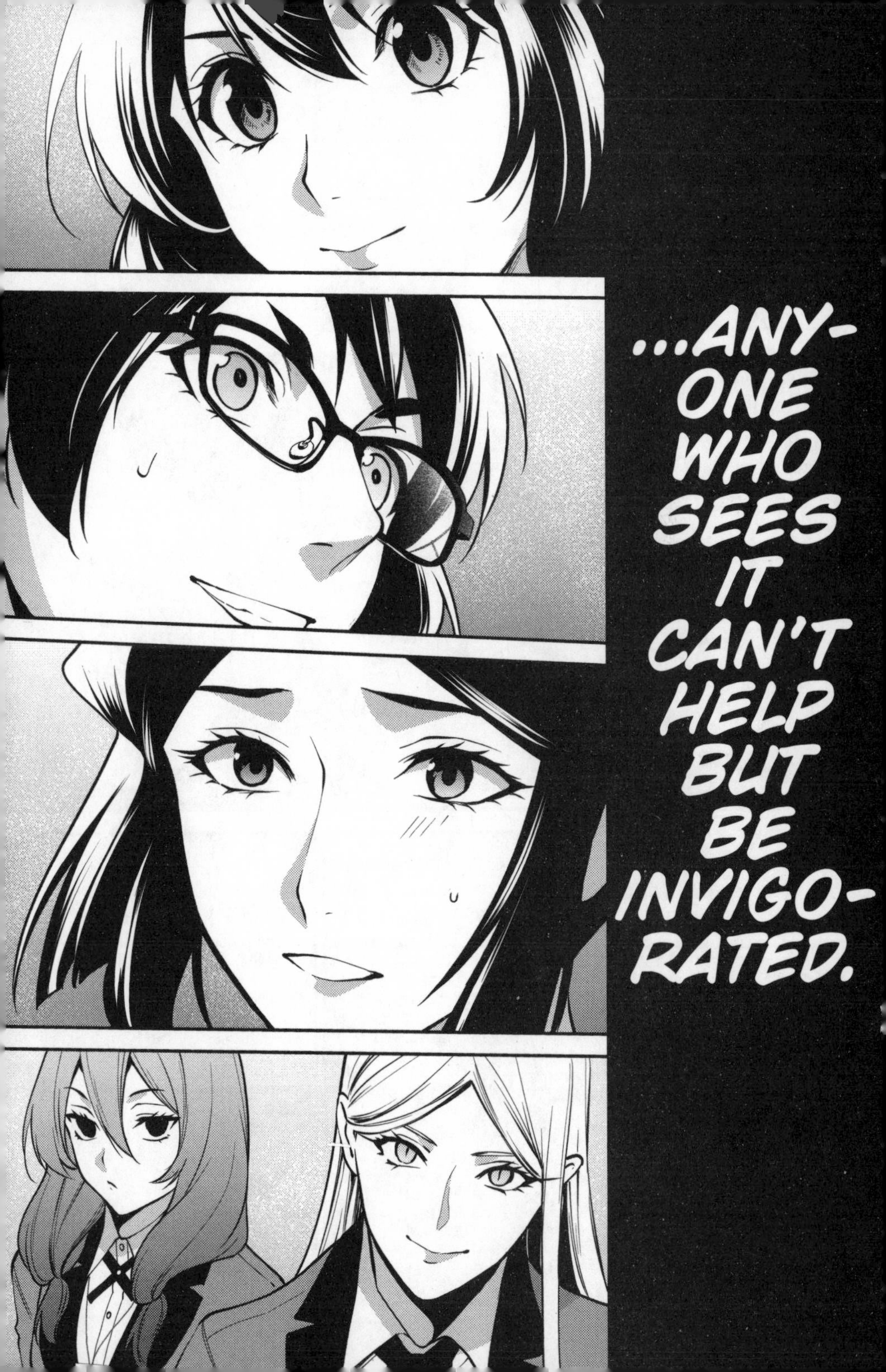
...ANY-ONE WHO SEES IT CAN'T HELP BUT BE INVIGO-RATED.

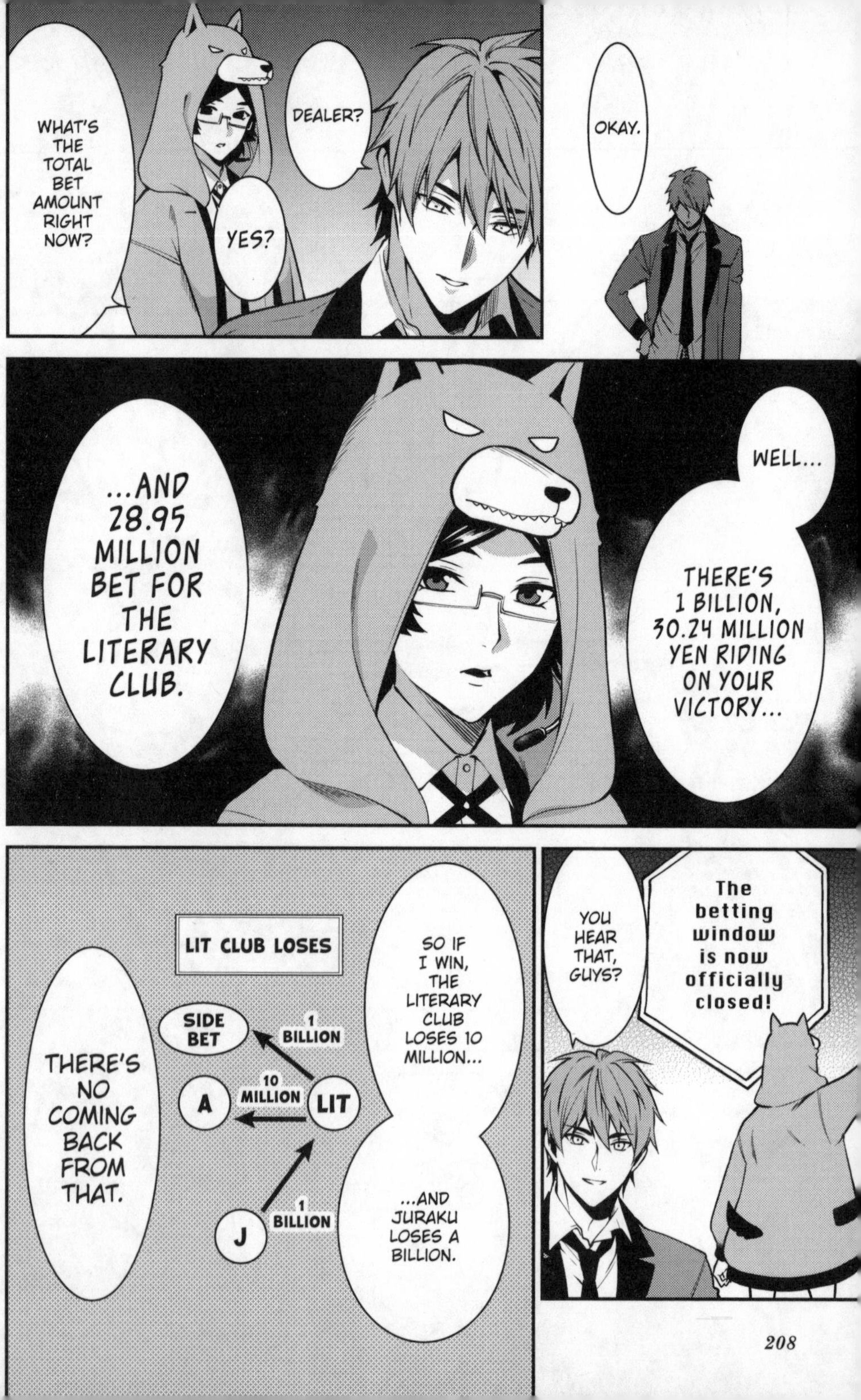
OKAY.
DEALER?
YES?
WHAT'S THE TOTAL BET AMOUNT RIGHT NOW?
WELL...
THERE'S 1 BILLION, 30.24 MILLION YEN RIDING ON YOUR VICTORY...
...AND 28.95 MILLION BET FOR THE LITERARY CLUB.
The betting window is now officially closed!
YOU HEAR THAT, GUYS?
SO IF I WIN, THE LITERARY CLUB LOSES 10 MILLION...
...AND JURAKU LOSES A BILLION.
LIT CLUB LOSES
SIDE BET
1 BILLION
10 MILLION
A
LIT
1 BILLION
J
THERE'S NO COMING BACK FROM THAT.

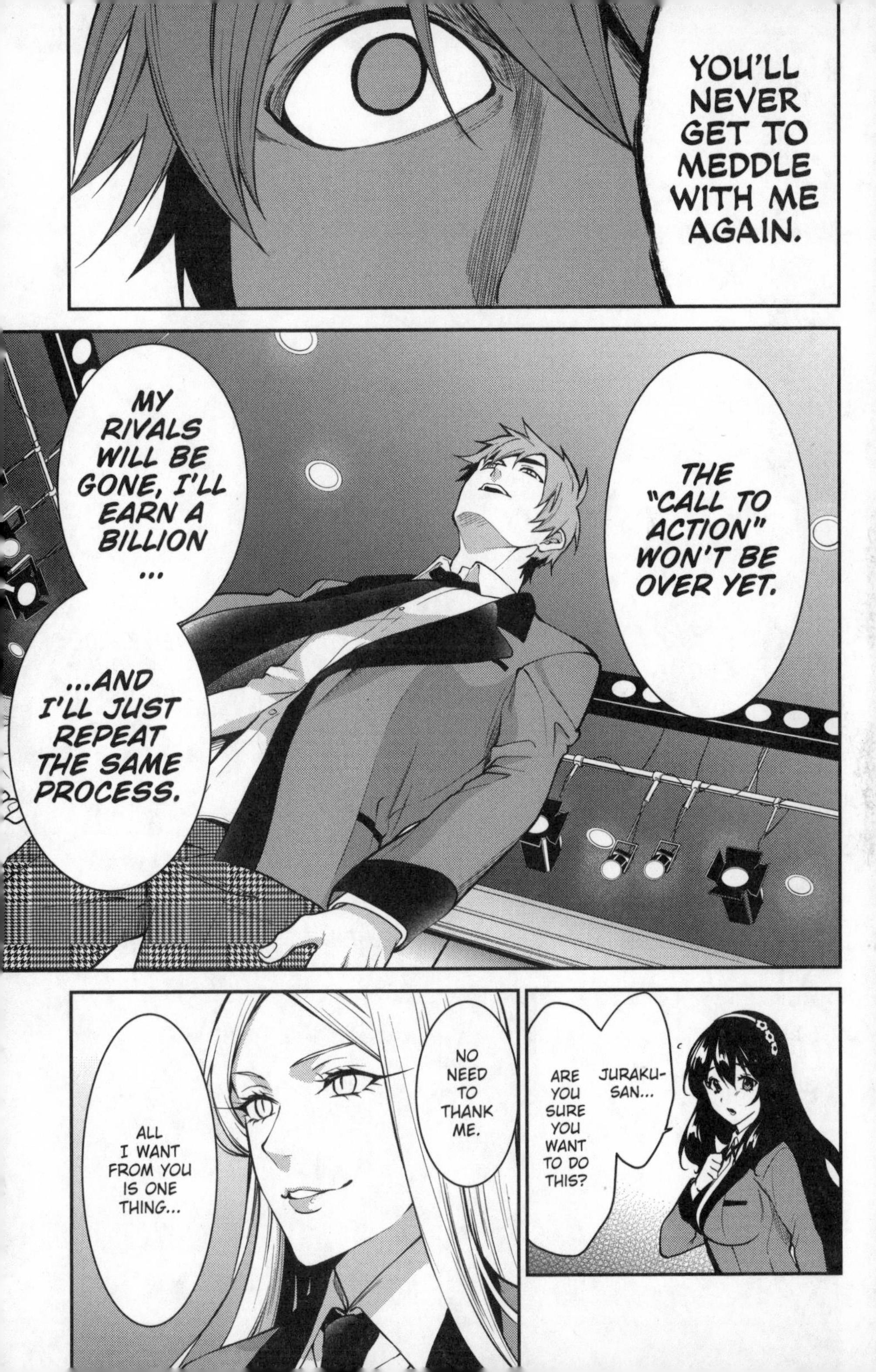
YOU'LL NEVER GET TO MEDDLE WITH ME AGAIN.
THE "CALL TO ACTION" WON'T BE OVER YET.
MY RIVALS WILL BE GONE, I'LL EARN A BILLION ...
...AND I'LL JUST REPEAT THE SAME PROCESS.
JURAKU-SAN...
ARE YOU SURE YOU WANT TO DO THIS?
NO NEED TO THANK ME.
ALL I WANT FROM YOU IS ONE THING...

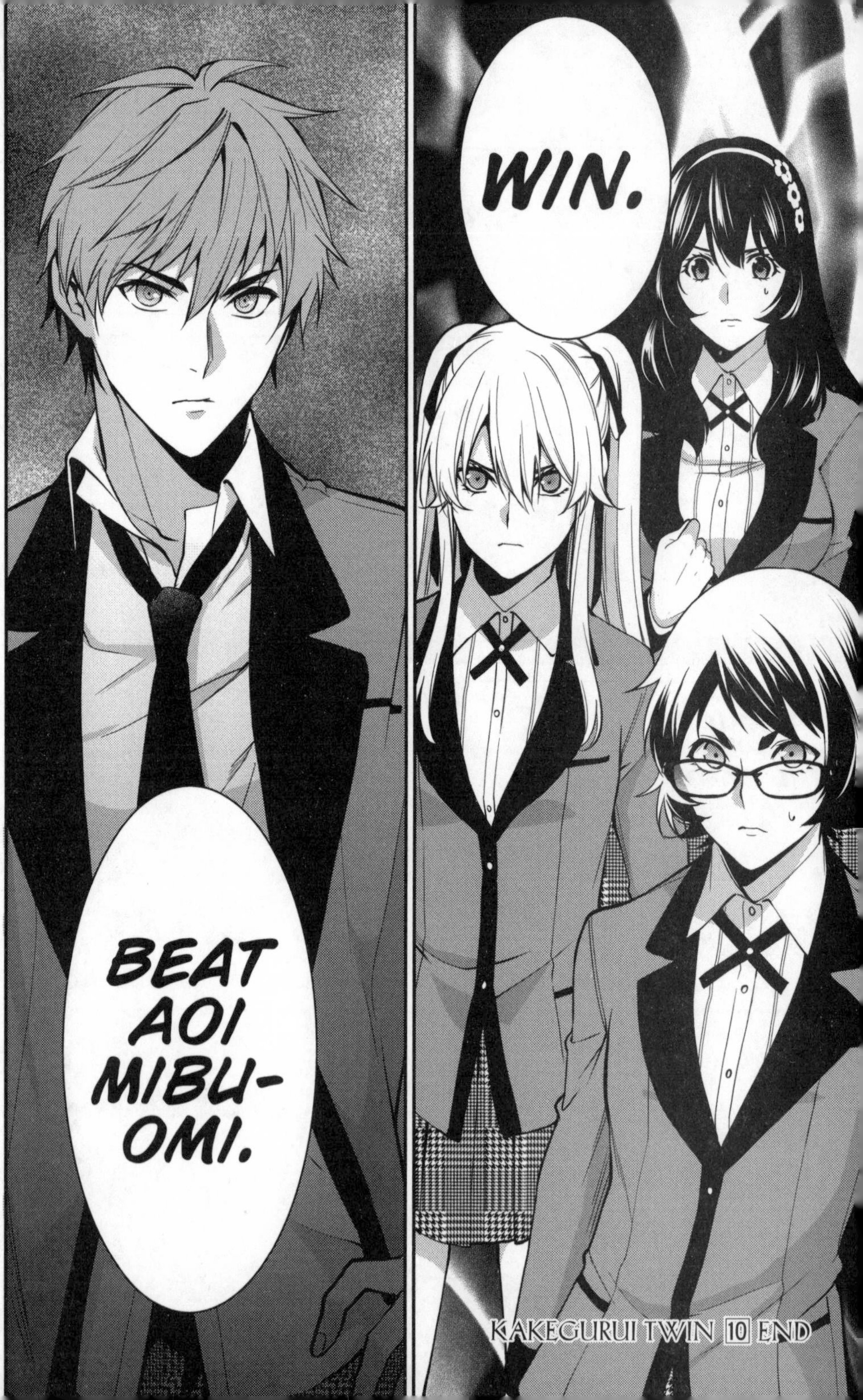
WIN.
BEAT AOI MIBU-OMI.
KAKEGURUI TWIN 10 END

TIME FOR SOME END-OF-THE-VOLUME BONUS COMICS!

THE FULL-BLOOM SECRET FILE

* This has no relation to the actual story.

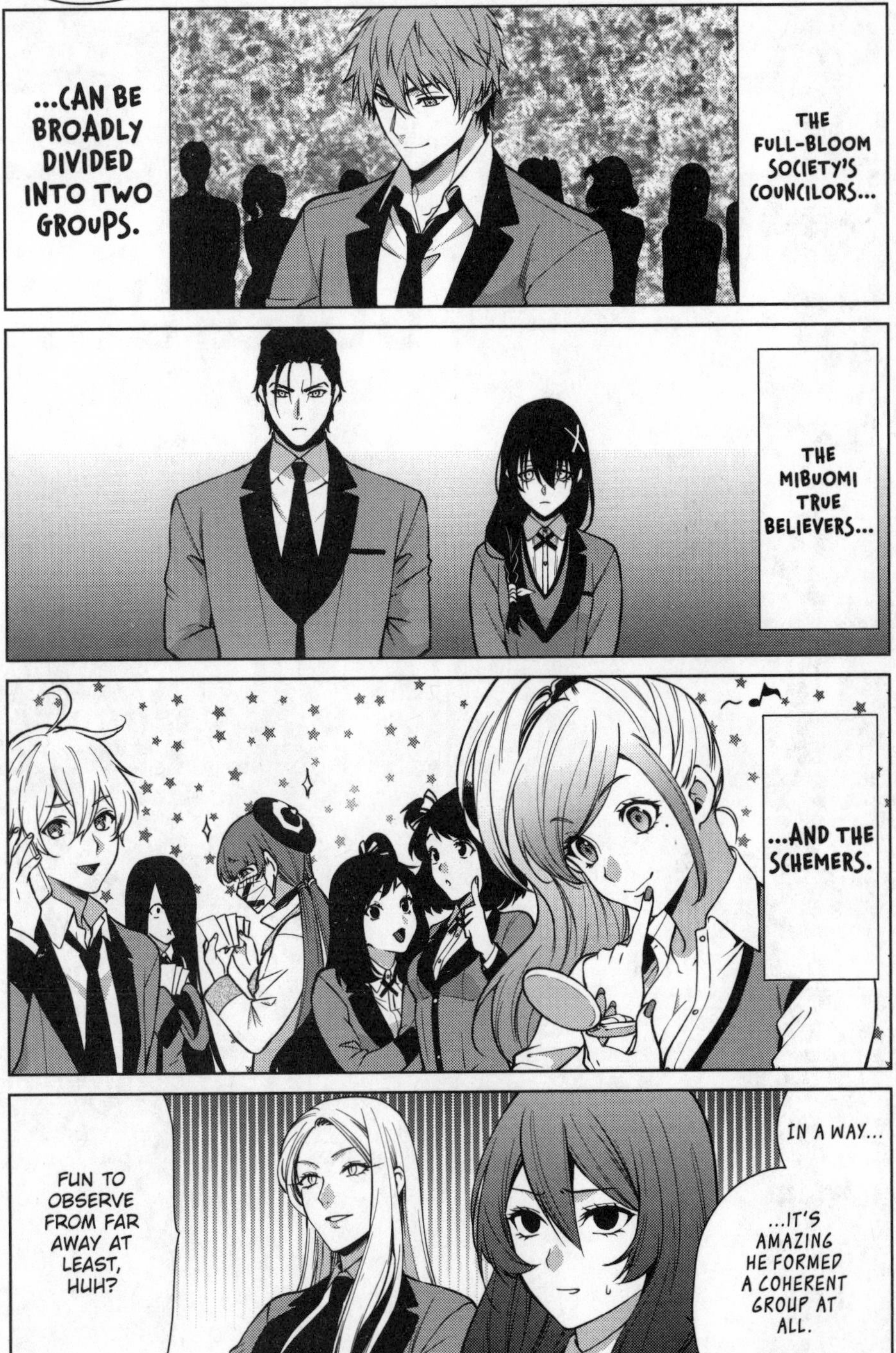
THE FULL-BLOOM SOCIETY'S COUNCILORS...
...CAN BE BROADLY DIVIDED INTO TWO GROUPS.
THE MIBUOMI TRUE BELIEVERS...
...AND THE SCHEMERS.
IN A WAY...
...IT'S AMAZING HE FORMED A COHERENT GROUP AT ALL.
FUN TO OBSERVE FROM FAR AWAY AT LEAST, HUH?

GAMBLING, THAT IS MY RAISON D'ÊTRE.

A counting game involving sets of cards.

It's a simple game, highly dependent on luck, but with cards being placed facedown and then gradually being revealed, there's a massive number of possibilities to think about.

To maximize your chances, you must do everything you can to the limit—part of what makes gambling fun in the first place. I'd love for the readers to try it out. Don't go betting real money on it, though.

Conquer

vs. vs. vs.

the Land

Thank you for picking up the tenth volume of *Kakegurui Twin*!

The tale of Mary has reached the auspicious Volume 10, and as a writer, nothing could fill me with more happiness. Looking across the whole *Kakegurui* franchise, Mary makes the most appearances in the story by far—but no matter how much we draw her, her behavior and reactions always seem so strangely fresh to me. Not even I thought she was a character who'd have this much depth, so I really look forward to the future. Aoi Mibuomi, of course, is her strongest opponent yet, and their gamble is still underway. I hope you'll look forward to the conclusion of that.

For this volume as well, I enjoyed untold help from Saiki-sensei, the assistants, our editors Sasaki-san and Yumoto-san, and everyone else involved in the production. Thanks to them, and also to our readers (and Tanaka too), we managed to get Volume 10 out. Thank you all very much.

See all of you in Volume 11.

Homura Kawamoto

KAKEGURUI TWIN X

◆ Special Thanks ◆

My editors
Kawamoto-sama

Ken'ichi Sato-sama
Kozue Tachikawa-sama

Volume 10!
Things are getting really exciting! And what's
more, it's "to be continued" in the next volume!
I can't wait to see how it'll turn out!
The cover features Mary with a male character
for the first time, so I had to feel around to
figure out what kind of distance they'd take.
Mary wouldn't want him too close, I thought—
but then again, Aoi would likely barge right
into her personal space, so...
It was fun to ponder over, but in the end, I got
the okay for this amount of distance. What
about the next volume, though? Hopefully
you'll join me as we watch over the conclusion
of this call to action.

Kei Saiki

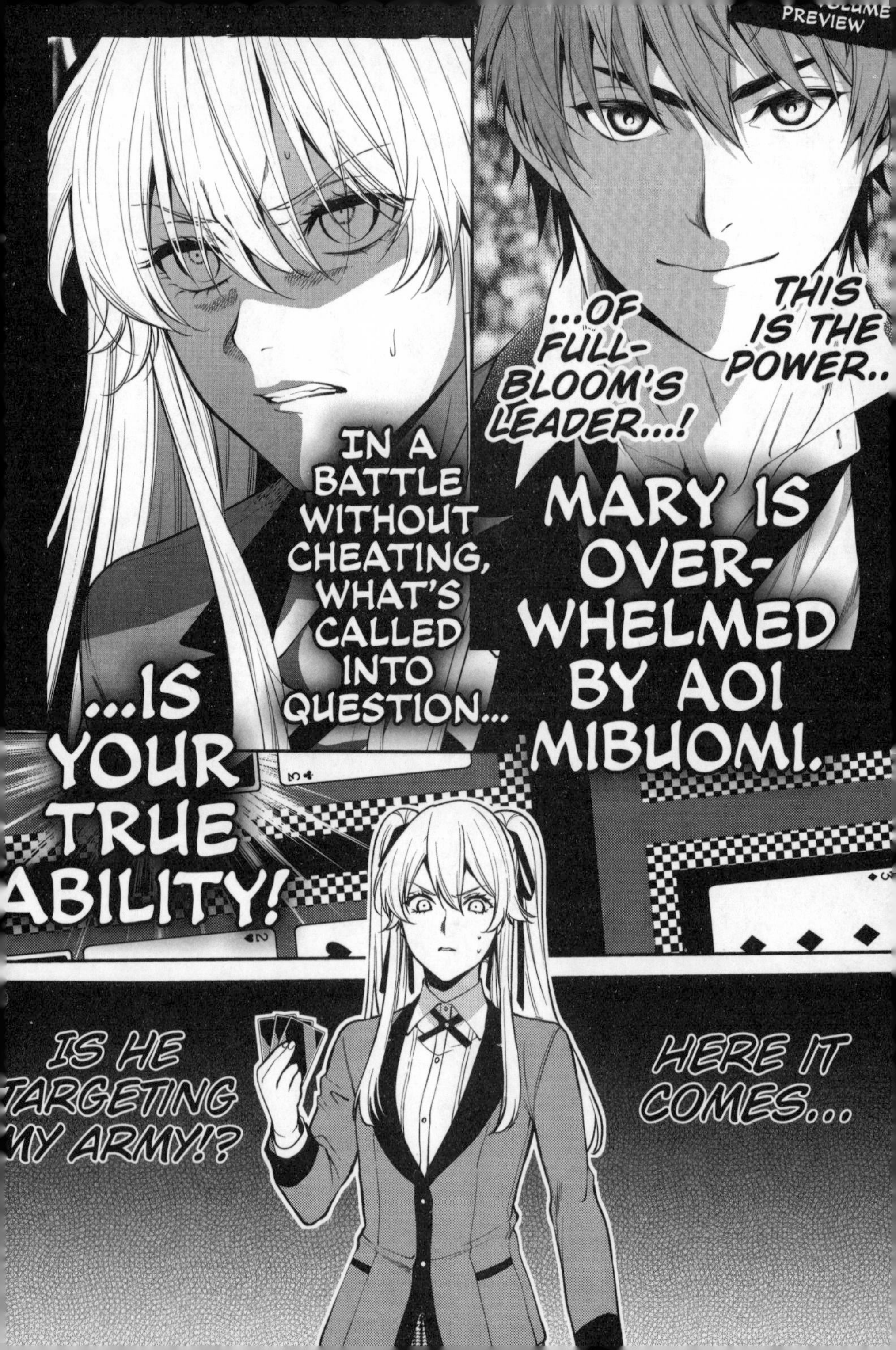
PREVIEW
THIS IS THE POWER..
...OF FULL-BLOOM'S LEADER...!
MARY IS OVER-WHELMED BY AOI MIBUOMI.
IN A BATTLE WITHOUT CHEATING, WHAT'S CALLED INTO QUESTION...
...IS YOUR TRUE ABILITY!
HERE IT COMES...
IS HE TARGETING MY ARMY!?

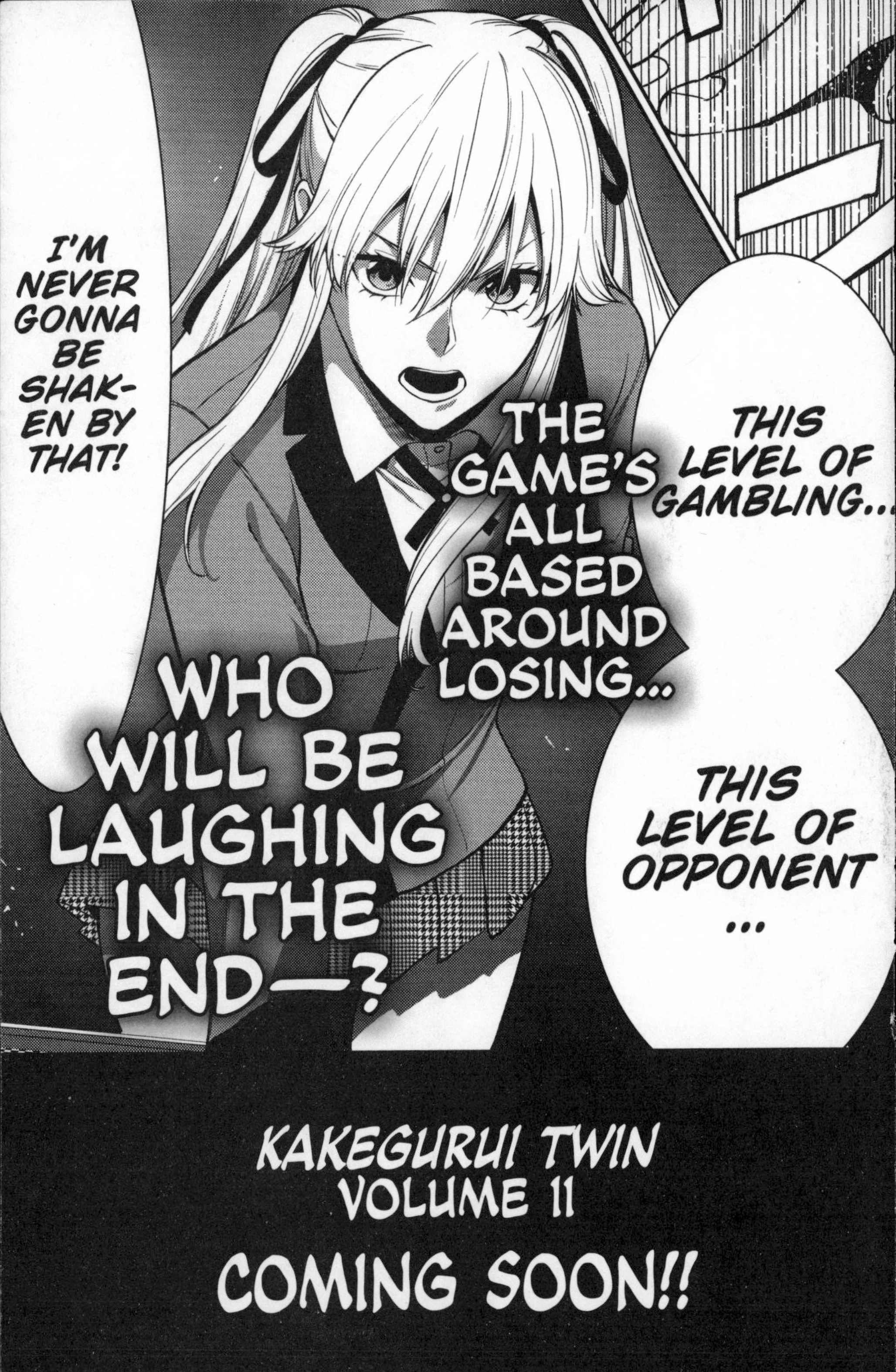
THIS LEVEL OF GAMBLING...
THIS LEVEL OF OPPONENT ...
THE GAME'S ALL BASED AROUND LOSING...
I'M NEVER GONNA BE SHAK-EN BY THAT!
WHO WILL BE LAUGHING IN THE END—?

KAKEGURUI TWIN
VOLUME 11

COMING SOON!!

Kakegurui Twin

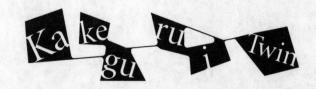

Translation Notes

Common Honorifics

no honorific: Indicates familiarity or closeness; if used without permission or reason, addressing someone in this manner would constitute an insult.

-san: The Japanese equivalent of Mr./Mrs./Miss. If a situation calls for politeness, this is the fail-safe honorific.

-sama: Conveys great respect; may also indicate the social status of the speaker is lower than that of the addressee.

-kun: Used most often when referring to boys, this honorific indicates affection or familiarity. Occasionally used by older men among their peers, but it may also be used by anyone referring to a person of lower standing.

-chan: An affectionate honorific indicating familiarity used mostly in reference to girls; also used in reference to cute persons or animals of either gender.

-sensei: A respectful term for teachers, artists, or high-level professionals.

-niisan, **nii-san**, **aniki**, etc.: A term of endearment meaning "big brother" that may be more widely used to address any young man who is like a brother, regardless of whether he is related or not.

-neesan, **nee-san**, **aneki**, etc.: The female counterpart of the above, *nee-san* means "big sister."

Yen conversion: While exchange rates fluctuate daily, a convenient conversion estimation is about ¥100 to $1 USD.

Hyakkaou Private Academy: In Japanese, *hyakkaou* means "one hundred flowers"—thus, all the classrooms in the school are named after different kinds of flowers.

Fido/Mittens: In the original, male housepets are called "Pochi"—a common Japanese name for dogs—and female housepets are called "Mike"—a common Japanese name for calico cats, which, due to genetics, are nearly always female.

PAGE 40

Koi-Koi is a Japanese card game played with a deck of Japanese cards called *hanafuda* ("flower cards"). Unlike the more commonly known French-suited cards, *hanafuda* decks consist of forty-eight smaller-size cards divided into months and seasons, as opposed to fifty-two larger cards divided into numbers and face cards. *Koi-Koi* involves matching different cards together to create sets (*yaku*), and is just one of many games that can be played with *hanafuda*.

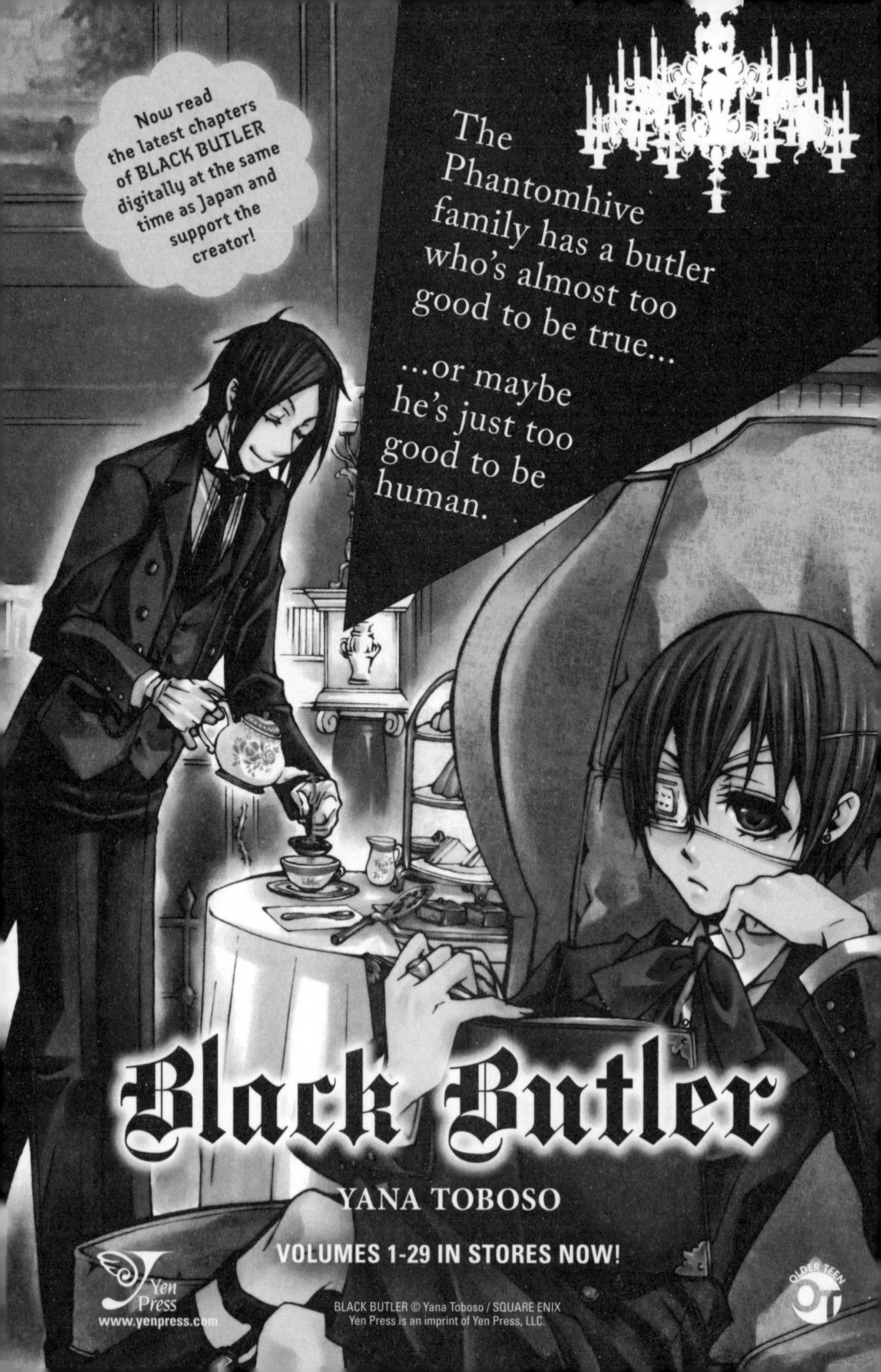
Now read the latest chapters of BLACK BUTLER digitally at the same time as Japan and support the creator!
The Phantomhive family has a butler who's almost too good to be true...
...or maybe he's just too good to be human.
Black Butler
YANA TOBOSO
VOLUMES 1-29 IN STORES NOW!
Yen Press
www.yenpress.com
BLACK BUTLER © Yana Toboso / SQUARE ENIX
Yen Press is an imprint of Yen Press, LLC.
OLDER TEEN
OT

MURDERER IN THE STREETS, KILLER IN THE SHEETS!

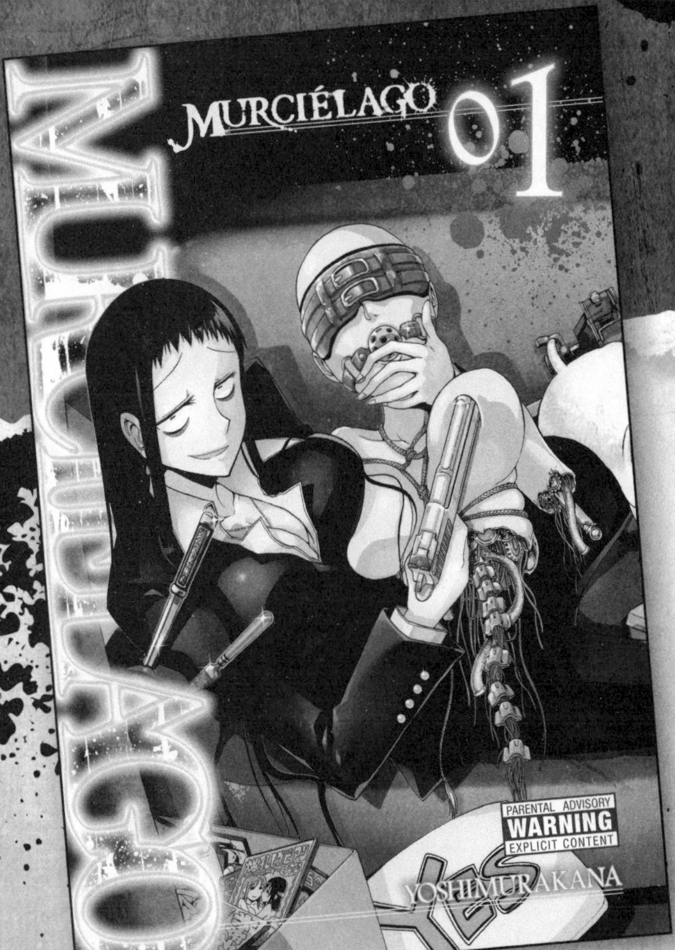
MURCIÉLAGO 01
PARENTAL ADVISORY
WARNING
EXPLICIT CONTENT
YOSHIMURAKANA

MURCIÉLAGO

VOLUMES 1-16 AVAILABLE NOW!

Yen Press

www.YenPress.com

Mass murderer Kuroko Koumori has two passions in life: taking lives and pleasuring ladies. This doesn't leave her with many career prospects, but Kuroko actually has the perfect gig—as a hit woman for the police!

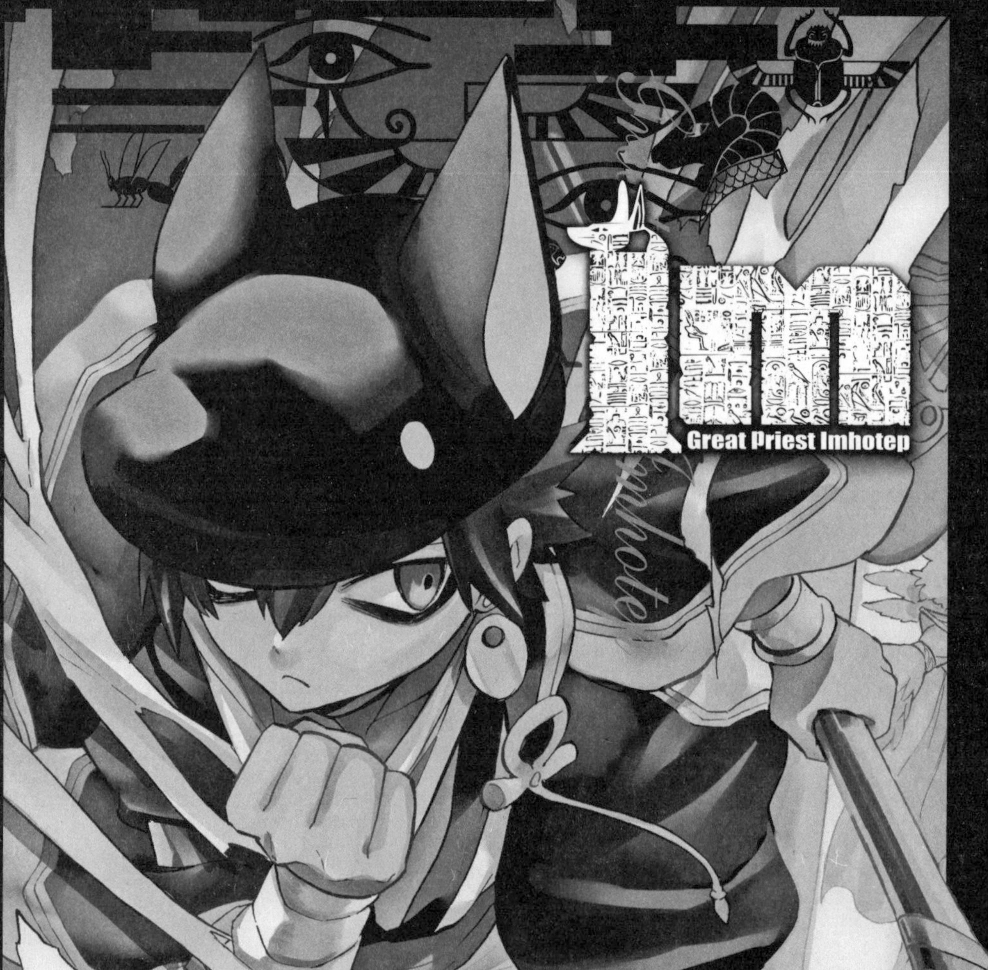
Im
Great Priest Imhotep
VOLUMES 1-9
IN STORES NOW!
Volumes 1-11 AVAILABLE DIGITALLY!

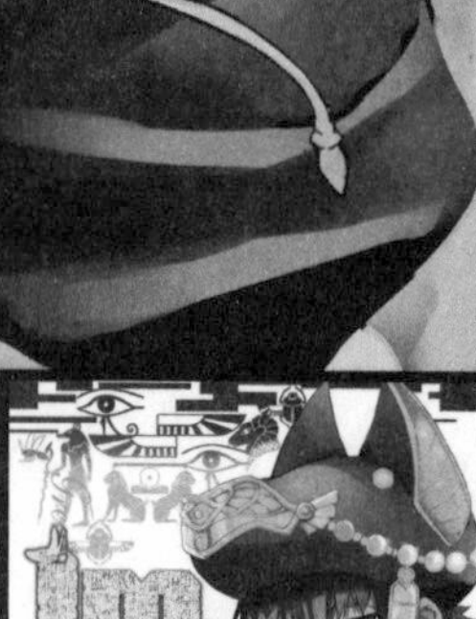
Im
Great Priest Imhotep
1
MAKOTO MORISHITA

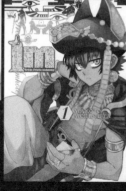

©Aidalro/SQUARE ENIX

封

Toilet-bound
Hanako-Kun

At Kamome Academy, rumors abound about the school's
Seven Mysteries, one of which is Hanako-san. Said to
occupy the third stall of the third floor girls' bathroom
in the old school building, Hanako-san grants any wish
when summoned. Nene Yashiro, an occult-loving high
school girl who dreams of romance, ventures into this
haunted bathroom...but the Hanako-san she meets
there is nothing like she imagined! Kamome Academy's
Hanako-san...is a boy!

Yen
Press

For more information
visit www.yenpress.com

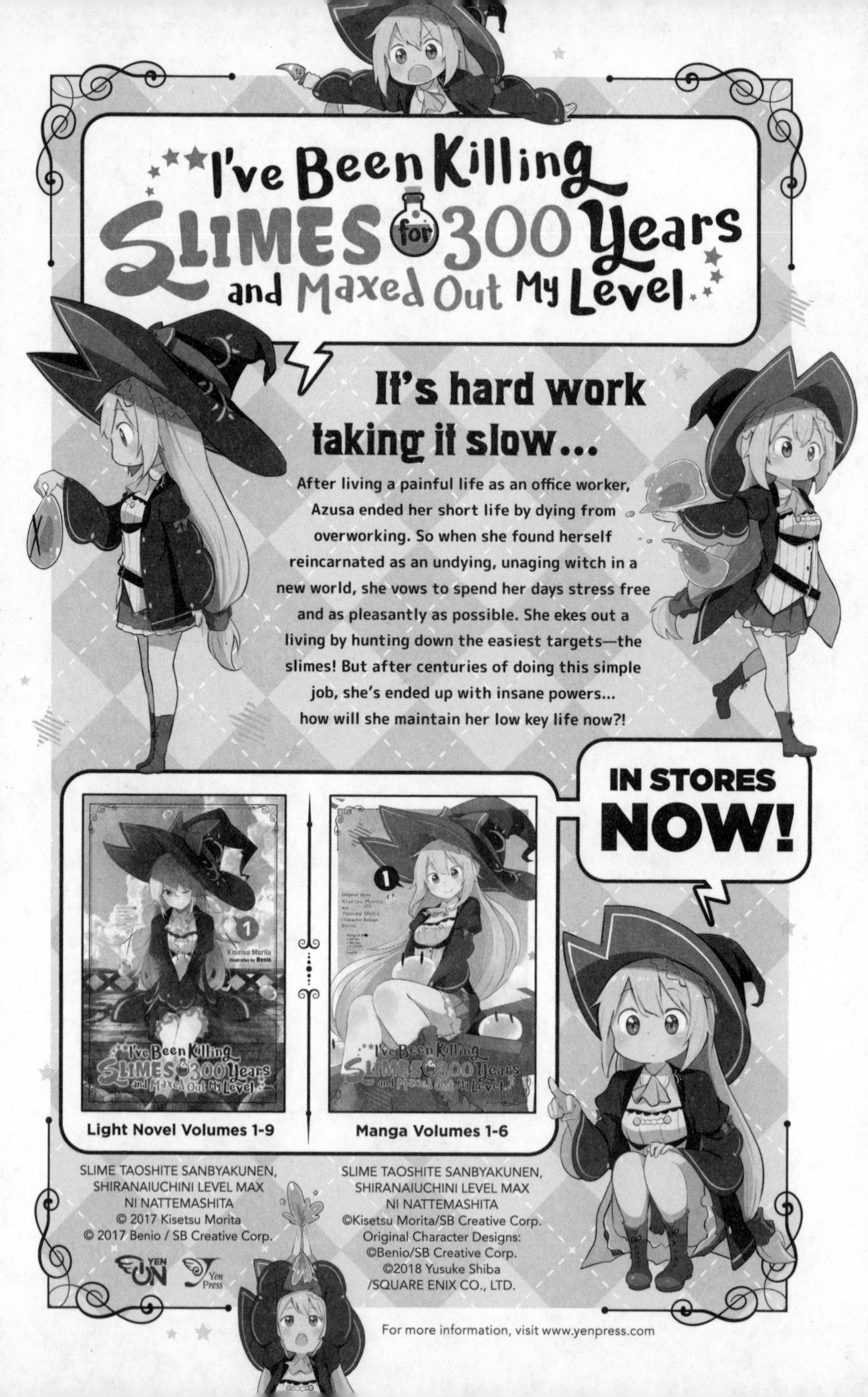

I've Been Killing SLIMES for 300 Years and Maxed Out My Level
It's hard work taking it slow...
After living a painful life as an office worker, Azusa ended her short life by dying from overworking. So when she found herself reincarnated as an undying, unaging witch in a new world, she vows to spend her days stress free and as pleasantly as possible. She ekes out a living by hunting down the easiest targets—the slimes! But after centuries of doing this simple job, she's ended up with insane powers... how will she maintain her low key life now?!
IN STORES NOW!
Light Novel Volumes 1-9
Manga Volumes 1-6
SLIME TAOSHITE SANBYAKUNEN, SHIRANAIUCHINI LEVEL MAX NI NATTEMASHITA © 2017 Kisetsu Morita © 2017 Benio / SB Creative Corp.
SLIME TAOSHITE SANBYAKUNEN, SHIRANAIUCHINI LEVEL MAX NI NATTEMASHITA ©Kisetsu Morita/SB Creative Corp. Original Character Designs: ©Benio/SB Creative Corp. ©2018 Yusuke Shiba /SQUARE ENIX CO., LTD.
For more information, visit www.yenpress.com

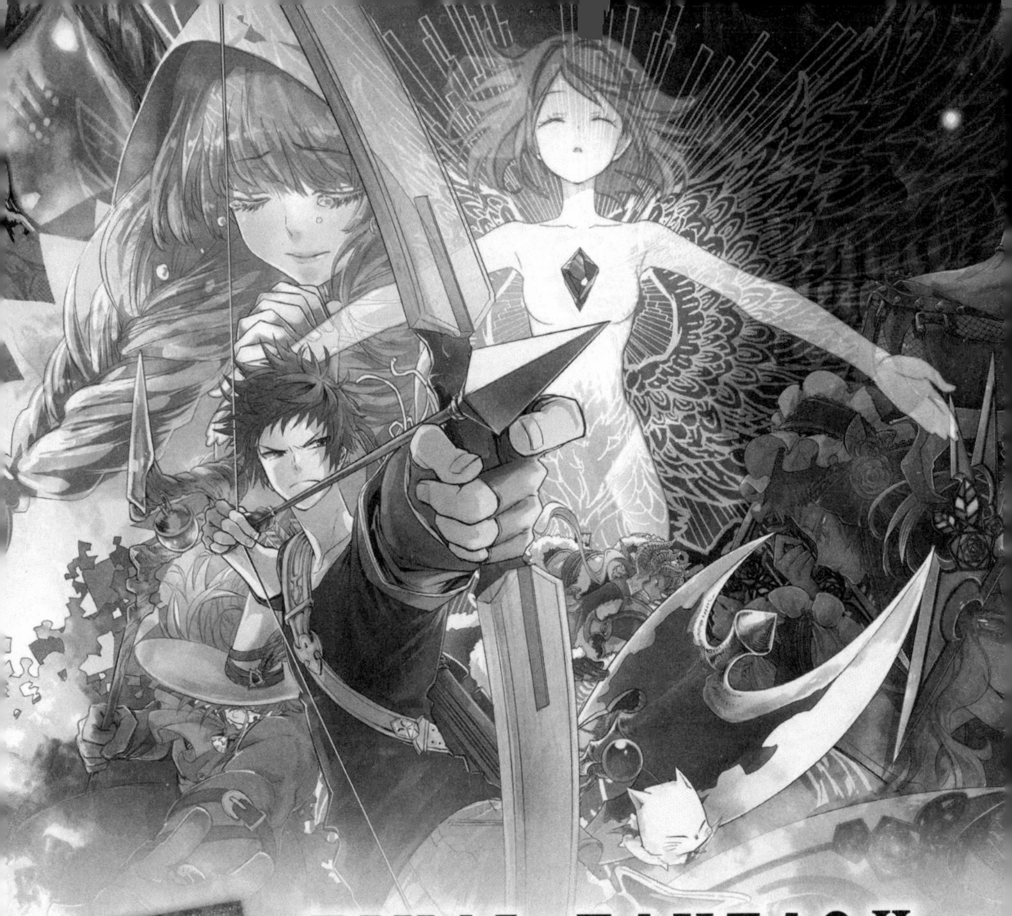

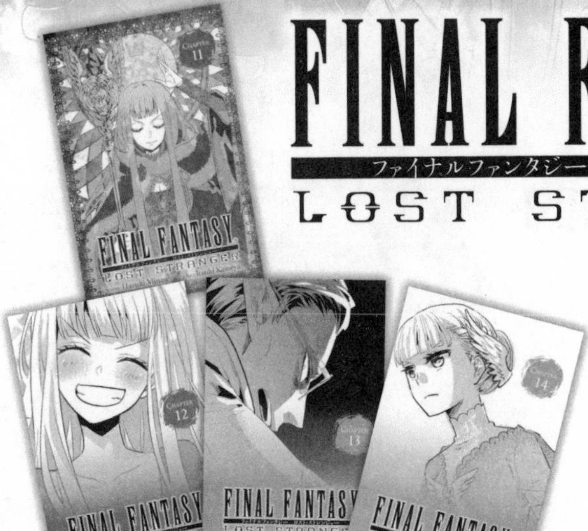

Chapter 11
FINAL FANTASY
LOST STRANGER
Chapter 12
FINAL FANTASY
LOST STRANGER
Chapter 13
FINAL FANTASY
LOST STRANGER
Chapter 14
FINAL FANTASY
LOST STRANGER

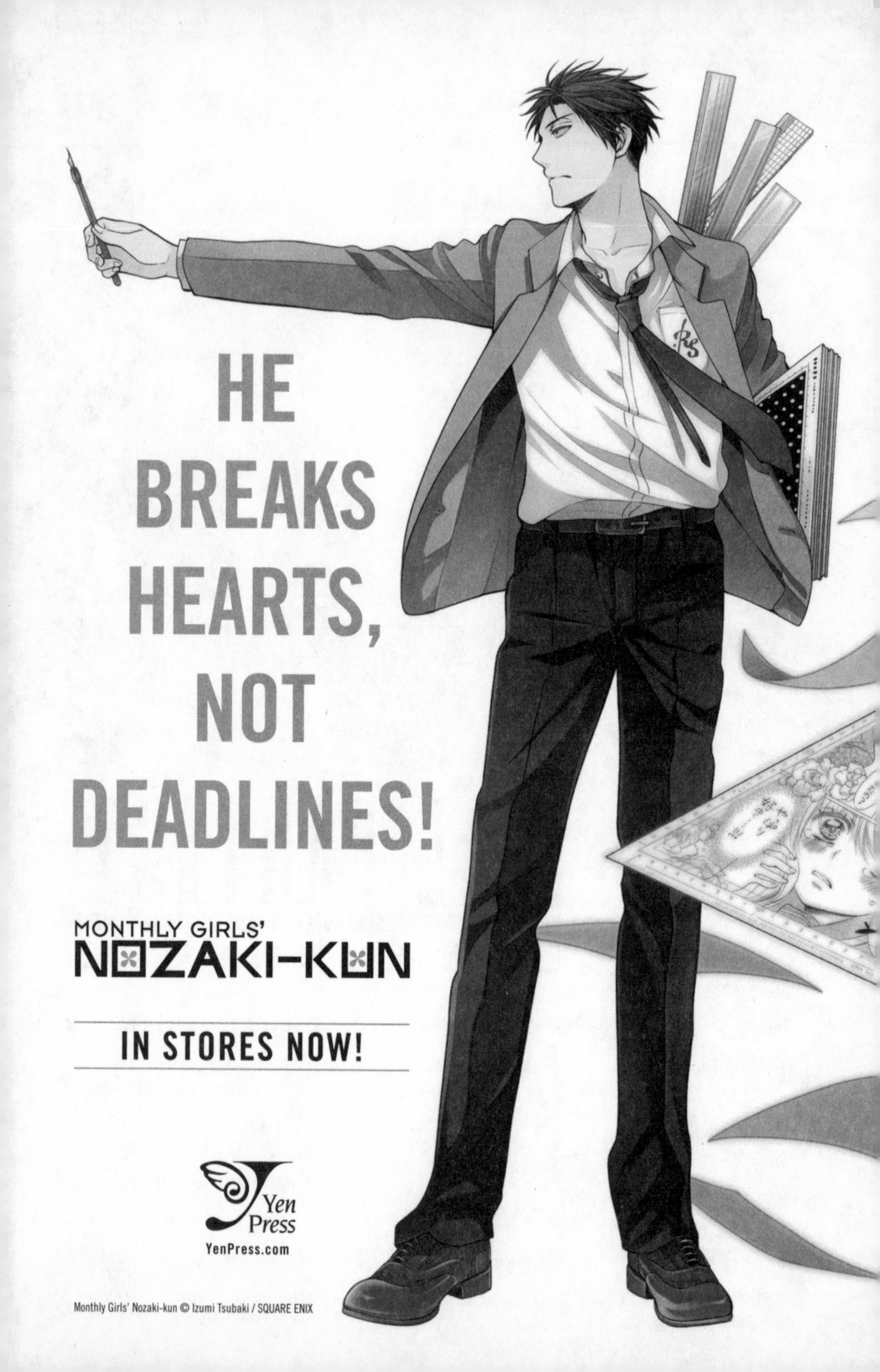
HE BREAKS HEARTS, NOT DEADLINES!
MONTHLY GIRLS'
NOZAKI-KUN
IN STORES NOW!
Yen Press
YenPress.com
Monthly Girls' Nozaki-kun © Izumi Tsubaki / SQUARE ENIX

Karino Takatsu, creator of
SERVANT x SERVICE, presents:

My Monster Girl's Too Cool For You

Burning adoration melts
her heart...literally!

In a world where *youkai* and
humans attend school together,
a boy named Atsushi Fukuzumi
falls for snow *youkai* Muku Shiroishi. Fukuzumi's passionate feelings
melt Muku's heart...and the rest of her?! The first volume of an
interspecies romantic comedy you're sure to fall head over heels for
is now available!!

STORY: **Homura Kawamoto**   ART: **Kei Saiki**

Translation: Kevin Gifford   Lettering: Anthony Quintessenza

This book is a work of fiction. Names, characters, places, and incidents are the product of the author's imagination or are used fictitiously. Any resemblance to actual events, locales, or persons, living or dead, is coincidental.

KAKEGURUI TWIN Vol. 10 ©2020 Homura Kawamoto, Kei Saiki/
SQUARE ENIX CO., LTD.
First published in Japan in 2020 by SQUARE ENIX CO., LTD.
English translation rights arranged with SQUARE ENIX CO., LTD.
and Yen Press, LLC through Tuttle-Mori Agency, Inc.

English translation ©2021 by SQUARE ENIX CO., LTD.

Yen Press
150 West 30th Street, 19th Floor
New York, NY 10001

Visit us at yenpress.com
facebook.com/yenpress
twitter.com/yenpress
yenpress.tumblr.com
instagram.com/yenpress

First Yen Press Edition: June 2021

Yen Press is an imprint of Yen Press, LLC.
The Yen Press name and logo are trademarks of Yen Press, LLC.

The publisher is not responsible for websites (or their content)
that are not owned by the publisher.

Library of Congress Control Number: 2018961911

ISBNs: 978-1-9753-2441-4 (paperback)
978-1-9753-2442-1 (ebook)

10 9 8 7 6 5 4 3 2 1

WOR

Printed in the United States of America